The political economy of education

The political economy of education

John Vaizey

with

Keith Norris

John Sheehan

and

Patrick Lynch

Manuela Ferreira Leite

A Halsted Press Book

JOHN WILEY & SONS

New York

First published in 1972 by
Gerald Duckworth & Company Limited,
43 Gloucester Crescent, London NW1

© 1972 John Vaizey

Published in the U.S.A. by Halsted Press,
a Division of John Wiley & Sons, Inc.
New York.

ISBN 0 470-89780-5

Library of Congress Catalog Card No.: 72-10688

Printed in Great Britain

Contents

Part five PRODUCTIVITY

Part six TEACHERS

To C.A.M. and our other
Portuguese colleagues

Acknowledgments

Acknowledgments are gladly made here to the Gulbenkian Foundation for permission to use copyright material. Acknowledgments were made in the Gulbenkian technical reports to owners of copyright granted to the earlier publication; to HMSO for some parts of paragraphs for the Plowden Report; to UNIDO for some paragraphs, on which some paragraphs of this book are based; and to many other people for detailed help with the Gulbenkian studies. These are repeated here. The authors also thank many people for special assistance. Lastly, Sheila Norris's secretarial and indexing skills are warmly appreciated.

Preface

THIS book is an attempt to study the economics of education and of educational systems in the broadest context. Much work in the economics of education has been concerned with a narrow interpretation of the economic consequences of educational institutions. Here we have tried to redress the balance by taking full account of the complexity of the issues.

The book is primarily for professional economists though it is hoped that others will also benefit from it. In this field, as in all other fields which economists till, the importance of the work lies in the detail, in the intimate familiarity with the nature of the soil. All the authors involved in this book are in close touch with the educational system; some of them have written of it elsewhere and have been directly concerned with systematic investigations of it. This is primarily a methodological and theoretical work that rests on a detailed knowledge of the daily life of educational institutions and their administration.

In the Spring of 1966 the Centre of Economics and Finance of the Gulbenkian Foundation asked me to undertake a research project on the costs of education and associated theoretical problems. The study began in the Autumn of 1966, in Lisbon, with the assistance of Dr. Manuela Ferreira Leite, a young Portuguese economist. The study had the deep concern and inspiration of Professor Carlos Alves Martins, the Director of the Centre and Professor of Economics at Lisbon University. In the Summer of 1967 the work got seriously under way, and John Sheehan, then in Brunel University, joined the project. Professor Patrick Lynch of University College, Dublin, became a consultant, and Dr. D. F. Cregan, Principal of St. Patrick's College, Dublin became consultant on educational matters. In the Spring of 1968 Keith Norris of Brunel University also joined the project. The work was completed in the Summer of 1970.

The results of the project were published initially by the Gulbenkian Foundation in Lisbon in a series of technical reports which were made available to libraries and selected specialists throughout the world. Despite this circulation the volumes, most of which are no longer available, have achieved the status of an underground literature. Now, with characteristic generosity and thoughtfulness the Gulbenkian Foundation has given permission for substantial parts of those reports to be reprinted in the present book. It is a new book, with added matter, and entirely rearranged. It represents a substantial body of new thinking about important matters. The authors are, as always, deeply indebted to the Foundation and to Professor Carlos Alves Martins.

A note must be added about the methods of work. I established the main outlines of the project, advanced the initial hypotheses, recruited the team and directed it. There were difficulties in organizing a complex piece of research and writing in Lisbon while working full-time in London. Dr. Ferreira Leite was the main link in this chain. John Sheehan and Keith Norris contributed much of the writing; their drafts were rewritten and co-ordinated; I then rewrote the final drafts for submission to the team and consultants.

John Sheehan is responsible, in great part, for Chapters 2-3, 8-10 and 12-15 and Keith Norris for Chapters 5-7, 19 and 21-22. The responsibility for the remainder has been mainly mine.

In 1962 I published a book, *The Economics of Education*, which gave a cautious, middle-of-the-road introduction to the subject; but because it questioned the basis of their reasoning, its main arguments were received with reserve by some extremist free-market economists. Since then an enormous bubble has been blown, which has now burst. The present volume is a detailed working-out of the themes presented in that book. The debt to Nicholas Kaldor and Joan Robinson is obvious.

John Vaizey
London, 1 July 1971.

1 Introduction

THIS book, which is concerned with the economics of education, and of manpower, is both empirical and theoretical in content. It contains an extended analysis of some of the concepts which have been used to explain the reciprocal connections of the economy and the education system. The connections between two social systems of such infinite complexity are bound to be over-simplified in any presentation, whether that presentation is mathematical or narrative in form, economic or sociological in character. The writers who tackle such big themes should do so in a spirit of some humility, hoping to be able to distinguish what is incidental from what is essential, but aware all the time that truth is many-sided, and that their versions are subject to continual qualifications and re-examination. As one of the most eminent historians of the age has written:[1] "without entering into philosophical methodological discussions, I must nevertheless make it clear that . . . lack of finality strikes me as both unavoidable and natural, and that the scientific method is not to blame. The scientific method strives above all to establish facts; there is a great deal about which we can reach agreement by its use. But as soon as there is a question of explanation, of inter-pretation, of appreciation, though the special method of the historian remains valuable, the personal element can no longer be ruled out . . . It is impossible that two historians . . . should see any historical personality, in the same light. The greater the political importance of a historical character, the more impossible this is". Pieter Geyl's remarks apply, *mutatis mutandis*, to economics and education. No relatively disinterested reader can fail to be struck by the variety of approaches, all claiming scientific "impartiality", to the question of the relationship of education and the economy. Indeed, one is tempted to formulate a rule, that the more partial an author is, the more he will seek to show that his work is "positivistic" and "value-free" (as though that had some merit in itself).

The present authors have made attempts to establish facts scientifically[2] and to examine the hypotheses which have been advanced to explain them—and to explain "facts" which are more open to doubt. They are more cautious in advancing hypotheses of their own. Economics is largely a negative discipline, devoted (like philosophy) chiefly to the eradication of error. Its positive statements tend to be so hedged about with qualifications as to be meagre

---

[1] Geyl, P., *Napoleon: For and Against*, London, 1965, p. 15.

[2] Vaizey, J., *The Costs of Education*, 1958; Vaizey, J. and Sheehan, J., *Resources for Education*, London, 1968; Lynch, P., *et. al.*, *Investment in Education*, Dublin, 1965; Norris, K. and Vaizey, J., *A Report on Unit Costs in Secondary Schools*, London, Acton Society Trust, 1969 (mimeographed).

guides to action.[1] This is not to decry the value of economics in policy formation. Practical men are generally naïve positivists,[2] filled with error.

This has been abundantly so in the economics of education. People taking decisions have sought an abstract, definitive and scientific criterion to give validity to their choices. Such a search is legitimate and understandable. The advance of human society has been partly the story of the replacement of the intuitive by the known. Certainly, the growth of knowledge about the costs of different kinds of education, and about the way education in its various forms is carried on, and about some of its effects, has had—and will have in the future— a profound impact on discussion and decision making. But there is bound always to be an area of choice—an area where interests differ, and are in conflict— where the search for an abstract criterion is a search for something that is not, cannot, be there.

In this volume, therefore, our conclusions have important intellectual and practical consequences. It has been shown, that the notion of costs is complex, and we have suggested how to make the data more reliable, and more useful, for planning and other purposes. The production function in education is examined in some detail and it is shown how it changes under the impact of new ideas of how to teach and how to learn, and the reciprocal effects of these new ideas with different factor scarcities and factor endowments. A study of teachers and their salaries complements this examination. The study of capital shows the complexity of the notion of different factor scarcities.

Our view is that up to a point there is value in many differing approaches to the economics of education, as might be expected in a subject with so many ramifications. The value of cost studies has been discussed, as has the question of international comparisons. The detailed study of cost functions, and especially of the changing details of how teaching is actually conducted, has outstanding importance. Economists have much to say, as we have shown, on the question of teacher supply and salaries. This is all in line with our fundamental view that economics has two sorts of contribution to make to policy-making. One is the heroic simplification—like Keynes' General Theory, or Leontief's input-output analysis—and the other contribution lies in the patient elucidation of the detailed circumstances of individual cases. Whether it is the fuel and power industries transport, oil, or the public budget, confidence in the reasoning can only be assured if the detailed analysis is convincing. In the study of the economics of education, let it be said, there are some contributions which carry little conviction on this score. What they say about education rings false: it is based upon superficial reading and faint memories of personal happenings. It is as though the deep study of the school—such as is found in Plowden, or in Husén's work—had never occurred. Those studies—like those by Anderson and Bowman, for example—which have this ring of deeply-observed truth about the school as such, carry a different tone, and merit deeper consideration, than those

---

[1] The exceptions, of course, are the heroic simplifications which led to philosophies of action, like laissez-faire, the General Theory and the Marxist theory of exploitation.

[2] Witness, for example, the crudity of the arguments for a European technology independent of that of the rest of the world.

that suggest a profound ignorance of the area which they purport to be about.

It must be said at once that such relevance, such an impression of an understanding of what it is all about, is not easily achieved. We all know too much about schools because we have all been to school and our children go to school. The glib, the superficial, the easy observation is far more prevalent than it would be in a more recondite field—nuclear energy, say—where only the expert can comment, and where ignorance is at once exposed for what it is. Nowhere is this superficiality more apparent than in the studies that purport to show causal relationships of a high order between educational expenditures and earnings later in life. Multiple regression analysis of complex data is a tricky tool to handle; it is quite as capable of showing that high earnings *cause* education as of proving the reverse proposition. Nevertheless, despite the wealth of evidence on the socio-economic relationships of education, a number of economists have been bold enough—over-confidently in our opinion—to make assertions about the relationships of education to income which our analysis and which much social research have shown to be highly implausible. It would be unwise for educational policies to be erected on such insecure foundations of unsound economic theory and bad statistical reasoning.

Nor have we overmuch confidence in long-term manpower forecasting as a means of deducing educational policies from economic data. The data, to begin with, are often not data. They are—usually—frail guesses. These guesses are useful as checks of reality, as judgements of the outside limits of probable developments. In particular fields—notably doctors and teachers—it is possible usefully to be far more precise than in other parts of the occupational structure. Short-term forecasts are, of course, far more likely to be reasonably accurate than long-term forecasts though, inevitably, they are less useful than long-term forecasts for the purposes of educational planning.

We have shown of all the methods so far used for educational planning the so-called "social demand" approach is much the best, if it is reinterpreted in the ways that we have suggested. It is this approach which is capable of incorporating the data and the insights from the research to which we have referred.

A great deal has been written about the economics of education. Here we want to ask a series of simple questions. The first is:

What is the direct economic impact of education?
This can be analysed at several levels:

1. The proportion of the labour force serving as teachers, ancillaries and students.
2. The proportion of different skilled groups in the labour force.
   The statistical difficulty is that of defining the labour force, because of unemployment, and fluctuations in the participation rates of different groups, the extent of overtime etc. The definition of the quantity of labour used in education depends primarily upon the evaluation of the potential labour time of students.

3. The use of other current resources—in most cases a fairly negligible proportion of the total volume of the resource available.
4. The proportion of the Gross National Product—or other national income accounting totals—used for education.
5. The proportion of the public budget, at different levels, used for education.
6. The proportion of private consumption which goes into education.

All these concepts will be discussed in later chapters. One thing, however, is evident. The short-term impact of education depends upon the level of unemployment and the participation-rates of different groups in the community in the labour force. If the level of unemployment is high and of participation low, then the multiplier effect of education will be considerable and its "cost" correspondingly negligible. If full employment prevails, then the "cost" is correspondingly higher. To give an example, in earlier research[1] it was shown that the price-falls of the 1920s and 1930s led to substantial increases in real expenditure on education. At the same time, with widespread unemployment, the "real" sacrifices of the current generation in providing education for themselves and their children were negligible. In the period of full employment up to the late 1950s in Britain, however, the growth of education in real terms was at the expense of other objectives.

This general conclusion needs to be qualified, of course, in the case of specialised manpower and equipment which may not have alternative uses. This especially applies to the women teachers who form so large a proportion of the teaching profession.

We suggest ways and means of analysing the short-term effects of the impact of education on the economy, we now ask our second main question: What are the long-term economic effects of education?

Over the longer term, of course, a number of considerations arise, which are very different in nature. The first of these, is how to measure the output of education. One "output" is also an input—and is also part of the productive process. This is the students' subjective enjoyment or distaste for the experience of education. While it is part of the Protestant ethic to postpone gratification, it is not inevitable that present satisfactions should be undervalued. Indeed, the drift of modern society is towards the revaluation of the moment; it is not necessary to be an existentialist to appreciate the strength of such a philosophical position.

The next consideration is the whole question of the evaluation of output. A provisional attempt was made to do this in the chapter on educational efficiency. An alternative approach is suggested here.

Hitherto in most work it has been customary to take for granted the question of output: to assume, that is, that if there are alternative methods of achieving the same objective, the objective would be equally well or badly attained by either route. This assumption of constant output enables comparisons of inputs and comparisons of techniques to be made easily, since the mathematical formula which is required is obviously much simpler, and because economists

[1] Vaizey, J., *The Costs of Education*, London, 1958.

then have no need to involve themselves in questions of measurement of output, which raise issues of psychological and other forms of evaluation that are much disputed.

The market mechanism solves most of these problems of output measurement, subject to the acceptance of one enormous simplifying assumption. In the neo-classical economic system, money prices both of input factors and of intermediate and final goods sold on the market represent scarcities, and the crucial assumtion is made that there is a constant marginal utility of money so that scarcities in one area can be compared with scarcities in every other area. It follows, there-fore, that if a teacher costs $20,000 a year and teaches 20 children, the cost of that education is equal to $1,000 per year per child, and in a perfectly competitive market system the education would be sold at that price to those children and—here we come to a second crucial assumption—it would, for the marginal child, be exactly worth the benefit that the child derives from it.

Now there are many merits of the neo-classical system. Chief among them is algebraic elegance and simplicity of policy prescription. If a paradigm of the market can be set up there is no need for proxies. Output is measured by the value that it is sold for, and inputs cost exactly what is paid for them. It follows that in a free and perfect market, the price of a year at school—say $5,000, would be "worth" $5,000 to the marginal family, and that is all there is to it. The diffi-culty with this type of analysis is that, first of all, it rests upon assumptions which may well be questioned, such as whether or not there are perfect markets for factors and perfect markets for intermediate and final products, and secondly it avoids all questions of economies of scale, of monopsony and of monopoly. But thirdly, and above all it leaves on one side the question of the allocation of resources within that very large part of economic and social life which is now the responsibility of public bodies.

Parenthetically, it is interesting that the size of the public sector in most of the advanced industrial democracies is strikingly similar. Furthermore, in all these countries, as indeed throughout the world, the bulk of education expenditure falls firmly within the public sector (excepting only the somewhat controversial instance of income forgone by students while they are studying). The problems of measurement of input, productivity and output, in the public sector, assume a similar importance for many countries despite differing ideologies, both econo-mically, socially and politically.

The technique which has become prominent for calculating the relationships of output to input in the public sector goes under the name of "benefit cost analysis" or—something similar—"cost effectiveness" techniques. These tech-niques date, in essence, from Pigou's work on the *Economics of Welfare*, in which he drew attention to the indirect as well as to the direct consequences of economic activity, and suggested that those effects which did not appear in the sector of society where money was the measure could be estimated by analogy with money costs. Thus, in the field of water conservation and in the field of public transport, calculations have been made of the costs of substantial public installations, and of the benefits that accrue both directly to the consumers of the products by these installations, and of the other indirect consequences.

Increasingly, there has been a movement for other public services to come within the orbit of this type of analysis; indeed, with the spread of target budgeting, both in Canada and in the United States, in which the objective is stated and alternative means of achieving the end are set out, the cost effective relationships become crucial determinants of public policy. It is therefore not surprising that the attempt has been made to bring these techniques into the field of education. Surprise is even less when regard is paid to the growing proportion of the national income which is devoted to education, which is now approaching in some countries 10 per cent, and to the crucial role that education plays in the provision of skills and in the determination of social mobility and other social characteristics of the population.

One point should be carefully noted. Benefit-cost analysis provides but small opportunity for contrasting different sectors of the economy; it is only applicable within sectors, and there to compare and contrast activities which closely resemble each other. And another point that will become critical in the analysis that follows may often be forgotten. The valuation that is put upon the non-monetary benefits and losses is subject to dispute, as it has not been settled by the market. So, one can never escape an index-number problem.

To examine in some detail the question of evaluation of output is to be concerned basically with three sorts of questions. The first is what can be defined as output? We have to remeber that one of the outputs, namely the student who emerges from a system, is at the same time an input and also part of the productive process. If we therefore take a generalised production function ($\pi=$ production, $S_i=$input, $S_0=$output) $\pi(S_i) \rightarrow S_0$ we find that there is a common element in all the symbols which are being manipulated. This is a matter which is fundamental. We have to consider very deeply the meaning of the words input, output and the ratio between input and output which is variously labelled "cost effectiveness" or "productivity". For example, the input to a given year in college is the student's experience of the work of the previous year. One of the benefits, or consequences, that arises from the input is the actual experience or enjoyment of the fear in itself. There is then the output, perhaps more conveniently measured, of the year which could be defined in terms of examination grades, or in other ways. It is important to understand that these three separate stages, as it were, are all closely linked with each other and in some sense indissolubly linked, so that to attempt to divide them out is, in a sense, to attempt to dissolve the indissoluble.

Far from knowing what is π and what is S_i and S_0, the formula could be rephrased in the form of ? (?)→? which would give a far more realistic description of the process of education as it is at present carried on than some of the calculations that have been made.[1]

What arises first is the question of evaluating student inputs. In the first place, it is possible simply to take numbers of students, but since the ability to study of different students is related to other socio-economic variables, the inputs of students have to be weighted by such matters as sex, race, socio-economic

[1] This is a formulation by Dr. P. Herbst of Oslo.

background and ability. Ideally, for comparing the progress of two students they should be similar in every respect. Now already the extreme unreality of the assumptions becomes clear in any basis of comparison, since measuring the ability or previous educational experience, or even the socio-economic background of different students is not, ever, an unambiguous or uncomplicated procedure.

Nevertheless techniques have been evolved for doing this which are well known, and by an analysis of variance substantial attempts at standardising student entry can be made. Furthermore, for any one institution differences from one year to another are not likely to be substantial. Nevertheless, at this stage of evaluating student inputs, there is an index number problem in the sense that the input has been weighted for different characteristics and the question of which weights to adopt will affect the outcome.

The next stage is to vary the procedures by which they are instructed, and Professor Torsten Husén has already said that so little is known about the different procedures of teaching that to contrast, say teaching by television with "conventional" teaching procedures is itself an extremely summary procedure.

Now the first and most important method of analysing outputs is, of course, by simple numbers, by which the number of students who go into a system is related to the number of students who emerge from it. Until recently, for international comparisons, this was virtually the only method that we had and simple though it may seem, the process of achieving statistical conformity for comparing different nations is still in its infancy. Despite this, the crude comparisons between such things as the proportion of the age group that go into higher education in different countries and the proportion of the age group that drops out in different countries seem to be important and significant indicators when there are gross differences. Another measure which seems to be important in the school system is the number of repeaters: in many countries it is a common habit for children to be forced to repeat a year and this has a cumulative and deteriorating effect on educational outcomes.

The next series of procedures are tests and grades and examination scores of all kinds. Here the investigator is faced with a number of complex problems. The first is the extent to which the examination results are consistent; evidence is widely known for many years that in the essay type of examination, or the oral examination which is common in Continental Europe, results given by different examiners are highly inconsistent, or even the same paper graded twice by the same examiner will be given widely different grades. It may well therefore seem that objective testing is more important. But objective testing raises difficulties when it is used intertemporally, that is from one year to another, because of the way in which knowledge changes, and also interculturally.

These tests, and achievements, have to be related to the inputs which are relevant. To take an example, in the mathematical achievement study it was found that the Japanese performed particularly well and the Americans and Swedes performed particularly badly. The Japanese concentrated on a small percentage of the age group, whereas the Americans and the Swedes were undertaking the heroic process of attempting to educate a whole age cohort.

It necessarily follows that the incorporation of substantially more students from the lower end of the socio-economic scale will lower the average attainment and the level of performance which can be expected will drop off. How are the levels of performance by different strata of the age cohort to be weighted? Again there are techniques for doing so, but the weighting that is adopted will affect the output measure.

The next range of objectives for which techniques of evaluation exist are changes in personality and attitudes. Again, here there are considerable difficulties, both in testing before admission and testing after the conclusion of the course, and problems not only of weighting changes in attitudes against the overt desire to change those attitudes, but also the problem of weighting character and attitudinal changes against academic performances. There is then a host of other values which are important and relevant: there is the general level of culture, sporting achievements, a whole range of activities which are assumed, or are said to be, the aim of activities in universities, schools and colleges. Probably the only answer that one can suggest for this relative weighting is the one of pragmatism that what is inevitable and necessary is for the agreed objective formulation to be presented, much in the way in which a Bergsonian welfare function would be formulated.

$$\omega(U^1, \ldots U^v)$$

In estimating the longer term economic effects of education, it has been suggested here that the influence may be less—and less precise—than has been suggested elsewhere. A great deal of this proposition rests upon two pieces of reasoning. One is that the observed effects of education upon social mobility are relatively small. A piece of evidence confirming what is adduced is the massive study of a group of Swedish students over a lengthy period by Professor Torsten Husén. He surveyed the work previously published, and then related it to his own study of a group of males in Malmo, Sweden, from 1938 to 1962. He writes: "Formal education has also been related to changes in occupational status during the same period. Relatively small differences are found between the various levels of formal education. This supports Anderson's theory that only a small part of a person's prospects of mobility can be explained by education."[1] "It is in any case safe to conclude, that education *as such* does not create income differences to the extent that has been assumed by those who have tried to estimate its rate of return, the 'effect' of education as such seems to be less decisive than had previously been assumed."[2] The second piece of reasoning concerns a matter of pure economic theory. It concerns the nature of capital—for upon that depends the validity of the notion of "human capital".

Capital has two aspects. It is the stock of the means of production in existence which embodies past and present technical know-how. There is no satisfactory or unambiguous way of measuring this stock as a total, but for some purposes rough comparisons of, say horsepower per man employed, or growth of value

[1] Husén, T., *Talent, Opportunity and Career*, Stockholm, 1969, p. 168.
[2] *Ibid.*, p. 159.

through time at a constant rate of profit may be useful to answer particular questions.

But, secondly it is the wealth owned by the citizens of a country, which is in turn divided into two aspects—the wealth of households and the earning assets of businesses.

As a matter of convention—but purely of convention—the return on household wealth, especially dividends and capital gains, which reflect the profits of firms, is identified with the "marginal product of capital". As Sraffa long since pointed out this term is itself hard to define. It is an attempt to identify profit with the benefit to society of the use of the means of production. Clearly, if a careful definition of the marginal product of capital were possible it would be useful.

Marginal productivity in its pure sense is physical output (corn) compared to physical input—man years of labour and hectares of land. The marginal product of labour applied to land includes wages and profits. In value terms, however, under competitive conditions, the marginal net product of labour is the value of output per head *minus* the cost of other factors. The rate of profit in this case has to be given before the marginal product of labour can be defined. Marshall pointed out that the net product of each factor has to allow for the cost of the others; for this reason marginal productivity does not provide a theory of wages.

The idea of marginal productivity is then extended to differential earnings of work. The executive or professor with a high salary must have a high "marginal product", though it is not wholly clear what relevance the word "marginal" has to the case, except in one case. It is true that high earnings are to a degree a reflection of scarcity. If there were a really open education system so that more talent emerged and it was all trained, the higher incomes of trained people would be sharply reduced and much greater equality would be observed in earned incomes. In this instance the "marginal" concept would be relevant. It is not that high earnings reflect (except tautologically) a high contribution to the social product; rather, they reflect scarcity relative to demand. They are scarcity rates.

The concept of "investment in human capital" can be used *as an analogy* with investment in the means of production *and* the means of consumption, such as housing, parks and other amenities. The analogy is correct in this sense: the stock of the means of production has to be kept up by continuous gross investment. Even if there were no growth in the national income (though with the change in the composition of final goods the notion of "growth" is itself not unambiguous), there would have to be an investment-goods industry to keep the stock in being. This is even more true of education and training than of capital goods, since machines and improvements in land may be permanent, and people are not. In a "growing" economy, the investment-goods industry is an expanding one.

Similarly, the stock of education embodied in the heads and behaviour of the population has to be kept up by an establishment of schools, teachers, books and equipment. To enlarge the "stock" requires a prior expansion of that establishment. The contribution of the "stock" to profit-earning industry is important since it provides trained personnel. *In this sense*, the provision of the stock is part of the infrastructure, like roads, which has usually to be provided by the public sector and which permits private capital to make a profit on investments, paid for by the taxpayers in general. The "stock" also makes possible the provision of public services, such as the health and social welfare services, and of course (as has been explained) there is a large re-investment in the educational establishment that maintains and enlarges the "stock".

The product of the "stock" is also an output of services to consumers—the worth, in itself, of education. To reduce the product to its contribution to profit-making industry is of course nineteenth-century manufacturers' utilitarianism at its most pedestrianly vulgar. It is not possible, of course, to assume that effectiveness of the product, even in that sphere of life, can be measured by its cost. The relationship between cost and profitability is measured in the private profit sector of the economy by the judgment of managers in terms of money spent and money to be gained. If the firms had to pay the full costs of training and educating their employees—as they do in a slave state—this criterion could be applied. It is fair to say that it would not give very exact results even in that instance. In a market economy, the cost is borne by the taxpayer, or by the family, hoping that their child will get a good job, and the profits are earned by the firms. But if there is a competitive system, any one firm is trying to keep up with the others. A firm would incur losses if it did not employ trained people. It does not earn a profit above Marshall's normal profit—by doing so.

So long as there is sufficient competition to keep the return of profit on capital from rising, increased output per man employed, which is broadly speaking due to technical progress embodied by means of gross investment into the stock of the means of production, accompanied by education and training which enables the labour force to operate the new methods, leads to rising real wages. But competition is not always sufficient to do this—and in a world of growing mergers and monopolies it is less and less likely to be so. And, it should be noted, the composition of goods offered as real wages is determined by the firms, and not by what people necessarily most need. In other words the supremacy of the market, which rests upon consumers' preferences mediated through perfect competition, is not seen in real life. Even within the private sector the marginal product idea is difficult to apply if this analysis is accepted.

Differential earnings, as argued earlier, may measure scarcity relative to demand. In this sense they mirror market—or more especially supply—conditions.

The broad division of gross investment into maintaining and enlarging the government apparatus, defence, industrial and agricultural equipment, the infrastructure (like transport), housing, schools and hospitals, is determined by the political system. It cannot by any device or technique be reduced to a calculus of productivity or profitability. The same reasoning applies to the analogy of gross investment with education and training. The division of the stream of output of education has to fit roughly to the stock of capital, so that the physical investment yields its output. Capital and education cannot have any productive effect without the other. There is no way of separating out the "marginal products" of each. Since education has mainly to be provided out of taxation, while industrial equipment is mainly provided out of profits, there is a chronic under-investment in education on any kind of reasonable judgment of the relative benefits to society, as Galbraith and others have argued for many years.

PART ONE

Capital and society

THE first part of this book is mainly about economic theory—chiefly "human capital". The issues are emphasised here because they affect the most profound questions of all—the role that education (in the broadest sense) plays in the economy, and the kind of economics best equipped to deal with such a question. Economics is not a settled body of conclusions. It is a process of argument. The argument sways to and fro. In this Part an attempt has been made to show it in all its strengths and weaknesses.

2   On human capital

IT IS easy to be misled by the observations of some economists on education; indeed, some of these observations have justifiably made educationists suspicious of the attentions of economists. This is especially the case with the concept of human capital, and a survey of the relevant literature on this subject is necessary if what economists have been saying about education is to be considered in a critical context. The concept of human capital has been widely used in various studies of the returns to investment in education and of the role of education in economic growth and development. These studies, which are analysed in the chapters that follow, have been made from both macro and micro-economic aspects, and in some cases, as will be seen, the macro and micro issues have become confused.

As the concept of human capital has been derived through analogy with physical capital it is necessary to examine some of the problems which arise in connection with the concept of physical capital, its measurement, and its use in certain types of economic analysis—especially in connection with the aggregate production function. The relation between these issues and the theory of human capital will then be set out. Finally the theory of capital (whether explicit or implicit) used in previous analyses of education and the economy will be examined.

The theory of capital

Neoclassical capital theory, especially as formulated by Irving Fisher, is an essential starting point, as the concept of human capital owes much to the neoclassicals. This theory is further developed in the work of Solow, Meade, Swan and others in conjunction with the aggregate production function, and the basic neoclassical postulates are accepted (implicitly at least) by Denison, Aukrust and others, whose analysis of modern economic growth and development is of importance from the point of view of this study because of the implications which have been drawn from it for education.

The first basic assumption is that the factors of production[1] can each be aggregated in terms of some standard unit, and can furthermore be compared directly by means of a price system. Secondly, the price system and competitive

---

[1] i.e., in this study labour and capital only. Land inputs are usually unchanging over time (especially in the more developed countries, where they are also relatively minor), and are treated as a constant. While input measurements are flow terms, measurements of stocks (especially of physical capital) may be necessary to derive them.

pressures are assumed to ensure that factors are employed optimally, i.e. that the marginal product and price of each factor are equal. On the aggregate level these relationships between inputs and outputs are summarized by a Cobb-Douglas production function:

$$Y = kL^{\alpha}C^{(1-\alpha)}$$

where Y = output
        L = labour input
        C = capital input
        k and α are constants ($\alpha < 1$).

The measurement of Y, L and C will be considered in more detail later; for the present some general, theoretical observations will be made.

The function shown above gives constant returns to scale, as the exponents of L and C sum to unity. This assumption is important in some empirical work, as will be seen later, and is made by Denison, at least as a working hypothesis.[1] The exponents (α and $(1-\alpha)$) are output elasticities which measure the share of L and C in total income. This may be shown if we differentiate the function to get the marginal product of labour ($\partial Y/\partial L$):

$$\frac{\partial Y}{\partial L} = \alpha k\, L^{(\alpha-1)}\, C^{(1-\alpha)}.$$

Under the usual assumptions about the market, this is also equal to the wage per worker. Multiplying by the total of labout units (L) to get total labour income, we have

$$L\,\frac{\partial Y}{\partial L} = L\alpha k\, L^{(\alpha-1)}\, C^{(1-\alpha)}$$
$$= \alpha k L^{\alpha}C^{(1-\alpha)}$$
$$= \alpha\, Y.$$

Similarly, total capital income is $(1-\alpha)\, Y$. These points are important as much empirical analysis[2] uses factor shares to measure output elasticities as well as the basis for weighting inputs, and it should be remembered that the aggregate production function, the marginal productivity hypothesis and all their attendant assumptions are basic to such studies, whether this is explicitly acknowledged or not. Thus, for instance Denison,[3] accepts this approach and the assumption that the exponents sum to unity, for the purposes of using income shares as a guide to marginal products. Later[4] he introduces the question of economies of scale (which is inconsistent with the use of α and $(1-\alpha)$ as exponents), and has

[1] Denison, E. F. (assisted by Jean Pierre Poullier), *Why Growth Rates Differ*, Washington, D. C., The Brookings Institution, 1967, Chapter 4, pp. 33-46.
[2] See especially Denison, *op. cit.*, and also earlier works: *Sources of Economic Growth in the United States and the Alternatives Before Us*, New York, 1962; Measuring the contribution of education (and the "residual") to economic growth, in *The Residual Factor and Economic Growth*, Paris OECD, 1964; Schultz, T. W., Education and economic growth, in *Social Forces Influencing American Education*, Chicago, 1961.
[3] *Why Growth Rates Differ*, *op. cit.*, Chapter 4.
[4] *Ibid.*, Chapter 17.

to proceed *as if* returns were constant when using income shares to analyse the respective roles of labour and capital in growth.

A type of production function analysis is used to analyse time trends of output and inputs. Output is measured at constant prices, using conventional national accounting procedures. Inputs are also measured at constant prices, using replacement costs or historic costs as a basis for capital measures, and man-hours as the basis for labour measures. The detailed theoretical and empirical criticisms of these measures will be dealt with later in this chapter, and in the next. At present only a brief description is given. Most of the empirical work of Denison and others, which finds that the weighted average growth of inputs is less than the growth of output, and that a "residual" due to technical change,[1] or education or some other factors, views such technical change as "disembodied", or as a function of time and not directly related to any investment.[2] Other models, notably by Solow,[3] use an "embodied" concept of technical change, relating such change to gross investment. Some of these distinctions will be clarified later.

All of the analysis described above has been within the conventional neoclassical framework. It has been attacked on many grounds, some of which, if accepted, invalidate the approach entirely, and some of which severely restrict its scope. First, there is the assumption of the measurability of capital which underlies it, or indeed any analysis which uses capital measurements on a macroeconomic scale. Professor Joan Robinson has demonstrated[4] the difficulties involved in choosing a method of measurement, and how some capital measurements will coincide only in an equilibrium situation which has persisted for at least as long as the lifetime of capital goods in existence, and which is expected to persist indefinitely.[5] Also, it is shown how in the real world these conditions are almost impossible to fulfil. There are four principal measurements, whose merits are considered by Professor Robinson:

1. *Physical quantities of capital goods.* This is an extremely crude method and obviously has severe limitations. For instance index number problems will almost certainly arise when it comes to aggregating, as the proportion of different types of capital goods will vary in different economies, and, unless there has been steady state of growth under similar conditions of net investment, the vintages of capital will vary also. Without anticipating the other

---

[1] "Technical change" should be distinguished from "technological change". The former includes all types of piecemeal improvements, learning effects and other general factors. The latter is linked with research and development and conscious promotion of technology. See Carter, C. F. and Williams, B. R., *Industry and Technical Progress*, London, 1957. See also Norris, K., and Vaizey, J., *The Economics of Science and Technology*, London, 1972.

[3] See Solow, R. M., Technical change and the aggregate production function, in *Review of Economics and Statistics*, Vol. xxxix, August 1957.

[2] Investment and technical progress, in *Mathematical Methods in the Social Sciences*, K. J. Arrow, S. Karlin and P. Suppes, eds., Stanford, 1960; Technical progress, capital formation and economic growth, in *American Economic Review, Papers and Proceedings*, Vol. lii, 1962.

[4] The production function and the theory of capital, in *Review of Economic Studies*, Vol. xxi, No. 2, 1953-4. See also *The Accumulation of Capital*, London, 1956, Chapter 11.

[5] The problem goes deeper than measurability because of conflicting views of what capital is. Some of these conflicts emerge when an attempt is made to measure capital.

types of measurement, it is obvious that little or nothing can be done without some type of *numeraire*, if we are not to be left with a long list of individual capital-good items, which is in a very real sense no measurement at all. Different techniques complicate matters further.

2. *Productive capacity of capital goods.* Capital measurements in terms of physical product are beset by some of the same problems as the previous method. Only when there is a stock of capital goods of "balanced" age composition[1] can one envisage a definite rate of output which can be maintained indefinitely (with a given amount of labour) from that stock. Different techniques and rates of investment give rise to the problems which were encountered in (1).

3. *Capital measured in terms of commodities.* (This may also be expressed in terms of money of given purchasing power over commodities). There are, in principle, three ways of making such a measurement. Capital can be measured according to its selling price in the market, or according to the present value of expected returns, or finally according to its historic cost, compounded to present value, and making allowances for profits already earned. When the economy has been in equilibrium throughout the lifetime of the existing capital stock, and when such equilibrium is expected to prevail, the three measurements will coincide. Otherwise they will diverge, because of interest rate and discount rate variations, and because of variations in the real wage—an important cost item. In addition, for the comparison of capital stocks of two economies in an equilibrium situation, there will be difficulties if real wages are different, because even if techniques are similar, real costs and real rates of return will vary, and thus capital values will diverge also. As this type of measurement involves prices, the rate of profit, without which value measurements of capital cannot be made, must be specified or imputed first.

4. *Labour time required to produce capital goods.* This is regarded by Joan Robinson as being the most significant measurement in many respects. As variations in the discount rate can alter the present value of past, or embodied, labour, therefore physically identical items of capital can be given different values and some ambiguity remains (this is in the case where with similar techniques, different wage and profit rates prevail). But these differences, which arise out of differences in the rate of profit, and which are independent of any variations in the physical productivity of capital, do have a genuine economic significance, because lower profit and discount rates signify a relatively plentiful supply of capital which is in a real sense less valuable in terms of relatively scarce labour. This measurement is a development of the labour theory of value of Smith, Ricardo and Marx.

These observations will be seen to be of importance in the following section, in view of the attempts which have been made to measure human capital and its role in economic growth.

---

[1] "Balanced" age composition implies an equal proportion of goods of each vintage, and is the result of a zero net investment equilibrium.

The argument of this chapter also follows that of Sir John Hicks who has criticized the production function approach, which lies behind the work of Aukrust, Denison, and Solow.[1] First (and this would appear to fit the case of "embodied" technical progress, though strictly speaking it could apply to any type of technical change), zero net saving,[2] with the technical progress, would involve increasing output and therefore, in a sense, an increasing stock of capital. Or, alternatively, if output is constant, "every technical improvement implies a loss of capital: *capital being measured in terms of the consumption that has to be foregone in order that the productive power that is embodied in the physical instrument should be replaced*".[3] Second, Hicks maintains that if one uses a production function approach and endeavours to fit it to actual experience, one "must somehow incorporate the loss of value, attendant on technological improvement, which emerged so clearly in our exercise, and which will clearly persist, however well it may be hidden away, in actual data. For when we are working with actual time sequences, we are not comparing equilibrium positions, for which the loss of value can be neglected. The economy that is being analysed is always in a state of transition, losing 'capital' by improvements, and offsetting that loss by accumulation. Much of the offsetting accumulation occurs quite passively, and remains unnoticed, but for a proper analysis it should be noticed, for it is always there. If we leave it out of account we inevitably attribute less of a rise in output to capital accumulation, and more to technical progress, than should be attributed—at least if one is using a production function technique . . . There is much to be said for the approach which reckons the concealed accumulation as true accumulation, performed by a wealthy economy very much in its sleep, by the reinvestment of its depreciation allowances on ever more productive terms."

Related to the problem of valuing capital is the marginal productivity theory of income distribution which was outlined above, and which is integral to the work of Denison, Solow, Aukrust and others. The basic criticism is Marshall's that the *net* product of each factor has to allow for the cost of the others. Marshall clearly stated that the marginal product of labour does not provide a theory of wages; nevertheless it is a useful *part* of such a theory.[4] There are many other well-known criticisms based on market imperfections (e.g. monopolistic, monopsonistic or non-maximizing behaviour, or government regulation) and divergences between social private costs and returns.[5] Some of these criticisms do not so much disprove the marginal productivity theory as obscure it; various imperfections and divergences may cancel each other, and the theory may give a reasonably accurate description of reality after all. Denison has recognized this and puts his justification of the income-shares marginal productivity hypothesis as follows: "on the average for all producing units, the tendency toward proportionality of

---

[1] *Capital and Growth*, Oxford, 1965.

[2] i.e., when gross investment equals depreciation at historical cost (assuming constant prices of consumer goods).

[3] *Capital and Growth, op. cit.*, p. 300 (italics in the original).

[4] *Principles*, Book VI, Chapter 1, § 8.

[5] Acknowledged or not, they derive from A. C. Pigou's perennial economic truths in *The Economics of Welfare*, 4th edn., London, 1932, esp. Part 2, Chapter 9.

factor prices and marginal products under conditions of reasonably high employment is sufficiently strong in the United States and, though perhaps weaker, in Western Europe for distributive shares to provide an adequate basis for the analysis of the relative contributions of the various factors to growth. The general similarity income distributions for different time periods and for the various countries that are derived ... somewhat strengthens its acceptability."[1]

If one accepts the view that technical progress, however it arises, is incorporated into the production process through investment in new machines or capital goods, and that furthermore labour-capital substitution is feasible when new investment is about to be made (*ex ante* substitutability) but not afterwards (*ex post*), there are some important consequences. First, the marginal product of labour will differ for capital of various vintages; it will be higher on new than on old capital goods. Second, if there is increasing output and real wages due to technical progress, and if we assume that there is no physical deterioration of capital goods, then the life of capital goods will be governed by the rate of income increase, which will determine the point at which quasi-rents on the older vintages become zero. At this point, the machines are replaced by new ones which due to technical progress yield a higher output and therefore a higher quasi-rent. Third, it follows that wages will not equal marginal product in the conventional sense, i.e. at the intensive margin, calculated by the output produced by employing one extra man on new machines. Instead, wages equal marginal product in an entirely different sense, i.e. wages are equal to the average product of labour on the oldest machines. (Because there is no *ex post* substitutability, all the labour employed on a machine is committed to it, and its average product is the basis for any marginal calculations).

If this model seems to be too inflexible, it might be worthwhile to examine the implications of *ex post* as well as *ex ante* substitutability. Labour will be progressively withdrawn from old machines as the real wage rate rises, in order to maintain equality of the wage rate with the marginal product of labour on all machines. The question is what degree of flexibility of labour inputs is it realistic to assume for various types of capital equipment? Complete *ex post* inflexibility is hardly realistic,[2] but neither is complete flexibility: indivisibilities and various institutional and legal constraints would suggest this. As long as there is *relative ex post* inflexibility of factor substitution, then there will be inequality between marginal product and the wage in the manner described above. Even though the shares of labour and capital in national income may still give an indication of the average contribution of labour and capital to production, it is almost certain that they will underestimate the marginal contribution of capital, which is the relevant measure when considering the effects of investment. This is another reason for believing that Denison and Aukrust have underestimated capital inputs and capital's contribution to growth.

One can extend this reasoning about the nature of technical progress and arrive

---

[1] *Why Growth Rates Differ, op. cit.*, p. 35.

[2] See Ranis, G., Factor proportions in Japanese economic development, *American Economic Review*, Vol. 50, No. 4, 1957. In Japan, even though the textile industry had similar machinery to the European industry, inputs of labour varied considerably, together with the quality of some raw material inputs and the methods of organization.

at another view of the contribution of capital and labour to growth. Not only may technical progress depend on new investment, but its rate of growth may depend on the rate of growth of output, or investment, or the total of all previous outputs, or some other variable. The essence of such a model is that it views technical change as the product of learning or experience.[1] In the Kaldor-Mirrlees model the rate of increase in productivity per man on the latest machines is a function of the rate of increase of investment. If the function is non-linear (and there are reasons to assume a *decreasing* function if the exogenous growth of ideas as well as investment opportunities is considered relevant) then it cannot be integrated into a production function, because technical progress will be linked not only with capital stock, but also with the rate at which capital was installed. This leads us back to the earlier arguments about the measurement of capital stock. There is however a further relevant point. New investment (in the Kaldor-Mirrlees type model) not only increases output directly; it also constitutes an increment of "experience" which contributes to technical progress and thus to the productivity of investment. Therefore there is an intertemporal divergence between private and social net product, and since calculations such as those of Denison and Aukrust measure actual private products and returns they will tend to underestimate the real (i.e. in this case the social) returns to investment.

"Human capital" theory

The theory of "human capital" may now be examined in the light of the previous section. In the following chapters, various attempts to measure education's contribution to growth, the "residual" factor, and rates of return to educational investment will be examined, particularly with reference to the theory which is set out here.

The concept of "human capital" has a long history; it is implicit in the work of Sir William Petty and some other seventeenth-century economists, who tended to regard a large and increasing population as a symptom of wealth, if not as synonymous with wealth itself.[2] More explicitly, Adam Smith agreed that if expenditure were to be undertaken, it would have to be rewarded by profits at least equal to the ordinary profits on capital investments of similar value.[3] This may be compared with the theoretical position taken up by Alfred Marshall, who argued that there was a similarity of motivation between the man who invested (physical) capital in a business, and who invested in his children's education, so that rates of return would be equalized at the margin, at least in theory.[4] In practice

---

[1] See Arrow, K. J., The economic implications of learning by doing, and Kaldor, N. and Mirrlees, J. A., A new model of economic growth, both in *Review of Economic Studies*, Vol. 29, June 1962.

[2] See Petty, Sir William, *Essay concerning the Multiplication of Mankind*, 2nd. edn., 1686.

[3] Smith, A., *The Wealth of Nations*, Book I, Part 1, Chapter 10. But the general position of the classical economists was to regard as national wealth the surplus only; wages were a cost. However the neoclassicals and Marshall generally include wages in the total of national income.

[4] Marshall, Alfred, *Principles of Economics*, Vol. I, ed. C. W. Guillebaud, London, 1961, p. 619.

however, rates of return would not be equalized, because of socio-economic influences tending to restrict investment in human capital. Also, Marshall was cautious in his use of the concept of "human capital" or "personal capital". A passage in the earlier editions of his Principles which gave a definition of personal capital was deleted in the fifth and subsequent editions Even though he did not delete the other references to investment in education, and even though it seems that he regarded the concept of "human capital" as useful in a limited sense, it is certain that he regarded the theory as unrealistic, and that further development would, if anything, lead to confusion. This was because he realized the importance of various socio-economic influences for investment in or expenditure decisions on education. Investment in human beings was certainly equivalent in some respects to a capital improvement, but the analogy with physical capital could become too forced if physical and human capital were considered jointly in all circumstances. Consequently, he was content to take a limited view.[1]

When more recent economists, especially the inheritors of the neoclassical tradition, are considered, it is apparent that the concepts of human and physical capital are much more closely linked. Thus T. W. Schultz has estimated the "human capital" stock in the USA for 1900 and 1957, and its contribution to growth.[2] The theory of capital used is similar to that set out above. While Schultz is regarded as the pioneer in this type of analysis, it is difficult to make a comprehensive theoretical analysis of his work—and of most other work in this field—as most of the theory is not explicitly set out. But it is clear that once calculations have been made of the stock of "human capital" and its growth,[3] the basic Cobb-Douglas production function analysis, the marginal productivity theory, etc. are all used freely. It is a simple neo-classical model, which abstracts from the difficulties noted earlier in this chapter. There are inevitably some complicating factors which cannot be overlooked at this stage. For instance, the use of factor shares to calculate contributions of labour and (physical) capital to growth cannot be used for "human capital", as labour income is not suitably disaggregated. This means that Schultz has to assume a certain rate of return (or one of several alternative rates) in order to calculate the income flow from a certain stock of "human capital". At this point the argument becomes inadequate for production function analysis, as the income flows are hypothetical. For rate of return analysis the procedure is invalid as it assumes rather than demonstrates a rate of return. These theoretical difficulties are difficult to disentangle from the work of Schultz, Denison, Aukrust and others, because the theory is mainly implicit. Consequently, a more detailed analysis must wait until the various empirical measures of "human capital" and returns are considered in the following few chapters.

Professor Mary Jean Bowman has proposed various measurements of "human

[1] See Blandy, Richard, Marshall on human capital: a note, *Journal of Political Economy*, Vol. LXXVI, 1968, pp. 874-5.

[2] Schultz, T. W., Education and economic growth, in *Social Forces Influencing American Education*, Chicago, 1961; Investment in human capital, *American Economic Review*, Vol. LI, 1961.

[3] The various calculations will be considered later, especially with reference to the theoretical issues raised in the present chapter.

capital", and considered them in a theoretical context.[1] She lists four basic methods of measuring human capital stocks and flows; stock and flow measurements can both be useful, depending on the questions which have to be answered. The four main types of question are:

1. What have total "human capital" inputs been over time, and what has been their effect on output? The appropriate measurement here is obviously flows, i.e. inputs.[2]
2. How large a part of society's total resources or total capital formation has been put into "human capital" in the past? This calls for a concept and measure of "human capital" as a store or stock.
3. What have been the rates of return to "human capital", i.e. to various amounts or levels of education? Like the previous questions this calls for measurements of stock.[3]
4. What will be the effect of past, present and prospective investments in "human capital" on the future national income? This type of question requires stock and flow measures, as well as additional information on vintage.

Some of Bowman's capital measurements are largely analogous to the four types of measurement set out by Robinson above. Firstly, one might measure the number of school-years, adjusted if possible for length of year. This is analogous to Robinson's Physical Quantities of Capital Goods measure, and is similarly invalid for comparing different stocks of capital, when the components of those stocks will vary. This is an especially acute problem when one considers the differences in content and structure between various levels and types of education. Secondly, one might use what Bowman terms "efficiency equivalence units", which weight years of schooling by the productivity or earnings of appropriate members of the labour force. An adjustment must be made for post-school experience; it is not clear how this can be done. This measurement is analogous to Robinson's Productive Capacity of Capital Goods measure. This type of measure is ambiguous unless capital goods have a balanced age composition, an especially realistic assumption in the field of human capital in the light of the evidence of rapidly increasing educational expenditure in nearly all countries. Thirdly, one might use "base-year lifetime earned incomes", i.e. the present value of the expected lifetime income yield of education. This measurement comes up against the difficulty (also found with Robinson's concept of capital measured in terms of commodities), that variations in the discount rate will cause variations in capital measurements. This difficulty, and the added difficulty that costs and discounted returns to education are not necessarily equated by the market, are admitted by Bowman. One might add that the stringent conditions laid down by Robinson for the coincidence of various capital measures (general

[1] Human capital: concepts and measures, in *The Economics of Higher Education*, Selma J. Mushkin, ed., Washington, 1962, pp. 69-92.

[2] This is the type of question asked by Denison, *op. cit.* But as will be seen later, he uses income differentials or returns and does not make any input measurements as such of educational investment.

[3] This is the type of question raised later. Thus the difficulties mentioned here concerning the measurement of "human capital", and the analogous difficulties with physical capital measurements become relevant.

B

equilibrium during the lifetime of existing capital and indefinite expectation of such equilibrium) are all the more important for "human capital" because of the time horizons involved, and the resulting sensitivity of measurements to the discount rate. Bowman uses a broad concept of human capital in this connection, i.e. non-educational components are included. Thus people with no education are considered. It is not clear what this broader concept exactly means as the non-educational components are not specified. Finally, there are two measures termed by Bowman as "approximations to base-year real costs" and "approximations to current real costs". The former measurement, which uses base-year prices and weights does not include quality change, and therefore a time series based on it would tend to diverge from a measurement based on the latter criterion. However, apart from all the conceptual difficulties concerning income foregone and opportunity cost, these measurements would appear to be of little use in a non-equilibrium situation, especially given the long time perspectives necessary when measuring "human capital".[1]

Bowman then discusses some of the practical problems in making these measurements, especially the cost-based measurements. There are three main problems: the "consumption-investment complex", the question of unemployment and opportunity costs, and the "under-educated"—those who leave school after a few years' study and probably lapse into illiteracy.

In the measurement of net human capital formation, depreciation is an important factor, according to Bowman. After adjustment for mortality rates, the original value of the human capital is allocated through time according to the proportion of its lifetime productivity which is used up. Obsolescence is not as important, because human capital is less specialized than physical capital; consequently obsolescence and depreciation may be treated jointly. Finally, rising earnings after the completion of education are better treated as pure capital appreciation rather than the result of further capital formation in the course of work (or informal "on-the-job" training).

The central point of the measurement of net human capital is the relation between earnings and productivity. This is an assumption which, as a later chapter on the socio-economic context of education demonstrates, is to be doubted severely. But, if for the moment, one leaves these doubts aside, and accepts, for the purposes of argument, the use of age-earnings data as being valid at least in principle as a means of estimating the rate of return to human capital, two further assumptions are necessary:

1. Within each education category the age-distribution of income must represent a stable historical life-cycle. Bowman would take the influence of unemployment into account by adjusting the data for "average" unemployment. She does not mention the influence of secular forces on income distribution which might be more important quantitatively and would certainly be more difficult to measure or forecast, if only because of the very long periods involved.

2. The age-distribution of private earned income must be proportional to

---

[1] See Robinson, Joan, *The Accumulation of Capital, op. cit.*, pp. 119-21.

social returns, i.e. if there is a discrepancy between private and social returns it must be proportionately equal in each age/income category. Bowman mentions some exceptions which may in fact be encountered, but does not attach much importance to them. This question is obviously a crucial one and will be discussed in greater detail in a later chapter.

The type of measurement finally advocated by Bowman is an earnings-based rather than a cost-based one. Thus, from the various adjusted age-earnings data, an estimate of human capital can be obtained by assuming a certain rate of return. The chief adjustments would be for mortality rates, unemployment, and, once estimates of gross human capital stock have been obtained, for capital consumption or depreciation. Bowman understandably concludes by recommending further studies on the measurement of human capital and of the relation between human capital, other inputs and growth, especially as it is recognized that existing concepts and measurements are inadequate.

Education, training and "human capital"

The foregoing sections have been concerned with "human capital" in the context of its relation with capital theory in general. A different approach is taken by Gary Becker, who starts with age-earnings and education data and who has constructed a general theory of investment in "human capital", which takes account not only of various types of formal education but also of on-the-job training, both formal and informal.[1] Although the approach is different, the theory and conclusions are in accord with conventional neoclassical capital theory. An important point is that, because of the long periods involved, discounted earnings are extremely sensitive to small discount-rate variations.

Becker's theory begins with the theory of the firm under perfect competition, where, in equilibrium, the marginal product equals the wage, or, more correctly:

$$MP_t = W_t$$

i.e. marginal product in period t (MP_t) equals wage in period t (W_t). Training (whether or not on-the-job, formal, or informal) will modify these equilibrium conditions; the important condition now remaining is that the present value of future receipts be equal to the present value of future expenditures. This means that actual marginal products and wages may diverge for some given period. Suppose training is given only in the initial period—"0"—, that there are n periods altogether, that k is the direct outlay on training, and that i is the rate of discount used. Then the marginal product-wage equation is given as follows.[2]

$$MP_0 + \sum_{t=1}^{n-1} \frac{MP_t}{(1+i)^t} = W_0 + k + \sum_{t=1}^{n-1} \frac{W_t}{(1+i)^t}$$

[1] See Becker, G. S., *Human Capital*, New York, NBER, 1964; also Investment in human capital: a theoretical analysis, *Journal of Political Economy*, Vol. LXX, October 1962, pp. 9-49.
[2] A more detailed analysis of the derivation of this and other equations is given in *Human Capital, op. cit.*, pp. 8-11.

i.e. $MP_0 + G = W_0 + k$ when the present value of future receipts minus the

present value of future expenditure $\left(\displaystyle\sum_{t=1}^{n-1} \dfrac{MP_t - W_t}{(1 + i)^t} \right)$, equals G.

G is the return from the outlay on training in the first period (if there were no initial outlay, then under the assumed equilibrium conditions G would be zero or infinity). There is an additional item however: MP, the actual marginal product of the labour being trained in the initial period is depressed on account of training, whether because of wasted time or material, or because of changes in the type of work done. Thus if one considers C which includes indirect expenditures or foregone receipts due to training, as well as direct expenditures (k), then, according to Becker:

$$MP_0^1 + G = W_0 + C$$

where MP_0^1 is the potential marginal product in period 0. $MP_0^1 - MP_0 = C - k$ = indirect expenditure on training. It might be argued that in equilibrium, the return on investment will cover its cost ($G = C$) and that consequently marginal product will equal wage. Becker proceeds to distinguish between different forms of training in order to show that this is not necessarily the case.

First there is general training, which raises, by a given amount, the marginal product of the labour being trained no matter what firm to which it should move. Specific training, on the other hand, raises labour productivity only in the firm which gives the training. Obviously there are degrees of specificity of training, and as complete specificity is not universal, training which raises marginal productivity of labour in other firms, but by a lesser amount than in the original training firm, is generally referred to by Becker as "specific".

Where training is general, individual firms will have no incentive to invest in it, unlike the employees themselves. Consequently, during training, wages will be depressed below marginal product, the returns in the form of higher wages in later periods being collected by the workers themselves. To the firm, returns (G) will be zero, as will net expenditure, i.e. any expenditure by the firm will be recouped through lower wages during training.

Thus in terms of potential marginal product:

$$MP_0^1 = W_0 + C$$

or in terms of actual marginal product:

$$MP_0 = W_0 + k.$$

By comparison with untrained workers, the earnings of trainees will start at a lower level but will rise more rapidly to a higher level, to an extent which will pay workers for the cost of training incurred in the initial period.

Where training gives specific skills, the costs may be borne by the employer, and the returns may be gained by him also. Becker argues that this is unlikely to happen in practice, however. First, it is alleged, most training is not entirely specific to a firm or industry.[1] Second, unless the worker is rewarded with some of the returns to training, his wage will be equal to his marginal product (and hence potential wage) in other firms and industries. This may (depending on circumstances) lead to high labour turnover, and extra payment to workers may thus pay the firm in the long run, by reducing labour turnover and the need for extra training expenditure. Therefore it seems likely that for many forms of specific training both costs and returns will be shared by firms and workers, even where there is perfect competition. Monopsony may lead to a larger share of costs and returns being met by firms.

Thus, even under perfect competition there is no need for the usual marginal cost—marginal productivity rule to prevail at any given period of time. This leads Becker to consider two further aspects: expenditure on full-time schooling. and rates of return to investment in "human capital".

Becker argues[2] that school costs and returns should be analysed similarly to on-the-job training because, in certain cases, they may be substitutes. Therefore he takes into account income foregone during education, actual earnings of the student (MP) and direct financial outlays on education (k). Then the *net* earnings of the student are actual earnings minus actual direct costs, i.e.

$$W = MP - k.$$

When foregone income is taken into account, MP^1 will be potential earnings of the student, and C the sum of direct and indirect (i.e. income foregone) costs. Therefore

$$W = MP^1 - C$$

i.e.

$$W = MP^1 - (MP^1 - MP + k).$$

This form of accounting may seem strange for school or college costs, but it is used so that it can be compared with on-the-job training costs, and so that a comprehensive analysis of the returns to "human capital" formation in general can be made, by summarizing net earnings of individuals and of firms which are due to all types of educational and training expenditures.

The concept of net earnings according to Becker enables one to calculate costs of education and training by considering only the next earnings resulting from two types of activity, one of which is unskilled labour and the other some type of skilled labour resulting from the education or training under consideration. Total returns can be considered either as the present value of the income differentials occurring in each period during the active life of workers in the relevant occupation or alternatively the internal rate of return may be calculated by discounting all the differentials to zero in the base period.

The objection may be made that "learning", which is costless, may have a considerable effect on age-income profiles and that consequently any calculations of returns based on observed income trends will include as returns the effects of

---

[1] This hypothesis is untested; it is possible that Becker underestimates the degree of specificity of training.
[2] *Op. cit.*, pp. 29-30.

"learning" as well as of "real" investment, i.e. a learning curve, which is upward sloping, will be imposed on a costs-returns curve, thereby increasing its slope. Becker argues, however, that "learning" is formally no different from other investment in training and education, especially because through its effects on income differentials it has an influence on the rate of return, and therefore on future investments, similar to that of past investments. But this argument oversimplifies matters as it does not seem to distinguish the *ex post* effect of returns to learning on income distribution from its *ex ante* effect on the flow of resources into investment in "human capital".

This distinction is of importance if uncertainty and the possibility of different learning effects for different occupations with similar training requirements are taken into account. Also, if "learning" is not conditional on education or training, it may be considered as a quasi-rent. This may be relevant if a rate of return is to be imputed to various education and training possibilities which give rise to "learning" effects. On the other hand, such "learning" effects may not be distinguishable (at least *ex ante*, which is important for decision-making) from returns to investment.

A long-term implication (according to Becker) of this or any theory which makes education and training depend on returns available is that with wages rising relatively to the price of goods, including the price of goods used in the education and training "industries", the rate of return should increase and induce more investment in education and training. This should, in turn, lead to a narrowing of income differentials. Thus, Becker would argue that the increased supply of skills in the USA during the past century was induced by higher returns and was not the effect of autonomous forces, or of free public education. Against this it may be argued that the foregone earnings component of costs will rise with wages, but Becker meets this argument by stating that he has assumed neutral technical progress which "implies . . . the same increase in the productivity of a teacher's time or in the use of raw materials, so even foregone earnings would not change".[1] This is doubtful in view of the evidence of increasing unit costs given later in this book and elsewhere.[2] As education tends to be labour-intensive, unit costs tend to rise relatively quickly over time. The quality of education and its effectiveness may also increase, but to assert this falls a long way short of asserting neutral technical progress.

After various reservations about the association between ability and the distribution of earnings, and about risk, liquidity, the state of knowledge, and capital markets, Becker draws four conclusions which, if his previous assumptions and arguments are accepted, help to clarify otherwise puzzling evidence concerning factor proportions and earnings:[3]

1. The skilled and educated tend to have steeper age-earnings profiles than the unskilled. Since these observed earnings included returns, but not costs, Becker concludes that the higher earnings in later years represent a return

[1] *Op. cit.* p. 53.
[2] See Vaizey, J. and Sheehan, J., *Resources for Education*, London, 1968, esp. the tables in Appendix B, pp. 152 ff.
[3] *Op. cit.*, pp. 59-61.

on the early years when *net* earnings were low (or perhaps negative). This is not at all clear since the relatively steeper age-earnings profiles seem to be associated with almost all middle class, but very few working class occupations. It would seem that various social and cultural influences also have to be taken into account if these age-earnings profiles are to be explained. The profiles vary according to class as much as according to education.

2. Paradoxical evidence (such as that put forward by Leontief) about the factor intensities of goods entering USA foreign trade can be explained if human as well as physical capital is taken into account. Goods which are at first sight comparatively labour-intensive may incorporate a high degree of skill, or technological effort, which is part of "human capital".

3. Studies of the elasticity of substitution between capital and labour are also affected. Wages may be high because of human capital investment and therefore a regression of physical capital on wages may give a biased estimate of the effect of wages on factor proportions. Becker is of the opinion that in fact physical capital is more complementary with human capital than with labour.[1]

4. Instead of economic growth being due primarily to physical capital investment and technological advance, it can according to Becker have its principal cause in the direct investment of earners in themselves. This is similar to much of what is implied by Denison, Schultz and others.

Obviously, any evaluation of Becker's theory must take into account the assumptions of perfect competition and profit maximization which are made at the beginning of his analysis. If these are not fully acceptable then the rest of his theory must lose much of its rigour. Also, as with Schultz, and others who have calculated rates of return to investment in schooling, the questions of correlation between other socio-economic variables and income must be considered. This is done later. Becker has attempted to make an allowance for the correlation between ability and other factors on the one hand, and earnings on the other. However the multiple correlations between education, class and income complicate the issue further.

Furthermore, as Becker's theory presupposes an earnings based measurement of capital, it cannot be regarded as unambiguous in the absence of general economic equilibrium. Unless there is steady-state or steady growth equilibrium, which persists for the long term, it cannot be taken for granted that the discount rate and the various earnings profiles will be constant. Therefore it cannot be assumed that capital values will be constant or fully determinate. Furthermore, discounted earnings streams are extremely sensitive even to small variations in the discount rate. Also, the data on physical capital, which are cost-based, cannot be compatible with the earnings-based "human capital" data, unless general equilibrium holds. But the real world is not one of general equilibrium. It is not enough, moreover, to say that it *tends* towards such an equilibrium. It is necessary for equilibrium to have persisted over the lifetime of existing capital stock both physical and human, and to be expected to persist indefinitely.

[1] See footnote, *op. cit.*, p. 60.

Therefore the different bases of human and physical capital measurements render comparisons or aggregation impossible. This fact of disequilibrium which is especially important due to the long time perspectives necessary when considering "human capital", makes human capital theory unrealistic in the context of other macroeconomic measurements. It has almost invariably been the case that human and physical capital measurements have been made from different standpoints, and that the stringent theoretical conditions necessary for the reconciliation of these have been lacking. Also, Becker's argument, by proceeding from marginal product to the firm or individual, which is in terms of money profit or money wage, seems to confuse it with marginal product to society, which is in terms of real output. This confusion is basic in any attempt to argue from education-earnings differentials and "returns" to the causes of economic growth.

Some conclusions

Three principal points should be made in conclusion. Firstly, the type of capital theory presupposed—usually implicitly—by those who have been responsible for the theory of "human capital" can be faulted on many grounds. There are the statistical and conceptual problems involved in the aggregate production function and there are post-Keynesian theories of economic growth, which imply a different view of capital theory, and which if accepted would compel a radically different view of attempts to calculate "human capital" and its rate of return. This is why the work of Hicks, Kaldor and Robinson has been given such attention in this chapter.

Secondly, when the attempts[1] to estimate human capital from earnings data are considered, it is clear that direct comparisons with physical capital quantities are hazardous. Data for physical capital are usually on a historic cost basis and are incompatible with earnings-based "human capital" data in the real world with all its disequilibria. Consequently a comprehensive aggregate production function analysis, combining separate inputs of human and physical capital with labour is almost entirely beyond the scope of existing data, apart altogether from whatever logical objections may exist.

Thirdly, there is the all-important question of the dual consumption–investment nature of education, the solution of which is a condition for any meaningful analysis of "human capital". This would appear to have been the source of Marshall's doubts on the realism of the use of a theory of "human capital"; he deleted that passage in his Principles which referred to the equivalence of "personal wealth" and "personal capital". Also, doubts have been raised by Eckaus[2] who argues that the consumption aspect of education invalidates the inclusion of income foregone in human capital measurements, and that not all education "capital" is fully utilized so that "human capital" stock may not be an economically meaningful concept. H. G. Schaffer argues that the consumption and investment effects of education are inseparable, and furthermore that the

[1] Notably that of Becker, *op. cit.*
[2] Eckaus, R. S., Education and economic growth, in *The Economics of Higher Education* Selma J. Mushkin, ed., Washington D. C., 1962.

motives of investors are almost invariably conditioned by social, cultural and other factors.[1] He also emphasizes the various socio-economic variables associated with income and earnings differentials, and notes that one of the earlier calculations[2] of rate of return was made with the reservation that several non-measurable but highly important variables must be accounted for before the results could be considered as final. Schaffer's discussion of the problem has, by emphasizing the influence of psycho-social factors, anticipated some of the results of recent research discussed later. The same of course could be said of Alfred Marshall whom Schaffer invokes. In reply to this argument, T. W. Schultz has made the observation that the current consumption element in education seems to be of minor importance,[3] and that the future consumption element is consistent with an investment view of education. It will be shown later that in view of the correlation of various socio-economic variables with income, earnings and education any such statement that education is simply investment does not do justice to the various complex influences involved.

It seems, finally, that Marshall's cautious approach towards the concept of "human capital" was justified, especially when contrasted with some of the more recent theories which would claim—in our view erroneously—to be in the same tradition.

---

[1] Schaffer, H. G., Investment in human capital: comment, *American Economie Review*, Vol. LII, 1961, No. 4. This is also dealt with in Chapter 5 below, Private Returns to Investment in Education.

[2] Walsh, J. R., The capital concept applied to man, *Quarterly Journal of Economics*, Vol. XLIX, February 1935, pp. 255-85.

[3] Schultz, T. W., Investment in human capital: reply, *American Economic Review*, Vol. LII, 1961. No. 4.

3 Economic growth and returns to education

FOLLOWING the analysis of the theory of "human capital", its relation to capital theory, and the relation between education and society generally, this chapter discusses various measurements which have been of the education-growth relationship and of returns to education. The statistical basis of some of these exercises will be considered, as will their theoretical basis in the light of the previous chapter.

First, a note of clarification is necessary on the terminology to be employed in this chapter. The term "returns to education" will be used in this chapter in a broad sense to mean the effect of education on economic growth, as for instance is found in the writings of Denison and others. Thus it includes the adjustment made to labour inputs to allow for increased education of the labour force, and certain "residual" elements in so far as these have been attributed to education.[1] "Returns to education" is therefore used in a macroeconomic context, or in conjunction with aggregate production function analysis. The effects of educational expenditure on aggregate demand and the general level of economic activity is not explicitly considered here. It is probably considerable, given the high levels of such expenditure, but is also difficult to determine exactly, because it must be considered jointly with policy on taxation and other forms of public expenditure.

In the following chapter however, where the "rate of return" to education or "human capital" is referred to, it should be understood as having no necessary reference to economic growth, or even to macroeconomic aggregates. It is quite possible in theory for investment in "human capital" to yield a positive rate of return to an individual in a stationary economy,[2] through its effect on the distribution of income. In a general sense therefore, "rate of return" to "human capital" or education is essentially a micro-economic concept and has a more precise meaning than the "returns to education" which are the subject of this chapter.

Schultz's estimates of "human capital"

T. W. Schultz has estimated investment in education in the USA during the

[1] As will become apparent in the following pages, treatment of the "residual factor" (roughly speaking the difference between the rates of growth of national product and of factor inputs) varies considerably, but when all possible adjustments have been made the final "residual" is usually linked with education, research and development, or some combination of both.

[2] In such a case, net investment would probably be zero, so one must speak of gross investment. This is usually the treatment given to "human capital" formation.

1900-1957 period, and has used the resulting estimates of stocks of "human capital" to attempt to quantify the contribution of education to economic growth.[1] The basis of his capital measurements is the school year, with an adjustment for the variations in length. During the period covered (1900 to 1957), the school year was lengthened in USA. The resulting stock of "human capital" increased by over 540 per cent between 1900 and 1957, while the stock of physical capital (on a historic cost basis also) increased by about 350 per cent in the same period. Furthermore, Schultz gives two reasons why this is probably an underestimate of the increase in "human capital". Firstly, education at the terminal date was more concentrated in the younger members of the labour force, who have a longer economic life ahead of them, and who presumably have acquired more up-to-date knowledge. Secondly, higher levels of education, which are relatively costly, have a higher weight in the total for the terminal year (1957), and, especially if productivity is related positively to costs, have the effect of augmenting the total of "human capital" relatively to a total which (like Schultz's) is unweighted for costs or returns. If the stock of "human capital" in terms of adjusted school years is weighted according to the 1956 unit costs of the various educational levels which contribute to it, the increase between 1900 and 1957 is raised from 540 per cent to 750 per cent.

The theoretical and statistical difficulties raised by such a measurement are considerable. As has already been pointed out certain question-begging assumptions about rates of return are necessary if the effects of this "human capital" investment are to be ascertained. Also, the adjustments which should in theory be made for utilization and age-composition of capital stock might be considerable; it has just been shown that a crude adjustment from physical to replacement cost measurements increased the growth of "human capital" from 540 to 750 per cent.

Leaving these difficulties aside, there are three possible interpretations of the data given by Schultz:

1. If education is to be regarded as an investment element it would seem that the rate of return was as high, or, indeed even higher than the rate of return to physical capital, as the stock of "human capital" increased more than twice as fast as that of physical capital. Furthermore, for the 1929-1957 period. Schultz calculates that the increase in stock of "human capital" per head of the labour force accounted for between 36 and 70 per cent of the otherwise unexplained increase in income per worker.[2]
2. If education is regarded as a consumption element, the income elasticity of demand for education is high (> 3) as educational expenditure increased much faster than real consumer expenditure.
3. If education is regarded as elements comprising both consumption and investment the previous two measures of its yield and elasticity are still

[1] Schultz, T. W., Capital formation by education, *Journal of Political Economy*, Vol. LXVIII, December, 1960; and also Education and economic growth, in *Social Forces Influencing American Education* (National Society for the Study of Education), Chicago, 1961, pp. 46-88.
[2] i.e. beyond that accounted for by increases in other inputs. The large variation in the proportion of growth attributed to human capital (i.e. between 36 and 70 per cent of "otherwise unexplained" growth) is accounted for by variations in the assumed rate of return.

of some interest but it becomes difficult to separate the consumption and investment components.

There are, of course, other complicating factors not considered by Schultz: the expansion of education may have been largely influenced by public policy, which naturally varies from country to country and from time to time in its responsiveness to consumer demand for education, or to investment opportunities in education. Moreover, educational investment may be complementary with physical investment,[1] and in this case, investment in both types of capital must be considered jointly.

Aukrust, Solow and the aggregate production function

Odd Aukrust and R. M. Solow have developed a theory which like Schultz's implies an important role for education in the economic growth process, but which is linked directly to the aggregate production function. Aukrust begins by criticizing the "conventional wisdom" which he says stems from Gustav Cassel and others, according to whom the rate of growth depends on the values of the marginal capital output ratio and of the savings (or investment) ratio. The conventional assumption was that the marginal capital output ratio was constant, and that variations in the savings (or investment) ratio therefore accounted for variations in the growth rate.

Aukrust observes that the capital output ratio in Norway had risen significantly in the postwar years, and that an increase in the investment/income ratio to record proportions had not been accompanied by a corresponding increase in the growth rate.[2] This leads Aukrust to give a relatively minor importance to physical capital as a factor in the growth process, and a correspondingly greater role to the other factors: labour and "organization".[3] A Cobb-Douglas function is fitted to the Norwegian data. It is possible to measure labour and capital inputs, but not "organization", so this factor is assumed to increase at a constant rate independently of other inputs. The function used is:

$$R_t = a K^\alpha N_t^\beta (e^{ht})^\lambda$$

where a, α, β and λ are constants,
                 $(e^h j)$ is the time trend of improvement in "organization",
then, $h\lambda = \gamma =$ the share of "organization" contribution to growth.

This is similar in form to Solow's "disembodied technical progress" function.

---

[1] See Vaizey, J., *Towards a new political economy?* Or some problems of some aspects of economics in the light of "human resource" concepts in *The Residual Factor and Economic Growth*, (ed.) J. Vaizey, Paris OECD, 1964; also Becker, G., *op. cit.*, p. 60.

[2] For another interpretation of the same Norwegian data see Denison, E. F., *Why Growth Rates Differ*, *op. cit.*, Chapter 10; and also Hill, T. P., Growth and Investment according to international comparisons, *Economic Journal*, Vol. 74, June, 1964, pp. 287-304. See also pp. 36-8 below where some of Denison's findings are discussed. From the data given by Hill, it appears that the Norwegian case of rising capital output ratio and constant growth rate was exceptional.

[3] Technical change and the aggregate production function, *Review of Economics and Statistics*, Vol. 39, August 1957.

The result of this investigation was that in Norway from 1948 to 1955, of a total growth rate of 3.39% per annum, 1.81% was due to "organization", 0.46% to capital and 1.12% to labour.[1] Hence, apparently, the relative unimportance of investment if the assumptions of the study are accepted. If net investment were zero, the growth of labour and "organization" alone would have ensured a growth rate of nearly 3%. Alternatively, to increase the growth rate to 4%, net investment would have to be nearly 20%, of National Income, i.e. gross investment would have to be about 30% of Income. Solow's results for the USA (1900-1949) are basically similar[2] except that capital appears to be slightly more important relative to labour and "organization"—or "technical progress" as Solow strangely prefers to call it.[3]

One obvious alternative to the hypothesis of disembodied or exogenous technical (or "organizational") change is to regard such change as a function of gross investment. Then, the "residual" would be a function of investment and it would even be possible for the rate of technical progress to vary if net investment were constant (or zero), depending on the rate of depreciation. This alternative model is mentioned by Solow in a reply[4] to Aukrust's article, and is further developed by him later.[5] Considered abstractly, technical progress can be assumed to be exponential in time, but its incorporation into the economic system depends on the rate of gross investment. Solow's vintage model is fairly complex, but in its simplest form, this type of theory gives a production of the type

$$Y = f(A(t)K, L)$$

where $A(t)$ is an increasing function of time. Hence technical progress is capital augmenting. Reality, however, is more complicated, for two reasons well known to students of post-Keynesian economics:

1. If the importance of education, stressed by previous models, is considered, technical progress may be to a considerable extent labour-augmenting.
2. The incorporation of technical progress in investment may be made *ex-post* as well as *ex-ante*. This weakens the link between investment and growth or actual technical change, except for the very long period, and is partly a return to the exogenous or "disembodied" view of technical change. It also leaves out of account the relationship between invention, innovation and technological change.[6]

---

[1] Aukrust measures labour input in man-years, and does not attempt to make the many qualitative and quantitative adjustments undertaken by Denison. The data, which refer to 1900-1955, exclude the war years of 1939-1945.

[2] *Op. cit.*, Solow analyses "Private non-farm activity" only. As government activity increased and agriculture decreased in relative importance over this period, offsetting each other, his analysis concerns a fairly constant and a very large proportion of total National Product.

[3] The various names—"organization", "technical progress" etc.—given to the residual is perhaps a further measure of our ignorance. Certainly the term "technical progress" is used in a loose and almost careless fashion, when compared with the sense in which it has been defined by Carter and Williams (*Industry and Technical Progress*, London, 1957).

[4] Investment and economic growth—some comments, *Productivity Measurement Review*, No. 19, November 1959.

[5] Technical progress, capital formation and economic growth, *American Economic Review, Papers, and Proceedings*, Vol. III, June 1962.

[6] See Carter and Williams, *op. cit.*

The relative merits of the "embodied" and "disembodied" technical progress hypotheses have been the subject of much controversy, which will not be pursued further here.[1] It is apparent however, that neither model is entirely satisfactory, because technical change is complex and does not occur simply as a function of time or gross investment or any other single variable. Furthermore, the work of Solow and Aukrust, like any example of aggregate function production analysis is subject to the criticisms made earlier, and which are especially relevant when considering "technical change" and its effects on the quality of different vintages of capital. This must make the aggregation problem all the more difficult.

Attempts to measure the "residual factor"

E. F. Denison's empirical measurements of the sources of economic growth and his international comparisons of growth rates of output and inputs[2] have been used to draw implications for the role of education in promoting growth and (implicitly at least), in attempts to develop a theory of human capital. One example of his work is of special importance as it emphasizes education rather than other factors.[3] However the theoretical framework is similar throughout, as are the basic statistical operations. The theoretical and statistical critique below applies to most of Denison's writings and to similar studies by Kendrick, Abramovitz and the United States Department of Commerce.[4]

In measuring the growth of inputs, Denison uses factor shares as weights, in accordance with the marginal productivity theory of income distribution.[5] The ways in which technical progress, learning, etc., can necessitate modifications to this theory have already been mentioned above. The growth of outputs presents relatively few problems; Denison uses Net National Product (or National Income) at Factor Cost, measured principally according to standard United Nations national accounting procedures. The following example[6] uses USA data for the 1929-1957 period; more recent data of Denison's show basically similar results, but were not intended to show the effects of education as explicitly.[7]

The result of the complex calculations of inputs was a growth of real national income of 2.93% per annum and a growth of total factor inputs of 2.00% per

---

[1] For a summary see Hahn, F. H. and Mathews, R. C. O., The theory of economic growth. A survey, *Economic Journal*, Vol. LXXIV, December, 1964. For some empirical evidence see Hill, T. P., Growth and investment according to international comparisons, in *Economic Journal*, Vol. LXXIV, June 1964.

[2] Denison, E. F., *The Sources of Economic Growth in the United States and the Alternatives Before Us*, New York, 1962; *Why Growth Rates Differ*, Washington, The Brookings Institution, 1967.

[3] Measuring the contribution of education (and the "residual") to economic growth, in *The Residual Factor and Economic Growth*, Paris, OECD, 1964

[4] *Long-term Economic Growth 1860-1965*, Washington, D. C., U.S. Department of Commerce Bureau of the Census, 1966.

[5] Denison stresses that the equality of factor rewards and marginal productivities tends to apply to large groups rather than individuals, i.e. that the theoretical conditions are fulfilled in a loose sense, sufficient to make them realistic assumptions (*Why Growth Rates Differ*, Chapter 10).

[6] From *The Residual Factor and Economic Growth, op. cit.*

[7] See, for instance, *Why Growth Rates Differ, op. cit.*, Table 153, p. 192.

annum, which means that there was an increase in output per unit of input approximately of 0.93% per annum. This "residual" was ascribed to various factors, most of which involved an element of arbitrary assumption: restrictions on optimal resource use, movements of factors from agriculture, local and national economies of scale, changes in the lag in application of knowledge. There is then a "final residual"—0.58% per annum—which is not fully explained, but is attributed to the "advance of knowledge". The precise significance of this residual (making due allowance for all the statistical operations involved in deriving it) is not clear; it is presumably linked with education (in the long run) but Denison also associates it with research and development expenditures, as well as other factors.[1]

Of the 2.00% increase in inputs, Labour accounted for 1.57% and Capital for 0.43% per annum. Inputs of land did not increase. Setting aside for the moment the statistical and conceptual difficulties in measuring the effect of reduced hours on labour efficiency, the increased experience and better utilization of women workers or the stock of capital et cetera,[2] there remains the important educational component, which caused labour inputs to grow at 0.93% per annum, or when labour is weighted by its share in total product, contributed 0.67% to the growth of real National Income. The method used to calculate this input increase was to take census data of the education (in terms of years) of the labour force. Where required, this data was extended by extrapolation, using the cohort method. Income differentials (for 1948) according to years of education received were then applied to the educational data for 1929 and 1957 in an attempt to measure the increase in inputs due to education. The differentials used were set at 60% of observed differentials, as it was assumed that the other 40% was due to other, non-educational factors. This part of the exercise is based on similar assumptions to those used in various calculations of rates of return to education which are examined below, namely that people are paid according to their marginal products[3] and that education and training account for these differences in productivity (and hence in income). It should be stressed that much of Denison's analysis rests on this crucial and by no means fully proven assumption.[4]

Thus, if Denison's calculations are accepted, almost a quarter (0.67% out of 2.93% per annum) of the growth in output between 1929 and 1957 in the USA was due to education, or more exactly, to the increased education of the labour force. Furthermore, when the "advance of knowledge" factor is considered it is apparent that Denison would regard 0.67% as the minimum contribution of education to the total growth rate of 2.93%. Beyond this it is not possible to say much else, as the advance of knowledge can be ascribed partly to non-educational

[1] *Why Growth Rates Differ, op. cit.*, Chapter 20, pp. 179-195.

[2] For a discussion of these see Measuring the contribution of education (and the "residual") to economic growth, *op. cit.*, pp. 13-23, and also *Long-Term Economic Growth, 1860-1965*, Washington, D.C., U.S. Department of Commerce, Bureau of the Census, 1966, which incorporates official data, as well as the results of work by Denison, Kendrick and others.

[3] Denison stresses that this condition holds true for large groups, rather than for individuals (*Why Growth Rates Differ*, Chapter 20).

[4] See Chapter 4 below for a fuller discussion of this question of the education income link.

items, or items linked with education (in the long-term at least), such as research and development.

This increase in output per unit of inputs has been termed as an increase in "total factor productivity"[1]—a term which Denison wisely avoids. The increase in the index of "total factor productivity" found in these studies is due apparently largely to expenditures on research, development, education, health and welfare items which are not officially classified as investment.[2]

Many of these items are both consumption and investment goods. The line between consumption and investment is often difficult to draw as it depends essentially on the uses to which goods are put rather than on any rigid classification of goods as such. When goods and services take the form of investment in man (and consumption by man, perhaps simultaneously) the statistical and conceptual difficulties of measurement and classification are compounded. This is the case with health, education and welfare expenditures. Expenditure on these items can amount to 12% or more of the National Income of a developed country, and their weight (compared with net investment as conventionally measured, for instance) is obvious. If the various difficulties in measuring them as inputs (which in fact they are) are overcome, the increase in the index of total factor productivity would become zero or almost zero. At most, there might be some small increase in total factor productivity due to economies of scale and learning-by-doing. For this reason this particular residual has been called "a measure of our ignorance".[3] The inputs measured by Denison and Kendrick are merely the known and measurable inputs. The precise contribution of several items classified as Consumption in the National Income accounts, but which are actually investments, is not known or measurable (given the present state of knowledge). If it were, the total factor productivity index or the residual would cease to exist, because on a macroeconomic scale the aggregate value of inputs equals the aggregate value of outputs. If purely consumption items are cancelled, this equality will still hold. If what is known and measurable is the criterion, then inconsistencies will arise as long as there is a difference in our relative ignorance of output and input measurement. This is what appears to be the case; it is difficult if not impossible to quantify and specify all inputs, and therefore the notion of "total factor productivity", like all measurements of productivity, needs to be handled with caution, if it is not to be rendered meaningless.

D. W. Jorgenson and Z. Griliches follow this line of reasoning in their analysis of aggregation and other problems arising from attempts to measure total factor productivity.[4] They start that "within the framework of social accounting the hypothesis is that if real product and real factor input are accurately accounted for, the observed growth in total factor productivity is negligible". While Jorgenson and Griliches do not attempt to measure the investment element in various inputs conventionally regarded as consumption, they nevertheless start

---

[1] Notably in Kendrick, J. W., *Productivity Trends in the United States*, Princeton, N. J., 1961.

[2] This is another example of the way in which index numbers need not refer to real quantities.

[3] By M. Abramovitz in a review of Denison's Economic growth in the United States and the alternatives before us, *American Economic Review*, September 1962.

[4] Jorgenson, D. W. and Griliches, Z., The explanation of productivity change, in *The Review of Economic Studies*, Vol. xxxiv, July 1967.

from a position similar to that put forward in the previous paragraph: the identity (in principle) of outputs and inputs. They test their hypothesis in a different way from that suggested above, i.e. they eliminate various statistical and aggregation errors in outputs factor and inputs as conventionally measured. The implications of their paper are important and will be discussed at length.

The conventional theory associates changes in "total factor productivity" or the "residual" with shifts in the production function,[1] while changes in the input and output variables, without any "total factor productivity" changes are regarded as movements along a given function. The (apparently) costless elements which shift a function must be separated from those which cause movement along a function. This necessitates detailed real input and output measurements derived from price and quantity data, and it is with the theory and practice of such detailed measures that Jorgenson and Griliches are concerned. They adhere to the basic framework of social accounting. Thus all prices are assumed to reflect private costs and benefits only,[2] and only market transactions and their counterparts are included.

Jorgenson and Griliches emphasize the importance of separating price and quantity changes. Their method is summarized here, using their own notation:

$$Y_i = \text{quantity of } i\text{th output}$$
$$X_j = \text{quantity of } j\text{th input}$$
$$q_i = \text{price of } i\text{th output}$$
$$p_j = \text{price of } j\text{th input.}$$

There are m outputs and n inputs. The value of total output and total input is identical for each period:

$$(3.1) \qquad q_1 Y_1 + q_2 Y_2 + \ldots + q_m Y_m = p_1 X_1 + p_2 X_2 + \ldots + p_n X_n.$$

Differentiating with respect to time, and dividing both sides by corresponding total value, one gets an identity between the weighted average sum of the rate of growth of output prices and quantities and the weighted average sum of the rate of growth of input prices and quantities:

$$(3.2) \qquad \Sigma w_i \left[\frac{\dot{q}_i}{q_i} + \frac{\dot{Y}_i}{Y_i} \right] = \Sigma v_j \left[\frac{\dot{p}_j}{p_j} + \frac{\dot{X}_j}{X_j} \right],$$

where

$$w_i = \frac{q_i Y_i}{\Sigma q_i Y_i}, \qquad v_j = \frac{p_j X_j}{\Sigma p_j X_j}$$

i.e. w_i and v_j are relative shares of value of ith output in total output and jth input in total input respectively. Thus it is necessary that:

---

[1] i.e. changes in the parameters (k and a in the terminology used earlier) as opposed to changes in the output and input variables only. They may be understood by analogy with shifts in (as opposed to movements along) a simple demand curve, to use an elementary example.

[2] This will have important implications in terms of the conclusions of Denison, Solow and others, as will be seen later.

$$w_i \geqslant 0, \quad i = 1 \ldots m$$
$$v_j \geqslant 0, \quad j = 1 \ldots n$$
$$\Sigma w_i = \Sigma v_j = 1.$$

The growth of the quantity of total output equals the weighted average growth individual output quantities. This follows from equation (3.2) and may be expressed as follows:

$$\frac{\dot{Y}}{Y} = \Sigma w_i \frac{\dot{Y_i}}{Y}.$$

Similarly for inputs:

$$\frac{\dot{X}}{X} = \Sigma v_j \frac{\dot{X_j}}{X_j}$$

and similarly for the growth of output and input prices:

$$\frac{\dot{q}}{q} = \Sigma w_i \frac{\dot{q_i}}{q_i}$$

$$\frac{\dot{p}}{p} = \Sigma v_j \frac{\dot{p_j}}{p_j}.$$

These are termed Divisia quantity and price indices,[1] and are central to the procedure of aggregation of outputs used by Jorgenson and Griliches. In terms of these indices, total factor productivity (P) is the relation of total of output (Y) to total quantity of input (X),

(3.3) $$P = \frac{Y}{X}.$$

Applying the Divisia indices given above, the rate of growth of total factor productivity may be expressed as follows:

(3.4a) $$\frac{\dot{P}}{P} = \frac{\dot{Y}}{Y} - \frac{\dot{X}}{X} = \Sigma w_i \frac{\dot{Y_i}}{Y_i} - \Sigma v_j \frac{\dot{X_j}}{X_j}$$

(3.4b) $$\frac{\dot{P}}{P} = \frac{\dot{p}}{p} - \frac{\dot{q}}{q} = \Sigma v_j \frac{\dot{p_j}}{p_j} - \Sigma w_i \frac{\dot{q_i}}{q_i}.$$

Definitions (3.4a) and (3.4b) are dual to each other and are equivalent to (3.2). If there is an identity between values of inputs and outputs, and if these values are separated into their price and quantity components, then a relationship between the quantity components (total factor productivity) will imply a similar

---

[1] After François Divisia, who formulated a theory of the objective price level or money index (*indice monétaire*), and thereby separated the effects of price and quantity changes which occur in time-series data. See several issues of the *Revue d'économie politique*, 1925-26; also *Économique rationelle*, Paris, 1928, esp. Chapter 14.

inverse relationship between the price components. This is expressed by the negative output terms in equation (3.4b).

These price and quantity indices are then integrated with the production function, with constant returns to scale and the necessary conditions for producer equilibrium.[1] The consequences of various errors of measurement for total factor productivity measurements are set out in detail.[2] While the various identities and equations set out above provide a framework for the subsequent analysis, it should be emphasized that inputs and output are measured independently and that growth of total factor productivity is not zero by definition so that zero (or very low) total factor productivity growth is a testable hypothesis.

Statistical data for the USA (1945-65) are used by Jorgenson and Griliches to apply the basic accounting framework and test hypotheses set out above. The results are summarized in the following table:

TABLE 3.1: *Rates of output, input and total factor productivity growth, USA 1945-65*

	R_o	R_{lk}	R_f	R_{lk}/R_o (%)
a	3.49	1.83	1.60	52.4
b	3.39	1.84	1.49	54.3
c	3.59	2.19	1.41	61.0
d	3.59	2.57	0.96	71.6
e	3.59	2.97	0.58	82.7
f	3.59	3.47	0.10	96.7

Source: Jorgenson, D. W. and Griliches, Z., *op. cit.*, Tables I-IX.

where R_o = rate of growth of total output (%)

         R_{lk} = rate of growth of total labour and capital inputs

         R_f = rate of growth of total factor productivity

         R_{lk}/R_o denotes percentage of output growth accounted for by input growth.

The initial measurements, with inputs measured at constant prices, are shown in line *a*. These measurements follow USA National Accounts practice. Factor inputs are assumed proportional to factor stocks, and are otherwise unadjusted. Inputs as measured account for 52.4% of output growth, before any adjustments are made.

The first adjustment is for errors of aggregation, when the constant price measurements of inputs and outputs are replaced by the Divisia indices mentioned above. These reduce the output growth rate and increase the input growth rate slightly, with the result that inputs now account for 54.3% of output growth. The results are shown in line *b*.

The second adjustment corrects a bias in investment goods prices. These were originally measured according to input prices in investment goods industries. The correct measurement is output prices of investment goods industries, which tend to show a slower rise (due mainly to productivity increases in these indus-

[1] *Op. cit.*, pp. 252-3.
[2] *Ibid.*, pp. 257-60.

tries). This implies a more rapid rise in real or quantity inputs of investment goods. The result (line *c*) now shows a higher increase in R_{lk} and that 61 % of output growth is accounted for by inputs.

The third adjustment gets rid of the assumption that the flow of input or factor services is proportional to factor stocks. Adjustments for capital utilization are made from data on the relative utilization of power sources. Labour adjustments are made according to hours worked and intensity of work (the latter being based on previous estimates by Denison). The result in line *d*, shows that inputs account for 71.6 % of output growth.

The fourth adjustment derives inputs of capital services from asset prices. The proportion between these will vary with taxation rates and the rate of return on capital. The price and quantity calculations of capital services take account of these variations. Also, a Divisia index of capital inputs is used in order to eliminate errors of aggregation, the result being that inputs then account for 82.7 % of total output growth.

The fifth and final adjustment concerns inputs of labour services. The original labour input index was simply the number of persons employed (this was subsequently adjusted for degree of utilization). It is assumed that the number of hours worked followed a uniform trend for all categories of labour. The various categories were classified according to years of formal education completed by the male labour force and were aggregated, according to hours worked and relative prices, into a new index of labour input. The resulting higher increase in labour input means that total inputs now account for 96.7 % of the growth in total output, i.e. that the "residual factor" has, for all practical purposes, vanished, especially when probable deficiences in the original data are taken into account.

The implications of this result are important. First, Jorgenson and Griliches (*op. cit.*, p. 274) conclude from the small "residual factor" "not that advances in knowledge are negligible, but that the accumulation of knowledge is governed by the same economic laws as any other process of capital accumulation". Research which attempts to measure directly the return to scientific research and development activities would help to clarify this. As there is no significant "residual factor", this statement of Jorgenson and Griliches seems to imply that education and training contribute to the "spread of knowledge" because of their effects on the earnings, and hence the productivity of the labour force,[1] rather than to the "advance of knowledge",[2] which is a "residual" item. The accumulation of knowledge would on this reckoning be embodied in the labour force and would appear as increased labour input. It is not clear from this how knowledge and physical capital accumulation are related.

Secondly it seems from Jorgenson and Griliches' results that private and social rates of return to investment are similar, because observed or private returns[3]

---

[1] This is measured in Jorgenson and Griliches final adjustment to the input data (see line *f* on Table 3.1 above).

[2] The terms "spread of knowledge" and "advance of knowledge" are used by Denison to mean returns or increases in labour productivity due directly to more education, and the effects of *R* and *D* and social returns on growth of output respectively. See especially *The Residual Factor and Economic Growth, op. cit.*

[3] i.e. actual income flows.

account sufficiently for inputs. Otherwise (assuming private were less than social returns), the observed contribution of investment would be lowered, and that of the "residual" would be raised. This diminution of the importance of the concept of social returns is of course in agreement with the first conclusion which diminished the importance of "advance of knowledge", a factor which would tend to raise social returns in so far as advances in knowledge are widely diffused. However it is to some extent in conflict with the growth theories of Kaldor and Mirrlees, and Arrow[1] where "learning" plays an important role, and therefore social returns tend to diverge from private returns.

Thirdly, the hypothesis that, on a macroeconomic scale, outputs and inputs are identical (if measured accurately) is confirmed, if labour inputs are adjusted for education-income variables. Otherwise accurate "conventional" input measurements, properly aggregated are all that are needed. This does not presuppose any difference from the methodology of Denison's work, according to Jorgenson and Griliches, but merely that various errors of measurements are corrected.[2] But the identity of inputs and outputs is nowhere put forward by Denison as a hypothesis—quite the reverse—and the assumption of such a hypothesis is a basic feature of Jorgenson and Griliches' work, especially when it is remembered that they do not rely on counting as inputs the investment element in various health, welfare and other "consumption" expenditures.

Returning to Denison's own measurements of capital, which form the basis of much of his analysis, the estimates of post-war capital formation and capital stock in Western Europe and the USA are on an historic-cost basis.[3] Both gross and net measurements are used, and the prices of capital goods for a certain year (which is not the same for all countries) are used as a base in order to derive constant price indices of capital stock.[4] An analysis is also made of net and gross investment as proportions of National Product.

These proportions are generally higher for Europe (excluding the United Kingdom) than for the United States. Denison points out that this does not necessarily mean anything as far as absolute volume of capital or growth of capital stock are concerned, because of differences in prices and in capital accumulation at the beginning of the period under review in the various countries concerned.[5] Later, he analyses investment ratios in terms of a common (i.e. United States) set of price weights, and quotes some data on international price relationships between capital goods.[6] These point to the fundamentally indeterminate nature of cost-based capital measurements and give substance to the reservations expressed by Joan Robinson, and by others.[7]

[1] The economic implications of learning by doing, *Review of Economic Studies*, Vol. XXIX, June 1962.

[2] *Op. cit.*, p. 272.

[3] *Why Growth Rates Differ*, Chapters 10-12, pp. 117-74, and Appendices H, I and J, pp. 406-25.

[4] In what follows, we shall deal only with fixed capital. Denison's analysis also includes inventories, but these do not present any extra conceptual problems.

[5] Denison, *op. cit.*, Chapter 10, pp. 121-2.

[6] *Ibid.* Chapter 12, pp. 161-3. The capital goods price data quoted by Denison are from Gilbert, Milton and associates, *Comparative National Products and Price Levels*, Paris, OEEC, 1958.

[7] Hicks, J., *Capital and Growth*, Oxford, 1965, esp. Chapter 24; see also Chapter 2, p. 18.

For example, at United States prices, expenditures on non-residential structures and equipment were 12.1% of GNP in 1962 in the USA, and 11.9% in Northwest Europe.[1] The percentage for Italy was also 11.9. However when the domestic prices of the European countries concerned were used to value investments and GNP, the ratio rose to 16.6% for Northwest Europe and 17.4% for Italy. If we regard actual GNP in 1962 as approximating to potential real income in these countries this means a rise of 39.9.% in Northwest Europe and 46.2% in Italy in the real or opportunity cost of investment at domestic compared to USA prices.[2] In addition, evidence is given of the relative price of producers' durables and non-residential construction in 1950, using both USA and various national European quantity weightings.[3] In 1950 using European quantity weightings, producers' durables were between 33% and 74% dearer in the Northwest European countries than in the USA, and were 147% dearer in Italy. When USA quantity weights were used the Northwest European percentages ranged between 16% and 46% dearer, and the Italian figure was 59%. These figures measure the excess of European over USA prices for producers' durables, *relative* to the price of all goods and services which make up GNP. For non-residential construction, divergences were neither as large nor as persistent; this item tended to be relatively dear when European quantity weights were used, and relatively cheap at USA weights.[4]

Furthermore there is evidence throughout the part of Denison's book that deals with capital and its contribution to growth that the proportions of capital of different kinds (residential and non-residential construction, producers' durables, inventories) vary in different countries, as well as the prices of various categories of capital goods, relative to one another and relative to GNP as a whole. For instance in the 1950-1962 period, investment in machinery and equipment as a proportion of total gross investment ranged from 33% to over 50% in Denison's sample of countries.[5] These variations have been analysed elsewhere[6] and their effect is well known. Also, if gross investment per employed civilian in various European countries is compared with the USA, two sets of values, depending on the use of USA or European price weights, can be found.[7] The resulting limitations on the interpretation of the data are fully recognized by Denison: "Investment ratios provided no information concerning the relative quantities of capital goods that the various countries obtained for their saving. GNP's are, of course, not the same in any two countries; and, even if they were, differences among the countries in price relationships could easily create the result that a country devoting a larger percentage of GNP to a particular type of invest-

[1] i.e. a weighted average of Belgium, Denmark, France, Germany, Netherlands, Norway and Britain.

[2] Denison, *op. cit.*, Table 12-8, p. 161.

[3] *Ibid.* Table 12-9, p. 162.

[4] Except in Denmark, and to a lesser extent, Belgium.

[5] *Why Growth Rates Differ, op. cit.* Table 10-1.

[6] Hill, T. P., Growth and investment according to international comparisons, *Economic Journal*, Vol. LXXIV, June 1964.

[7] *Ibid.* Table 12-10, and Appendix H. This is analogous to the multiple values found when comparing educational expenditures in various countries later.

ment than another country obtained less capital goods for its expenditure."[1] The point here, however, is that the observed price and quantity variations in gross physical investment over a considerable time (and therefore variations in the structure of capital stock) are a vindication of the theoretical objections examined in chapter 2. The same reservations hold for measurement of "human capital", partly because of our ignorance of some of the prices and quantity variables involved, and also because the rapid growth in the size of and changes in the structure of the educational system, which must make any attempt at measurement of "human capital" stock very hazardous. For instance some of the adjustments made by Schultz (an example is the conversion from a type of historic cost to a replacement cost measurement) produced wide variations in measurements, which have been noted earlier in this chapter.

The statistical information gathered by Denison, therefore gives some grounds for doubting the validity of other measures of "human capital". Denison's own theoretical framework is itself unsatisfactory however. First, its implicit assumptions, in terms of the theory of capital outlined in the last chapter are inadequate, especially when post-Keynesian theories of economic growth are considered. Secondly, further statistical analysis of aggregate input and output data[2] by Jorgenson and Griliches has shown that the "residual factor" may be reduced to insignificant proportions (the returns to education are important nevertheless, as they are incorporated in the labour input measurements). Thirdly, if one considers the necessary identity of inputs and outputs on a macroeconomic scale, the residual becomes a "measure of ignorance", the important point being that as ignorance changes, so will the "residual" and total factor productivity. *Total* factor productivity is a contradiction of the other assumptions made by Denison and Kendrick; the notion that health, welfare and education expenditures contain investment elements implies that they relate to factors of production, and that the "conventional" factors of labour and capital which are the basis of "total" factor productivity are not really comprehensive totals at all.

Theoretical aspects of "human capital" measurements

The various attempts to measure returns to education and total factor productivity in connection with returns to education on a macroeconomic scale must now be considered in terms of capital theory, i.e. in connection with the concept of physical capital and the various measurements which reflect this concept.

Denison states his basic position in the following terms: "some analysts would like to measure changes in the capital stock by use of a different definition than that adopted in this study. By that definition capital goods in the stock at different dates would be equated by their ability to contribute to production at a common date, the capital stock would grow faster, and a larger contribution of capital to growth would be computed. This procedure would classify gains in production resulting from advances in the ability to design capital goods as

---

[1] *Why Growth Rates Differ, op. cit.,* p. 121.
[2] Jorgenson and Griliches use different data from Denison, but they imply that, over a long period, the "residual" will not be significantly large.

contributions of capital. In my classification these gains are counted as part of the contribution of 'advances of knowledge'. Since it is impossible to construct a capital stock series of the alternative type, I do not attempt to isolate gains from advances in the ability to design capital goods from the gains provided by other advances in knowledge that permit more output to be obtained with the same use of resources. My classification seems to me not only unavoidable but also desirable because it permits the contribution of capital to be identified with the process of saving, and the contribution of capital to be identified with determinants such as research, of changes in the "state of the arts". But in any case, no matter of principle, only one of classification is involved."[1]

Denison argues that it is impossible to construct a productivity measurement of capital stock, whether in physical or value terms. It can be argued even more forcibly that a meaningful measurement of the type advocated by Denison is impossible. Denison's own data, show the international price differences of capital goods. International price differences in education, and the strong likelihood of relative price movements over time,[2] make calculations of both physical and human capital stocks equally difficult. Furthermore, because of these price movements, the advantage claimed by Denison for his method, i.e. that it permits the contribution of capital to be identified with the process of saving, is not entirely apparent. When the relative prices of investment and consumption goods vary, investment goods of given specifications can have different values in terms of consumption. While investment and saving will always remain identical, this will hold only in a relative sense, and not in the sense that the saving necessary for a given (physical) piece of capital equipment has the same opportunity cost in terms of consumption goods at different times or in different countries. Conversely, a given amount of real savings will finance different physical amounts of capital as prices vary. In addition, technical change will mean that given amounts of savings will tend to finance new investment which may be of constant cost, but which will have a higher productivity in a later period than in an earlier one. This technical progress may also change the physical characteristics of capital and one is thus left with the alternative of saying either:

1. that the value or amount of capital has risen because its productivity or expected earnings have risen, or
2. that the amount of capital is unchanged in so far as its cost in terms of consumption foregone is unchanged, and that increasing output is largely ascribable to "technical progress" or some such measure, and not necessarily to increased capital inputs.

The latter alternative, which is statistically more convenient is the one chosen by Denison, Aukrust, Solow and others as the basis for their work. It is apparent however, from the earlier analysis, especially that part which is concerned with Hicks' criticism of the aggregate production function and the concept of capital

---

[1] *Why Growth Rates Differ, op. cit.*, p. 144.

[2] There is some evidence for such changes in price structure in post-war Europe and the USA in Gilbert, Milton and associates, *Comparative National Products and Price Levels*, Paris, OECD, 1958.

usually associated with it, that the measures of capital stock used are not economically meaningful. The former alternative is more difficult to use in empirical analysis, but probably gives greater insight into the issues involved in measuring capital and its contribution to growth. Furthermore, while a measure of capital in terms of consumption foregone makes some sense when applied to current flows of investment, it makes none at all when applied to the capital stock, for reasons given in the previous chapter. A similar criticism would of course apply to any input flows derived from consumption-foregone capital stock measurements for the purposes of aggregate production function analysis.

From this discussion it is apparent that the various macroeconomic measurements of the "residual factor" will tend to overestimate the "residual' or "human capital" element (or whatever it may be called) at the expense of physical capital input. This is because the rise in real capital inputs (in terms of productivity) may well be underestimated (on account of the likelihood of divergence between marginal products of factors and factor prices), which will probably underestimate the role of investment. Also the question of "experience" or "learning" will introduce a distinction between private and social returns, the latter being higher in a dynamic economy. While all these arguments depend on viewing technological progress occurring through "embodiment" in new investment, the dependence is not total. It is reasonable to expect some technical or organizational change to occur exogenously and these arguments leave room for such change. But it is also reasonable to expect the rate of new investment to have a bearing on technical change, and therefore some macroeconomic studies may underestimate the importance of physical capital and overestimate that of the "residual" or of "human capital".

If the concept of embodied technological progress is extended to human as well as physical capital a new perspective emerges on rate of return analysis. If the value of physical capital cannot be measured unambiguously because of embodied technological change, then there is a case for arguing that the same holds true of human capital. And where capital values cannot be properly expressed it can be argued that a rate of return cannot be calculated properly either.

Whatever weight is to be placed on Schultz's estimate of human capital formation in the United States,[1] one thing is clear: the large increase in enrolments and in expenditure in the USA during the twentieth century undoubtedly indicate a rise in the amount of education embodied in the labour force. Furthermore, if we look at the marginal increments to the labour force, there is every indication that this rise will continue in each age-cohort, as it enters the labour force.[2] There is also the more general evidence, presented later of the large post Second World War increase in educational expenditures in many countries. This period was also one of high economic growth when investment in physical capital

---

[1] *Education and Economic Growth, op. cit.*

[2] See Denison, E. F., Measuring the contribution of education (and the "residual") to economic growth, *op. cit.*, Table 2. The educational qualifications of the labour force (measured in terms of percentages completing various numbers of years of education) have increased steadily from 1910 to 1960. However the educational qualifications of those leaving school and college in 1960 are much higher than the average 1960 figures, and are roughly equivalent to the estimated qualification structure of the labour force in 1980.

and rates of output grew relatively quickly, as well as investment in education. To this must be added some of the considerations put forward by those who have written about the theory of manpower planning as an aid to development. For instance Michel Debeauvais who writes; "In the industrial countries economic and social development has revealed chronic shortage of high-level skills, and future requirements of engineers, technicians or physicians have to be forecast. *Even in the developing countries, where unemployment and underemployment mean that there is a manpower surplus, the dearth of skilled workers is acknowledged to be one cause for the disappointing results of investment, or at least the level of returns.* An increasing number of countries are therefore endeavouring to strike the proper balance between material investment and the training of workers."[1]

The evidence of the association of educational with physical investment, together with the observation on the causes of low rates of return quoted above, suggest complementarity between capital and labour as factors of production. Labour incorporates certain aptitudes and skills which are necessary for economic development and for the operation of physical capital so often associated with economic development. If this is the case, then the relevant question is of investing in the appropriate mix of human and physical capital so as to give the highest rate of return; rates of return to one factor may not be a complete guide as increased investment in, say, higher education of a certain kind could raise the rate of return on both physical and human capital in general. Such an approach has been advocated by J. Vaizey,[2] and it is apparent that as a result much of neo-classical capital theory, and also the basis for most attempts to measure the sources of economic growth and their significance, have to be modified.

---

[1] Manpower planning in developing countries, *International Labour Review*, Vol. 89, No. 4, April 1964. (*Emphasis added*).

[2] Towards a new political economy or certain aspects of economic science viewed in the light of "human resource" concepts and the problems posed by them, in *The Residual Factor and Economic Growth*, Paris OECD, 1964.

4 The socio-economic background of education

DR. CLARK KERR has referred to the paradox that socio-economic research in education has revealed.[1] On the one hand some economists claim to have found a correlation between education and lifetime earnings, and to have established a causal relationship between the two. On the other hand sociologists and psychologists appear to have established that the main social effect of the school is to emphasize and to reinforce existing psychosocial differences. How can education contribute substantially to earnings differentials if its observed effects on social mobility are small?

The resolution of this paradox depends upon several steps in an argument. The first step is to show that the correlation between education and lifetime earnings, while it certainly exists, does not of itself prove that education causes the earnings, and that there are strong theoretical reasons for holding that at the very least, the point is unproven. The second step is to examine the psycho-sociological studies, to see what they say, and whether they establish the point that the influence of the school is not very important. It will be seen that, generally speaking, Kerr's view of the evidence is undoubtedly correct. The third step in the argument is to indicate that the mathematical statistical basis of attempts to sort out the independent effects of related variables, such as education level, intelligence, socio-economic background, race and sex, is more complex than has been assumed in some economic studies.

Much of this report is concerned with the validity of the arguments concerning lifetime earnings and education. This discussion will not be repeated here. It has been established that the complexity of the notions of "capital" and "returns" together with other serious matters, make it implausible that education "causes" earnings on anything like the scale that has been asserted. Further, it is worthy of note that the relative stability of the income distribution through time, and its similarity in countries with comparable GNP per capita is *prima facie* evidence that another explanation must be sought for the total pattern of income differentials than the amount of education—however measured—embodied in the population. While for any one man or woman, education may be—and often is—a major factor in determining his or her life-chance, what is true for the individual cannot be true for all, because the rapidity of changes in the educational output and occupation structure would have been reflected in changes in the income distribution—changes that have not occurred. It is argued in this chapter that

[1] In a paper read to the Australian Conference on Planning in Higher Education, Armidale, N.S.W., August 1969.

the evidence about education and its socio-economic context is sufficiently compelling to suggest that an explanation of the income effects of education along the lines suggested by rate of return analysis is not only implausible but unnecessary.[1]

An illustration of the difficulties of interpretation of the data is given by the calculations of the rates of return to men and to women from education. At one time women had no access to the professions and other well paid jobs. They had little or no formal education. Gradually, most occupations have been opened to them, though—outside the socialist countries—their participation rates in the better paid groups are still low.[2] Their average earnings are lower than men's, and in some cases their wage rates, for the same jobs, are lower too. Though women are known to have the same general ability as men, and there is little evidence that their efficiency is less than men's,[3] except that in many countries there is a significant period of withdrawal from the labour force for child rearing, there are far fewer women than men in well paid jobs.[4] This difference in employment opportunities in part reflects and in part is reflected in the situation in higher education, where in England and Wales, for example, only 27% of graduates are women.

Two policy recommendations could be made, to eradicate these sexual differences, if it were desired to do so. One is that legislation should be enacted and administrative action taken to ensure an eventually equal participation of women in well paid and highly valued posts, at men's rates of pay. This is in line with I.L.O. convention 100. This has, in fact, been the trend in most countries, since 1960. The other is to try to ensure a higher participation of women in higher education. Both courses should be followed for, unless more jobs are created, the educational policy would probably be unsuccessful, and unless there were a bigger flow of qualified women, the jobs could not be filled. It could be argued that by perfecting the labour market, the non-inherent differences between men's and women's opportunities would be eradicated. It could also be argued that without legislative and administrative action, approaches to equality would never have been achieved, or would be achieved in the future. A law—if it could be enforced —that wage rates and earnings for men and women doing similar jobs should be equal, and that access to good jobs should in fact be equal, would radically alter lifetime earnings calculations. In the absence of such a law, calculations based on existing (cross-sectional) data will tend to provide arguments to perpetuate unequal access by men and women to higher education.

A similar series of considerations applies to the earnings of whites and blacks in the United States. In the absence of positive steps on job opportunities and

[1] H. F. Lydall, in *The Structure of Earnings* (Oxford 1968) suggests that education plays a significant part in determining the income distribution. But this explanation is along different lines from rate of return analysis, and suggests that the social advantages and disadvantages of different occupational groups are the heart of the matter. This issue is further considered in the forthcoming work, *Inequality*, by John Vaizey.
[2] They are under-represented for example in medicine, law and engineering, and in executive and administrative posts, and over-represented in teaching, nursing and clerical jobs.
[3] Even the Royal Commission on Equal Pay (London, HMSO, 1947), which sought enthusiastically to justify unequal rates, found no serious evidence for the lower efficiency of women.
[4] In 1969, in the United Kingdom, there were two women cabinet members out of 23, and one woman high court judge out of 65.

educational opportunities, the rates of return calculations would tend to provide arguments to perpetuate the white/black educational differentials, if only because they would give a lagged response to the earnings opportunities presented by government intervention in the job situation.

An interesting parallel may be drawn, too, with the opportunities presented to the products of the private and state sectors of education in Great Britain. From the evidence given to the Public Schools Commission[1] it is clear that a disproportionate number of "top" jobs—"top" both socially and financially—are held by private sector ex-pupils, and that their lifetime earnings are therefore higher than those of public sector ex-pupils. The respective private rates of return depend, also, of course on the respective private opportunity costs. These rates of return would be profoundly affected, however, by any decision to ensure—by legislative and administrative action—higher proportions of public sector ex-pupils in public sector employment (notably the home civil, defence and diplomatic services).

It might be argued against these considerations that, while suggested legislative and administrative action can fundamentally affect earnings differentials, to do so violates the principles of marginal productivity. This is not in fact the case. Marginal productivity doctrine takes the wage differential pattern as given and varies the input of labour into different occupations until the marginal return is equal in all occupations. It is true, of course, that this principle is thought to operate optimally in a context when wages respond flexibly and quickly to supply and demand considerations in a perfect market. All hindrances to this flexibility are "imperfections". Whether it is wise to call all actual determinants of wages "imperfections" is another question: it is a little like the theological doctrine (which is probably an heretical one) that the only legitimate purpose of sexual intercourse is procreation. A perfect labour market, with wage differentials going up and down like yoyos, would be implausible to imagine. It would also invalidate *a priori* the use of cross section data to yield lifetime earnings profiles.

A major source of data on the relationship of education to other social, psychological and economic variables is a United States government document, published in 1966.[2] Its principal author, James Coleman, was sponsored by the U.S. Office of Education, under the Civil Rights Act, 1964, to investigate the "lack of equality of education opportunity" among racial and other groups in the U.S. In the original intentions of Congress in writing the law, gross material inequalities were probably dominant. The Office of Education, however, and the authors of the survey, interpreted their brief very widely, to cover many aspects of inequality of opportunity. According to Coleman[3] three of the definitions of inequality of opportunity were of "inputs" to the school: (1) facilities, curriculum, teachers, (2) educational and socio-economic backgrounds of the pupils, (3)

---

[1] *First Report of the Public Schools Commission*, London, HMSO, 1968.

[2] Coleman, James S., *et. al.*, *Equality of Educational Opportunity*, Washington, Government Printing Office, 1966, and the invaluable discussion of the Report, in *Harvard Educational Review*, Vol. 38, No. 1, Winter 1968. Since the main *Report* is relatively inaccessible, references (whenever possible) are to the Review.

[3] *Review, op. cit.*, p. 18.

"morale" of the school—and two were of the effects or "outputs" of schooling—attainment and socialization or integration. The Report suggested that the most important factors in attainment were the backgrounds of fellow students, and the least important were facilities, with teacher quality midway between, whether the attainment concerned was that of Negroes, or the relative attainment of whites as against Negroes. It may not be an unfair conclusion that in assessing inputs to education in terms of their effectiveness, neither amounts spent, or even length of school life (the conventional measures) are as significant as the social milieu of the students.

The major source of education inequality in the U.S., measured by achievement, was not as bad (as had been expected)[1] large inequalities in educational facilities. It was, quite simply, that children from poor homes, going to the same or similar schools as the better-off, did worse. It was their background that was on average dominant. The research findings should be related to another study[2] which revealed different patterns of aptitude for different American ethnic groups (Chinese, Negroes and Puerto Ricans), and that levels of aptitude varied with social class. According to a further study, whose results are heavily in dispute, the ability of different racial groups varies mainly for genetic reasons.[3] Whether the attainment results are due to genetic or socio-cultural factors does not greatly matter for the present purpose; it is sufficient that the calculations suggest that education *per se* affects attainment—and hence lifetime earnings—to a lesser degree than might be supposed. "The correlation of socio-economic status with pupil achievement generally runs high—so high indeed that it is difficult to tease out with certainty how much impact schools *per se* are having on pupils."[4]

It may well be, of course, that the cross sectional data which is the basis of most of these studies[5] yields a more conservative result—understating the school—than a longitudinal study would. There is some evidence that this may be the case.[6] This is contradicted by the Douglas results,[7] and the difference between the longitudinal and the cross sectional data is in any case small—one standard deviation over three years of study for age 15 to age 18. Furthermore, one of the conclusions of critics of the Coleman Report, who would like to show that the schools are more effective than Coleman's study found them to be, is that it is the *hard-to-change* characteristics of the school which are more important than its *easy-to-change* characteristics.[8] The implications of this for economic studies of the effects of the school needs to be spelt out. It is that changes in the school are hard to achieve, even with substantial expenditure and that, generally speaking,

[1] Moynihan, Daniel P., *Review, op. cit.*, p. 24

[2] Lesser, G. S., Fifer, G. and Clark, D. H., Abilities of children from different social class and cultural groups, *Monographs of the Society for Research in Child Development*, Vol. xxx, No. 4, 1965.

[3] Jensen, *Harvard Educational Review*, Vol. 39, No. 2, Spring 1969, and Vol. 39, No. 3, Summer 1969.

[4] Dyer, Henry S. in *Review, op. cit.*, 1968, p. 42.

[5] But see Douglas, below.

[6] Shaycroft, Marion F., *The High School Years: Growth in Competitive Skills*, Pittsburgh, 1967.

[7] Douglas, J. W. B., *The Home and the School*, London, 1964 and London, 1969.

[8] The phrases are Dyer's.

there is at least a generation's lag between the decision to seek more education for a given group, and its implementation. It has usually been said that education is a long term social force; short term economic analysis, with its emphasis on virtually instantaneous response to small changes in the rate of return is almost certainly understating the degree of "stickiness" in the situation and, therefoie, overemphasizes the market solution and underemphasizes the administrative solution to the problem of the socio-economic educational disadvantages of the poor.

The Coleman studies, together with other studies, suggest that a key variable in the equation of differential educational attainment is the social class composition of the student body.[1] This social class composition accentuates parental motivation for children's education achievement. An important study by Wilson of the Bay area of California showed that, after allowing for personal background, neighbourhood context explains what otherwise appears to be a relatively simple set of social data.

Bowles disagrees with the interpretation of the Coleman Report that would imply that spending more on the schools would have relatively small consequences for education attainment.[2] His reinterpretation of the raw data would imply that such an improvement in attainment would result from higher expenditures, but that discrimination in the labour market against Negroes[3] also needs to be dealt with, "the earnings gap considerably exceeds the learning gap".[4]

It is well established, probably beyond reasonable doubt, that educational differences mostly reveal themselves before secondary and higher education begin: that is, that by and large, an individual's life chances are mainly determined before his secondary education begins. The Crowther, Newsom and Robbins Report are unanimous on this point, as is other social research.[5] It is beyond dispute that the exceptional individual can emerge fruin obscurity at almost any age. It is also beyond dispute that the individuals concerned are exceptional. It is held by some authorities that these deeply entrenched differences are genetic in origin,[6] while others regard them as the results of proundly important socio-cultural conditioning at a very early age. The Plowden Report, which presents an authoritative interpretation of the evidence, suggests that an oversimplification of the issue is to be avoided.[7] This has also been argued by P. B. Medawar, who considers the complex ways in which nature and nurture may interact: "as recently as 30 years ago, many geneticists were still worried and confused

---

[1] *Review, op. cit.*, pp. 19-22.

[2] Bowles, S., *Review, op. cit.*, 1968, pp. 89-99.

[3] And, by implication, other disadvantaged groups.

[4] Bowles, p. 98.

[5] *15 to 18* (The Crowther Report), London, HMSO, 1959. *Half our Future* (The Newsom Report), London, HMSO, 1963. *Higher Education* (The Robbins Report), London, HMSO, 1963. See also J. W. B. Douglas, *op. cit.*, and Floud, J. (ed.), *Social Class and Educational Opportunity*, London, 1956.

[6] Jensen, *op. cit.*, following Sir Cyril Burt, *Age, Ability and Aptitude*, London, 1954, holds that about four-fifths of I.Q. is genetic. Halsey, Bernstein, and other writers hold that for operational purposes it is prudent to assume that intelligence is culturally determined. In fact, intelligence is so complex a concept that a simple nature/nurture breakdown is impossible.

[7] *Children and their Primary Schools* (The Plowden Report), Vol. i, London, HMSO, 1957, Chapter 2.

by the problem of assessing, in precise terms, the relative contributions of nature and nurture—of heredity and environment or up-bringing—to the overt ('phenotypic') differences between our mental and physical constitutions and capabilities. Both nature and nurture exercise an influence, of course; but L. T. Hogben and J. B. S. Haldane were the first to make it publicly clear that there is no *general* solution of the problem of estimating the size of contribution made by each. The reason is that the size of the contribution made by nature is itself a function of nurture. (I use the word 'function' in its mathematical sense). If someone constitutionally lacks the ability to synthesize an essential dietary substance, say X, then the contribution made by heredity to the difference between himself and his fellow men will depend on the environment in which they live. If X is abundant in the food he normally has access to, his inborn disability will put him at no disadvantage and may not be recognized at all; but if X is in short supply or lacking, then he will become ill or die. The same reasoning applies to other, much more complicated examples. If people live a simple pastoral life that makes little demand on their resourcefulness and ingenuity, inherited differences of intelectual capability may not make much difference to their behaviour; but it is far otherwise if they live a difficult and intellectually demanding life. How often has it not been said that the stress of modern living raises the threshold of competence below which people can no longer keep up or make the grade? This is not to deny that some differences between us are for all practical purposes wholly genetic, wholly inborn. A person's blood group is described as 'inborn' not just because it is specified by his genetic make-up, but because (with certain known exceptions) there is no environment capable of supporting life in which that specification will not be carried out. We shall not go far wrong, however, if we treat these cases as exceptional. Most differences between us are determined both by nature and by nurture, and their contributions are not fixed, but vary in dependence on each other."[1] Whatever view is taken of the nature/nurture controversy, it is known that the differences are of a profound nature, and are well-established and almost ineradicable at the Jesuitical age of seven. One of the consequences of the elucidation of the complexities is that "standardization", by difference equations and multi-factoral analysis, for ability, social class, sex, race and other variables, is a highly complex and controversial affair. It is considered further below, where it is established that some attempts to isolate "educational" from other socio-cultural and psycho-sociological characteristics, are misguided. As G. F. Peaker has commented,[2] "in marshalling the evidence to test conjectures about the reasons why some children make more progress in school than others, a prime difficulty is to know what evidence is relevant, and to what extent". He also draws attention to the vast numerical complexity of multiple regression analysis of this type. "There would be no purpose in an inquiry if we knew this at the outset. The difficulty lies mainly in the right application of the phrase 'other things being equal' . . . it is natural to think that the way to explore this question is to replace the simple two-way table (which relates two variables) . . . by a number of tables . . . Continuing on these lines, we

---

[1] *Encounter*, November 1969, pp. 90-1.
[2] *Plowden*, Vol. II, pp. 179-80.

should need 59,049 tables for 10 variables, and more than two hundred billion for 30 variables . . . It might be thought that it would be safe to take the variables in the descending order of their simple correlation but . . . this is not the case. It is not the case because the relevance of a variable depends not only upon its simple correlation with the criterion, but also on its correlation with its fellows, and with their correlations among themselves. This makes it impossible to guess the order of importance. All the variables in the picture have to be considered before any of them can be declared irrelevant . . . for a practicable method it is necessary to involve some rather complicated algebra which, together with electronic computation, enables a solution to be found . . . Before the inquiry it was plain, as a matter of common sense and common observation, that parental encouragement and support could take a child some way. What the inquiry has shown is that 'some way' can be interpreted as 'a long way', and that the variation in parental encouragement and support has much greater effect than either the variation in home circumstances or the variation in schools."

The Plowden Report gives the results of an extended, extensive and sophisticated inquiry into the relative effects of schooling and other factors on educational achievement.[1]

It would be unfair to say that the Report takes the view that schooling was unimportant. On the contrary, as Peaker observes, "the reasons why the school variables play so small a part is not, of course, that schooling is unimportant"[2] and he cites (in a different context), "Mr Pickwick's views on brandy and water as a prophylactic—that where it failed it was because the sufferer had fallen into the vulgar error of not taking enough of it".[3] Nevertheless, ". . . experiences during the early years of childhood, especially the amount and quality of environmental stimulation, are as important for the realization of full intellectual potential in later years as they are for emotional stability".[4] On this general point of the supremacy of early experience over later experience the evidence seems virtually unanimous. This implies, of course, that in general the later experiences reinforce the earlier. To suggest an *independent* influence (on earnings for example) of later stages of education would seem to involve a misconception of the nature of the effects of the education. To imply that anyone could rationally (in the full as opposed to the tautological sense of that word) calculate a rate of return on expenditure on university education which was truly independent of earlier experiences is to take a view of the process of decision-making about life choices that is as breathtaking in its simplicity as it is crude in its formulation. To the view that people behave "as if" they made these calculations, no response is possible. It is as literally irrefutable as it is inherently untestable.

In its sophisticated analysis of differing influences on educational attainment, the Plowden Report offers what must be regarded at this time as the most authoritative commentary on the subject. The results of its extensive surveys, and its review of the state of knowledge of the topic, are contained in Chapters 2

[1] *Plowden*, Vol. II, Appendices 3 to 7.
[2] *Op. cit.*, Vol. II, p. 180.
[3] *Op. cit.*, Vol. II, p. 181.
[4] *Plowden*, Vol. II, p. 84 (medical evidence).

C

and 3 of Volume I of the Report, which summarize the detailed studies reported in Volume II.

The first point that the Report established in this context is the great variability of growth rates of children measured by different indices. To use I.Q. or any other single measure as a standard of overall ability, or readiness to learn, or maturity, is an error. "The picture of the growing child emerges as one in which each of a number of facets of physical, intellectual and emotional behaviour is developing slowly or fast, according to the individual and his circumstances. The various facets may only be linked loosely one with another. Thus a 12-year-old boy may be beginning puberty, be amongst the strongest of his contemporaries and be skilful at games; but he may still be behind his contemporaries in certain intellectual attainments, not necessarily because he will eventually have little ability in this direction, but because he is developing slowly in these respects."[1] It follows, therefore, that decisions taken at any age ought not to be irrevocable; and that to regard a choice made at the age of 12, or 16 or even 18, as the full considered result of a mature judgment would be unwise, if only because the data and experiences of subsequent growth in some or all of the developing facets of the individual's life will modify the judgment. For the purpose of this volume, the point is a major one: to standardize a group by I.Q. is not to standardize what people think they are standardizing.

The next point is that the complex of characteristics commonly called intelligence is greatly variable, making "standardization" for I.Q. an even more dubious matter. "Biologists are now much clearer than they were 30 years ago about the manner in which hereditary and environmental factors interact to produce a characteristic, be that characteristic stature or the score in an intelligence test. What is inherited are the genes. Except in very special instances, such as the blood groups and a few diseases, the chemical substance that any given gene causes to be produced is not directly related to any characteristic of a child or an adult. All characteristics have a history of continuous developmental interactions, first of gene products with other gene products, then of more complex molecules with other molecules, then of cells with cells, of tissues with the environment of the mother's uterus, and finally of a whole complex organism with an equally complex environment during the whole of growth after birth. It is now believed that all characteristics are developed in this way: none is inherited. And none can develop without the necessary genetic endowment to provide the basis, a basis as essential for characteristics which are learned as for those which are apparently not learned. The effect of this new biological outlook is of particular importance when we come to consider the question of changes in measured intelligence."[2]

The Plowden Report then establishes that height, weight, the incidence of disease, and maturity vary with socio-economic class (even within a relatively socially homogeneous country such as England) and that these differences are important. "Environmental and hereditary factors interact inextricably to produce these differences between socio-economic classes. One set of factors tends to reinforce, not cancel out, the other. Socio-economic classes are heterogenous

[1] *Op. cit.*, Vol. I, par. 19.
[2] *Plowden*, Vol. I, par. 29.

and artificial, and it is not so much the family's occupation or income that is operative here as its attitudes and traditions of child care, its child centredness, its whole cultural outlook. As the more intelligent and forward-looking parent moves up the social scale, so his children's conditions improve: the less intelligent, less ambitious and more passive parent creates conditions which give less stimulation and support to the child's physical development. Similar considerations apply to intellectual development. Intelligent parents, who have themselves gained educational and social advantages, tend to make effective use of the educational, social and medical provision for their children. There is a strong association between the circumstances which affect the nutritional conditions underlying progress in physical development and those other conditions which nourish, as it were, intellectual and emotional growth. The significance of these facts for education lies largely in the light they throw on the progress, or lack of it, made towards equalizing even the simple circumstances of life between children of different social classes."[1] To these facts may be added variations in emotional development, and the growth of language skill, which are also intimately related to family background and to socio-economic class, and which are crucial to educational attainment.

All of these factors—physical, emotional, linguistic—affect general ability or "I.Q.". Thus I.Q. is not constant, it varies with growth and, above all, with experience. "Thus the notion of the constancy of the I.Q. is biologically self-exploding as well as educationally explosive. The description of the causes of I.Q. variation given above shows that strict constancy of the I.Q. could not be achieved under any circumstances. The nearer the approach to the ideal state in which each person's environment became perfect for him throughout his whole growth, the nearer, it is true, would be the approach to constancy. But even then, long term gains and losses due to the different rates of intellectual development would remain. The I.Q. has indeed its educational uses, but these can only be properly evaluated if we have a clear, not over simplified idea of what I.Q. test scores represent, on what they are based, by how much they vary, and for what reason."[2] Furthermore, in pointing to the use of intelligence tests to indicate academic potential the Plowden Report comments: "Most psychologists agree that there is no sharp distinction between measured intelligence and educational attainments. Both are the product of genetic and environmental factors; both are learned. Intelligence refers to generalized thinking powers which have developed from experience in and out of school: attainments are more directly influenced by the school curriculum."[3]

With all these limitations of the tools for measurement, it is nevertheless clear that the complex of characteristics called measured intelligence is profoundly affected by social conditions. "Other research has shown a marked association between parental occupation and measured intelligence, although it has of course always been clear that exceptionally able children, dull children and children who are failing to realize their potential are to be found in each occupational group.

[1] *Plowden,* Vol. I, par. 37.
[2] *Op. cit.,* Vol. I, par. 60.
[3] *Plowden,* Vol. I, par. 64.

There is some evidence that the gap between the measured intelligence of the children of manual workers and of middle class parents begins to widen at a very early age and that the causes are both genetic and environmental." Hindley found evidence for the widening gap, admittedly on a small sample, in the pre-school years. The polarization continues, according to Douglas, at the primary stage. At 11 the scores and achievement of children from the different classes are further apart than they were at eight. In England, the process persists in the secondary school. The Robbins Report on higher education referred to the evidence about primary and secondary schools, and concluded that the handicaps imposed on the children of manual workers throughout the years at school did not seem to have been getting less. When the classes were compared, "it looks as if the relative chances of reaching higher education have changed little in recent years".[1]

This conclusion is formidable, and will be further considered in the concluding section of this chapter where the evidence for higher education is surveyed. The significance of the Plowden survey was that it attempted—with many qualifications and limitations—to quantify the various influences in education performance. It was found that between schools, 35% of the total of educational performance was "unexplained" (and might, therefore, reasonably be supposed to be due to "intelligence", or "drive", or whatever), while 28% was due to parental attitudes, 20% to home circumstances, and 17% to the state of the school.[2] If the 35% "unexplained" were allocated to the other elements, then about a quarter of educational performance was due to the school. From other evidence, this would be an overestimate. For education at secondary and higher levels it would be a considerable overestimate. It suggests, therefore, that a considerable mistake has been made in the procedures for estimating the effect of education *per se* on lifetime earnings, even if the economics underlying the calculations were correct. (Even within schools, the observed effect of the school was the same while the "unexplained" proportion was larger).

The conclusion from the evidence seems inescapable that by the end of primary school, when most people's ultimate performance in education and in life is already, for the greater part, fully determined, the differentials between people have been largely established by genetic and environmental influences. It is only over the very long term that these factors can be varied. The influence of the school, though crucial in individual cases, and important in almost all, is not of the same significance as the genetic and the environmental factors. When this evidence is added to the other considerations adduced in this Report, reasonable doubt may well have been thrown upon the calculations and the formulae that underline them, which purport to show that education "causes" great differences in lifetime earnings.

The evidence from studies in higher education confirms the conclusions just reached. Christopher Jencks and David Riesman have surveyed the available material in some detail,[3] in the major authoritative study of the results of research

[1] *Op. cit.*, Vol. I, par. 83.
[2] *Plowden*, Vol. I, par. 91 and Table 1.
[3] Jencks, C. and Riesman, D., *The Academic Revolution*, New York, 1968, especially Chapter 3, Social stratification and mass higher education.

on the interaction of social stratification and the growth of higher education. Their analysis proceeds from the conclusion, reached on other evidence, that the process of certification—by degrees, diplomas, grades and marks—is inseparable from American higher education. Other evidence suggests that this is generally true in other countries, though the formal process of certification may be separated from the teaching (as in the French *baccalauréat*). This process of certification is one of the means by which the social stratification process is assisted by the higher education system. Despite the American allergy to discussion of social class,[1] the evidence is that socio-economic class divisions are as profound there as elsewhere in the western industrialized countries.[2] After reviewing the evidence, the authors say: "What does this imply about social class in America? It seems clear that technological change and improvements in human skills have increased the productivity of the labour force, and that the increase in productivity has led to rising living standards for virtually all Americans. While some occupational groups have not gained as much as others, occupational groups have not gained as much as others, occupations with lagging wages have been mostly shrinking in size. Both old and new workers have gravitated toward occupations in which wages were rising fairly rapidly. The net result is that the distribution of goods and services has remained relatively constant despite the rise in absolute living standards. It should be noted, however, that if both the rich and the poor increase their income at about the same rate over the years, the absolute gap between them will necessarily grow. Between 1947 and 1962, for example, 80th percentile income was always between 4.0 and 4.5 times as much as 20th percentile income. But the absolute gap grew from $4,650 to $6,988 (1962 dollars). Still, if the income distribution is taken as a crude index of the distribution of occupational skills, responsibilities, and prestige, it also seems fair to conclude that these latter have not been redistributed to any significant extent since 1945. In that case it also follows that the relative size of various social classes has remained essentially unchanged for the past twenty years. Nor is there much prospect of change in the near future."[3]

The conclusion that follows from this is that if pure talent, in a genetic sense, or education, were to lead to social promotion, it must also be accompanied by some social demotion, otherwise the higher social classes would grow from generation to generation. While this does happen, it is not as common as might be supposed.[4] As the authors comment: "The best data on social mobility is that presented by Blau and Duncan in *The American Occupational Structure*. They find a simple correlation between the occupational status of fathers and sons of .34 for those born 1897-1906 and .37 for those born 1927-36. This means that if a father ranked in the 84th percentile of the occupational distribution, his son had typically fallen to the 64th percentile."[5]

Jencks and Riesman suggest that "social" and "cultural" classes are increasingly approximating to each other and that—as the Plowden Report suggests—it is

[1] *Op. cit.*, p. 64.
[2] *Op. cit.*, pp. 65-9.
[3] *Op. cit.*, p. 72.
[5] *Op. cit.*, pp. 73-4.
[4] *Op. cit.*, p. 74, note 18.

"cultural" values that express social differentiation and affect the educational progress of the student. As they say: "While schooling may be an instrument for changing men's values and more especially for disseminating the attitudes and skills that characterize the upper-middle class, evidence for this is by no means definitive. Instead, the relationship between schooling and cultural class may often work the other way. Young people's ultimate cultural class may be almost entirely determined by factors such as genetic ability, family structure, social connections, and so forth. Schools and colleges may simply be a sifting device for separating those whose talents and inclinations will land them in one cultural class from those whose talents and inclinations will land them in another."[1]

Their conclusions, drawn from an extensive review of the literature on education, income and social mobility are:

1. The overall level of educational attainment seems to be rising, just as the overall income level is. The overall level of cultural sophistication is probably also rising, though not at anything like the same rate as the standard of living.
2. The distribution of years of schooling is more equitable than the distribution of income, and unlike the income distribution is moving toward greater equity. The absolute attainment gap between the well educated and the poorly educated is growing, however, just as the absolute income gap between rich and poor is growing.
3. The distribution of educational resources, like the distribution of income, does not seem to be getting notably more or less egalitarian. What this implies for the distribution of intellectual competence is debatable, however, just as it is debatable whether a stable distribution of income indicates a stable distribution of occupational power and responsibility.[2]

These conclusions are still controversial. Nevertheless, the evidence is sufficiently strong to suggest that: "The overall relationship between education and occupational status has not changed much over the years, though earning a B.A. may be growing more important than it once was and a high school diploma less so. The relationship between education and income also seems to be fairly stable. The relationship between educational attainment and social mobility seems to be both modest and stable."[3]

All this is not sufficient—far from it indeed—to prove that education, *per se*, has *no* effect on income. What it does is strongly to suggest that education's effects are more subtle than has been supposed by the proponents of the view that it directly affects the income distribution, and to suggest that education tends to reinforce, rather than to diminish existing social inequalities. As Jencks and Riesman illuminatingly suggest: "A good portion of the apparent impact of schooling is, we would suggest, anticipatory socialization. Sending a bright child to school, in other words, is like telling him he has a rich maiden aunt and will

[1] *Op. cit.*, p. 76.
[2] *Op. cit.*, p. 76.
[3] *Op. cit.*, p. 85.

eventually inherit a fortune. The aunt and her money have no direct effect on the child's life or growth. But the *idea* of the money—even if it is non-existent—may have a considerable effect, for the child may feel he has special opportunities and responsibilities. So too with schooling. What actually happens from day to day in a school or college may have relatively little effect on the students—though it certainly has *some* effect. But a good student's knowledge that he can go to college and that a college degree will be a passport to a good job and a comfortable standard of living may have a significant effect on him. He may even adopt the attitudes and acquire the skills he thinks he will need in the world he expects to enter. The fact that he may not really be able to enter this world may be irrelevant at this stage, just as the actual terms of his aunt's will are."[1]

It is in this context, that we return to a consideration of the more purely economic questions. Jencks and Riesman, however, must be allowed the last word. Commenting, as sociologists, on the economics of education, they say: "Cost-benefit analysis need not, of course, support the status quo in all its aspects. But an economic analysis of educational 'outputs' which assumes that present income differentials represent real differences in productivity and which allocates educational resources on this premise can hardly be expected to imply the need for radical changes in income differentials."[2]

[1] *Op. cit.*, pp. 87-8. See also p. 133, where Jencks and Riesman say: "Coming of age in America can be a race for the top. It is seldom a sprint, however, in which victory goes to the naturally gifted or enthusiastic. It is a marathon in which victory goes to those who train the longest and care the most. And it is here that the upper-middle class child has the crucial advantages. He is trained for the contest from birth, and more often than not he is convinced that losing it will mean metaphorical if not literal death.

"For the lower-class or working class child, going to college is a step up in the world, a way of improving on the conditions in which he or she was raised. It may be desirable but it is hardly indispensable."

[2] *Op. cit.*, p. 152, note 116.

5 Private returns to investment in education

MOST of the literature on returns to education is concerned with the return to expenditure viewed as an investment, rather than with the type of aggregative study discussed in the previous chapters.

Two types of calculation of these returns have been attempted. One method is to calculate the return to the individual's investment in education by comparing the costs incurred by the individual, and the returns received by him as a result of this education: the resulting rate is termed the private rate of return. The other method, which will be the subject of the subsequent chapter, is to derive the social rate of return by treating expenditure on education as a social investment and to calculate the costs incurred by, and the returns accruing to society.

In both cases the relationship of returns and costs to other returns and costs are held to be basis of rational decision making. Thus it is held by some advocates that social rates of return to education should play a part in the formulation of educational expenditure policy. The private rates of return are held to govern, as a matter of fact, at least partially, the individual's decisions on his education. This contention, and the meaning that can be assigned to private rates of return, are the subject matter of this chapter.

The total costs to an individual of any education, E, are divided into monetary expenditures borne by him, and opportunity costs. Monetary expenditures include such things as educational fees, books, and equipment. The opportunity costs to the individual of undertaking education is usually measured by the income that he would have received had he been employed. For compulsory education there is no opportunity cost as long as the laws forbidding the employment of children cover all children of less than school leaving age: in developed countries this is normally the case.[1] The total costs have to be compared with the returns to the investment. What are these returns? All published evidence shows that, in large samples and taken as a group, the educated earn more than the less educated. This holds true over more or less the whole educational range. Thus in Britain post-graduates earn more than graduates, who in turn earn more than holders of the Higher National Certificate.[2] These differentials tend to hold true for all age groups. As the calculation of the rate of return

[1] Except for part-time employment.
[2] *Survey of Earnings of Qualified Manpower in England and Wales 1966-1967*. Statistics of Education, Special Series, No. 3, London, 1971.

to education is a marginal analysis the returns to education E are taken to be the extra post-tax lifetime earnings associated with education E over the lifetime earnings associated with the immediately lesser amount of education, say education D. It is accepted by those making such calculation that not all of the extra earnings are due to education but that some is due to innate ability, drive, socio-economic background and other influences. This point will be returned to, but here it is noted that in most (but not all) calculations only a proportion (however derived) of the extra earnings of those with education E, are appropriated to the education. The rate of return of education E, is now the rate of discount which when applied to the stream of extra lifetime earnings just equates them to the total costs of that education.[1] In principle such rates of return can be calculated for different amounts and different types of education. Indeed the calculation of rates of return is something of a growth industry. Rarely a month passes by without the return being calculated to yet another level of education in yet another country. This growth is surprising when one looks at the weaknesses of the data and the many factors which are potential sources of error.

In the case of the private rate of return we will confine attention to the returns side of the analysis. We consider first the data used. Ideally, in deriving the rate of return of an investment, made in year t, in education, E, one needs the excess earnings of those with education E over those of people with some lower education, D, in each of the years $t + 2, \ldots, t + n$, where n is of the order of the magnitude of 45 years, This data is not, and clearly could not be, available, and second-best material has to be substituted. The substitute used is cross-section data showing at a given point in time (t) the earnings of individuals of various ages and with differing amounts of education. Thus, for example, although in principle the extra earnings of the individual in year $t + 45$ are required, the proxy data used are the earnings in year t, of people who were educated to levels E and D in year $t - 45$. The rate of return calculated for education now is thus based on rates of return on past education. There are a number of influences causing divergences between the (desired) time series of future earnings and the (actually used) lifetime earnings derived from cross-section data. Over time, income levels increase in money terms: only increases in real incomes are relevant as all investment decisions are rationally made in terms of constant prices. If all real incomes increase in the same proportion, then absolute income differentials will increase and hence so will the rate of return. Thus use of cross-section data understates the rate of return. Secular increases in income can be allowed for, however, as long as an estimate of the future increase is made, although in most calculations this is not done. Another factor leading to possible understatement is that present graduates from any education may tend to be better educated than those in the past leading again to wider income differentials. On the other hand it could be argued that as more people are educated less extra earning ability will accrue to the educated. The normal practice of those engaged in making such calculations, in most cases where possible divergences occur, is to assume that influences in different directions

---

[1] See Appendix to this chapter for a formalization.

cancel out. This might be so but it is important to make clear these (often implicit) assumptions.

A further disadvantage of cross-section data against life-cycle earnings data is that the former is affected by movements of the economy.[1] In life-cycle earnings data, which relate to a period of 45 to 50 years, the influence of cyclical changes might be expected to (approximately) cancel out, whereas cross-section data is taken for a single year, and the earnings differentials would differ according to whether the data was for a boom or a depression year. As M. W. Reder[2] has shown, skill differentials tend to narrow during periods of excess demand for labour and broaden during slumps. Ideally one would choose a "neutral" year, in the cyclical sense, for the data but it often comes from sources (e.g. censuses) whose timing is outside the investigators' control. The inaccuracy introduced is not likely, however, to be very great and perhaps insignificant when compared to the other sources of error. When comparing returns, not to differing amounts of education but to differing types of education (e.g. various disciplines at University), the use of cross-section data assumes that differentials between occupations will be constant over the next 45 years: this seems implausible.[3]

The most fundamental problem is how much of the observed income differentials between people of different educational attainments are in fact "due to" education. It is accepted as a matter of common sociological knowledge that there is a very close correlation between the amount of education a person receives and his innate ability, the income of his parents, the educational attainment of his parents, his social class, race and sex. Furthermore, of course these other factors are themselves highly correlated. These inter-relationships have been discussed in Chapter 4. Thus there arises the problem that an income differential due, for example, to parental income differentials may be mistakenly attributed to education. In early calculations, although this difficulty was recognized, all income differentials were assigned to education. This was the case in what may be considered the pioneer study of J. R. Walsh in 1935:[4] Walsh used 1926-1932 data to estimate the profitability of high school and various types of college education in the United States. Walsh recognized the problem of innate ability causing some of the observed differences in earnings but saw no way of isolating the separate effects, but referred only obliquely to the other variables.

More recently, however, attempts have been made to determine what proportion of the observed income differentials are due to education. One of the best documented is that by Becker.[5] The estimates relate to 1939 and are of the return to USA college education. On the basis of figures unadjusted for other influences, and using 1949 tax rates, the internal rate of return was calculated as

[1] For a contrary view see Blaug, M., The rate of return on investment in education in Great Britain, in *Manchester School*, Vol. 33, No. 3, 1965, p. 224.

[2] Reder, M. W., The theory of occupational wage differentials, *American Economic Review*, Vol. xlv, December 1955, pp. 833-51.

[3] Although due to discounting the early years receive most "weight" in the calculation.

[4] Walsh, J. R., The capital concept applied to man, *Quarterly Journal of Economics*, Vol. xlix, February 1935, pp. 255-85.

[5] Becker, G. S., *Human Capital*, New York, NBER, 1964, especially pp. 79-88. The theoretical foundation of this work has been discussed in Chapter 2.

13.0%. Cross-section data are used: if allowance is made for a secular increase in real incomes of 1% a year the calculated return increases to 14%, and to 15.3% if a 2% a year increase is allowed for. Becker then attempted to adjust these rates for ability and for father's occupation. Data provided from a survey carried out by the Bell Telephone Company showed that those who did not go on to college ranked lower in their high school class than those who did. On the assumption that they would similarly have ranked lower in college had they gone on to college, those with only high school education would have earned about 7% less than those who in fact had gone on to college.[1] Seven per cent lower earnings account for about 20% of the income differential of college graduates, and the effect is to reduce the rate of return from 13.0% to 11.5%. Data from another study, by Wolfle and Smith yielded rather similar results. Three other studies were cited by Becker. These were a study of college drop-outs, a study of the incomes of brothers, carried out in the 1920s, and a multiple regression analysis by Morgan and David. These studies indicate that smaller adjustments could be made to allow for the influence of intelligence (as measured by I.Q. as opposed to class rank) and for father's occupation. The total evidence was rather limited but Becker concluded that 2/3 of the earnings differentials between college and high school graduates appear to be attributable education. It has been suggested above that the studies cited by Becker do not have the authority of some other major social studies of ability, attainment, and social class.

Denison,[2] derived a similar coefficient from one of the five sources cited by Becker, the study by Wolfle and Smith. This appropriation of about 2/3 of observed income differentials to education seems to have become accepted as the norm. This estimate is based on what is admitted as being rather fragile evidence and on evidence for only one country. Furthermore there are severe statistical difficulties involved in attempting to "standardize" for social background and other variables. One of the crucial assumptions of multi-variate analysis is that the explanatory variables in an equation are not themselves related. Where the explanatory variables are highly correlated—as clearly education, ability, and socio-economic class are—it becomes very difficult or impossible to disentangle their separate efforts. There are several instances of multicollinearity from a more or less hopeless case where the explanatory variables are linked by some equation, to the more likely case where they are highly but not perfectly related. In the latter case it is possible to make estimates of the parameters but the standard errors will tend to be large.[3] The estimates made of the effect of education alone are based on slender evidence, ignoring major studies, and the standard error of the estimates is likely to be large even if the position is accepted, for the purposes of argument, that education, ability, socio-economic class, educational attainment

---

[1] How this conclusion was reached is not clear.

[2] E. F. Denison in Vaizey, J. (ed.), *The Residual Factor and Economic Growth*, Paris, OECD, 1964, pp. 93-111.

[3] For a general survey of the problems involved see Johnstone, J., *Econometric Methods*, New York, 1963, pp. 201-7. Merrett, S., in *The Rate of Return to Education, a Critique*, Oxford Economic Papers, 1966, pp. 289-302, examines in some detail the econometric difficulties in the specific case of education. His conclusion is that research into the rate of return to education should be discontinued.

of parents, etc. are not so hopelessly and inevitably inter-related as to defy separation of the individual effect of each factor.

Further margins of uncertainty, and imprecision, arise from what is termed the "consumption-investment" problem. The difficulty in this case is that rate of return analysis treats education as an investment, whereas to many individuals education is at the same time a consumption expenditure. "Such expenditures, more often than not, are at least in part consumption expenditures as far as both the economic motivation of the investor and the economics effects on the individual and on society are concerned."[1] Thus as education is (partially) consumption not all the costs incurred should be included when calculating the rate of return: in particular, of course, income foregone ceases to represent the opportunity cost. Conceptually the way to avoid this problem is simple: in the calculation either deduct from the costs the consumption element[2] or add the consumption element to the returns.[3] In practice, of course, there is no chance of identifying the consumption and investment elements and so no correction is made.[4] The result is that calculated rates of return are underestimated because of this factor. Thus further imprecision is introduced: the margin of uncertainty can clearly be large. If, for example, 2/3 of education expenditures are viewed as consumption then counting all costs and returns as related to investment underestimates the return by a factor of 3.

The results derived from private rates of return to investment in education have to be interpreted with a great deal of caution. This is not unusual in itself for many economic measurements, but in this case the range of inaccuracy may be so large as to render the estimates literally meaningless. Further, as has been argued in the previous chapter, estimating the returns to education may be attempting to attribute to education something—higher lifetime earnings—which is not in any determinate sense caused by education.

Those authors who have presented these, and similar, calculations see the data as adding substance to a theory of demand for education. In the same way as consumer demand theory seeks to explain consumer behaviour at the micro-level, and investment theory seeks to explain the pattern and level of investment, so a theory of private demand for education is developed to explain how much, and what type of, education individuals wish to invest in. It is cast in the neo-classical mould, postulating that people behave according to some "rational" economic calculus, and defining "rational" as a continual conscious (or unconscious) comparison of rates of return.

According to this view the "rational" person is supposed to invest in an education for himself up to the point when the internal rate of return from that education is equal to the rate of interest reflecting his subjective time prefer-

---

[1] Schaffer, H. G., On investment in human capital, *American Economic Review*, Vol. 52, December 1961, pp. 1026-35.

[2] There has been some discussion as to whether the consumption elements are positive. See Blaug, M., *op. cit.*, pp. 218-20.

[3] Because of the discounting factor these methods would not yield the same results, but this is hardly important in view of the impossibility of measuring the "consumption" element.

[4] Schultz, T. W., *The Economic Value of Education*, New York, 1963, pp. 54-6.

ence.[1] Thus, in England, for example, a 15-year-old boy would ideally discount the extra earnings he would expect from staying on in the sixth form and, comparing with the costs to him of remaining at school, calculate the rate of return. Unless this exceeded his time preference rate he would leave. Assuming he stays, he repeats the calculation when he is 18 carrying out the calculation for University or other forms of Higher Education. Of course at both stages he should carry out a series of calculations, one for each of the various combinations of subjects he could read. However, as he probably had to undertake some specialization when he was 13-years-old, he should (or perhaps his parents should[2]) have carried out similar calculations then. In this way he maximizes the returns from his education. Such calculations are clearly not consciously made—lack of information rules them out from the start—but the notion retains its value if students act *as if* they made such calculations.[3] If they do, then the theory, and the results, have predictive value. One way to test an economic theory, of course, is to compare what the theory would predict with what actually happens. The evidence on the demand for education is not necessarily inconsistent with the hypothesis offered by an economic calculus but neither is it inconsistent with others. With the data at present available, it is just not possible to reject with any certainty any of the various hypotheses which have been put forward.

Becker[4] illustrates the predictive effects of the theory of demand for education. Here two examples will be given. It will be seen that the evidence is not inconsistent with the "rational" economic calculus hypothesis, but that neither is it inconsistent with other hypotheses that can be put forward.

Consider first differences in enrolments in college (USA) between white and non-white males. As stated earlier the estimated unadjusted rate of return to college education for urban white males is put at 14.5%. The "best" estimates of the unadjusted return received by non-white males are 12.3% in the North and 8.3% in the South; on the assumption that all non-whites go to Negro colleges (which is largely the case). If non-whites go to white colleges then because the latter are more expensive, the rate of return falls, in the North to 7.3%. Thus Becker argues, the prediction is that a lower proportion of non-whites would go to college. He tests this on the basis of a "supply schedule" (*S*, in Figure 5.1) relating the percentage of high school graduates going to college, to the return from college, and which assumes away the psychic returns of a college education.

Now *if* non-whites and whites had the same supply schedule, then given the lower returns, Becker would expect a lower proportion of non-white high school graduates to go to college. He then cites evidence that "in 1957, about one-third of all non-white male high school graduates over 25 had some college while a little

---

[1] See Appendix to this chapter. The problem of family investment raises insuperable philosophical problems concerning the nature of the Unit of Welfare as one of the present authors has pointed out: Vaizey, J., *The Economics of Education*, London, 1962, pp. 28-9.

[2] The ambiguity is, of course, fatal to the argument.

[3] For an exposition of what exactly is meant by the *as if* methodology see the analogy of the pool player in Friedman, M. and Savage, L. J., The utility analysis of choices involving risk, *Journal of Political Economy*, Vol. 56, August 1948, pp. 279-304.

[4] Becker, G., *Human Capital, op. cit.*, pp. 94-113.

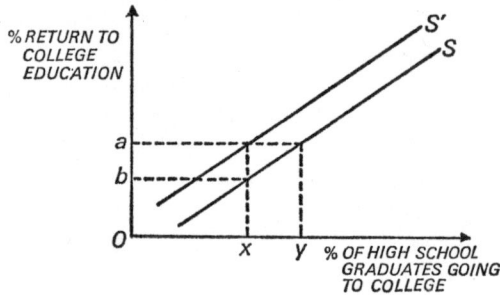

FIG. 5.1

over two-fifths of all white male graduates did". But of course if the supply curve of non-whites is to the left of that of whites (*S'*)—as all the sociological evidence would suggest—then this means nothing. In Figure 5.1, the observation that $x\%$ of non-whites, and $y\%$ of whites go to college can be explained by a lower return ($b\%$ rather than $a\%$) from college education to non-whites, assuming that whites and non-whites have the same supply curve: or alternatively that the returns are the same but that the two groups have different supply schedules. It could also be explained by some intermediate alternative—non-whites receive lower returns and have a different supply schedule. But Becker would still argue "the relatively small differences in the fractions going to college is impressive support of the evidence indicating that the difference in gains is not very great. For *many fewer* non-whites would go to college if this supply curve were much to the left *and* if they gained much less from college."[1]

As a second example consider differences in enrolment between men and women The rate of return to college education for women is stated to be several percentage points less than for men. Thus, on the hypothesis, one would expect a lower proportion of women to go to college: this is in fact the case. Thirty per cent of women high-school graduates go to college whereas 40% of male graduates do. This could equally be explained through marriage patterns, and prejudice against women in higher education. Further, however, the rate of return to non-white females from college education is stated as being greater than that to white females, which is consistent with the higher college enrolment ratios of the former.

On a more aggregate scale it has been suggested that knowledge of private rates of return are useful in forecasting the social demand for education. This contention is examined later and it is argued there that even if the calculated figures are accepted as reasonable approximations, they provide very little—if any—help to forecasters, partially because of the great difficulties in deriving a demand curve and partly because other hypotheses seem to the present authors to be more plausible and meaningful interpretations of the data.

The position thus is that the available empirical data are not yet adequate for

---

[1] Italics in original.

a choice to be made between the various contending hypotheses concerning the demand for education. It is argued here that the accuracy of the figures is probably too low to assign any great weight to them. Leaving this aside for one moment, however, the question whether people base demands for education on some economic calculus of the type outlined in the cited studies is a point incapable of resolution at the moment. This is not to say that earnings factors do not enter into decisions made by individuals about their education. It is just more probable that people weigh up, in some crude and emotional way, various kinds of factors, and make a lunge at a decision. Further than that one cannot—and perhaps should not—go.

APPENDIX: INVESTMENT CRITERIA

In several places in this part reference is made to the discounting of future returns (outlays) and to the calculations of the returns to investment, notably to investment in education either by the individual or by the State. In this appendix the methods of calculation are outlined and the problems involved briefly discussed.

Where the returns to any expenditure accrue over a period of time it is necessary to adjust the returns to take account of the fact that a given sum of money receivable in the future is worth less than that sum receivable now. Thus it is not possible to simply add sums of money receivable at different periods of time. Thus consider a loan of £P_0 at interest rate i, compounded annually.

After one year the lender receives back his principal plus interest, £$P_0 + iP_0 = P_0(1 + i) = P_1$. Thus

$$P_0 = \frac{P_1}{(1 + i)} ;$$

P_0 is the present value of P_1 receivable in one year's time.

If P_1 is re-lent for another year then after two years the lender receives £$P_2 = P_0(1 + i) + i[P_0(1 + i)] = P_0(1 + i)^2$. Thus present value of P_2 is

$$\frac{P_2}{(1 + i)^2} = P_0$$

and in the general case,

$$P_0 = \frac{P_n}{(1 + i)^n}.$$

This is the basis of all discounting calculations. In the literature on the economics of education two methods of calculating returns to an investment appear:

1. *The internal rate of return method*

If C_n = costs of an investment in year n
   R_n = net returns from the investment in year n.

Then the internal rate of return (r) is the rate that equates the costs and returns. Thus solve for r in:

$$\frac{C_1}{(1+r)} + \frac{C_2}{(1+r)^2} + \cdots \frac{C_n}{(1+r)^n} = \frac{R_1}{(1+r)} \quad \frac{R_2}{(1+r)^2} + \cdots + \frac{R_n}{(1+r)^n}.$$

This equation may not have a unique solution.

The investment criteria: (i) invest as long as $r > i$, where i is the rate of interest reflecting the opportunity cost of the investment expenditure; (ii) rank alternatives according to their internal rates of return.

2. *The net discounted value method*

To calculate *NDPV*, discount the costs and returns by the appropriate discount rate (d):

$$NDPV =$$
$$-\frac{C_1}{(1+d)} - \frac{C_2}{(1+d)^2} - \cdots \frac{C_n}{(1+d)^n} + \frac{B_1}{(1+d)} + \frac{B_2}{(1+d)^2} + \cdots \frac{B_n}{(1+d)^n}$$

The investment criteria: (i) invest as long as *NDPV* is positive; (ii) rank alternatives according to *NDPV*.

The criteria compared

Where they yield different results the solution given by *NDVP* is conceptually the correct one. This can be shown in the following example:[1] consider two alternatives A and B with the same cost. Their *NDPV* at different discount rates are plotted below.

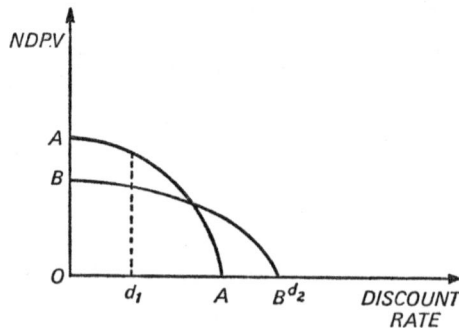

FIG. 5.2

The lines cut because the time distribution of the returns of the two investments differ: at high rates of discount B has the greater *NDPV* and vice-versa. Thus B yields (relatively) more of its returns in the near future: at high rates of discount

[1] From Baumol, W. J., *Economic Theory and Operations Analysis*, New Jersey, Englewood Cliffs, 1965, p. 443.

A's returns which accrue in the more distant future are discounted heavily. Say the discount rate is d_1; then on *NDPV* criterion choose A as it has greater *NDPV*. On the other criterion choose B as its internal rate of return (d_2) is greater. Yet A must be the correct choice for it adds the greater amount to the resources of the owner of the amount invested.

The choice of discount rate

This is crucial to both methods. At what rate should returns be discounted in the *NDPV* method, and what discount rate should the internal rate of return be compared with?

Conceptually, for an individual, it should represent the opportunity cost of the investment, i.e. it should be the rate of return on the next best alternative. With imperfect capital markets and a variety of interest rates the precise rate to be chosen is not clear, but for long term investment (e.g. education) the yield on undated government stock can be taken as a fair approximation.

The literature on the rate relevant to the government investment expenditure is large.[1] Theoretically the rate should reflect society's time preference and also the opportunity cost of funds drawn from the private sector. In the real world the two do not coincide, the latter always tending to be the greater,[2] and a policy decision is required to select the rate. In practice the choice tends to be arbitrary, but again often tends to approximate the yield on undated government stock.

---

[1] For a list of references see Prest, A. R. and Turvey R., Cost benefit analysis: a survey, *Economic Journal*, Vol. 75, No. 300, 1965, pp. 697-700.

[2] Baumol, W. J., On the social rate of discount, *American Economic Review*, Vol. 58, No. 4, 1968, pp. 788-802.

6 Social returns to investment in education

In most countries education is financed, wholly or partly, by the Exchequer. Since the Exchequer has many other claims on its budget an obvious question is how much education should the State finance? As resources at the disposal of the Exchequer are necessarily limited a choice may have to be made between the allocation of extra resources to education, to health services et cetera. There is, in addition, the question of appropriately allocating resources in the non-market sector of the economy. In this context estimates of the social returns to education assume significance, for a possible answer to both questions lies in traditional resource allocation theory. This theory suggests that the State should invest in education up to the point where the social returns equal those from other State expenditures and to the social opportunity cost of the capital employed. Difficulties of measurement and, more important, political factors preclude this method of determining expenditure priorities, but social rates of return might appear to be able to offer guidance about the allocation of resources within the educational sector, even where the total resources to be allocated to education are decided on some other grounds. Calculations might indicate, for instance, that a greater social return would be forthcoming from expanding (say) primary education rather than some other level of education, or that the education of (say) linguists offers a higher return to society than education of (say) botanists. The use of social rates of return might thus be a useful tool in determining the shape of the development of an educational system.

The form of the calculation for social rates of return is the same as in the case of private rates of return—the rate which when applied to the stream of social returns just equates them to the social cost. The difference between private and social rates lies in what is included in the costs and the returns. To private outlays is added expenditure by the State on education: thus in the calculations that have been made the social costs consist of educational costs incurred by individuals plus educational costs incurred by the State[1] plus the opportunity costs incurred by individuals. The latter are a large component of the total costs: Schultz[2] estimates that 59% of the total resource costs of four years of college education are opportunity costs. However, the use of income foregone to measure opportunity costs, and the use of opportunity costs in an aggregate measure is open to serious objection.[3]

[1] Excluding transfer payments.

[2] Schultz, T. W., *The Economic Value of Education*, New York, 1963, p. 29.

[3] pp. 23-30, and see also Bowman, M. J., The costing of human resource development, in *The Economics of Education*, E. A. G. Robinson and J. Vaizey (eds.), London, 1966, pp. 421-50, and the discussion of her paper, pp. 689-708.

Whereas the returns to an individual from education are calculated from after-tax lifetime earnings differentials, the social returns are calculated from pre-tax differentials. Basically, therefore, the same data are used in both sets of calculations and the weaknesses of using cross-section data are common to both. The addition of public expenditures and public (tax) receipts are usually the only two changes made to the calculation of private returns to convert them to social returns. The calculations are therefore for the social return to education in a narrow sense of the term as only direct returns to the immediate beneficiaries are included. External benefits and costs i.e. those accruing to other than the immediate beneficiaries are excluded. The application of the term "social rate of return" to measures excluding externalities is unfortunate, and has given rise to some confusion. The measures relevant to public investment decisions are those which include externalities and which further make adjustments to allow for deviations of wages and prices from their competitive levels. Calculations of "social rates of return" rarely include either externalities or such adjustments. It is thus incorrect to refer to such calculations as cost benefit analyses: they are simply investment appraisals and as such are not, by themselves adequate for decision making in the public education sector. To avoid ambiguity the measures which convert from private rates of return by adding public expenditure and receipts will be termed "social rates of return" in the narrow sense, as opposed to the "true social rates of returns".

Weisbrod[1] has classified the other beneficiaries into three groups:

1. Residence related. For example, children's attendance at school enables mothers to enter employment. As an illustration of the possible benefits Weisbrod assumed that one million of the 3.5 million working mothers with children six to eleven years old in the USA (1956) would not have worked in the absence of school. Thus if each had earned $2000, "the value of the care service of elementary school may be estimated as roughly $2 billion a year". This was about 25% of the total resource cost of elementary schooling. Other residence related beneficiaries include neighbours—the higher social values of educated children may, for example, improve neighbourhood environment—and the future family of the educated person. It has already been emphasized that children of educated parents are likely to enjoy high lifetime earnings.
2. Employment related. The education of one worker may confer benefits on other workers. Thus if it is assumed that education develops flexibility and adaptability then, where production requires properties, others will benefit —their productivity will be increased—from the employment of educated people. As Weisbrod points out, this argument depends crucially on the assumption that education does in fact develop the properties of flexibility and adaptability.
3. Society in general. Here Weisbrod grouped cases where the benefits are widely diffused and where it is hard to identify the beneficiaries. An example

[1] Weisbrod, B. A., Education and investment in human capital, *Journal of Political Economy*, Vol. 70, No. 5, Part 2, pp. 106-23.

is literacy. Literacy is of value not only to those possessing it, and to the employment and residence related beneficiaries, but to other people as well. Without widespread literacy the transmission of information by the written word would dwindle; "and it seems fair to say that the communication of information is of vital importance to the maintenance of competition and, indeed, to the existence of a market economy, as well as to the maintenance of political democracy." Also, some minimal level of arithmetic competence is clearly necessary for the functioning of a money economy. It has also been argued that there is some presumption that the more educated members of a society are, the more likely is it that that society will be law abiding; in so far as this is true, education confers benefits on society in general. External benefits of education also arise from the basic research promoted in higher education institutions, by the extent to which benefits of research are understated by the salaries of those who undertake it.

As the external diseconomies of education are not likely to be large, the social rate of return including external effects will be greater than the social rate of return in the narrow sense. Further, the difference may be very large, which introduces the question of measurement of the external effects. It is possible to value some externalities, the case of working mothers for example, but as many are intangibles, they may be difficult to quantify—let alone value unambiguously.[1] Where calculations like these are used as a basis of decision making, a statement of intangibles is presented to the policy maker, with the calculation for those benefits that can be both enumerated and evaluated. The fact that it is not possible to evaluate all the external effects of education is not peculiar to the calculation of social returns to education: it is a major problem in evaluating all public investment. The benefits of education are, however, very widely diffused which makes the problem more acute. It has been suggested that although the indirect returns to education cannot be completely measured, an upper limit can be put on the true social rate of return, the lower limit being provided by the social rate of return in the narrow sense. Thus Becker[2] argues that the upper limit is provided by macroeconomic studies of the returns to education. Denison calculated that .58 percentage points of the U.S. annual growth rate between 1929 and 1957 were due to growth of knowledge and .67 percentage points were due to education. Since the social rate in the narrow sense was calculated as 13%, the maximum to be imputed for indirect effects is about 12%, and the upper limit of the social rate of return is thus about 25%. This series of steps depends of course on an acceptance of the calculation of the residual, which was discussed earlier, and still leaves a considerable range of indeterminacy. Indeterminacy in these matters is, of course, inevitable—and is a major source of doubt as to the value of this work. However, even this step does not get us much further on, for the economic objectives are but one set of the objectives of education. The only benefit reflected by the calculated social rates of return in the narrow sense is

---

[1] For a discussion of valuation problems and of cost benefit analysis in general see Prest, A. R. and Turvey, R., Cost benefit analysis: a survey, *Economic Journal*, Vol. 75, No. 300, 1965, pp. 683-735.

[2] Becker, G., *Human Capital*, New York, NBER, 1964, pp. 119-20.

the contribution education makes to the earnings of those who receive education: these extra earnings are held to reflect extra output. All the other objectives of education are, of necessity, ignored. There are purely educational objectives and there are social objectives—intellect may be valued for its own sake: one goal may be the lessening of inequality in educational opportunity or to render young people more able to fit easily into society: and so on. Thus economic factors are not the only ones to be taken into account in policy decisions: probably no one pretends they are. The point is that, perhaps more than any other major public sector, it is not at all clear that the economic factors are even the most important.

It was suggested earlier that calculations of social returns might be useful in determining the total resources to be devoted to education, and also in determining the allocation of resources within the education sector. These contentions are discussed in the remainder of this chapter, where the assumptions on which such calculations are based will also be examined.

By calculating social returns to different levels and different types of education an optimal allocation of resources within the education sector might be arrived at, or, more probably, extreme cases of misallocation could be identified. In a perfect competition situation, of course, the social rates of return to each (say) level of education should be equal. It is convenient to take an example of such calculations and centre the discussion around it.

Before turning to the example it is worth noting that calculations of the social rate of return in the narrow sense always tend to yield lower figures than calculated for private rates. The addition of expenditure on education by the State, which is not discounted, more than offsets the extra returns that arise through using pre-, rather than post-tax data, many of which are heavily discounted. Unless the unlikely assumption is made that the external benefits are just equal to the difference between the private and social rates of return, it is probable that the State (if it acted on these criteria) would supply a different, and lesser, amount of education than private returns calculations might imply.

J. A. Smyth and N. L. Bennett[1] have calculated social rates of return (in the narrow sense) to four educational sectors in Uganda—primary (seven years), lower secondary (four years), higher secondary (two years) and University (three years). Over 80% of those possessing at least school certificate qualifications are employed in the government sector, and the discounted lifetime earnings of those in the three latter sectors were derived from government salary scales, adjusted to allow for the rather higher salaries ruling in the private sector. Those with only primary education were assumed to have age-earnings profiles similar in shape to those of the more educated, and those with no education to have earnings unaffected by age: in both cases estimates were made of their earnings in peasant farming and in wage employment. The present value of the earnings, representing benefits, was derived using a discount rate of 12% and using convergent series, i.e. assuming that a person works for ever. The cost of each education was then estimated and the benefit cost ratios calculated. These

[1] Smyth, J. A. and Bennett, N. L., Rates of return on investment in education: a tool for short-term educational planning, illustrated with Ugandan data, in *World Year Book of Education, 1967*, London, 1967, pp. 299-322.

calculations were then translated into rates of return shown in Table 6.1.

TABLE 6.1 *Rates of return on investment in different education sectors, Uganda, 1965*

University	.	.	.	12%
Higher Secondary	.	.	.	78%
Lower Secondary	.	.	.	22%
Primary	.	.	.	66%

Source: Smyth, J. A. and Bennett, N. L., *op. cit.*, p. 319.

Three points about the results can be made immediately. All the results are too high because of the use of convergent series. Secondly the returns to higher secondary education are considered to be freakish as the market for such leavers is very small: most of them pass on to university. Thirdly the return to university education may tend to be (relatively) understated; this point is returned to later. The lesson of the results taken at face value is clear, however. It is that Uganda should have expanded primary relative to higher education at that time.

What are the implicit assumptions that have to be fulfilled before changes in educational policy are warranted on the basis of such results? J. B. Knight— referring specifically to the Ugandan figures—has argued that two conditions should be met: "(1) the earnings of different educational categories of labour must measure the net marginal *social* benefit of their differential education and (2) the relation between earnings differentials and the rate of expansion of educated manpower must be known."[1]

Condition (1) breaks down into several parts. It is known that at least part of earnings differentials are due not to education but to other factors.[2] In the Ugandan case this is apparently less important than in developed countries.[3] In the general case, however, some adjustment should be made and this, as argued above, introduces a range of inaccuracy into the results. Secondly earnings may not even reflect marginal *private* products: for equality between the two all firms must be profit maximizers. This condition clearly does not hold in Uganda where most of the people whose earnings have been used for the calculations work for the government or other public bodies and the issue thus becomes whether the marginal productivity theory of distribution is a reasonable approximation to the facts. The argument has been rehearsed many times before and there seems little point in discussing it further here. Neild's comment will simply be re-stated: ". . . the division between those who believe in the marginal productivity theory of distribution and those who do not (is) a matter of faith: it (is) not something that could be resolved by discussion (or conversion)".[4]

[1] Knight, J. B., Earnings, employment, education and income distribution in Uganda, *Bulletin of the Oxford University Institute of Economics and Statistics*, Vol. 30, No. 4, 1968, pp. 267-97.
[2] See Chapters 4 and 5.
[3] Knight, J. B., The determination of wages and salaries in Uganda, *Bulletin of the Oxford University Institute of Economics and Statistics*, Vol. 29, No. 3, 1967. See especially pp. 254-258.
[4] In Vaizey, J. (ed.), *The Residual Factor and Economic Growth*, Paris, OECD, 1964, p. 273.

Thirdly, even if one accepts—which the authors do not—that wages reflect marginal private products, before they can legitimately be used to measure social benefits they should also reflect marginal social products. To accept wage rates as measuring marginal social benefits is to accept the values placed upon men by the market, tradition, and institutional factors. As Smyth and Bennett point out ". . . the level of earnings of Uganda's univesity graduates is probably as much a reflection of ex-British colonial salary scales as a reflection of their potential 'worth' to the Uganda economy". In another way the use of earnings data may underestimate the social benefits of university education to Uganda. "The trouble is that the earnings of the higher educated underestimate in a peculiar way the contributions of such people to the gross domestic product: some of the earnings of the uneducated are, in fact, earned for them by the highly educated. The District Agricultural officer with five thousand peasant cotton growers under his wing can be a crucially important factor in the development of cotton culture in his locality, in so far as he is a major agent in the dissemination of technological information relevant to the local agricultural economy."[1] Salaries in developed countries, similarly, are ambiguous measures of "worth": in what sense do teachers' salaries in the United Kingdom, for instance, measure their "worth" to the economy? It is also well known that the high salaries earned by some professional groups are solely due to market imperfections: although corrections can be made, in principle, for such imperfections. The point here is, however, that corrections of this sort do not appear to have been often made in calculations of the social rate of return. There still remains of course a further major cause of divergence between private and social products—the existence of externalities—which has been discussed above, though when considering decisions of resource allocation *within* the education sector, externalities present less of a problem, since they may not differ significantly between levels of education.

The second of Knight's conditions is that the relation between earnings differentials and the rate of expansion of educated manpower must be known. Given present data, calculations can usually only be made for average rates of return whereas what are needed are marginal rates. If the results are used for relatively short-term policy making and for small changes, then this may not be too serious —although it is in the nature of things that because of the time lags involved, a long-term view involving major shifts is necessary.

The true social returns to investment in education are, then, more difficult to calculate with any accuracy than the private returns. All the difficulties encountered in the private calculations recur and there is in addition the measurement of the external benefits to contend with.[2] There are also the difficulties of adjusting ruling salary levels for labour market imperfections though these problems are, perhaps, no more serious than in cost benefit analysis. The externalities give a large range of indeterminacy to the calculated results, as Becker has indicated. Even if the upper limit is accepted as that suggested by the Denison-type calcu-

---

[1] Smyth, J. A. and Bennett, N. L., *op. cit.*, p. 320.
[2] Nor, as J. Vaizey's *The Costs of Education* (London, 1958) shows, is public and private expenditure on education easy to calculate.

lations, the true social returns to education (in the cost-benefit sense) may be anything up to twice as great as the figure calculated net of external benefits. The operational significance of so vague a number cannot be great. When considering resource allocation within the education sector the external benefits problem may not provide so severe an obstacle. Some external benefits are quantifiable and the view may justifiably be taken that the others may not vary in such a way within the sector as to invalidate the quantitative results. Nevertheless, because of the serious difficulties encountered in the calculation of the social rates of return, it is clear that large differences in the return to different levels or types of education would have to be apparent before the results have any great significance for educational policy making.

The usefulness of the results of these kinds of calculations in aiding decisions on resource allocation between different parts of the public sector seems precluded by the problems of externalities. Prest and Turvey have summarized the position: "It is no good expecting those fields in which benefits are widely diffused, and in which there are manifest divergencies between accounting and economic costs or benefits, to be as cultivable as others. Nor is it realistic to expect that comparisons between projects in entirely different branches of economic activity are likely to be as meaningful or fruitful as those between projects in the same branch. The technique is more useful in the public-utility area than the social-services area of government. Comparisons between, say, different road projects are more helpful than those between, say, road and water projects: and both of these are likely to be more helpful than applications in the fields of education, health, research and so on."[1] It is the present authors' view also that, even within education, the usefulness of such studies is very limited.

[1] Prest, A. R. and Turvey, R., *op. cit.*, p. 731.

7 The social demand for education

Social demand in general

THE Robbins report[1] had as a guiding principle the axiom that "courses of higher education should be available for all those who are qualified by ability and attainment to pursue them, and who wish to do so". A goal implicit in Dutch planning is stated as: "If a sufficiently qualified citizen stands at the door of any type of school he must be admitted, and it is the responsibility of the appropriate government authorities to anticipate his requests so that school capacity will be adequate to accommodate him."[2] The educational system is thus seen as adapting itself to student pressures, and also to student choices, for no attempt is made to force or persuade students to enrol for any particular subject. Starting as it does from the inputs into the educational system the social demand approach is thus a complete contrast to the manpower approach which starts with outputs and which expects that the educational system will be changed according to the projected manpower requirements of the economy. For clarity the two types of projection have been considered separately but neither conceptually nor practically are they mutually exclusive: it is clear, for instance, that manpower influences will affect in some way the social demand for education.

The social demand for education is given greatest emphasis in the planning of the more developed countries, perhaps because with their higher living standard they attach less importance to satisfying incremental material needs. Thus the "consumption" element of education is given relatively more weight than the "investment" element. Discussion here is confined to more developed countries; the examples cited are from Western Europe where demand factors have taken a decisive role in many forecasts. A notable exception however, has been the forecasts made in the MRP countries which have been largely based on manpower considerations.[3]

Most published forecasts of future student numbers have dealt with only one part of the educational system, or have dealt separately with the various parts. Recently there has been dissatisfaction with this approach for it tends to ignore, or obscure, the interdependencies between the different parts of the system. This dissatisfaction has stimulated the development of models of the whole educational system so that, for example, the implications of changes in secondary education for higher education can be determined and the consequential policy

[1] *Higher Education*, London, HMSO, 1963, p. 8.
[2] *Educational Policy and Planning: Netherlands*, Paris, OECD, 1961.
[3] Except in Portugal.

decisions made. Ultimately the result of present work in developing such models would ideally be, as a recent OECD report[1] has stated, a computable model of the whole system which would be able to:

1. demonstrate how the educational system would develop, assuming no change in its structure;
2. demonstrate the effect on all branches of the system of a given policy decision;
3. show the developments, or changes, in the system needed to attain certain targets.

In this chapter attention will be confined to models of the educational system that implicitly incorporate a social demand approach to education, what have been termed "demand for places models". Such models do not exclude manpower influences nor is it desirable that they should do so: thus the models can show the implications for the educational system of a given set of manpower requirements. However, models of the demand for places type should be distinguished from those which are essentially concerned with the outputs rather than the inputs of the system: these are basically of the manpower forecasting type. The best known example is the Correa-Tinbergen model.[2] Having derived manpower coefficients it shows that growth in the economy may typically lead to disequilibria in the (three sector) educational system. The model has subsequently been refined and developed by Tinbergen and Bos.[3]

In the following section the model of the educational system developed by Stone[4] is outlined. This model is described in order to indicate the approach used in demand for places models, and in order to provide a framework in which to discuss various forecasts of future enrolments which have been published and in which to discuss various forecasts of future enrolments which have been published and in which to discuss the social demand for education. It is not the purpose of this chapter to survey educational models,[5] and a general outline of the mechanics of demand for places models,[6] is in the present context less useful.

The following section describes in some detail projections of the social demand for education. The remaining sections of this chapter examine various factors influencing the growth of the social demand: particular attention is given, in the final section, to economic influences.

[1] *Methods and Statistical Needs for Educational Planning*, Paris, OECD, 1967, p. 21.

[2] Correa, H. and Tinbergen, J., Quantitative adaption of education to accelerated growth, *Kyklos*, Vol. 15, 1962, pp. 777-86.

[3] Tinbergen, J. and Bos, H. C., A planning model for the educational requirements of economic development, in *The Residual Factor and Economic Growth*, Paris, OECD, 1964, pp. 147-69.

[4] Stone, R., A model of the educational system, *Minerva*, Vol. III, No. 2, Winter 1965, pp. 172-86.

[5] For a comprehensive survey see Correa, H., A survey of mathematical models in educational planning, in *Mathematical Models in Educational Planning*, Paris, OECD, 1967, pp. 21-93: see also the papers by R. M. Stone and P. L. Dressel in the same publication.

[6] See *Methods and Statistical Needs for Education Planning*, op. cit., pp. 17-31.

Stone's "demand for places" model

The purpose of Stone's model is to derive "the present implications of future levels of educational activity as determined by the evolution of the demand for places on one hand and the economic demand for the products of education on the other". It is essentially a sub-model of the whole economy but it is described here as a separate entity. The scope of the model extends to all schools (excluding nursery), colleges, universities, and other institutions that provide formal training leading to qualifications e.g. professional bodies. The model is of the input-output type: the primary inputs are 5-year-olds and the final outputs are those leaving (graduating from) the system from any one of the processes (educational stages); these and the flows within the system being represented by an input-output accounting matrix.

The model, under the assumption that the student passes to a new process each year, can be outlined as follows.

Represent the stock of pupils by the vector s, whose elements represent the number of pupils in each process.

Each year some will die: if $\hat{h}$ is a diagonal matrix of survival rates then during the year $(I-\hat{h})s$ will die and $\hat{h}s$ will survive. Thus:

$$(7.1) \qquad\qquad s = (I - \hat{h})s + \hat{h}s.$$

If p is the vector whose elements represent the probabilities that a student in (say) process j will be in process $j + 1$ next year, then of the survivors $\hat{p}\hat{h}s$ will continue in the system next year and the rest, $(I - \hat{p})\hat{h}s$, will leave.

Thus the last term in (7.1) can be divided:

$$(7.2) \qquad\qquad s = (I - \hat{h})s + \hat{p}\hat{h}s + (I - \hat{p})\hat{h}s.$$

The last two terms of (7.2) can be re-written:

1. If Es represents next years initial stock of students in each process, (E being an operator that advances the variable to which it is applied by one unit of time, here a year), and J is a matrix with all elements zero except those above the main diagonal, which are one, then

$$\hat{p}\hat{h}s = JEs.$$

2. The last term is simply the proportion $(I - \hat{p})$ of the survivors who leave the system. It is the vector of graduate leavers, g.

Thus substituting in (7.2)

$$s = (I - \hat{h})s + JEs + g$$

which can be re-written

as

$$(7.3) \qquad\qquad s = \hat{h}^{-1}JEs + \hat{h}^{-1}g$$

or as

$$s = Ts + T\,\Delta s + \hat{h}^{-1}g$$

where $T = \hat{h}^{-1}J$ and $\Delta = E - 1$, the first difference operator.

(7.3) is the flow equation of an open, dynamic, input-output model. Given any present stock of pupils (and their distribution among processes i.e. the vector s) it can predict the future flow of graduate leavers from the system. Or, of course, for any flow of future leavers it indicates the required present stock.

To determine the evolution of the system over time, the exogenous demographic component, the birth and survival process has to be included. The following equation is derived:

$$s = \hat{q}n_2,$$

where $\hat{q}$ is a vector of enrolment ratios, and n_2 is the vector of numbers in each student age group, derived from the birth and survival process, the details of which do not concern us here. By applying the operator E to this expression (or more correctly to the expression when the term for n_2 is substituted) future student numbers can be calculated. The important point is that the enrolment ratios are functions of the transition probabilities. For compulsory education they are both equal to one and for the first year of voluntary education they are also equal. In subsequent years of voluntary education the elements of q are a function of past elements of p. Thus given the time path of q, and hence p, the evolution of the population and an initial population vector, future values of the student population by process, i.e. s, can be calculated.

Ignoring the survival rates, which are clearly not an educational variable, the key parameter that has to be estimated is p, the vector of transition probabilities. Under the assumptions of the model their value is 1 up to the compulsory school leaving age. Subsequently the value of the p_j obviously lies between 0 and 1. Given adequate data the present values can be derived but the crucial point is how they move over time. A model that uses current transition probabilities in its projections is unlikely to be very helpful. The values of p_j above the leaving age imply values for voluntary enrolment ratios and it will be seen when various projections are considered that the estimation of these is the most hazardous step in the process. The major determinant in Stone's model is taken from epidemiology. "The suggestion made here is that higher education[1] should be regarded as a series of epidemic processes in which changes in the demand for places depend, in part, on the number infected and so liable to infect others and, in part, on the number not yet infected and so liable to catch the infection." A simple example is given to show how this notion is used in the determination of p_j over time. Assume a single sequence of higher education consisting of three processes, e.g. staying on in the Sixth Form, going to University, and postgraduate study, and let p_1 be the proportion of school leavers who stay on in the Sixth Form, p_2 the proportion of Sixth Form who go to University, et cetera and define:

$$p = p_1, p_2, p_3.$$

---

[1] i.e. education after compulsory school leaving age.

Then the evolution of student numbers can be given by the three difference equations

$$\Delta p_1 = a_1 p_1 (1 - b_1 - p_1)$$
$$\Delta p_2 = a_2 p_2 (1 - b_2 - p_2)$$
$$\Delta p_3 = a_3 p_3 (1 - b_3 - p_3)$$

which can be written in matrix form as

(7.4) $$\Delta p^* = \hat{a} \hat{p}^* (i - b - p^*).$$

This can be explained as follows: the change in p_1 from one year to the next is related by the factor of proportionality (a_1) to the proportion who attended this year (p_1) and to the proportion who did not attend this year but who had the ability, and similarly for p_2 and p_3.

(7.4) can be re-written as

$$E p^* = \hat{p}^* [i + \hat{a}(i - b - p^*)]$$

where E is an operator as defined above.

This system of equations give rise to growth curves: the trend of the increases in p will be that at low values of p the increases in p will be small but for intermediate values of p will be high, falling off in value as the value of p becomes near to unity. That the change in proportion of pupils at each stage who will move on to a further stage should follow such a pattern is intuitively attractive but it will be seen that, despite supporting evidence, forecasts often rely on straight line projections.

A development of the model in the University sector is to disaggregate the total social demand into the demand for places in different departments. Here the epidemic model alone ceases to be adequate. Stone suggests that the choice of subject is determined by a combination of three factors: the difficulty of each subject, the employment and earnings prospects arising from each subject, and the contagious effect.[1] He is not very specific about the strength of the economic factors nor the weight that should be given to them: this is important, however, and it is discussed further below. This is clearly a point at which the sub-model links up with the economy as a whole.

The remainder of this model of the educational system is concerned with the resulting demand for economic inputs, particularly teachers, and their supply: these points are not relevant here, but are discussed in the chapter dealing with the supply and demand for teachers.

Possible refinements to the model, discussed by Stone, are:

1. Treating different socio-economic classes separately, as the evidence shows that the various social classes are at different stages of educational penetration, i.e. above the school leaving age the p_j differ according to social class.
2. Improving the simple representation of students moving from process to process. Partly this involves allowing for the existence of different streams, but more important allowing for variations in the time students spend in a

[1] No evidence is produced in support of this contention.

process. In the model outlined above the same transfer probabilities are used for those entering a process for the first time and for repeaters.[1]

Stone states that the effect of such modifications, however, is not to alter the conclusions significantly.[2] It should be emphasized that the model was chosen because it provides a useful framework for discussion and it is not presented as a definitive work. Thus Stone argues that the input-output framework will have to give way to a programming formulation, and in subsequent articles[3] he has outlined a demographic accounting system.

In these the demographic factors are no longer exogenous and the flow of pupils through the education system are placed in the context of a complete demographic model: at the moment this has only been attempted for the under 19 age group, and is a long way from completion.

Trends of voluntary enrolments

In the event projections are not normally made for the whole system. For clarity the system will be divided into three parts, compulsory education, voluntary education in schools, and higher education, although this is not, of course, meant to imply that projections are made in such divisions.[4]

Underlying the educational forecasts are demographic forecasts. The demographic estimates are provided for the educational planners by the government actuary's department, and usually have to be accepted as given by the planners.[5] Estimates of future births have to be made on assumptions regarding variables that are inherently unstable, such as average age of marriage rates, and size and spacing of families, and as is well known, such estimates are subject to wide margins of error. Demographic research is often under-supported and it is not surprising that many predictions have been hopelessly wrong. However, it is difficult to see what educational planners can do except accept the estimates of the government actuary, where these are available.[6]

The estimation of the future school population receiving compulsory education would appear to be straightforward, 100% of the cohort, but this is rarely the case. In less developed countries compulsory enrolment ratios are often less than 50% and even in Western European countries there is divergence between the legal and the actual situation: in Portugal, for example, in 1961 only 79.2%

[1] The simple assumption often has to be made. In Thonstad's model (*Education and Manpower*, London, 1969), which is of the Markov chain type, allowing for repeaters having different transition ratios would involve introducing second (and higher) order Markov chains and thus further significantly increasing the amount of computation.

[2] In England the number of repeaters is small, except in further education and hence modification (2.) above is not as important as in countries where repetition ratios are higher.

[3] Stone, R., Input-output and demographic accounting, *Minerva*, Vol. IV, No. 3, Spring 1966, pp. 365-80: and Stone, R. and G., and Gunton, J., An example of demographic accounting; the school ages, *Minerva*, Vol. VI, No. 2, Winter 1968, pp. 185-212.

[4] The chapter on the supply and demand for teachers is concerned with schools only, and hence considering school education separately here is convenient.

[5] Although sometimes with reservations: see *The Demand for and Supply of Teachers, 1963-86*, London, HMSO, 1965, pp. 32-4.

[6] In Ireland no estimates were available to the producers of the report, *Investment in Education*, Dublin, Stationery Office, 1965, who made their own population forecasts.

of the age group 7-10, for which schooling was compulsory, were enrolled and in Sweden in 1963 only 88 % of the 14-year-olds were in school. It can be argued that such a divergence will tend to be greatest where the legal situation is based more on idealistic or prestige grounds than on economic and cultural considerations.[1] Enrolment for compulsory education is also likely to be relatively low where the legal minimum age for entering the labour force is lower than the school leaving age. In such circumstances there is an opportunity cost of compulsory education which does not exist where the two legal requirements coincide. There is also a purely statistical reason why compulsory enrolment ratios are unlikely to be precisely 100%. Whereas figures for enrolments are derived directly from school sources, the population by age-group is calculated by interpolation of census data, except of course in census years. Thus as the figures are on different statistical bases any coincidence would be rare. As national education plans are largely concerned with the State (or maintained or aided) sector, the proportion of children below the school leaving age who attend private schools also has to be estimated: this proportion, however, changes only slowly over time and does not present much difficulty. The estimation of future compulsory enrolments although not as simple as they might appear are, however, clearly likely to be more accurate than the forecasts of voluntary enrolments.

In recent years voluntary enrolments in schools have increased rapidly in European countries as shown by the table below.

TABLE 7.1 *Growth of voluntary school enrolments in selected Western European countries, 1955-1965*

	School Leaving Age	Growth Rate per Annum (%)
Belgium	14	7.7 (a)
Denmark	14	8.6
England and Wales	15	9.5 (b)
Italy	14	7.1 (a)
Norway	14	10.7 (c)
Portugal	13 (d)	9.2
Sweden	16	10.6
W. Germany.	14–15	—2.6 (a)
Yugoslavia	15	9.2 (c)

(a) Second Cycle of Secondary education, 17-18 year olds.
(b) 1956-66.
(c) 1955-64.
(d) 1955-63. 15 years for 1964-65. Applies to pupils who have not yet reached a certain minimum standard.

Sources: UNESCO Statistical Year Book 1966, Paris, UNESCO, 1968.
Statistics of Education, 1966, Vol. I, London, HMSO, 1967.
Study on the Demand for and Supply of Teachers, Paris, OECD, 1967 (mimeographed).

[1] Tinbergen, J., Educational assessments, in *Economic and Social Aspects of Educational Planning*, Paris, UNESCO, 1964, pp. 165-205.

The fall in voluntary enrolments in Germany is largely explained by a rapid reduction of enrolments in part-time "berufsschulen" which were at a high level in 1955, the figures for Germany[1] being derived from attendance figures unadjusted to full-time equivalent pupils.

Given the demographic forecasts the planner has to apply projected enrolment ratios to obtain future school populations, by age-group. The estimation of the ratios presents many difficulties, particularly as past trends may be a poor guide to future changes: here attention will be concentrated on two aspects. What is the effect of raising the school leaving age and secondly, following Stone, what is likely to be the growth curve of voluntary enrolment ratios?

The effect of changes in legislation will have been taken into account in estimates of future enrolments, although being political decisions their timing may not be known.[2] Experience has shown that the result of raising the school leaving age is to raise the social demand for education at the next level, although the extent of the increase is difficult to forecast. Published projections for England and Wales have not taken explicitly into account the raising of the school leaving age from 15 to 16 in 1973 in projecting enrolments of the over 16-years-old age range. The Ninth Report of the National Advisory Council on the Training and Supply of Teachers stated that in its projections, "in the absence of any firm basis of calcuation, no allowance has been made for any possible secondary effects of the higher school leaving age on this trend"[3] (of more pupils staying on voluntarily). It is still not possible to integrate the effect of raising the school leaving age explicitly into projections of voluntary enrolments. However to the extent that present voluntary enrolment ratios reflect anticipation of the forthcoming change, the effect is implicitly included by projecting present trends in these enrolments.[4] Different assumptions about the effect of legislation can yield very different results. This can be illustrated by reference to estimates by Armitage and Smith.[5] In the projection, which is made solely for illustrative purposes, the transition proportions ruling in 1963-64 are assumed to stay constant through the projection. This isolates the effect of the decision: if increasing transition proportions were allowed simultaneously then the difference between the two estimates would be significantly increased. Two limiting assumptions about the behaviour of those who are forced to stay on at school when they would otherwise have left are: (1) "they will take the characteristics of the people who stay on at present voluntarily, i.e. their future movements will be determined by the same transition proportions";[6] (2) that they leave as soon as possible.

The resulting voluntary enrolments i.e. enrolments in schools of 16-19-year-olds in 1988[7] number 860,800 and 596,000 respectively. The upper limit assump-

[1] And also for Belgium and Italy.

[2] Forecasts for England and Wales made before January 1968 were invalidated when it was decided to postpone the raising of the school leaving age.

[3] *The Demand for and Supply of Teachers, 1963-86, op. cit.,* p. 36.

[4] *Statistics of Education, 1969, Vol. 1,* pxvi, London, 1970.

[5] Armitage, P., and Smith, C., A computable model of the Educational System, illustrated with British data, in *The World Year Book of Education, 1967,* London, 1967, pp. 423-39.

[6] Using the earlier terminology, they all become infected.

[7] Based on raising school leaving age in 1971.

tion yields enrolments 44% greater. Reality will lie between the two assumptions but the example illustrates the wide range of possible results. One possible hypothesis is that voluntary enrolment trends are relative to the school leaving age. Thus if the school leaving age is now 15, the annual increase in the proportion of 17-year-olds at school after the leaving age is raised will be the same as the present annual increase in the proportion of 16-year-olds at school.[1] The authors of the Ninth Report were presumably provided with forecasts based on various assumptions but, as stated earlier, as there is no firm evidence on the effect of the change, chose to assume that it would have no effect. Admittedly quantitative evidence which seems to indicate a correlation between legislation enforcing compulsory education and voluntary enrolment ratios has to be interpreted with caution; the increase in ratios might have occurred in any event, and in making comparisons it has to be remembered that exceptions are often granted in legislation. These points are well illustrated by data presented by Stigler.

TABLE 7.2 *Average by states of percentage of children enrolled in schools by age and maximum age through which attendance was compulsory, 1940*

Maximum age of compulsory attendance	Age of children			
	15	16	17	18
	URBAN			
18	94.4	88.8	76.6	49.8
17	90.7	81.1	67.8	43.8
16	92.7	81.0	66.5	41.0
15	85.6	72.8	54.6	33.0
14	80.8	67.2	50.2	30.6
	FARM			
18	90.3	81.5	68.8	45.4
17	79.0	66.1	51.6	32.5
16	81.1	66.5	51.1	32.4
15	72.4	57.6	40.9	25.2
14	73.0	58.1	40.8	24.1

Source: Stigler, G. J., *Employment and Compensation in Education*, NBER, Occasional Paper No. 33, pp. 67-70.

It will be noted that enrolment ratios for children of less than the maximum school leaving age is in every case less than 100%. In many States exceptions were granted to legislation e.g. for children of widows, or for children over some minimum age who had employment. The figures presented seem to support the contention that the higher the school leaving age the higher the level of enrolments, both compulsory and voluntary, for in both urban and farm areas the

[1] Moser, C. A. and Layard, P. R. G., Planning the scale of higher education in Britain: some statistical problems, *Journal of the Royal Statistical Society*, Series A, Vol. 127, Part 4 1964, pp. 473-513.

D

absolute level of enrolment was higher in states with a higher leaving age and declined more slowly with age. The data, however, is not standardized for socio-economic differences between states and hence is open to the contrary interpretation that legislation simply reflects the conditions that lead to high enrolments. Thus Stigler states that: "if we classify states by per capita income and the racial composition of the children—both of which are in a sense more fundamental and persistent than school age legislation—within the cells there is no evidence of a correlation between legislation and school enrolments". He concludes that the influence of legislation on voluntary enrolments is relatively weak.

Cross-section analysis of this type may, however, not be relevant to the problems faced by those projecting enrolments who are concerned not with inter-area differences but with the effect across all areas of a change in legislation. Thus it seems fairly common ground among the European countries that have raised their school leaving age since 1955—Spain, Austria, Sweden, Yugoslavia—that enrolment ratios increase. This is particularly likely to happen where the difference between number of years of compulsory schooling and the years of attendance necessary to obtain an academic certificate is small: in England and Wales where normal academic schooling ends at 18 the difference will be only two years. Projections that ignore the effect of changes in legislation on voluntary enrolment ratios may tend to underestimate the future social demand for education.

The basic problem remains that of projecting enrolment ratios: changes in legislation only serve to make these basic forecasts more critical. Into the model (partial or complete) underlying projections of enrolments clearly a trend pattern of enrolment ratios has to be integrated. Where statistical work is being done for an advisory body various estimates of enrolments may be provided based on various trend projections of enrolment ratios. Precisely how choices are made between the alternatives is not clear. In England and Wales published estimates were, until 1969, based on straight line projections. A weakness of straight line projection of these ratios is that a trend in a ratio cannot be linear indefinitely, unless of course the ratios are constant over time, but such projections have the advantage of simplicity. There are of course alternatives. Consider Stone's contagious hypothesis. The increases in transition probabilities, p_j, vary from low value when the transition probabilities are small, through high intermediate value to small values when the probabilities approach unity. The data available is for enrolment ratios (q) rather than transition probabilities (p). But the former are a (lagged) function of the latter and will tend to follow the same growth pattern. Enrolment ratios for three ages, 15, 16, 17 are given below for England and Wales: there is discontinuity in the series for 15-year-olds in 1964 due to a change in the school leaving regulations.[1]

Estimates of future enrolment ratios in England and Wales were until 1969, based on straight line projections. This is a simple interest growth model, the increase in the enrolment ratios being the same every year. In Table 7.3 the annual increases in enrolment ratios (Δq) are presented in the second column

---

[1] The Christmas leaving date was abolished.

TABLE 7.3 *Voluntary enrolment ratios: England and Wales* (%)

	Age 15			Age 16			Age 17		
	Enrolment ratio (q)	Δq	$\dfrac{\Delta q}{q}$	Enrolment ratio (q)	Δq	$\dfrac{\Delta q}{q}$	Enrolment ratio (q)	Δq	$\dfrac{\Delta q}{q}$
1954	22.8	—	—	10.4	—	—	4.9	—	—
1955	23.6	.8	3.5	11.1	.7	6.7	5.1	.2	4.1
1956	24.8	1.2	5.1	11.8	.7	6.3	5.5	.4	7.8
1957	26.2	1.4	5.6	12.8	1.0	8.5	6.0	.5	9.1
1958	27.7	1.5	5.7	13.5	.7	5.5	6.7	.7	11.7
1959	29.2	1.5	5.4	14.6	1.1	8.1	7.0	.3	4.4
1960	30.9	1.7	5.8	15.4	.8	5.5	7.6	.6	8.6
1961	31.4	.5	1.6	15.9	.5	3.2	8.1	.5	6.6
1962	34.0	2.6	8.3	16.2	.3	1.9	8.5	.4	4.9
1963	36.2	2.2	6.5	18.6	2.4	14.8	8.8	.3	3.5
1964	50.0	—	—	19.0	.4	2.2	9.8	1.0	11.4
1965	52.8	2.8	2.9	20.4	1.4	7.4	10.3	.5	5.1
1966	54.7	1.8	3.5	22.0	1.6	7.8	11.0	.7	6.8
1967	56.8	2.2	4.0	23.6	1.6	7.3	12.2	1.2	10.9
1968	59.8	3.0	5.3	25.9	2.3	9.7	13.3	1.1	9.0
1969	61.6	1.8	3.0	27.9	2.0	7.7	14.5	1.2	9.0

Source: Statistics of Education, 1969, Vol. I, London, HMSO, 1970, p. 80.

Notes: a) The enrolment ratios refer to maintained schools only.

b) The figures for 15-year-olds after 1963 contain some compulsory enrolments: see text.

for each of the three age groups. If the column referring to the 15-year-olds is examined it can be seen that although there is considerable year to year variation there has been a tendency for the Δq to increase over time. Unfortunately the break in the series in 1964 makes it difficult to interpret the whole series, as after 1963 over half of the 15-year-olds were waiting until the school leaving date, and were thus not "voluntarily" enrolled. However when the totals are broken down—which is only possible for boys and girls separately—the voluntary enrolment ratios appear to follow a growth pattern consistent with pre-1964.

The figures for 16- and 17-year-olds are of particular interest for the absolute level of enrolment was still small in 1954 and so on Stone's hypothesis the increases would be expected to be small in the early years and increasing over time. This is quite clearly the case, being particularly noticeable for 17-year-olds. So for 16-17-year-olds the data for recent years suggest that linear extrapolation will tend to underestimate enrolment ratios in the future.

As a result of this tendency towards underestimation the Department of Education and Science abandoned linear projections in 1969. The method subsequently adopted is described in *Statistics of Education*, 1968, *Vol. 1*, p. xix: "The proportion of children who stay at school after compulsory school age to a later age, has been accelerating over the past eight years (1961-1968). An exponential trend has been fitted and extended to 1970 (ages 16 and 17), to 1972 (age 18) and to 1974 (age 19). Thereafter, to 1990, straight line growth has been assumed at tangents to the respective curves. This applies to each sex and to maintained schools as well as to all schools." The resulting forecasts of enrolment ratios are considerably higher than the earlier estimates, based entirely on straight line growth. The 1968 and 1969 estimates are compared in Table 7.4.

TABLE 7.4 *Estimated enrolment ratios: England and Wales*

	age	1970	1975	1980	1985	1990
1968 forecast	16	25.76	48.04	51.92	55.66	59.50
1969 forecast		30.17	48.90	55.18	61.23	67.71
1968 forecast	17	13.65	16.23	19.29	22.27	25.33
1969 forecast		15.90	20.40	25.49	30.78	36.32
1968 forecast	18	4.60	5.51	6.55	7.54	8.55
1969 forecast		5.30	6.70	8.33	10.00	11.73

An alternative simple model is to assume compound interest growth: in this case the proportionate increase in enrolment ratios is constant. The proportionate increases $\left(\dfrac{\Delta q}{q} \right)$ are shown in the table and it can be seen that although there is again considerable year to year variation (see the 1962-64 figures for 16-year-olds for example) this model fits the data much better. Whether its predictive value will be any better is another matter, for if Stone's contagiousness hypothesis is in any sense correct, even the simple annual increases, (Δq), will at some stage begin to decline. Without calculating the parameters of the model it is not possible to say when this will occur although it will occur first in the series for 15-year-olds where enrolment ratios are highest.

The fact that estimates are based on some projection of a time trend, enrolment ratios being presented as a function of time, simply emphasizes our present ignorance of the determinants of the social demand for education. Until our knowledge improves estimates have to be based on extension of past trends and inaccuracy is inevitable.

Discussion of projections of the demand for higher education will be based on the Robbins report,[1] often considered the classic example of a social demand projection for Higher Education. It has been shown in the early pages of this chapter that the projections in the report are based on the desirability of providing higher education for all qualified applicants. Manpower influences play no part in the projections of total enrolments, although in the estimates of places to be provided for teacher training, and of the places in each faculty manpower considerations were taken into account. A brief outline of the statistical work which yielded estimates of future social demand is now given.

The report was predominantly concerned with full-time courses of University

[1] *Higher Education, op. cit.* See especially Chapter 6 and Appendix I.

level, provided either in Universites or in Colleges of Technology or Polytechnics. The Committee has as its starting point the then existing excess demand for higher education defined as the excess of applicants with greater than the minimum entry qualifications[1] over places available: 83% of entrants to higher education had at least three Advanced level passes. The projection was based on providing enough places in the future to eliminate this excess demand. Two crucial assumptions were made: that the minimum entry requirements would remain unchanged, as would the then existing policies regarding student maintenance. The estimation of the number of qualified applicants in the terminal years of the projection[2] can be divided into several stages:

1. Demographic. Estimates of the future size of the 18-year-old age groups were provided by the Registrar General and the Government Actuary's department. The increase in the age group accounted for about 7% of the increase in qualified applicants in 1980-81.[3]
2. To the age groups must be applied the proportion that will attain the minimum entry requirements, to obtain the number of qualified school leavers. This is the most important step, accounting for about 60% of the increase and the most difficult. It is compounded of two factors: (a) the increase in the number staying on at school voluntarily to which is applied; (b) the proportion of final year school students who attain the minimum entry requirements. The estimates were based largely on past trends: "the proportion of the age group obtaining these qualifications will continue to grow up to 1980 by annual increments nearly as large as the average since 1954".
3. To stage 2 must be applied the proportion that in fact apply for higher education; little statistical data was available on the numbers of applicants and assumptions had to be made of the number of qualified people applying. It was assumed that the application rate would be 10% higher. This factor provided 13% of the expected additional demand for places.
4. The residual 20% is accounted for largely by alterations in the length of courses and increases in the number of students from overseas.

It is now clear that the report underestimated the growth of the social demand for higher education. The number of qualified applicants in 1969 will be 26% greater than was forecast for that year in 1963. The forecasts of the proportions staying on at school into the Sixth Form were reasonably accurate, but the Committee underestimated the proportions who would attain the minimum qualifications.[4]

Various influences on voluntary enrolments

It is probable that in most countries future development of the educational system is based on projections of the social demand for education. Leaving aside political

[1] Two passes at the Advanced Level of the General Certificate of Education.
[2] 1973-4 and 1980-1.
[3] All the figures in this description refer to the projections for 1980-1.
[4] For a detailed statistical analysis see Layard, R., King, J., and Moser, C., *The Impact o, Robbins*, London, 1969, especially Chapter 3.

factors, its main attraction over the other criteria, manpower requirements and rates of return to social investment in education, is its apparent simplicity. This simplicity is, however, artificial: the method of projecting past trends is used not because there is any *a priori* reason why they should continue but because of lack of knowledge of the relative importance of the various sociological and economic influences on the trend.[1] Trends are treated as a function of time out of ignorance. This is true whether the projection is for one part of the system or whether it is part of an educational model. In Stone's model, for example, the transition probabilities change over time according to a stochastic process, reflecting ignorance of the quantitative importance of the various factors. Given this ignorance it is not surprising that projections have not been notably accurate, the tendency being to underestimate the growth of enrolments. For this reason it has been argued that rather than to continue to make such mechanistic projections, effort might be better rewarded in research into the factors affecting the number of voluntary enrolments.[2] It is not difficult to list factors likely to influence the future demand:

1. Economic factors. For example the effect of changes in fees charged (if any), of changes in opportunity costs of secondary education as indicated by the labour market for school aged youth, and the possible effects of changes in the relative earnings of educated people. Changes in the level of economic activity, partly though their effect on the above factors, may influence the level of voluntary enrolments. These factors are considered more fully in the next section.

2. Changes in educational organization such as changes in entry requirements for academic secondary schooling and less rigorous selection methods. There is evidence that in comprehensive schools easy transfer between streams provides encouragement to children who would not normally have entered for academic certificates. The introduction of academic certificates different from the traditional level[3] also encourages this.

3. Various socio-economic factors. Cross-sectional studies have shown that a high parental real income is associated with parental persuasion of children to stay on voluntarily at school: hence what is the effect of rising *per capita* income over time? It is also known that the children of parents with a high level of educational attainments are more likely to remain at school after the compulsory leaving age: as the average level of educational attainment increases over time will this exert a similar influence?

4. Changes in government policy. The effects of changing the school leaving age and of changes in the stringency with which compulsory education requirements are applied. Changes in maintenance grants or loans to students will affect the demand for higher education.

[1] It is possible to argue that as the term projection necessarily implies a simple continuation of past trends, and concern with influences on the trend is irrelevant.

[2] Hansen, L., Educational plans and teacher supply, *Comparative Education Review*, October 1962, pp. 136-41.

[3] For example the Certificate of Secondary Education introduced in England and Wales in 1965.

5. When considering enrolments in one sector of the system changes in other sectors must be taken into account: this is of course part of the case for educational models.

Many other possible influences could be listed and some would argue that not all those just mentioned are relevant. But that is beside the point: what is at issue is the quantitative importance of these factors. In the next section the economic factors are discussed more closely, in particular the possibility of deriving a demand curve for education is examined.

The previous section has described various projections based on the social demand approach and we are now in a position to look more closely at the social demand for education and its determinants. The social demand for education is the aggregate of the private demands for non-compulsory education. This has been expressed more precisely by Correa:[1] "the demand for authorization to attend a specific educational institution, on a given level, and for certain subject matter". It should be noted that in section 1 of this chapter we have also discussed projections of compulsory enrolments which, strictly speaking do not arise from social demands: we can justify this on a practical level as we wish to describe the methodology of forecasting total enrolments so as to enable a discussion of forecasts of teacher demands[2] later. It should be noted, too, that in countries where (at least) elementary education is free and compulsory, enrolment ratios are always less than 100%. In highly developed countries the difference is often small and the reasons trivial, but in less developed countries ratios fall a long way short of 100%, in some cases being less than 50%. One reason for this, as suggested earlier, is that there is an opportunity cost of education to children of elementary school age in these countries, whereas this is usually not the case, for legal reasons, in more advanced systems. Hence the same sort of influences may be important for compulsory schooling as for voluntary. The subsequent discussion will be, however, of the social demand for education, as defined above by Correa.

Economic aspects of social demand

In this section some economic influences on the social demand for education are looked at more closely. The starting point is the demand by an individual for education. The individual considered will be the student, although there is, of course, an abundance of evidence that in this respect students are strongly influenced by their parents. In considering the determinants of the individual's demand the problem is immediately met that education has been termed both a consumers' good and an investment good. As a consumer good education is demanded in some sense for its own sake and as an investment good because it yields an economic return through higher lifetime earnings, or greater opportunities to increase the recipients' economic welfare. These two types of benefit from education are very closely bound up, and in the general case there is no chance of separating them. Leaving this aside, for the moment, and taking the

---

[1] Correa, H., *The Economics of Human Resources*, Amsterdam, 1963, p. 56.
[2] Of school teachers only.

demand for education, generally—as a consumption and an investment good—there is little possibility of deriving a price demand curve, because there is no explicit price to which the student or his family can respond. An exception is private education, but this is a small sector and does not centrally concern us here. In the countries we are concerned with education is normally provided free, and the taxes paid to meet the costs of the system do not vary with the benefits received. "It seems quite unlikely that they are ever conceived of as the prices of education, nor would a rational man so consider them."[1]

Thus two difficulties are immediately encountered in an attempt to derive a demand curve, in the normal sense of the term, of an individual for state-provided education. One can proceed, however, if education is solely considered as an investment good: if this assumption is made then rate of return analysis would seem to provide a way of deriving a demand schedule for education. The analogy is with the Keynesian investment demand schedule: this is derived from the marginal efficiency of investment (MEI) schedule which reflects the diminishing marginal returns to investment. On this theory of investment the firm invests up to the point where the market rate of interest[2] is equal to the marginal efficiency of investment: hence the MEI schedule is the demand schedule. It has been shown, that some writers argue that individuals make, at least in part, their education decisions in a similar way. According to this view, in the case of the private demand for voluntary education, the individual would "buy" education up to the point where the returns from the last unit of education are equal to his subjective time preference rate. Such an approach, postulating that the individual acts according to some rational economic calculus, depends on all the usual neo-classical assumptions (such as perfect foresight) as well as diminishing marginal returns to education. (Before examining this contention it should be mentioned that as education cannot be bought in infinitely small units the function relating returns to an individual of education will be a step function: and as education cannot be bought, or rather it does not make sense to buy, education in equal time units the horizontal steps will not be equal). The contention that there are diminishing marginal returns to education can be examined on *a priori* grounds. Thus according to G. Becker and B. Chiswick,[3] "one factor decreasing the marginal rate of return, at least eventually, with increases in the amount invested is a presumed diminishing marginal product from adding more capital to a fixed human body". In a later article Chiswick[4] argues that this "presumed" decline in the marginal rate of return is due to "the rise in opportunity costs with additional schooling and the imperfect substitution of direct for time costs, the finiteness of an individual human being's life and perhaps the limited capacity of the human mind". In both cases the writers are explaining why the marginal returns may decline *eventually*: but do returns

[1] Eckaus, R., Economic criteria for education and training *Review of Economics and Statistics*, Vol. 46, 1964, p. 182.

[2] As long as this represents the opportunity cost of the capital employed.

[3] Education and the distribution of earnings, *American Economic Review*, Vol. 56, No. 2, 1966, pp. 385-69.

[4] Minimum schooling legislation and the cross-sectional distribution of income, *Economic Journal*, Vol. LXXIX, 1969, pp. 495-507.

decline over the normal length of education and intensity of education? From a policy point of view this is the question that needs answering. Although this can be discussed on *a priori* grounds—for example it seems doubtful whether the finiteness of the individual's life can cause returns to decline over the normal range of education as earnings in the distant future are heavily discounted— whether the returns decline or not is basically an empirical point. Unfortunately as we have seen, the calculated rates of return are not noted for their accuracy. However, it seems fair to those who would support this sort of approach if for this purpose we take the figures at face value. The most complete data on internal rates of return to various amounts of schooling has been provided by Hansen.[1]

Hansen's data is for the USA for 1949, the basic source being the 1950 Census of Population which provided distributions of incomes of males by age and level of schooling. Three tables of internal rates of return are calculated, the social returns and the private returns both before and after tax. The latter are the rates relevent to the decision of an individual on how much schooling to "invest" in. The results are unadjusted for ability, socio-economic class, et cetera.

TABLE 7.5 *Internal rates of return to private resource investment in schooling after tax, United States, males, 1949**

	From:		a	b	c	d	e	f	g
To:	Age		6	8	12	14	16	18	20
		Grade	1	3	7	9	11	13	15
a	7	2	†	...	...	...	...	...	...
b	11	6	†	†	...	...	...	...	...
c	13	8	†	†	†	...	...	...	...
d	15	10	27.9	33.0	24.8	12.3	...	...	...
e	17	12	25.2	28.2	22.2	14.5	17.5	...	...
f	19	14	17.2	17.5	13.7	9.4	8.5	5.1	...
g	21	16	17.2	17.3	14.4	11.5	11.4	10.1	16.7

* All rate-of-return figures are subject to some error, since the estimation to one decimal place had to be made by interpolation between whole percentage figures.

† This indicates an infinite rate-of-return, given the assumption of costless education to the individual through the completion of eighth grade.

[1] Hansen, Lee, Total and private rates of return to investment in schooling, *Journal o, Political Economy*, Vol. 71, 1963, pp. 128-40.

The marginal rates of return are the boxed figures and we see immediately that these do not decline as more schooling is purchased. The individual clearly cannot make decisions based on the marginal rates: for example if his subjective rate of time preference were 6%, and he is deciding how much education to invest in after grade 8, then he would stop at grade 12, despite the fact that grades 15-16 yield 16.7%. The individual can, however, look at education in large blocks and the corresponding average rates of return: these are obtained by reading down the columns. Thus if the decision age is again taken to be 13 (grade 8), the average rate of return on education up to age 15 is 12.3%, to age 17 is 14.5% and to the terminal education age of 21 the return is 11.5%. Thus on this basis he "invests" in the complete block of education as long as his time preference rate is less than 11.5%.

Unfortunately this method of basing demand on the average return gives nonsense results if the marginal returns do decline as one receives more education. Consider the following hypothetical example: the averages are not, as they should be, weighted, but this makes no difference to the argument.

TABLE 7.6 *Theoretical example of internal rates of return to investment in schooling*

To grade	From grade 1	From grade 3	From grade 5
2	30	...	...
4	25	20	...
6	18	12	4

If the individual's subjective time preference rate is 10% then whether he makes his decison at grade 1 or 3 he invests in education (on the average criterion) up to the terminal grade. However this necessarily means that he purchases education in grades 5-6 which yields only 4%: clearly this is not worth buying. Thus there can be no general investment rule, and, in the general case, no demand schedule. Where the marginal returns both increase and decrease with education received, or where they increase, the average return is the relevant one because of the interdependency between various grades. In the first example, to obtain the 16.7% return on grades 15-16 the individual *has* to "invest" in grades 13-14 which yield only 5.1%: on the marginalist approach he would cease his education at grade 12 as long as his preference rate was more than 5.1%. Where returns decline with education the marginalist approach yields the correct "investment" decisions.

In Britain data relating earnings to education have only recently become available from censuses and have previously come from *ad hoc* surveys. As a result the data were often in a form unsuitable for rate of return calculations. D. Henderson-Stewart has calculated the rate of return to three years (voluntary) secondary education as 13%, and to three years higher education as 14%. The data on which these findings were based were very crude,[1] however, and the 1% difference is not significant.[2]

Further figures of rates of return to various levels of education in Britain have been presented in a much quoted study.[3] They are not easy to interpret for these purposes as the different educational levels do not represent a typical progression but there seems to be little evidence that returns diminish on additional increments of education.

Similar conclusions emerge from the most recent available data for Britain. These were the first results to be based on census data—or at least on a follow up survey to the 1966 sample census. A multitude of different rates were calculated; those most relevant to the present discussion are presented below.

TABLE 7.7 *Social rates of return to education in Britain: Males 1966-67*

Incremental comparison	%
Advanced level/unqualified . . .	6.9
First Degree/Advanced level . .	10.4
Masters Degree/First Degree . .	0.8
Doctorate/First Degree . . .	0.7

Source: Morris, V., and Ziderman, A., The Economic Return on Investment in Higher Education in England and Wales, *Economic Trends* May 1971.
Notes (1) The figures include an "ability adjustment" of .66.
(2) The figures are not adjusted for secular growth of real incomes.

The figures are for the social rate of return in the narrow sense. However there is no reason to suppose that the private rates would show a different pattern, although they would of course be higher. Once more we see that the marginal returns do not diminish. The return to a degree is greater to that of advanced level, whereas both postgraduate qualifications return less than first degrees.

Thus the available data offer no support for the contention that an individual would receive diminishing marginal returns from "investment" in education. However, because of the interdependencies between different levels of education, the returns to early levels of education tend to be understated. Weisbrod has

[1] The source was a random sample of male heads of households, aged 20 or more, that was made by a market research company in 1964. The data related income (not earnings) to terminal education age and to present age. There were only two terminal education ages, and no distinction was made between various types of education, or between full and part-time education. The present ages of those in the sample were grouped in ten year ranges and of course there was no information on those aged less than 20. The earnings of those who were educated beyond the age of 19 were largely estimated independently of the sample data.

[2] Yet the results have been widely quoted, despite the author's concluding statement: "All the results . . . should be looked upon as being purely provisional and valuable largely as an illustration of the technique of calculating the rate of return from cross-section data." Henderson-Stewart, D., *Appendix: An estimate of the rate of return to education in Great Britain.* in "Manchester School" Vol. 33, No. 3, 1965, pp. 252-62.

[3] Blaug, M., Peston, M., and Ziderman, A., *The Utilization of Educated Manpower in Industry*, London, 1967, Chapter 7.

developed an approach[1] which takes into account the interdependencies and adjusts the rate of return to any level of education according to the value of the value of the "option" it gives of continuing education further and thus receiving further returns. The result is normally to increase the returns to intermediate levels of education as at worst the value of the option to continue is zero; it clearly cannot be negative as it need not be used. The returns to a given level of education, say level j, are given by:

$$R_j = R_j^* + \sum_{=k}^{n} (R_\alpha^* - \bar{R}) \ \frac{C_\alpha}{C_j} \cdot P_\alpha$$

The total returns to education level R_j now comprise two parts. The rate of return over cost for education unit j as in usual rate of return analysis plus the value of the option of continuing: this is the second expression in the above equation. For each subsequent level of education α, the option value is calculated as follows: the term in brackets yields the "supernormal" rate of return on level α as given by the excess of the rate of return[2] over the discount rate used. This is weighted by two factors: the cost of education as a proportion of the cost of education j, and secondly by the probability of a person with education level j reaching level α. These expressions summed over all subsequent education levels, yield the option value of level j. Clearly the value of the option will decline the higher the educational stage reached. Thus Weisbrod calculated that recognition of option values increased (in 1939) the return on elementary education from 35% to 54%, but the value of high school education, when including the value of the option to continue to college, increased only from 14% to 17.4%. Referring back to the example of the student deciding on how much education to "invest" in, inclusion of option values modifies but does not fundamentally alter the conclusions reached. If we take the marginal returns from Hansen's data then all but the last figure[3] will be increased, but the fluctuations will be slightly smoothed out but not eliminated. Thus the conclusion stands that investment decisions according to marginal calculations would be very difficult, or impossible, to make.

Two attempted theoretical derivations of the demand curve for education will now be considered. Blaug[4] is concerned with the aggregate demand curve for education. This is the horizontal summation of the (sort of) individual demand curves discussed above. The basic premise is the same: people demand education as long as the rate of return from education (R_E) is greater than some market rate of interest, in this case the average yield of equities and debentures (R_B). "Hence we can draw the demand curve for education as a positive function of the internal rate of return on investment in education and a negative function of the average yield of equities and debentures." The resulting demand curve drawn on the

[1] Weisbrod, B. A., Education and investment in human capital, *Journal of Political Economy*, Vol. 70, 1962, pp. 106-23.

[2] As in normal usage.

[3] Although, as Weisbrod argues, even the return on the last grade of education may be increased, if a value for the option of independent work is imputed.

[4] Blaug, M., An economic interpretation of the private demand for education, *Economica*, No. 33, 1966, pp. 166-82.

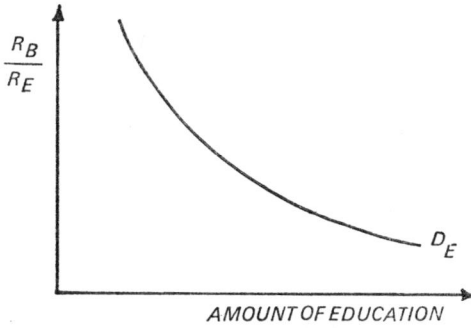

FIG. 7.1

usual assumption of *ceteris paribus*[1] is as follows:

The horizontal axis is presumably measured in man-hours of education demanded. The individual demand curves from which the aggregate curve is derived cannot, however, have this horizontal axis; leaving aside part-time further education it is not possible to buy education in such a way, i.e. it is not possible to vary one's demand within a given year, one undergoes a year's education, or a course considerably longer, or one does not. Therefore the horizontal axis must be that implied by the earlier analysis, i.e. school grades. Although clearly, given the present age of each individual, his decision as to how many years education to undertake can be converted into man-hours, the problem of how the individual makes this decison remains. The aggregate demand curve thus glosses over the difficulties in deriving the individual demand curves: the implicit assumptions must be that the individual at any given decision age refers to the average returns up to any terminal education age, that interdependencies are ignored, and that the returns vary smoothly with education received.

An alternative is not to start from the individual's demand curve but simply from the individual's "yes/no" decision on any education. This has been done by Campbell and Siegel.[2] They deal with the demand for higher education—undergraduate enrolments in four year institutions. "Ordinary investment theory would have the individual compare his expected rate of return with some appropriate interest rate. An education will be purchased if the expected rate of return exceeds the rate of interest. The education will not be purchased if the interest rate exceeds the rate of return. An aggregate demand schedule for enrolments may then be derived by arraying individuals according to their expected rates of return (from highest to lowest). The total number of enrolments demanded will equal the aggregate of all enrolments for which the rate of return exceeds the rate of interest. Variations in the rate of interest will lead to inverse variations in the number of enrolments demanded." This clearly avoids the first aggregation problem, but it does not avoid the interdependency problem, i.e. how did the

---

[1] *Ceteris paribus* as usual includes the tastes of consumers, i.e. all the sociological factors. It has been argued above that the influence of these factors is very strong.

[2] Campbell, R., Siegel, B., The demand for higher education in the United States, 1919-64, *American Economic Review*, Vol. 57, No. 3, June 1967, pp. 482-94.

individual make the decision to demand education up to the pre-college level. Neither does it entirely escape the consumption-investment problem, as the authors admit.

The difficulties involved in deriving a demand curve for education and of using it to forecast the social demand can now be summarized. It is not clear how the individual faced with the interdependencies between various educational levels, even if he did attempt to act according to a rational economic calculus, would make his decisions. There thus may be no individual demand curve for education and hence, logically, no total demand curve derived by aggregating. The approach also considers education simply as an investment good; in practice there will be great difficulty in separating the consumption and investment elements.[1] thus "consumption" spending on education about which little is known will tend to obscure the workings of influences on "investment" spending on education. A way out of this latter difficulty is for the student to impute a monetary value to these real benefits but it is very difficult to imagine how this could be done. A further objection to the economic approach is that it treats the sociological variables as essentially subsidiary to the economic variables: at the present state of knowledge, however, it is not possible to choose between the various explanations of the social demand. Clearly economic factors do play a part, but it is the authors' view that any approach to the social demand for education which concentrates largely on such factors, with all the empirical and analytical difficulties inherent in it, is unlikely to be of much assistance to those making projections.

A further question is whether once—on whatever basis—the decision has been made to enrol for (say) higher education, economic factors influence the subject read.[2] Evidence on this cited by Correa[3] "does not allow the conclusion that the number of graduates in the several specializations has a clear relationship with the income received by professionals in the same specialization". For example the most obvious direction of influence would seem to be that occupations in which income was increasing relatively would attract an increasing number of graduates: yet of the professions examined the incomes of lawyers showed the smallest increase, yet the numbers entering the profession showed the greatest increase. However the data on which these results are based do not permit strong conclusions to be drawn. On the other hand neither does it offer much help to the model builder.

Some conclusions

Economic factors are, in any case, as have been seen, only part of the story, and sociological factors have played an important part in the rapid increase of the demand for education in European countries in recent years.

The effect has been one of contagiousness: this may be the explanation as well.

[1] For a discussion of this see Chapter 5 and the references there, particularly Schaffer, H. G., Investment in human capital: a comment, *American Economic Review*, Vol. 52, 1961, pp. 1026-35.
[2] See Stone's educational model, this chapter, p. 96 ff.
[3] Correa, H., *op. cit.*, pp. 83-6.

Barna,[1] after emphasizing how far the demand for education is removed from demand as in orthodox economic theory, has drawn an analogy with the demand for consumer durable goods. The demand for ordinary household commodities is very stable but it is difficult to forecast the demand for durable consumer goods. Income and price are important variables but alone they cannot explain the increase over time of the demand for (say) washing machines. It could be explained, however, by models of a learning process, consumers imitating each others' habits.[2] "The model which explains the spread of durable consumer goods is then similar to a model which explains the spread of a disease. I think that the growth of demand for education may be explained by a similar model . . . but probably the factors are even more complicated."

A further stimulus to the demand is that the educational requirements of any given occupation may increase over time: there is evidence that this has occurred in the United States.[3] This may occur where the supply of (say) graduates is greater than required given the existing educational requirements of various occupations: hence graduates are forced to take jobs of lower status than they had anticipated, and in future the educational requirement of these jobs is upgraded. In such circumstances employers and professional bodies may also seek to upgrade requirements for status reasons. Hence supply creates its own demand. This process may be wasteful of resources. It may also create social and educational problems. As a former presidential adviser has said in the United States: "we must meet head on the problem we are creating by making a four year college degree the prerequisite almost any kind of employment short of digging a ditch".[4]

When all of these influences, whose relative importance is not known, are considered it is very apparent that the choice of transition ratios to use in projections is very difficult. Clearly constant base year ratios are inadequate. The problem is exactly the same whether it is a model builder deciding what pattern of ratios to incorporate in the model, or a policy maker faced with the decision of selecting between various forecasts based on different assumptions. Clearly past trends must influence the decision: yet transition ratios tend to be unstable, yielding no obvious trend, in years of rapid educational expansion. Yet it is in just these years that forecasts take their greatest importance. In the last analysis the forecaster simply has to take a view.

As presumably was always apparent the use of education models still leave the forecaster with the crucial problem of estimating the future values of the parameters, notably transition ratios: it is a truism to say that a model can only yield results as accurate as the data which is used. The over-riding advantage of the sort of educational model being used and developed is that the inter-relationships between the sectors of the educational system are clearly allowed and hence the implications of changes in one sector for another sector can be identified and

---

[1] T. Barna, in discussion of paper by Moser, C. A. and Layard, P. R. G., *op. cit.*, p. 518.

[2] As Duesenberry has argued, consumers' utility functions are not independent of those of other consumers. Thus utility is a function not only of the amount of goods one consumes but also of the amounts consumed by others.

[3] See *Economic Aspects of Higher Education*, Paris, OECD, 1964, pp. 25-7.

[4] Califano, J., *Washington Post*, 4 May, 1969.

quantified. Given the time lags involved, for example in the training of teachers, such knowledge is essential for planning purposes. The major stuctural weakness of the demand for places model is that the transition probabilities (ratios) are not in the strictest sense demand parameters, but are some combination of supply and demand parameters. This is particularly true of the transition ratios between schools and higher education: where there exists excess demand for higher education then the transition ratios are in effect constrained demand parameters. If more places were provided in higher education institutions then more school leavers would attend and the transition ratios would increase. Hence projections based on existing ratios (or on past trend of ratios) would underestimate future enrolments in colleges were there any expansion. Any expansion of higher education could also be expected to increase transition ratios at earlier levels of voluntary education. Thus transition ratios between second and third levels of secondary education might increase with the increased chances of a place in a higher education institution. This difficulty is not unsurmountable and in this and other respects such models clearly have not approached the end of their development phase. There are other possible improvements to these models.

For example it is common ground that to forecast accurately transition probabilities (ratios) it will be necessary to deal with different social groups separately. This is a proposed refinement to Stone's model and Thonstad also suggests this as a possible improvement: "In sociological investigations, the influence upon the propensities to study of parental social class and parental education is emphasized. Separate transition matrices could possibly be used for pupils coming from different social and geographical environments, and influences of changes in the parental occupational and educational structure could thus be accounted for."[1] An analysis of the relevant sociological factors and a survey of the basis data needed is provided in *Methods and Statistical Needs for Educational Planning op. cit.*, Chapter 3.[2]

There are two powerful constraints, however, on this development. At the moment in most countries there is a lack of basic data, for example on the effect on transition ratios of increasing parental income. Secondly some of the refinements suggested, for example using separate matrices for pupils coming from different social backgrounds, greatly increases the amount of computation. The resulting model would be very complex and in cases could conceivably come up against the constraint of computer capacity, but probably more important against financial constraints. Thus possible improvements for these reasons may be minimized: this is perfectly acceptable as obviously the influence of some variables, and the payoff from including them, will be very small. At the present state of quantitative knowledge of the relative importance of the many influences, however, which ones to discard may not be at all obvious.

The conclusion thus is reached that at present not enough is known to enable confident projections of the social demand for education to be made, although the

---

[1] Thonstad, T., *op. cit.*, p. 62.

[2] This chapter also briefly discusses models of diffusion processes, of which Stone's model is an example.

situation will improve as more data is collected. If it is possible, however, to accurately assess the demand as a function of time, by some stochastic process for example, then lack of knowledge of the factors at work may not be serious from the point of view of those who have to make the future supply plans. Similar remarks apply to correlations between Gross National Product *per capita* and enrolments: if there is a close correlation then what the causal relationships are do not matter as far as projections are concerned.[1] As long as the effect is known, ignorance of the cause may be less serious.

---

[1] For example, M. C. Kaser, Education and economic progress: experience in industrialized market economies, in *The Economics of Education*, E. A. G. Robinson and J. Vaizey, (eds.), (London, 1966, pp. 89-173), found a correlation of .64 between secondary enrolments and GNP *per capita*. In England, however, no correlation between either growth of Advanced Levels or staying on at school and changes in GNP was found by Layard, King and Moser (*op. cit.*, p. 33).

PART TWO

Manpower

Skills and manpower are the two obvious consequences of the education system that directly affect the economic system. What is the nature of the relationship, usually known as the labour market; which connects the two? In these chapters an attempt is made to answer this question. The question is also considered later, in part 6, which deals directly with teachers, who are usually the largest group of educated people in the labour force.

8 Education, skills and the demand for labour

THE following three chapters are concerned with various aspects of the relationship between education and manpower. This chapter will be concerned principally with the labour market, and the possibility of using market indicators as guides to labour scarcities and, in turn, to developments in education and training.[1] The following chapters are not, on the other hand, concerned with the market mechanism, but rather with a type of education and manpower planning exercise which is based largely on the view that market forces and indicators are inadequate or even to an extent irrelevant.

Since the problem in this chapter is one of skill and wage differentials, one would expect it to be dealt with more explicitly in partial studies, i.e. in studies of the demand for special categories of manpower. Therefore the chapter will be concerned with such issues rather than overall educational planning as such. Nonetheless, there may be some conclusions which are relevant to the more aggregate type of analysis considered later.

M. W. Reder[2] provides a theoretical framework for the relation between the demand for labour and skill substitution. He starts by postulating that firms may be unable or unwilling to increase money wages in response to some kinds of labour shortages. Instead, downgrading of requirements, internal promotion, or on-the-job training may be used to meet shortages. This is often related to reluctance to bid labour away from other firms, or to disturb wage rates negotiated with trade unions. When there is labour slack, the union rate may be above the market rate, in which case job rationing is not unlikely. Expansion of the aggregate demand for labour will produce skill shortages, and part of the response to this situation will be the substitution of lower skills for higher (at given relative wage rates). It is possible to envisage a chain of substitution, which must stop when it comes to unskilled labour. When all labour reserves have been drawn on,[3] it may well happen that unskilled labour is more scarce

---

[1] The principal concern of these chapters is with education rather than specialized training. When dealing with labour markets and shortages of certain types of manpower, it is, however, necessary to place considerable emphasis on training. One important category of skilled manpower—teachers—is considered separately and at length later.

[2] The theory of occupational wage differentials, *American Economic Review*, Vol. XLV, December 1955.

[3] The labour force may expand in a boom as various people, such as housewives, are attracted into the labour market. Only in a very pronounced boom such as that caused by the two world wars will the labour force reach its maximum, exhausitng all possibilities of substitution. The "social minimum" wage may prevent employment of some marginal, unskilled low productivity workers, thus putting another constraint on the expansion of the labour force.

than various categories of skilled labour, because (unlike the latter) no further substitution (or downgrading of requirements) is possible. This greater relative scarcity of unskilled labour will lead to a narrowing of skill differentials in times of excess demand for labour.

Reder's hypothesis is tested for USA data on building and manufacturing wages covering the first half of the present century. It is found that differentials narrowed rapidly during the war years and during the post second world war period which were, in general, boom periods. Also, differentials broadened during the 1919-21 slump. These trends seem to confirm the hypothesis. However, differentials continued to narrow during the great depression of the 1930's. This is explained by the growth of trade union power during that period and also by a (probable) increase in the social minimum relative to other wages.[1]

There are international and inter-regional aspects of this question also. In advanced economies the predominance of manufacturing industry results in a wide range of skilled and semi-skilled occupations, which means that a series of small steps of substitution is feasible. Not so with a more traditional economy where the gap between skilled and unskilled is large. Observation by Reder of the relatively backward southern states of the USA and the western states (relatively advanced) shows that differences, both in terms of skill and training and also in terms of earnings differentials, are higher in the former region. Finally, the above hypothesis is not inconsistent with the observation that the annual earnings of the unskilled fluctuate more than those of the skilled during economic cycles. This is because Reder's analysis was in terms of hourly (or some other period) rates and corrects for the greater fluctuation in hours and employment experienced by the unskilled.

This analysis of Reder may explain why many economists and manpower planners minimize the relevance of the price mechanism. It may simply give no indication of the relative demand for various skills—and in some cases may give a perverse indication. Thus some non-market assessment of "manpower needs" rather than "manpower demand" may be a necessary basis for educational planning.

The arguments on the other side state simply that manpower shortages, being a market condition, are reflected in market prices, given reasonable institutional flexibility. Thus Blank and Stigler[2] dismiss the often alleged "shortage" of engineers in the USA (at least in the pre-1954 period) by demonstrating the relative decline in engineers' earnings. Also, Jewkes[3] has dismissed the notion of a shortage of scientific manpower in the United Kingdom during the 1950's on somewhat similar grounds: average earnings of chemists and physicists rose at about the same rate as average industrial salaries, and somewhat less than the average industrial wages. As a result, he distinguishes "unmet need" from "shortage". Determining the former is almost impossible and almost invariably involves value judgements; the latter, if it should occur, will be reflected in relative earnings.

---

[1] Which might be expected when wages are falling.

[2] Blank, David J. and Stigler, George J., *The Demand and Supply of Scientific Personnel*, New York, 1957.

[3] Jewkes, J., How much science, *Economic Journal*, Vol. 70, March 1960.

The findings of Blank and Stigler have been questioned by W. L. Hansen,[1] on the grounds that in some cases they compared average with starting salaries, and interpreted some evidence selectively. Also, during the 1939-54 period the educational level of the labour force as a whole rose appreciably relative to that of engineers. This might lead to a decline in engineers' relative earnings irrespective of any disequilibrium in the labour market. According to Hansen, a reinterpretation of the data confirms the absence of a shortage and the possibility of a surplus until 1950. From 1950-58, however, the relative salary trends indicate a growing tendency for a shortage of engineers to emerge. Furthermore, the increasing enrolments of engineers, both in absolute and relative terms, during this period indicate a response to the earnings trends.

Arrow and Capron[2] provide a further analysis of the demand for higher level scientific and technical manpower in the USA during the 1950-58 period. The empirical evidence (of Blank and Stigler, and Hansen) suggests surpluses or, more recently, shortages of engineers at current salary rates. However, in a situation where demand is increasing continuously, current rates may refer to equilibrium rates of a previous period and the shortage may be more than temporary. Arrow and Capron then formulate a "dynamic shortage" theory, which starts from the observation that there may be a lag in taking on new personnel because (*a*) of the lag in perceiving needs and taking decisions and (*b*) there may be a reluctance to raise salaries as this entails increased costs for present as well as extra employees.[3] The "dynamic shortage" model makes the rate of change of price (i.e. of earnings of engineers and scientists) a function of the shortage or surplus, i.e. $\frac{dp}{dt} = g(D - S)$. Further, if demand continually increases (i.e. if the demand curve shifts to the right), a situation can arise where equilibrium price is greater than actual price, due to adjustment lags. Thus, a dynamic shortage is not necessarily apparent from present price movements, which is a reason for questioning the findings of Blank and Stigler, and Hansen, who inferred surpluses and shortages from such data. The magnitude of a "dynamic shortage" will depend on (*a*) the reaction speed of the market (*b*) the rate of increase of demand and (*c*) the elasticity of supply and of demand. According to Arrow and Capron these variables behaved in a way to make a "dynamic shortage" likely.

As will be apparent from the following chapter, the degree of substitutability of various manpower categories is important for any manpower or educational plan. In the engineer case (which is of special interest because of its links with technology and productivity, and which has been the subject of much controversy), a shortage could lead to substitution in two dimensions: (*a*) vertical

---

[1] Hansen, W. L., The "shortage" of engineers, *Review of Economics and Statistics*, Vol. 43, August 1961.

[2] Arrow, K. J. and Capron, W. M., Shortages and salaries: the engineer scientist case in the United States, *Quarterly Journal of Economics*, Vol. 73, No. 2, 1959.

[3] This is consistent with some aspects of Reder's theory, although Reder solves the initial reluctance to raise wages by substitution of skills, and Arrow and Capron by a lagged response. This is partly because the latter are dealing with high level scientific and engineering manpower where the degree of substitution may be more limited and the trade union factor (which inhibits any wage movements for fear of upsetting differentials) weaker.

substitution where sub-professionals, i.e. technicians, take the place of graduates or professionals (technologists), (*b*) horizontal substitution where other professionals are recruited—such as physicists, chemists, et cetera—especially in the research and development field where they are likely to be more suitable. This substitution will be a complicating factor in the relationship between shortages and earnings. In particular, ease of substitution may inhibit earnings increases for engineers, and may be another reason for the Arrow-Capron phenomenon of simultaneous shortage and stable relative salaries.[1] However, it would not explain the other phenomenon which has been noted especially in the United Kingdom, i.e. a large and continuing gap throughout the entire 1950-65 period between vacancies or firms' requirements (as revealed by surveys) on the one hand, and applicants or jobs actually filled, on the other. These phenomena are analysed further by Peck,[2] who compares the employment, status and relative earnings of engineers in the USA and the United Kingdom. Evidence given by Peck[3] shows that in the 1956-64 period engineers' salaries rose considerably faster than overall salaries in the United Kingdom. This is a reversal of the earlier trend noted by Jewkes, and presumably signifies a shortage in the sense meant by him.[4] However, taken in conjunction with the analysis of Arrow and Capron, it is reasonable to infer a shortage of engineers throughout the entire 1950-64 period, as one would expect a lag in the adjustment of salary scales—especially where, as in Great Britain, there is a degree of oligopsony in the scientific and technical manpower market.[5]

A cross-section analysis of technician, technologist, and scientists' earnings does not agree with the other, intertemporal indicators of shortage. According to the time-series data given by Peck, one may argue that engineers (technologists) are relatively scarcer in the United Kingdom than in the USA, on the evidence of firms' requirements, employment patterns and the degree of substitution. However, whereas USA engineers command, on average, a premium of 9 to 11% in earnings over scientists, they are at a slight discount in the United Kingdom. This is partly explicable by the fact that nearly all USA engineers are graduates, whereas about half of U.K. engineers are non-graduates, though trained to similar standards. Graduate engineers in the U.K. earn a slight premium over scientists, whereas non-graduates earn about 11% less than graduates. Even so, the premium earned by graduate engineers over scientists is very small (they earn the same as physicists, and slightly more than chemists), so that the training differences are not enough to explain the apparent discrepancy between salary differences and scarcity. Comparing engineers and technicians, the latter earned about 60% as much as the former in the U.K. in 1960, whereas the USA

---

[1] Although, on the other hand, it can be argued that ease of substitution eliminates shortages.
[2] Peck, Merton J., Science and technology, in *Britain's Economic Prospects*, Washington, D. C., The Brookings Institution, 1968.
[3] *Op. cit.*, pp. 453-56.
[4] See above, p. 108.
[5] This is confirmed by Payne, *Britain's Scientific and Technological Manpower*. Fifty industrial firms provide 25 per cent of Britains engineering employment. Also the government employs 16.8%, nationalized industries 14.5% and education 6.6%; see *Report on the 1965 Triennial Manpower Survey of Engineers, Technologists, Scientists and Technical Supporting Staff*, London, HMSO, 1966.

ratio was 68 % in 1964. In the U.K., technicians are generally a higher proportion of the labour force in the important engineering, metal and chemical industries than in the USA (with professional engineers the trend is reversed). Also the technician/technologist ratio in manufacturing is significantly higher in the U.K. These data are thus in agreement with the relative salary data. Then, various complicating factors arise because of differences in standards, which may be higher (especially for technologists, despite the high percentage of non-graduates) in the U.K.[1]

From all this evidence, some important, if negative, conclusions emerge. First, the relative trend of earnings does not always register shortages or sur-pluses of manpower; where it does there may be a considerable lag. This gives rise to the need for other criteria of the type used by manpower planners. Second, substitution is possible to some extent, but by dampening price changes it may make the ultimate solution of manpower shortages more difficult. Thus, Britain finds it difficult to fill engineering faculties despite the shortages of engineers. Third, international comparisons may be unreliable or inconclusive: U.K. graduate engineers, although o tensibly scarcer and more highly trained than their USA counterparts, do not command a similar premium over scien-tists. It is not possible to say to what degree differences in substitutability or status account for this.

In view of this, it is not surprising that actual demand forecasts have not usually used the labour market or prices as guides. These criteria usually indicate only the existence rather than the extent of a shortage or surplus, or at best a likely trend of shortages and surpluses to increase or decrease. Various attempts have been made to forecast the requirements for scientific and technical manpower in the United Kingdom. There have also been numerous forecasts of the demand for teachers; these constitute a special aspect of the manpower problem and are dealt with in another part of this book. The long-term forecasts made for the 1956-66 and the 1961-70 periods assume either a fixed relationship between the growth of output and the need for scientific and technical personnel, or else a certain trend growth in the proportion of such personnel in the total labour force.[2] The question of salaries is apparently considered a minor factor, even though scientists and engineers generally work in either managerial, research and development, or production jobs, and the question of salaries is obviously relevant if one considers the interplay between technological develop-ment and the allocation of manpower between these areas. In general the same comments apply to these forecasts (especially concerning the relation between growth, technology, occupations and education) as to the larger and more comprehensive forecasts.

---

[1] Peck, *op. cit.*, gives a fuller discussion of these issues. He does not mention some other difficulties in the international comparisons, such as the differences in definition (as well as training) of technicians. There are subordinate issues here to the question of the price mecha-nism, what it signifies, and how (or if) it works.

[2] See *Scientific and Engineering Manpower in Great Britain* (Office of the Lord President of the Council), London, HMSO, 1956; also *The Long-term Demand for Scientific Manpower* (Advisory Council on Scientific Policy, Committee on Scientific Manpower), London, HMSO, 1961.

Medium-term forecasts (for 3-year periods) have also been made.[1] These rely largely on surveys of employers' needs and intentions. The question did not refer to relative salaries, and did not make any assumption about the course of economic growth. While a 3-year period may be too short for educational planning purposes (unless the trends indicated by the surveys are assumed to continue), they may be useful in achieving a better balance by subject specialization in the output of engineers even if they cannot enable overall shortages to be rectified.

Moser and Layard,[2] in the course of their observations on the forecasting of demand for scientific and technical manpower in Great Britain, mention the crucial questions of skill and professional substitutability. They emphasize the distinction between "needs" and "demands", which sometimes arises when making forecasts. "Demands", i.e. market demand may be according to Moser and Layard a function of price, and is often expressed through surveys of firms and of their manpower requirements. "Needs" are an entirely different matter and are not linked to market variables. An important piece of information given by Moser and Layard is that in 1961, 210,000 of the 260,000 qualified scientists and engineers in the British labour force were in occupations which related closely to their scientific education. This included a large proportion in managerial and sales positions. But it excludes 17,000 with scientific and technological training, who were classified as "technicians", i.e. who were working at a lower level than their qualifications would indicate. These factors are an argument for "overproduction" of scientists and engineers, in the sense that generous allowances must be made for posts in managerial and sales activities (whether or not these are related to science and technology) and for drop outs and partial failures, to whom the 17,000 technicians referred to above might correspond.[3]

At the other extreme is the long-range (30 year) projection made by Vermot-Gauchy[4] of the supply and demand for engineers in France. A detailed analysis is made for the 1955-1960 period and the results are then projected to 1985, when equilibrium is finally reached. A table giving the supply of engineers in 1965 is classified into 10 training groups (mainly relating to subject specialization), 10 industrial sectors as well as further divisions relating to engineers in military service, outside France and retired. Demand for 1965 (giving actual shortages when compared with supply) and for 1960 is shown separately for each category, using aggregate and sectoral product projections, productivity trends et cetera as criteria. Together with statistics of retirements and transfers, educational and training requirements are calculated. There is a certain "balan-

---

[1] See, *inter alia*, two publications by the Committee on Scientific Manpower: *Scientific and Engineering Manpower in Great Britain, 1959*, and *Scientific and Technological Manpower in Great Britain, 1962* (both London, HMSO); also Moser, C. A. and Layard, P. R. G., Planning the scale of higher education in Great Britain: some statistical problems, *Journal of the Royal Statistical Society*, Series A, Vol. 127, Part 4, 1964.

[2] *Op. cit.*, especially pp. 493-543.

[3] Another case for "overproduction" of highly skilled manpower is given in the subsequent chapter in connection with manpower requirements of the Irish economy. The factor of labour mobility seems to be central to this question.

[4] The supply and demand for engineers, in *Forecasting Manpower Needs for the Age of Science*, Paris, OECD, 1964.

cing intake" which is just enough to equate demand and supply; and divergence from this will lead to progressive shortages or surpluses. As there is an initial shortage (1955), actual intake must be greater than balancing intake to compensate, and will fall eventually when the shortage is rectified. Needless to say, making these projections for a 30-year period involves some heroic assumptions. notably that the rate of economic growth and the rate of growth of demand for engineers will both be similar in the 1960-85 period to the 1955-60 period. Perhaps, due to the need to allow for a large degree of unpredictable technical change, the long-term part of the forecast could have been put in more flexible and general terms. However, for short and medium term work, Vermot-Gauchy's forecast is an extremely rigorous and useful example of technical manpower and educational planning. The term "technical" should be stressed, as like the British forecasts mentioned above, there is no consideration of market prices (or even administered prices) and their influence on supply and demand.

A major dilemma which should be apparent from these examples is that caused by (*a*) the necessity of considering the long-term because of the long production period of scientific and technical personnel[1] and (*b*) the inevitable imprecision of such long-term forecasts due to technical change, changes in relative earnings (including relative earnings abroad, which might induce a significant net migration of skilled manpower), and substitution possibilities between various categories of scientific and technical personnel.

If we for the moment anticipate some of the conclusions of the following chapter, it will become apparent that, apart from the objection that education should not be subordinated to economic or manpower needs, the most obvious defect of the manpower approach is its apparent inflexibility. This is emphasized especially by those who would advocate rate of return analysis and (implicitly) rely on labour market forces to clear shortages of manpower. Against this point of view is the argument given by some manpower forecasters (and contained implicitly at least in all such forecasts) that the long production or education period will lead to a cobweb cycle, i.e. that even if manpower supplies respond to labour market forces, the inevitable lags involved will lead to over-response and surpluses of manpower.[2] Also there is the evidence (cited above) of Arrow and Capron and others, that prices are not necessarily an indication of current scarcities. This defect is further emphasized by the tendency of the manpower approach, through its assumption of fixed coefficients, to underestimate the elasticity of substitution between inputs in the production process.

These various objections can be met (in principle at least) (*a*) by incorporating price data as well as survey data and job analysis into estimates of current manpower requirements and shortages, (*b*) by interpreting manpower require-

---

[1] It will be taken that "long-term" refers to periods of 10 years or more. Thus some of the British forecasts, especially the 1961-70 forecast, are more medium than long-term, especially in view of the long production period of British scientists and engineers, due to early specialization.

[2] See, for instance, Bombach, G., Long-term requirements for qualified manpower in relation to economic growth, in *Economic Aspects of Higher Education*, Paris, OECD, 1964.

ments as minima in order to allow for possible migration and other factors,[1] and (c) by avoiding the mistake of making projections or forecasts which are too detailed for too long a period. Such exercises are unnecessary as detailed specialization usually comes at a comparatively late stage in education. Broad educational requirements (or minima) should be easy to forecast, especially at the non-specialist and secondary education levels, for the medium and long-term. For short-term analysis, more detailed work is possible, both from the point of view of estimating demands and adjusting supplies.

These considerations will assume greater significance in the following two chapters, which are concerned with forms of planning rather than with markets. At this stage, two conclusions may be stated. First, it seems that the market mechanism does not provide adequate data for manpower planners. It may, however, be a useful, if limited, indicator in some circumstances. Secondly, forecasts of "needs" or requirements for highly qualified manpower are of value, in the absence of adequate market mechanisms. The assumptions underlying these need to be considered carefully, however. They also may fulfil the important function of improving the quantity and quality of data relating to manpower and education which, as the following chapter shows, is seriously inadequate.

---

[1] Not the least of which are the objections of those who would advocate a "social demand" approach to education, and who would object to manpower *constraints* on educational development.

9 Education and manpower—developed countries

EDUCATION has already been examined as an investment process, analogous to physical investment, from which a return may be derived. It was seen that the analogy is not always valid, and it should be apparent that even where it is, certain problems remain concerning the planning of education[1] and the wider question of the role of education in economic growth and development. Also, in the previous chapter it was evident from the analysis of the relationship between income differentials and the supply and demand for skills, together with their implications for education and training, that the labour market did not provide an unambiguous guide to the balance between the supply of and demand for various skills and professions. Consequently it is necessary to examine that approach to educational planning which emphasizes the manpower requirements of the economy directly, largely ignoring the question of costs and returns to education and income differentials. This has been termed "technical" manpower planning, as opposed to the more "economic" approach of the previous chapter.[2] The present chapter will deal largely with the theory and practice of such "technical" manpower and educational planning as developed by the OECD which has, to a considerable extent, been a pioneer in this field, rather than with the special planning exercises envisaged by Vimont, Moser and Layard and others, in the previous chapter. The latter generally apply to higher scientific and technical manpower only, and often to training rather than education.

A general outline of educational and manpower planning

The basic methodology of the type of educational and manpower planning used in the OECD Mediterranean Regional Project has been described by H. S. Parnes.[3] A summary of Parnes' general theoretical work is necessary as a basis for comparison with the various applications which have been made in the MRP and other OECD projects.

---

[1] The chapter on social demand also raised some problems which are relevant to manpower and educational planning.

[2] These terms have been used by John Vaizey to differentiate the basic approaches to manpower planning; see The labour market and the manpower forecaster—some problems, International Labour Review, Vol. 89, April 1964, pp. 353-70. The "economic" approach does not usually involve planning in the same thorough sense as the "technical" approach. It has in practice tended to take the form of partial analysis of labour market trends, of the type encountered in the previous chapter.

[3] Forecasting Educational Needs for Economic and Social Development, Paris, OECD, 1962.

The MRP was to ascertain the educational needs of various southern European countries as well as the costs and other implications of meeting these needs. Unfortunately, as Parnes remarks, "need" in this context is an ambiguous term: "There is no such thing as a 'need' for education (either by an individual or a society) except in terms of the values and goals that happen to be held and the total amount of resources available for the pursuit of those goals. A country's 'needs' for education, in other words, depend upon the criteria selected and even then can be ascertained only in reference to a host of competing needs. The commitment of resources to education represents, at least at the moment, the loss of potential resources to other activities."[1] Therefore, one must ascertain the educational implications of economic or of general cultural goals. Both of those criteria are necessary, but the economic aspect is stressed because it presumably gives more definite and quantifiable results. In this case, manpower requirements were the key factor in determining economic "needs" for education. (Again, one presumes that it was favoured over a rate of return analysis as the forecasts yielded were more expressible in quantitative terms).[2]

The method to be used to calculate such requirements may be summarized as follows. An analysis of the manpower structure, classified by industry, occupation, age and education is made for a certain base year. Then, a similar set of calculations is made for a target year, based on forecasts of GNP, productivity, population growth, etc. If the age-structure of the labour force in the base year is known, then calculations can be made which give the gross changes required in the labour force for various occupations and industries. Obviously, the existence of an economic plan (even if only for part of the educational planning period) is a help in the estimation of the manpower requirements. In practice, according to Parnes, the available information is almost certain to be less than what is ideally required, and its comprehensiveness will vary between sectors and occupations. Besides censuses and special sample surveys of individuals and enterprises, a combination of trend projections, adaptations of pre-existing records and surveys, comparisons with more advanced sectors and industries, and informed judgement about future changes will have to be used, according to circumstances. The resulting manpower forecast must of course be consistent with demographic trends. Its degree of disaggregation is more important for higher level occupations where a considerable amount of specialized training may be required, and where costs may be important in proportion to the number of people involved.

The next step in the operation of forecasting which is described by Parnes is the critical one from the methodological viewpoint. This is the conversion of manpower to educational requirements. Any difficulties which may have been encountered in the first stage are also found in economic forecasting and in planning generally—especially the forecasting of productivity trends. Productivity is also important in the next phase as it is linked with technological advance,

---

[1] *Op. cit.*, p. 12.

[2] It is apparent that Parnes intends the term "need" to mean something similar to "unmet need" (as opposed to "shortages" which are indicated by price movements) as the latter term is used by Jewkes. See Jewkes, J., How much science? *Economic Journal*, Vol. 70, March 1960; see also discussion in previous chapter.

and technology will determine to a large extent the inputs of various categories of labour required, and therefore the education and training required.[1] Parnes demonstrates the difficulty of this exercise by quoting figures for the USA, Canada, France, and England and Wales, which show the varying educational attainments of certain professional and managerial sections of the labour force, whom one might expect to have university degrees, or at least some post secondary school education.[2] Significant proportions did not complete secondary education, and these proportions varied from country to country.

The more detailed aspects of the planning process, especially those relating to statistical requirements and operations, may now be set out. There are various ways of measuring labour requirements, as will be seen when some of the country reports of the MRP are referred to later, but whichever one is chosen there are certain basic minimal data requirements[3] which may be classified as follows: on the demand side, assuming the total planning period is 15 years, 5-yearly estimates of the demand for university graduates, post-secondary school graduates, higher secondary, lower secondary and primary school graduates are needed. Furthermore, scientific and technical graduates need to be estimated separately at the university and post-secondary levels. Where possible, additional breakdowns should be made in the various higher scientific and technical fields, the reason for these (as well as medical and teacher estimates) being the special type of institutions necessary in some cases, or at least the special and expensive facilities necessary, as well as the close link that often exists between education and occupation (closer than that which exists in, say, many areas of management or administration). Requirements for medical personnel and teachers (the latter must be made at the end of the exercise) should also be calculated separately. These demand requirements for education are expressed by Parnes in terms of the required labour force composition at various dates, i.e. in terms of stock. The flows necessary to attain such levels can be estimated in conjunction with the supply side of the exercise.

Future manpower supplies can be estimated either in educational or occupational terms. The former procedure is less complex,[4] and is also more suitable as demand forecasts have already been expressed in educational terms. Consequently the educational supply forecasts referred to by Parnes will be analysed here.

The first forecast is of manpower supplies over the plan period (assumed to be 15 years) assuming no change in educational policies and a continuation of existing demographic and other trends. If the school leaving age is at least 15, the size of each age-cohort of the labour force in the plan period is known quite accurately and is not dependent on variations in the birth rate. Starting from information on the educational qualifications of the labour force in the base

---

[1] Especially if one accepts the assumption, inherent in this type of manpower forecasting, that relative prices of various kinds of labour and capital are unimportant, i.e. that elasticities of substitution of factors are low.

[2] *Op. cit.*, Appendix D, Table 1.

[3] Parnes, *op. cit.*, Table, p. 41, and paragraphs 95-7.

[4] Because (*a*) the education-occupation relation is not fully known, and (*b*) occupational mobility is difficult to measure and forecast.

year,[1] it is necessary to estimate total entrants into and withdrawals from the labour force during the plan period. The following is an outline of the necessary measurements given by Parnes.[2]

Entrants to the labour force come mainly from the educational system. Consequently forecasts of enrolments will have to be made for the plan period. These must be classified by sex, as enrolment patterns and labour participation rates vary. From these enrolments, the number of graduates from each level of the system (excluding those who pass on to a higher level) can be calculated, and labour force participation rates for the appropriate age/sex groups applied to these in order to calculate additions to the labour force. Also, estimates will have to be made of entrants (usually re-entrants) to the labour force who do not come directly from the educational system. These may be difficult to count, but their number is likely to be relatively small.

Withdrawals from the labour force may be calculated by applying mortality and retirement rates to each age-cohort (population and labour force age-cohort statistics usually cover five-year age intervals), making the assumption that level of education has no significant effect on the mortality and retirement rates for a given age group—unless, of course, separate statistics exist for these categories.

Withdrawals and entrants should be counted gross; thus any temporary withdrawals who re-enter the labour force during the plan period will be cancelled. Estimates should be made for all the categories included in the demand forecasts, i.e. including separate estimates for medical personnel, teachers and various categories of higher scientific and technical personnel. For these estimates, entrants should be calculated on the basis of existing training facilities and recent graduate trends, as appropriate. Withdrawals, retirements and deaths should be estimated for both the initial stock and for new graduates or entrants during the plan period. Professional association records may provide suitable data in some cases.

Thus for the terminal year of the plan period there are two manpower inventories: one based on estimated requirements and the other on estimated supplies. If the forecasts indicate a shortage of manpower in each category except the lowest (this is the most likely case) then the expansion in educational enrolments which is necessary to meet the deficiency can be calculated by either of two methods.

First, the absolute number of graduates required at each level may be calculated, by taking the cumulative totals of labour force requirements for each type of graduate at the terminal date. This needs to be adjusted by labour force participation and mortality rates for each education/sex category in order to arrive at graduate requirements for the total population. Then, assuming a certain number of years for construction of extra facilities and training of teachers, a certain number of classes will graduate before the terminal date. The extra graduate requirements in each year will be calculated according to this number. Total enrolments at higher, and later at lower levels, can be built up, using certain assumptions (usually based on past trends) about wastage, repe-

---

[1] Classified in the same manner as the demand forecasts in the preceding paragraphs.
[2] *Op. cit.*, pp. 42-9.

tition, et cetera. Throughout the exercise the extra and existing forecast enrolments may be distinguished. The result should be internally consistent, i.e. the number in the lower levels should be enough to supply the requirements both of higher levels and of the labour force. More important, especially during a period of rapid expansion, the number of required enrolment for each age-cohort, must not, of course, exceed the population forecast.[1]

The second method, which is simpler, is to plan the production of labour force entrants in the same proportion as labour force requirements, according to educational levels. Wastage rates between levels, and labour force participation rates will give an idea of total graduate requirements at each level. From these figures, and again using various assumptions about drop-outs, enrolment estimates can be derived. Thus "output" of graduates is designed to become, initially, proportional to requirements, and, eventually, equal to requirements.

In addition, various calculations of enrolments in special higher technical and scientific fields should be made. The estimation of requirements for teachers is especially important,[2] particularly from the aspect of consistency referred to above. For instance, expansion of university enrolments may require expansion of lower and especially upper secondary enrolments (depending on drop-out and wastage rates, and the possibilities of improving them). But the teachers for these levels must come from the universities, before the planned expansion is carried out. Thus, expansion will have to be phased gradually, or else pupil/teacher ratios will have to be somewhat flexible. Another example is when increased primary enrolments require more places not only in teacher training colleges, but also in the secondary schools which supply these colleges. Furthermore, the extra teachers in training colleges and secondary schools will make further demands on higher education.

All the statistical requirements presuppose that some solution can be found to the problem of converting manpower to educational requirements. As will be seen later, much of the criticism of the education-manpower planning approach is concerned with this point. Parnes gives some examples of how the problem might be solved.

First, there is a detailed analysis by R. S. Eckhaus of 4,000 job titles drawn from United States official sources, and classified according to both general and vocational development required. Each type of development is divided into several degrees of proficiency.[3] From this extremely detailed breakdown some idea of educational requirements for the proficiency corresponding to job descriptions (and therefore to manpower requirements) may be ascertained. The main defects of this method are obviously the extremely laborious nature of the calculations, which, coupled with inadequate data, make the work less

---

[1] There is also the question of consistency within the educational system, i.e. expansion at one level requires expansion at other, higher levels if enough teachers are to be supplied. This is dealt with separately below.

[2] Parnes, *op. cit.*, pp. 61-2.

[3] General development is analysed in terms of degrees of reasoning, language and mathematical development. Vocational development is classified according to categories representing various periods of vocational training or experience required to achieve a certain average proficiency on the job.

E

worthwhile. Parnes advocates statistical developments in an attempt to improve the accuracy and scope of the method. A more fundamental difficulty is the impossibility of dividing into two mutually exclusive categories the time required for general and vocational development.

Secondly, less ambitious and laborious approaches might rely on surveys of firms in various sectors of the economy which sought information on actual and desired qualifications for various jobs, on the likely changes in job content and on the likely demand for labour of various categories during the plan period. Alternatively, a more difficult assessment of the relation between job content, education and training, and job performance might be sought.

Thirdly, international comparisons with more advanced countries may be used as a guide, but this is difficult because of differences in educational systems. None of these methods overcomes the fundamental difficulties: occupational categories tend to be relatively broad and encompass varying educational requirements; for any one requirement, varying combinations of education, training, experience, etc. may be possible.

According to Parnes, it would seem that the chief virtue of the manpower approach is that it enables definite quantitative targets to be set. These can be understood, however, as minima, in the light of manpower requirements. Furthermore "cultural" or political factors, which are strictly outside the influence of the economist or educational planner, may add to these requirements. Thus Parnes seems to envisage that manpower planning could become part of a broader, "social demand" approach to education.[1]

Having seen the general approach of the "technical" manpower planner, it is of interest to turn to the various applications of this type of exercise, particularly those undertaken by the OECD, in order to see how, and if, the difficulties involved have been overcome.

Some applications of the method

In general, the Spanish MRP report[2] follows closely the approach put forward by Parnes. First, the structure of the present (1960) educational system is analysed as a basis for the forecasts, and for various reforms which are proposed. Second, a projection is made of GNP for 1975, which is disaggregated into sector and industrial group projections. Third, the occupational structure of the labour force is analysed for 1960, and a forecast is made of the 1975 structure, taking into account the GNP calculations, Finally, educational qualifications of the various categories of workers in various sectors of the economy are set out for 1960 and 1975, making allowance for the elimination or reduction of existing deficiencies by the latter date. This serves as a basis for calculating enrolment, school building, and other requirements to meet the needs of the economy.

The GNP calculations were disaggregated into Primary, Secondary and Tertiary sectors, each of the latter two being in turn divided into four industrial

---

[1] See the chapter on the social demand for education (Chapter 7).
[2] *The Mediterranean Regional Project: Country Reports, Spain,* Paris, OECD, 1965.

groups.[1] The active population was divided into nine groups corresponding to level of qualification, and was cross-classified according to economic sector. The degree of disaggregation would seem to have been limited by the data as a complete classification of the labour force was not given for some sectors.[2] This lack of data, which is a problem in many such manpower studies, obviously adds to the conceptual and methodological difficulties, which will be discussed below, involved in converting manpower to educational requirements.

Forecasts of educational needs were made partly on the basis of international comparisons, partly on comparisons with advanced sectors of the Spanish economy, and partly on a direct basis (e.g. doctors, teachers). The following passage summarizes the view which is taken of the education-occupation link: "In fact it is impossible to fix a quantitative relationship between a desired rate of economic growth and the corresponding improvement in the level of education, for the simple reason that the necessary information is lacking. Nevertheless, the occupational structure of the active population for 1975 constitutes a solid basis for assessing the necessary changes in the level of education, since occupation is the most important factor in determining what the proper level of education should be. This does not mean that changes in occupational structures can be directly translated into changes in the level of education, if only because the level of education in the immense majority of occupations was too low in 1960 ... Nor should the level of education in 1975 be necessarily the same throughout a given occupation. Some jobs in the same occupational category require greater knowledge than others. These differences are especially marked amongst administrative, executive and managerial workers, and clerical and sales workers ...

"We cannot therefore expect a fixed relationship between occupation and level of education. This would mean a society in which everybody after leaving school would remain forever in the same occupation. It is quite a different thing to assume that normally a certain standard of education is necessary for certain posts, leaving a margin for those who obtain similar training through the work itself."[3]

Thus the Spanish MRP report, while accepting in practice the basic methodology of the manpower approach to educational planning, and while making manpower–educational forecasts, is careful to emphasize that the occupation-education link is not adequately known. Also, the last sentence quoted in the preceding paragraph implies an important role for on-the-job training, a point made earlier.

A second example of manpower and educational planning is provided by the EIP (Educational Investment and Planning) project of the OECD which attempted to produce forecasts of educational activity for various northern European countries. The Irish EIP report[4] will be analysed in Part Four of this book in connection with unit costs and the methodology of cost projections; it is

---

[1] Spanish MRP Report, *op. cit.*, Table 39.
[2] *Ibid.*, Tables, 47 and 43.
[3] Spanish MRP Report, *op. cit.*, pp. 98-9.
[4] *Investment in Education*, Part I, Dublin and Paris, OECD, 1966.

analysed here with regard to its general forecasts of educational and manpower needs and its special comments on the supply of and demand for certain specialized categories of manpower, notably technicians.

As a first step, the structure of unemployment and migration is examined in order to trace categories of manpower which may be in excess demand or supply.[1] Generally, unemployment was much higher (nearly 15%) among the social groups comprising unskilled and unspecified workers, than it was for the whole labour force (about 5.7%). For every other social group, unemployment was lower than average.[2] Furthermore, although unskilled and "unknown" or unspecified workers and their families were about 30% of the total population, they accounted for 83% of male and 61% of female unemployment in 1961.[3] Although immigrants formed only 3.4% of the total labour force, they formed 18.9% of the total male labour force in the administrative, managerial and executive categories and 11.8% in the professional and technical categories.[4] As these occupations usually demand a comparatively high level of education or training, there exists some basis to suppose a shortage of certain highly educated people. Of course the report stresses that this phenomenon could be associated with foreign investment and therefore no conclusive proof is possible. On the other hand, the educational and occupational attainments of emigrants (who are numerically far greater than immigrants) was low, only 5% being in the professional business, managerial and clerical categories, and 66% having left school at or before the age of 14. These indicators point to a surplus of unskilled manpower and perhaps to a shortage of certain types of highly qualified people.

Bearing these considerations in mind, the report proceeds to forecast manpower demand for 1971 and 1976, using the census year of 1961 as a base. Generally, a "historical" approach was used, taking past trends as a basis and modifying them where necessary; it was supplemented in places by international and inter-industry comparisons or by surveys. Emigration was a significant variable, especially when estimating flows from the educational sector. Immigration was small by comparison. The demand forecasts were classified according to three economic sectors (agriculture, industry and services) and seven categories of occupation.[5] These were checked for consistency with population forecasts and were, in general, derived from the assumptions laid down in the *Second Programme for Economic Expansion*.[6] The result was a significant expansion in all categories of manpower except farmers and agricultural workers. In addition

[1] *Ibid.*, pp. 177-81.

[2] *Ibid.*, Table 7.1 (*a*), p. 178.

[3] *Ibid.*, Chart 6.7, p. 172 and Table 7.1 (*b*), p. 178. Although the unemployment percentages refer to the labour force, classified by social group, and the population percentages to total population, the differences are so large that there is little doubt about the concentration of unemployment.

[4] Immigrant females, who were 3.4% of the total female labour force, accounted for 23.9% of females in the administrative, et cetera category and 7.1% of the professional and technical category; see Table 7.3, p. 179, *op. cit.*

[5] There were professional and technical, employers, managers and salaried employees, skilled manual, intermediate non-manual, farmers, agricultural, forestry and fishery workers, and other (mainly unskilled) workers.

[6] Dublin, Stationery Office, 1964.

a more detailed forecast was made of the demand for professional and technical and for scientific and technical manpower for which 14 different categories were identified.[1] Only one seventh of the total demand for manpower was for expansion, the rest being replacement demand. This is especially true of occupations with low educational content, where emigration and withdrawal rates are high. The report is quite explicit about the way in which demands for manpower, especially highly qualified manpower, should be regarded as minima. Such manpower is highly mobile, especially in Ireland where there are many factors making for outward mobility. Consequently it is necessary to "over-produce" highly qualified manpower, i.e. to educate and train more than is demanded by domestic sources.

The crucial operation of transplanting occupational data to their educational equivalents is approached cautiously. Unlike the scheme set out by Parnes, and used in the Spanish MRP report, no estimate of the stock of manpower with various levels of education is made because of the lack of data and the importance of accounting for those outside the labour force, and because of on-the-job training (whether formal or informal) which makes such calculations less meaningful. Consequently an estimate of the demand for various occupational groups classified by level of education required is made in flow terms. As the occupational groups are broadly based, they are not associated with any single educational level; thus, for example, 65% of entrants to the group professional and technical manpower will have third level qualifications and 35% senior cycle secondary qualifications.[2]

Thus a pattern of demand for various categories of education in the 1961-71 period is built up. This is confronted with estimated supplies, which are derived from the analysis of the educational system and the forecasts of its expansion (under policy conditions existing at the time) which were made in the earlier part of the report. Allowances are made for non-labour force supplies and demands, which cancel (emigration being the balancing item). The results show an overall balance in supply and demand,[3] but there are some large imbalances in the various constituent items. Supplies of third and senior second level students are slightly greater than demand. But there is a large shortage (76,000 out of a total labour force demand of 186,000) of people with lower second level qualifications and a correspondingly large surplus of people with no second-level qualifications (70,000 more than the 160,000 demanded) over the 10 year period. This would suggest that a greater expansion of lower secondary education is needed, and it is interesting to note that in Portugal and Spain this level of education is expected to expand more rapidly than any other, and at a faster rate than that projected for Ireland.

The Irish report is essentially a partial analysis; it takes as hypotheses certain trends in economic development and emigration, and it sets certain educational

[1] *Op. cit.*, Table 7.6, p. 189.
[2] *Op. cit.*, Table 8.1, p. 199. People are classified according to highest level of education completed. Consequently some may have a partially completed education at a particular level which will not be counted. This leads to some underestimate of the educational attainments of the labour force.
[3] *Op. cit.*, Table 8.4, p. 201.

qualifications as being desirable for certain occupations. Then a conservative estimate is made of likely demands on the educational system over a 10 year period, and it is shown that the result is a serious shortfall of certificants at a certain level. These are the people who might be expected to train as technicians, which are also in short supply in Ireland. Because of this the report also analyses the supply of and demand for technicians.[1]

In this respect, the Irish report indicates the complexity of the manpower approach, and examines many factors not dealt with by other studies. Consequently the analysis is extremely difficult to summarize as so many adjustments and allowances are continually made for institutional and other special factors. It illustrates the extreme difficulties in carrying out forecasts for certain categories of manpower where (unlike for teachers, for instance) educational–occupational categories are loosely defined, and where on-the-job training is probably of very great importance. Certain problems which were encountered are worth noting, and they may be of general interest:

1. The number of technicians was not accurately known (OECD estimates ranged between 2,920 and 5,680). This uncertainty was partly a function of the informal nature of much of the training, and partly of the uncertainty as to what was meant by "technician".
2. The various sources of supply of technicians gave rise to confusion, as individuals may have undergone different types of training and thus have been double-counted. This pointed to the need for an individualized data system.
3. The distinction between technician and technologist, which formed the basis for part of the demand forecasts, was not always clear (some highly qualified technicians appeared to be equivalent to technologists). It is especially doubtful whether these categories were well enough defined to make international comparisons of technician/technologist ratios meaningful, not only because of confusion about the level of training corresponding to various qualifications, but also because of lack of correspondence between the description of various fields of study.[2] The latter point is important because the ratio of technicians to technologists will vary in different industries and types of specialization.

A critical view of education and manpower plans

For a critical view of this type of manpower approach, some of the other OECD country reports are useful. The Portuguese MRP report[3] is of interest in this respect, particularly as it was developed from an earlier study[4] which was the

---

[1] *Op. cit.*, pp. 208-21.

[2] For instance in Canada the terms "technician" and "technologist" are used in an exactly reverse sense to the usual OECD meaning.

[3] *Mediterranean Regional Project: Country Reports, Portugal*, Paris, OECD, 1966.

[4] *Análise quantitativá da estrutura escolar portuguesa, 1950-1959* ("*A Quantitative Analysis of the Portuguese Educational System*"), Lisbon, Centro de Estudos de Estatistica Económica, 1963.

basis on which the Mediterranean Regional Project was originally proposed and developed. The report gives two important methodological objections to the education–manpower planning exercise.[1] First, the fact of technical change means that relationships between output and occupational structures will not be stable or predictable—especially as internal cross-section comparisons will be more hazardous. Secondly, there is the difficulty (which was admitted by Parnes) that no automatic progression from occupational category to corresponding educational qualifications exists. Technical change and changes in productivity also give rise to statistical problems, especially when measuring output per head in different sectors of the economy. The methodology of Parnes is rejected in favour of a combination of criteria based partly on general economic needs, and partly on enrolment targets which are essentially of a social demand nature.

Thus the Portuguese MRP report is not an exercise in manpower planning in the "technical" sense that Parnes and others would intend. This is because there are no detailed projections or forecasts of manpower requirements or of their educational equivalents. Instead base-year education statistics, together with observations on the position of more advanced countries are used as a basis for calculating the desired increase in enrolments. The increases eventually required, for the 1951-55 to 1971-75 period, are large: 1024% in lower secondary, 460% in upper secondary, 303% in teacher training, 787% in intermediate, and 151% in higher education.[2] Once the needs of the terminal year have been decided on, the calculation of enrolment, graduate, entrant, teacher requirement, and cost trends is similar to that involved in any "technical" manpower planning exercise.

A further example of the tendency to combine social demand and manpower criteria is found in the Netherlands EIP report.[3] Indeed this report could be described as being almost entirely based on social demand criteria, with a few, mainly critical, comments on the relevance of manpower requirements to the exercise. First, it is stated as a basic goal of the whole plan "to provide adequate education for all individuals and groups to the highest levels that they demand".[4] A piecemeal approach is used, and only the demand for university graduates of two categories, doctors and engineers, is analysed in any detail. For doctors, changes in consumers' tastes, in consumers' incomes (in order to calculate income elasticity of demand) and in medical fees are the principal variables analysed. The latter is a neutral factor as it is assumed that the "real price" of doctors' services will remain constant. (This assumption was necessary because of the lack of data). For engineers, the regression of the number of various types of engineer on GNP for the 1900-56 period was used as a basis for forecasting. No details were given of the methods of forecasting used for other categories of graduates such as law, economics, geography, languages, etc. The report comments that its approach, "which does not take into account all occupations at the same time may lead to the wrong conclusions. This objection, however,

[1] See Portuguese MRP report, *op. cit.*, pp. 41-6.
[2] *Op. cit.*, Table 2, p. 23.
[3] *Educational Policy and Planning in the Netherlands*, Paris, OECD, 1967.
[4] *Op. cit.*, p. 27.

is not as serious as it may sound. There are a number of checks on the validity of forecasts; in the case of university personnel, for example, there is the numerical relation between this type of personnel and the category immediately below university engineers and college engineers, between the number of engineers and that of graduates in science. Forecasts of the number of university freshmen as a percentage of qualified grammar school leavers should be checked for other competing demands for these leavers, etc.

"Forecasts covering all types of occupations and/or levels of education would only give one additional and rather meaningless checkpoint, i.e. total supply and demand of workers regardless of their level of education. This checkpoint, important as it may be in planning as part of economic planning, is not of much use in manpower planning in relation to educational planning."[1]

The checks which are made for consistency in the Netherlands report are obviously important if the piecemeal approach is to be of use. But if these checks are made systematically and comprehensively, it is doubtful whether the method could be described as "piecemeal" any longer. Thus the approach tends to resolve itself into a more global or general form than at the outset. Furthermore, as the Netherlands report says, while the overall type of confrontation between manpower supplies and demands may not be of much use in manpower planning considered merely as part of educational and not economic planning, it should be apparent that manpower planning by its very nature is linked with economic as well as educational planning. For instance, in the Irish EIP report, the economic plan or programme provided the basis for calculating manpower requirements. Where such plans have been lacking (for instance in some of the MRP countries) the educational and manpower planners have had to, so to speak, construct their own—at least to the extent of making specific forecasts of economic growth and structural changes.

This view is taken by R. Hollister, who, in his review of the Mediterranean Regional Project, states that "the rationale of the manpower requirements approach is to put educational decision-making in line with economic decisions".[2] Of Hollister's various criticisms, there are three which are of outstanding importance and which need lengthy consideration:

1. It may not be possible to forecast productivity and occupational structure trends sufficiently accurately.
2. Manpower supplies and demands may be interdependent.
3. Not enough is known about occupational–educational relationships.

It will be seen that these issues are interrelated and that they raise further questions concerning the optimum degree of disaggregation, and the adequacy of available data.

The estimation of productivity change, especially productivity trends in various sectors, depends on technological change. This cannot be forecasted accurately, as the Portuguese MRP report demonstrated. Furthermore, Hollister

[1] Netherlands EIP report, *op. cit.*, p. 100.
[2] Hollister, R., *A Technical Evaluation of the First Stage of the Mediterranean Regional Project*, Paris, OECD, 1967, p. 31.

points out that inaccurate productivity forecasts will invalidate the most careful disaggregation of occupational trends. Previous trends have shown that productivity change is irregular, and this adds to the difficulties in forecasting.

The question of interdependence of manpower demands and supplies raises two further important issues, according to Hollister:

1. If input coefficients are flexible, then variations in relative supplies of factors or types of factor (e.g. labour of various degrees and types of skill) may be difficult to distinguish from the effects of variations in demand. This is the familiar identification problem in econometrics.

2. The variability of input coefficients and the indentification problem may lead to a situation where the planner is confronted by indeterminacy. Hollister found that among the MRP countries, labour-output coefficients did appear to be flexible. One might add that this indeterminacy may have the effect of making manpower planning extremely difficult; there is, however, the offsetting advantage of a greater range of choice. This could be of importance if technological change is, as has been suggested above, unpredictable.

The question of educational-occupational relationships is, according to Hollister, the weakest link in the analytical chain which constitutes the manpower requirements method. Technological change, as well as affecting productivity, can change education and training requirements for certain occupations,[1] and also the previous problem of flexible manpower coefficients and supply effects will inevitably react on educational–occupation relationships. Analysis of the country MRP reports has shown that educational requirements during the plan period are extremely sensitive to change in educational–occupation specifications for the whole labour force. The method used in the Irish EIP report of calculating requirements for the flow of new entrants only, will, according to Hollister, reduce this sensitivity, which would seem to be exceptionally important as so little is known about the independent variable.

On the degree of disaggregation to be used, Hollister concludes that the question is still an open one. In theory, disaggregation is essential for manpower planning; in practice, the MRP did not gain much from the disaggregation of GNP forecasts by economic sector. The answer to this question probably depends on the availability and reliability of the data, which as nearly all manpower studies show, falls short of the ideal. For instance, some of Hollister's statistical evidence suggests that differences in education–occupation coefficients were due to discrepancies in the definition of various categories (or at least in the interpretation of such definitions) as well as any actual differences related to economic and technical factors.[2]

---

[1] An example given by Hollister is how the introduction of electronic data processing can change the requirements for clerical personnel: some may require more, and others less complex training than previously.

[2] See especially *op. cit.*, Table 1, pp. 112-13, where the distribution of employment by occupational category shows such wide inter-country variations, often inversely related to the level of economic development, in the proportion of skilled workers of various types in some economic sectors.

Hollister and some of the OECD country manpower studies agree on the most basic theoretical difficulty, namely the inflexibility which the technical manpower approach requires. The previous chapter has shown that the labour market is not always a reliable guide to scarcities and manpower needs. Still less is it the flexible and perfect market of some economic textbooks. This means that there is a need for some sort of manpower planning. But the criteria are not as easy to specify as some of the "technical" exercises seem to imply. There seem to be three major requirements: the quality and quantity of the relevant data must be improved radically; more flexibility must be built into the planning process (it is easy to say this in principle, but difficult to apply in practice); and "social demand" (however it may be specified) should be taken into account, leaving manpower *requirements* as minimum demands, as suggested by the term.

10 Education and manpower— developing countries[1]

In the less developed countries of Africa, Asia and Latin America, where a high proportion of employment and economic activity is in the subsistence sector, and where the enrolment rate even at the primary level is only about 50% of an age-cohort, the methodology of manpower forecasting may be quite different in some respects from that outlined in the previous chapter.

First, the choice may have to be made between universal primary education and literacy on the one hand, and the development of secondary and higher education to provide the necessary skills for economic development, on the other. This is because the low educational attainments and income of such countries often set budget or teacher supply constraints at such a level that one of these goals will have to be sacrificed or at least compromised.

Secondly, the fact of economic backwardness gives such countries a wide choice of technologies, as well as "intermediate" labour intensive technologies which have sometimes been advocated as being more suitable to their circumstances of relative scarcity of capital and technological capabilities and relative abundance of labour. These choices will obviously affect the demand for skill and the type of education and training needed to meet such demands.

Thirdly, the use of expatriate manpower in high-level occupations may give less-developed countries access to otherwise unavailable skills. This has to be set against the relatively high cost of such manpower (which comes from high-income countries) and the political forces which often demand its replacement, thus creating greater than ever pressures for the rapid expansion of second and third level education.

Finally, the subsistence sector, which is often large, is outside the scope of such manpower forecasts, at least as far as educational planning is concerned, as it has no necessary link with formal education (the need to train agricultural advisors is an important exception to this). Therefore the type of global planning of educational development of the entire labour force which is the basis of many OECD plans is not always appropriate.

---

[1] It is not proposed to make any rigid distinction between "developed" and "less-developed" countries. The latter generally include much of Asia, Latin America and all of Africa (except South Africa). They are characterized by high levels of illiteracy and low enrolment rates at the primary level, rather than by low income per head for the purposes of this chapter. The need to import teachers is another important, though not universal, characteristic. These aspects of underdevelopment are discussed further below.

There is, in addition, the difficulty that most data are available only for very recent years with the result that time trends are impossible to ascertain. Also data concerning the labour force, output and productivity is often incomplete or non-existent, especially for the subsistence sector.

F. Harbison and C. A. Myers have compiled a series of "human resource" and other indicators of development for 75 countries.[1] As well as using a composite index based on enrolment ratios in second and third level education, they use as indicators GNP per head, ratios of various categories of qualified manpower (including teachers) to population, percentage of population in agriculture, and various other enrolment indicators. Significant correlations are found in most cases among the various "human resource" variables and between the "human resource" and more general economic variables.[2] The countries concerned in this chapter are those with low levels of human resource development in the Harbison and Myers classification.

When compared to the European countries which were discussed in the previous chapter, Latin America is in general underdeveloped. Some of the problems arising from manpower planning in Latin America circumstances were discussed at an OECD seminar held at Lima in 1965.[3] In particular, the problems of such planning in Peru, when compared with the Spanish MRP project (discussed in the previous chapter), show some characteristics which are found in manpower and educational planning exercises in many underdeveloped countries.[4] First, the presence of a dual economy means that the primary sector, which is largely subsistence and outside the market economy, is outside normal manpower censuses, except in the general sense of constituting a large source of surplus, unskilled labour. Therefore the manpower planning exercise is not global; it tends to be concerned largely with the secondary and tertiary sectors, which are relatively small. Secondly, enrolment rates at all levels are so low, and illiteracy such a large problem that a tendency emerges to set general social goals rather than more limited manpower and economic goals for the educational system. Thirdly, data on labour skills, productivity and sectoral employment was extremely scarce.

The Peruvian example is instructive, as it suggests some comparisons with African and Asian countries, as will become apparent below. But it should not be taken as a model for all Latin America. Argentina, which is discussed in the same report,[5] is by contrast more developed than many of the MRP countries, both economically and (especially) educationally. Furthermore it has been the object of a long and detailed manpower–education project along MRP lines.[6] It is interesting to note the wide disparity of conditions in Latin America. For instance, according to the Harbison-Myers classification, Peru is in level II,

[1] *Education, Manpower and Economic Growth*, New York, 1964.
[2] The exceptions were mainly indicators based on percentages enrolled in certain branches of third level education.
[3] See the report on the Lima Seminar: *Problems of Human Resources Planning in Latin America and in the Mediterranean Regional Project Countries*, Paris, OECD, 1967.
[4] See the Lima Seminar report, *op. cit.*, esp. pp. 85-94.
[5] *Op. cit.*, pp. 103-22.
[6] *Education, Human Resources and Development in Argentina*, Paris, OECD, 1967.

just above Pakistan, Jamaica and Turkey, and just below Iraq, Mexico, Thailand and India.[1] Argentina, by way of contrast is in level IV, above Norway, Denmark and Sweden, and just below Israel and West Germany. Granted that the precise ranking of the two countries may not be significant their general position (with 24 countries separating them) undoubtedly is, when one considers the countries with which they are grouped.

Many African countries are near the bottom of the Harbison-Myers scale for a variety of reasons: they were without significant access to the developed countries until the late nineteenth century in many cases; when such access was available in a colonial context, the use of expatriates for skilled jobs obviated any consideration of the need to develop human resources for economic development. Consequently this need has been felt suddenly with the post-war trend towards independence. A typical example (important because of the way in which it has been documented) is Tanzania where there has been a sustained attempt to integrate educational and economic plans. The result is a type of manpower approach to educational planning which is described by G. Skorov as having the following priorities: "(a) to meet the economic requirements for high-level manpower; (b) to ensure that the quality of primary education is maintained at a level adequate to lay the foundations of permanent literacy; (c) to progress towards the long-term aim of achieving self-sufficiency, both qualitative and quantitative, in the supply of school teachers".[2]

There have been some preliminary surveys of manpower needs in Tanzania,[3] but these have suffered from the defect of being based on inadequate information about existing manpower stocks, or else from lack of integration with any overall development plan, in which case estimates of economic growth and therefore of demand for technical and scientific manpower especially, must be regarded as tentative. Also, certain categories (self employment, some clerical jobs) were not within the scope of some of these studies. Another report, the Thomas survey,[4] was more comprehensive and was specifically geared to the needs of Tanzania's development plan. Like the earlier reports it was confined to higher level manpower, i.e. manpower with secondary or higher education qualifications, and in some cases with professional training as well. The partial coverage of the survey may be seen if one compares the total number in employment in 1965, which was 334,000, with the total of high level manpower covered by the survey, which was only 29,500. Furthermore, the former figure relates

[1] Harbison and Myers, *op. cit.*, pp. 46-7. Another point which emerges—witness the relatively high rank of India—is that economic and educational development are not rigidly liked. Where educational development is relatively high one expects to find intellectual unemployment, especially where such development is concentrated on arts and low at higher levels. India and some Latin American countries provide examples of this.

[2] *Integration of Educational and Economic Planning in Tanzania*, Paris, UNESCO-IIEP, 1966, p. 40.

[3] Hunter, G., *High Level Manpower in East Africa. Preliminary Assessment*, London, 1962; *High level Manpower Requirements and Resources in Tanganyika*, Dar-es-Salaam (Government Printer), 1963.

[4] *Survey of High-Level Manpower Requirements and Resources for the Five-year Development Plan 1964-65 to 1968-69* (Prepared under the direction of Robert L. Thomas), Dar-es-Salaam, 1965.

to wage and salary employment, which accounted for only about 6.5% of the economically active population.[1]

The method used in Tanzania is that employment of high level manpower in the public sector is derived from estimates of the ministries concerned, modified by the Planning Directorate. For the private sector, forecasts of productivity, employment and GNP are used, together with estimates of the proportion of high level manpower in the labour force of each sector. This proportion is assumed to vary with output. The result gives a certain net increase for the period 1965-69. To this must be added allowances for retirements, deaths, and in the case of expatriates (who form a large proportion of highly-skilled manpower, especially at the professional level) an allowance for replacement or "Africanization". This latter factor is a matter of government policy, and there is a target rate of replacement for various categories of expatriates. The result is a doubling of requirements for manpower with graduate, professional, technician and second level qualifications between 1965 and 1969. Educational expansion is to be tailored to these requirements; it is calculated however, that second level education will not be able to supply enough "C" manpower (65% of which is skilled office occupations) and that some upgrading of skills or else training of people with primary education will have to fill the gap. Together with this apparent shortage of second level graduates one must consider the estimates for total employment in the 1965-69 period. There will be an estimated 110,000 vacancies in paid employment during the period, and apart from higher-level graduates there will be over 230,000 graduates from primary schools. These represent only about 20% of an age-cohort, as the total number of entrants to the labour market is estimated at about 1,150,000.[2] Thus less than 10% of entrants are likely to get paid employment; the rest will presumably remain in the subsistence sector. This raises problems concerning the primary school curriculum. If it were given a rural and agricultural orientation, especially in the rural areas, it would be more in line with the probable future occupation of pupils. On the other hand, there are doubts about the effectiveness of such measures, expressed by UNESCO, the FAO and the Addis Ababa conference of African States.[3] Also, there is the danger that such a move might drive urban and rural areas further apart.

Skorov makes several observations on the low absorptive capacity of the Tanzanian economy and the problems posed by it. A type of "intermediate technology", with investment of about £100 per work place would spread scarce capital resources more widely and probably create more jobs. But in the long run there is the danger that it would widen the technological (and income) gaps between developing and developed countries.[4] Furthermore little is known about such technologies, or what people mean exactly when they talk in such terms as "intermediate technology".

[1] Skorov, *op. cit.*, p. 18.
[2] *Op. cit.*, p. 58.
[3] See UNESCO/ECA Conference of African States on the Development of Education in Africa. *Final Report*, Addis Ababa, 1961.
[4] Skorov, *op. cit.*, pp. 62-3.

Similarly, in Uganda, where a manpower survey was carried out by the Central Planning Bureau, the coverage was limited. For instance it was estimated that by 1961 there would be a demand for 9,000 level I personnel (university graduates or equivalent) and 36,000 level II personnel (higher secondary graduates or equivalent); numbers in 1963 were about 3,000 level I and 7,300 level II.[1] By comparison, the total population was about 7 million. In the case of Uganda the high level manpower requirements were derived by assuming a fixed relationship with GDP, and the relation between the different grades of high level manpower was also assumed to be a certain ratio by the target date. Clearly, this approach has its defects; it would appear to rely too much on the assumption of arbitrary targets, and to neglect questions such as the relation between capital, technology and skill formation which are highly relevant.

Similarly, for other African countries, manpower planning tends to involve relatively small numbers of highly educated and trained personnel for the modern sector.[2] This does not diminish the importance of such planning, even though lack of data may make certain types of analysis difficult. Given the large disparity between unit costs at different levels of education the choice of educational "mix" is important; each extra pupil in secondary school may cost as much as ten primary school pupils, who may have to forego any chance of education. Furthermore, over-expansion at the secondary and higher levels could give rise to the phenomenon, so common in parts of Asia, of the unemployed graduate. Therefore, there is much to be said, when the modern sector is small and has limited absorptive capacity, for linking educational plans to manpower needs. However, it is clear that as in the case of the developed countries, not only is further study needed on the theory and concepts connected with manpower and development, but also a great deal needs to be done to obtain the data which is a prerequisite of any attempt to plan.

The partial coverage of human resource planning in some of the less developed countries brings one back to consideration of the studies of supply and demand (or "need") for highly qualified manpower in Chapter 8—but in a very different context. First, the use of expatriate workers, and the need to develop education and skills where very little exists preclude reliance on the price mechanism as an indicator of manpower needs or as the sole inducement to the development of human resources. This is quite apart from social and institutional factors which may render the price mechanism useless in any case. Therefore the type of forecasting used by Moser and Layard, Vermot-Gauchy and others will be of some use in less developed countries. Second, it will be often necessary to consider political factors, many of which add to the difficulties of the manpower planner both in the sense that they put extra pressures on an already overburdened educational system and also in the sense that they are formulated in an imprecise way. A prime example arises from the use of expatriate manpower in many African countries. But perhaps it is vain to expect too much precision in this type

[1] Chesswas, J. D., *Educational Planning and Development in Uganda*, Paris, UNESCO-IIEP, 1966, pp. 24-6.
[2] See, for instance, the Zambian manpower plan: *A Report on Manpower Education and Training in Zambia*, Lusaka, 1966.

of manpower analysis (as in other types), as this may lead to "frail guesses" instead. What is more important is a sense of co-ordination and strategy among educational and economic planners, so that their well-intentioned efforts do not run to waste in the overproduction of some categories of university graduates which exists in some countries alongside poor quality at all levels of education and low enrolment ratios even at the primary level.

PART THREE

Outlays

This Part considers what is spent on education, and an explanation is offered for the extraordinary rise in expenditure since the end of the Second World War.

11 Increases in outlays on education and their socio-economic causes and consequences[1]

Outlays

THE proportion of National Income devoted to expenditure on education has tended to rise as National Income *per capita* rises. This trend is evident in practically every country for which information can be obtained, and seems to occur at every stage of economic development. The following table shows the trend of educational expenditures as a percentage of GNP in several of the more developed countries. The trend in Table 11.1 below is quite clear.

While good statistical data for many developing countries is not available, the trend of expenditure on education is upwards there also, as can be seen from Table 11.2 below. It also emerges from this table that a very high proportion of resources is going into education in some—especially African—countries. Despite the extreme lag in income levels behind the countries in Table 11.1, there is a tendency for more resources to be directed to education than has occurred in the richer countries. This phenomenon is associated with aspects of labour market considerations which has been analysed in another part of this study, and also with the inflow of foreign aid payments, especially to Libya and the former French territories.

This increasing share of education in the National Product of most countries is, as far as can be seen, a post 1950, certainly a post Second World War phenomenon.[2] (We do not discuss here whether this is a cause or a consequence of the economic development that occured from 1947 to 1966). All of this must be regarded as a cause for concern about effective use of resources because it is plain that the trends outlined in the foregoing tables cannot continue indefinitely. Concern with the trend of unit costs will therefore become increasingly important, for as one recent writer has put it: "managers of educational systems will thus have smaller annual increments to work with, and a smaller area of man-

---

[1] Earlier versions of part of the chapter were presented to a Colloquium at the American Embassy in London in April, 1968, and at Calgary University, Alberta, in July 1968. An earlier version of the later part of the chapter was presented to a seminar of UNIDO, in New York, in June 1967, and was published in *Planning for Advanced Skills and Technologies*, UNIDO, New York, 1968.

[2] For instance in Ireland, public expenditure on education was 3.1% of GNP at factor cost in 1927, 3.2% in 1930, 3.6% in 1940, 2.5% in 1945 and 2.8% in 1950—see *Investment in Education, Ireland*, OECD, Appendix v, Section E, Table E6. In the United Kingdom, current public expenditure on education was 2.1% of National Income in 1925, 2.3% in 1930, 2.4% in 1935, 2.0% in 1940 (see (Vaizey, J., *The Costs of Education*, London, 1958).

TABLE 11.1 *Education expenditure as a percentage of GNP of more developed countries*

Year	United Kingdom	Ireland	Portugal	United States	France	Netherlands
1950	3.1	2.8	—	3.0	—	2.9
1955	3.2	3.2	1.4	4.2	2.8	3.6
1960	5.1	3.7	1.8	4.9	3.3	4.7
1965	5.8	4.0	2.9	6.3	5.7	5.7
1975*	6.0	4.4	4.6	6.8	5.7	7.0

* Projected. The USA figures refer to 1974, the French to 1970, the Irish to 1971. Education expenditure is net of transfer items. Public education expenditure only is included for Portugal; private expenditure would account for an extra 0.5% of GNP in 1960 and 0.3% in 1975 (approximately).

Sources: United Kingdom: Vaizey, J., *Resources for Education*, London, 1968. The figures have been adjusted to include capital expenditure. The 1975 projection uses the assumptions set out in W. Beckerman and associates—*The British Economy in 1975*, Cambridge, 1965, pp. 102 and 494. Since the growth of the British economy is likely to be less than projected for 1975, the percentage of expenditure on education may be greater, as the indications are that educational spending will be up to expectations by 1975.

Ireland: *Investment in Education*, OECD, Paris, 1966, Part 2, App. V, Table E6. Figures refer here to GNP at market prices. The 1970-71 projection is from Part 1, Ch. V.

Portugal: *MRP Report on Education in Portugal*, OECD, Paris, 1966, also the Portuguese version of the same report, Lisbon, 1963.

United States: *U.S. Digest of Educational Statistics 1965*. The 1974 projection is an IIEP estimation, cf. Coombs, P. H.—*The World Educational Crisis—A Systems Analysis*, IIEP, Paris, 1967. Vol. II, Table 11.105.b.

France: Poignant, R.—*L'Enseignement dans les pays du Marché Commun*, I.P.N., Paris, 1965.

Netherlands: *Educational Planning in the Netherlands*, OECD, Paris, 1966.

oeuvre—this because the increments of educational budgets are usually heavily committed in advance, especially with respect to rising salary bills".[1]

The increasing pressure on resources may be further illustrated because education in both developed and developing countries has in recent years been absorbing an increasing percentage of government expenditure, although increasing increments of educational expenditure may tend to diminish. And all the time the tendency of government economic and social activity to assume greater importance in Europe and North America has continued since the Second World War, and governments' share in total expenditure has been positively associated with economic development.[2]

As countries move from primary to secondary production, and, in turn, to

[1] Coombs, P. H., *The World Educational Crisis—A Systems Analysis*, IIEP, Paris, 1967.
[2] See, for instance, Kuznets, S., *Modern Economic Growth: Rate, Structure and Spread*, New Haven and London, 1966, pp. 406-7, and 426. It appears that the increasing importance of education and health expenditures accounts for nearly all of the increase in the share of government expenditure in the National Income of the more developed countries.

TABLE 11.2 *Trend of expenditure on education as percentage of Gross Domestic Product at market prices of less developed countries*

Year	Colombia	Mexico	Venezuela	India	Burma	Uganda	Kenya	Tunisia	Libya
1950	1.1	0.4	1.2	0.8	0.8	—	—	—	—
1954	1.2	0.8	1.7	2.0[1]	1.8	3.4	2.5[5]	—	—
1960	2.5[2]	1.3[2]	3.7	2.3	1.6	3.4	4.6[5]	—	2.4[2][5]
1963	2.8	1.6	3.5[3]	2.4	2.0	2.8	4.8[5]	5.8	3.7[5]
1965	2.2	1.9	4.0	2.6	2.5	2.7	5.6[5]	4.3	5.9
1967	2.3	2.5	4.0	—	3.0	2.9[5]	—	5.0[4]	3.6

Source: Statistical Yearbook, UNESCO, 1969.
Notes: [1] 1955, [2] 1961, [3] 1965, [4] 1966, [5] as percentage of Gross Domestic Product at factor cost.

the development of the tertiary sector, the tertiary sector's expansion will inevitably include a considerable amount of expansion of expenditure on education. In this context, the study of unit costs and of efficient resource use is of increasing importance both in developed and in all types of developing economies.

Later in this study a considerable development of the concept of a production function in education is undertaken, in order to see how factor combinations change, and in response to what forces. These forces are, of course, relative prices, government regulations, educational ideas and so on. They combine to give an "educational technology" (or given combination of resources per unit) for different educational systems.

This rising expenditure on education is associated with the shift in consumption expenditure towards young people and children, and with the rising demands for qualified manpower which a more productive economy requires. The second part of this chapter is concerned with some of these matters.

In this work a rising demand for education is assumed, as forecast by various OECD reports and other documents. Two main points may be noted however:

1. The reason for assuming a rising demand is principally because of assumed manpower requirements. This reason may be supplemented to a greater or lesser extent by "social demand" or by political factors. The manpower requirements approach has revealed the need for a large expansion in education before 1975 in the MRP countries, and also in Ireland and, to a lesser extent, the Netherlands. There are criticisms of this approach, arising mainly from lack of data, and from indeterminacy—demand may well be a function of supply.[1] Although forecasts may need revision, the general upward trend is obvious and can hardly be disputed. "Social demand"[2] is

[1] For an analysis of these criticisms see Hollister, R., *A Technical Evaluation of the First Stage of the Mediterranean Regional Project*, OECD, Paris, 1967, especially pp. 32-40, and pp. 47-81.
[2] According to Hollister, *op. cit.*, "demand not associated with education required for productive objects".

also rising; this is especially evident for a country such as the United Kingdom, where past expansion in education leads to a greater awareness of the benefits to be derived from education, whether these benefits be directly "productive" or not.[1]

2. The pattern of the rising demand may also be relevant. Expansion tends to be greatest in the more advanced sectors of the educational system. While the pattern of expansion is by no means uniform, the relatively large primary (first level) sector in most countries will generally have a decreasing *relative* size. As this sector has relatively low unit costs, the effect on educational costs of the pattern of educational demand will be important.[2] The demand projections for education, drawing mainly on MRP—and EIP—OECD forecasts are set out in the following paragraphs.

There has been a marked rise in the demand for education throughout the post-war period. Table 11.3 below illustrates this trend in enrolment in Ireland, Portugal, Quebec and in England and Wales. As there was practically full enrolment in these countries in primary education throughout this period, (except in Portugal in the earlier part of the period), enrolments at this level follow demographic trends for the relevant age-group. Enrolments at higher levels far outstrip any population increases.

Thus in England and Wales, and Ireland there is a slight rise, or even a fall, in primary school enrolments between 1955 and 1965. At the secondary level there were increases of 50% or more during the same period. In England and Wales this is partly a reflection of the high birthrate in the immediate post-war years, but partly due to a strong trend towards nore secondary education. The very large rises for Portugal and Quebec in secondary enrolments in the 1955-1965 period (over 250% in Quebec and over 150% in Portugal) are obviously too great to be due to any demographic influence and are evidence of a strong increase in the demand for secondary education.

More important for planning purposes are the forecasts which have been made, by the OECD and others, of the demand for education in the period up to 1975. Some of these forecasts are summarized in Table 11.4 below; in every case there is a very substantial increase at the Secondary and subsequent levels.

The questions that arise are: (1) why has this growth occured, and (2) what have been and what will be its socio-economic consequences?

Socio-economic background to rising educational outlays

In recent years many of the more confident assertions about the relationships and inter-relations of education and the economy, between education and

---

[1] For instance in Beckerman, W. and associates, *The British Economy in 1975*, Cambridge, 1965, J. Vaizey and R. Knight make forecasts of educational requirements for 1975 which depend much less on manpower and much more on social and political objectives (such as the extension of compulsory education) than do the MRP reports. Also, the EIP report Educational Policy and Planning in the Netherlands (OECD Paris, 1967) bases many of its requirements on "fundamental goals" in Chapter 2. These goals are largely non-economic.

[2] This point is developed further in the following chapter.

TABLE 11.3 *Indices of educational enrolment (England and Wales, Ireland, Portugal, Quebec), 1945-1965*

Year	Republic Of Ireland			England and Wales		Quebec		Portugal	
	Primary	Secondary (1st cycle)	Secondary (2nd cycle)	Primary	Secondary	Primary	Secondary	Primary	Secondary
1945	94.8	76.3	70.1	79.3	52.7	—	—	67.6	80.0
1950	93.6	85.5	76.6	79.5	89.2	72.0	69.7	74.6	80.3
1955	100.0	100.00	100.00	100.00	100.00	100.00	100.00	100.00	100.00
1960	102.5	129.7	131.4	91.3	141.7	117.9	204.6	106.8	175.1
1965	102.3	159.3	182.5	92.9	146.8	135.0	369.5	110.0	267.0

Sources: Ireland: *Investment in Education*, Part II, OECD, Dublin and Paris, 1966, General Statistical Tables.
England and Wales: 1945 and 1950, Vaizey, J.—*The Costs of Education*, London 1958, pp. 219, 220. 1955, 1960, 1965, *Statistics of Education,*
    1956, Part I, HMSO, London, p. 44.
Quebec: *Report of the Royal Commission of Inquiry on Education in the Province of Quebec*, Vol. V, Table XVIII.
Portugal: *Estatisticas da Educação, 1967*, I.N.E. Lisbon, 1968, p. XXII.

Note: All Direct Grant school pupils in England and Wales are shown under "Secondary". A few of these are in the primary departments of grammar
    schools. Their number is small, however, about 0.3% of primary or 0.5% of secondary enrolments.

TABLE 11.4 *Some forecasts of educational enrolments*

(Average daily enrolment '000)

	United Kingdom (NIESR)			Ireland (EIP)			Portugal (MRP)		
	1960	1975	Annual % change	1964	1971	Annual % change	1961	1975	Annual % change
Primary . . .	4,414	6,108	+2.2	493.3	509.7	+0.5	887.2	800.0	—0.8
Secondary (general) .	3,206	4,308	+3.0	94.6	124.6	+4.0	160.0	561.0	+9.3
Secondary (technical and vocational . .	498	1370	+6.7	30.6	43.0	+5.0	70.0	263.0	+9.8
Higher. . . .	144	426	+7.5	16.8	23.6	+5.8	24.1	47.0	+5.0

Sources: United Kingdom: Estimates by J. Vaizey and R. Knight in *The British Economy in 1975*, Cambridge, 1965, Ch. XIV.

Ireland: *Investment in Education*, Part 1, OECD, Dublin and Paris, 1966, Tables 1.2, 3.1, 3.2.

Portugal: *The Mediterranean Regional Project: Country Reports, Portugal,* OECD, Paris, 1966, Table 32.

Notes: a) Education in Britain includes independent schools and therefore the figures differ in coverage from Table 11.3 above.

b) Technical education in Britain includes part-time students, and refers to *further education,* which is not quite the same thing as technical education in Ireland or Portugal. From a manpower point of view however, this procedure seems justified. The full-time equivalent (counting the part-time element as 1/5) is 167,000 students in 1960 and 365,000 in 1975.

social change, and social change and productivity, have been examined, and the present state of knowledge on the subjects concerned is somewhat less confident than it was.

This applies less to the relationship between economic growth and education than to other relationships. The *locus classicus* of this work is Denison's examination of the relationships between economic growth in the United States and in some other western countries, to education.[1] The basis of this work has been much discussed and part of what follows is an examination (necessarily abbreviated) of some of the major points of debate.

Examination of census and other data shows a relationship between education and earnings. The key question is what is this relationship. Clearly, there is a multiple correlation between education, earnings, social background, race, sex and occupational grouping. Yet standardisation for all these factors has so far still left a positive relationship, in which it appears plausible that education (in some sense) causes higher earnings.[2] This has to be related to sociological evi-

---

[1] Denison, E. F., assisted by Jean-Pierre Poullier, *Why Growth Rates Differ*, The Brookings Institution, Washington D.C., 1967.

[2] See Hansen, W. L., Total and private rates of return to investment in schooling, *Journal of Political Economy*, Vol. LXXI, April 1963, pp. 128-40; Renshaw, E. F., Estimating the returns to education, *Review of Economics and Statistics*, Vol. XLII, August 1960, pp. 318-24; Blaug, M., The rate of return on investment in education in Great Britain, in *Manchester School*, 1965, pp. 205-62; Schultz, T. W., *The Economic Value of Education*, New York and London, 1963.

dence[1] that the relationship between social mobility and education is not nearly as high as had once been expected *a priori*.

Most of the data available are cross-sectional data, but it is possible (on certain assumptions) to calculate the life-time earnings pattern for different typical individuals. The life-time earnings have to be standardised, of course, for price changes and life-expectancy. These life-time earnings properly discounted, can be expressed as a rate of return on the cost of education. The cost of education may be measured in a variety of ways, but usually in this work it is calculated at what is called the opportunity cost, that is to say total educational costs plus income foregone as a result of the loss of earnings which would have been made had the students been in employment when they were at college or at high school.

Denison's study of growth rates depends primarily on the marginal productivity theory of income distribution, i.e. on the hypothesis that the factors of production are rewarded in proportion to their marginal products. Denison analyses the growth of output in the USA and in European countries. He then makes a detailed analysis of the growth of land, capital, and labour inputs. In accordance with the marginal productivity theory, each factor is weighted by its share in National Income throughout the calculations. The adjustments to labour input include allowances for changes in employment, hours of work, age-sex composition of the labour force, amount of education received. The adjustments to capital take account of international movements, and detailed measurements were made of all types of capital goods. After these calculations there remains a residual, as the rate of growth of output is greater than the weighted average rate of growth of factor inputs. Parts of this residual are then ascribed to economies of scale, various improvements in resource allocation, reduction in the age of the capital stock, reduction in trade barriers et cetera. The final residue is called "advance of knowledge". This presumably is linked in some way with education, as is the "spread of knowledge" component, i.e. the effect of increased amounts of education on the productivity of the labour force.

The whole procedure depends on the acceptance of the marginal productivity theory of income distribution, and the aggregate production function. These in turn presuppose that one can measure the stock of capital.

As Harry Johnson has said: "The essence of it is to regard 'capital' as including anything that yields a stream of income over time, and income as the product of capital. From this point of view, as Fisher pointed out, all categories of income describe yields on various forms of capital, and can be expressed as rates of interest or return on the corresponding items of capital. Alternatively, all forms of income-yielding assets can be given an equivalent capital value by capitalising the income they yield at an appropriate rate of interest. By extension, the growth of income that defines economic development is necessarily the result of the accumulation of capital, or of 'investment'; but 'investment' in this

---

[1] For example Anderson, C. A., A skeptical note on educational mobility, *American Journal of Sociology*, Vol. 66 (1), May 1961; also *Children and Their Primary Schools* (The Plowden Report), Vols. I and II, HMSO, London, 1967, where such evidence is implicit in many of the investigations undertaken.

context must be defined to include such diverse activities as adding to material capital, increasing the health, discipline, skill and education of the human population, moving labour into more productive occupations and locations, and applying existing knowledge or discovering and applying new knowledge to increase the efficiency of productive processes. All such activities involve incurring costs, in the form of use of current resources, and investment in them is socially worth while if the rate of return over cost exceeds the general rate of interest, or the capital value of the additional income they yield exceeds the cost of obtaining it. From the somewhat different perspective of planning economic development, efficient development involves allocation of investment resources according to priorities set by the relative rates of return on alternative investments."[1]

Ultimately, therefore, the intellectual basis of the work is standard neo-classical theory. The complex statistical work may be recalculated, using different weights; but this is not a matter of substance.

The statistical work is, however, necessarily based on certain assumptions which may be questioned. In so far as the relationship between earnings and past education is concerned, if the labour market is a series of non-competing markets, then it follows that considered aggregatively the relativities in wages and salaries are due to factors which do not accurately reflect marginal productivities. The labour market does not correspond, even approximately to the perfect consumption model.

A further basic assumption of the reasoning is refuted by Kaldor, namely the existence of a production function of this type. Kaldor has said that "All such estimates are derived from hypothesis concerning the so-called 'production function' and the price system, (it is a mild description to call them 'strong assumptions') which have no theoretical or empirical basis whatever". Instead he uses a technical progress function in which marginal factor rewards are not equated to marginal productivity.[2] The technical progress function relates the rate of increase of output per man on the latest investment to the rate of increase of investment, rather than relating output per man to capital per man, as in the orthodox production function. As new investment affects the rate of technical progress, it gives rise to external economies which cannot be appropriated by the investor. "Thus, if reality corresponds to these models, econometric calculations of capital's contribution to growth based on actual factor shares will therefore lead to an underestimate."[3] Kaldor also argues that as technical progress is expected to diminish the rate of return from existing investments, new investments will be made subject to a "pay-back" criterion, and that this— together with a decreasing rate of return and a changing price/wage ratio over time—means that marginal products and marginal factor rewards are not necessarily equated at any time.[4] As Neild said: "It was evident . . . that the

---

[1] Vaizey, J. (ed.), *The Residual Factor and Economic Growth*, OECD, Paris, 1965, p. 221.
[2] See Kaldor and Mirrlees, A new model of economic growth, *Review of Economic Studies*, June 1962, also *The Residual Factor and Economic Growth*, OECD, Paris, 1964, pp. 155-60.
[3] From a discussion of technical progress functions in Hahn, F. H. and Matthews, R. C. O., The theory of economic growth—a survey, *Economic Journal*, Vol. 74, December 1964.
[4] *The Residual Factor and Economic Growth, op. cit.*, See comments by N. Kaldor.

division between those who believe in the marginal productivity theory of distribution and those who do not was a matter of faith; it was not something that could be resolved by discussion (or conversion)."[1]

Supposing for a moment, however, that these major statistical and conceptual difficulties are ignored, then (as has been shown above) the evidence on returns to education suggests that there is a comparability with the rates of return on physical capital. Further, the "residual" factor, of which education is the major component, contributes most to growth. These results have been found to prevail in the United States, and in many other Western countries.

It follows, therefore, that too little has been devoted to "human capital" (in the United States and elsewhere), and that therefore a reallocation of resources away from physical capital to human capital would have accelerated growth.[2]

These conclusions are not necessarily valid for other countries, as the calculations for India seem to suggest. But generally speaking, "human capital", and, specifically, education should (as a result of this work) be included in any policy for growth. This policy is not accepted, however, in short-term macro-economic work and there is no sign of it in short-term macro-economic forecasts.

Clearly no less important than the quantity of education is its quality. The problem as discussed above, is to assess its quality, or the content of education, by criteria other than just crude years of schooling. But in the absence of such studies, the material that is available at present must be accepted as a basis for discussion.

Is there a diminishing marginal rate of return on extra years of education? Using aggregative data (especially cross-section data as a time-series) makes it difficult to assess the increment of output which is attributable to additions to education. *A priori* it might seem that increments should give smaller and smaller returns; the rate of return should tend to fall the more education any one man (or community) receives. On the other hand, there is little evidence to suggest that in wealthy societies the returns to education are lower than the returns to education in low-income societies. A suggestion is offered below (which deals with complementarities) which throws doubt on the reasoning just discussed.

There are, therefore, doubts about the figures presented, and doubts about the reasoning on which they are based. Technologically progressive societies, which also tend to have had periods of high and sustained growth, tend to spend between five and seven per cent of their national income on education. Since the proportion of the Gross National Product spent on education has risen throughout the world in the past twenty years, the potential growth rate is also rising. The evidence for these two general propositions suggests a positive causal relationship.

Historically, many instances of this correlation have been given: the German

---

[1] *The Residual Factor and Economic Growth, op. cit.*, pp. 138 and 273.

[2] Denison (*op. cit.*, pp. 287-88) includes Research and Development expenditure as a factor in advancing knowledge, i.e. as a component in the final "residual". However he maintains that it is not an important factor, and observes (p. 288) that increased R and D expenditure, in the USA was not associated with an increased residual.

technical education system in the later nineteenth century, the American high school and land grant college system at the same period, the Japanese education system after the Meiji era, the Soviet education system, are examples that have been often quoted. But much historical work lays emphasis on quality, or on the education of élite groups. There is little evidence that the volume of education played any part in the British industrial revolution. Indeed in many cases—India is an example—the education system has hindered development. One has to be very careful to separate out arguments about volume and about quality: arguments about education for all from arguments about education for key groups.

Social scientists are not yet in a position to assent to, or to deny, the general propositions which have been advanced by some economists and historians about the relative importance of education compared with other factors in economic development. This will require far more detailed work and will require many research projects to be undertaken.

Thus the nature of the contribution of education to economic growth, and the reciprocal relationship between education and economic growth, is a matter for further study, and existing findings are subject to much refinement. It appears that in the process of economic growth skilled manpower plays a critical role in the development of the socio-economic structure.

Rough forecasts can be made for the requirements of manpower over the next twenty or thirty years, though most manpower forecasts are for far shorter periods. Manpower forecasts can be re-interpreted into educational categories. As will be argued below, this is in itself a complex and (arguably) invalid procedure.

In this work, manpower forecasting has already been considered. Detailed manpower forecasts for long periods ahead have little validity, either conceptually or in practice. The only satisfactory ones are those for specific types of skill in the short period, or for specific industries, where the degree of error should be tolerable. Manpower forecasts for the economy multiply existing forecasting errors.[1]

The major task that manpower forecasting has been used for is to predict the likely ranges of demand for different types of qualification; and it is therefore (to a degree) a substitute for a critical discussion of the content of education. As one of the present authors has said; "Implicit in the manpower programmes may well be a view of the nature of the future economy and the society which would not be acceptable. And secondly, the discussion is about the implicit values and outlook which are associated with a particular structure of education. In the developing nations the educational system derived from manpower targets characteristically has a larger higher education system, and above all a larger secondary education system, than that which would be derived from the pressure of parents and politicians, which tends to be a more orthodox pyramid in shape. The opponents of this mode of reasoning underlying present manpower

---

[1] For these reasons the Portuguese MRP report did not accept the methodology of the manpower forecasting approach: see *The Mediterranean Regional Project, Portugal*, OECD Paris, 1966, pp. 41 and 42.

plans, and education policies drawn from them, call attention not only to the whole range of extremely dubious assumptions, which are made in devising these manpower targets, but also to the fact that unless the manpower is most carefully fed into jobs in the developing economy, the leads and lags which develop may well be worse than the maladjustments which would arise in an almost un-coordinated development of the education system. Thus, for example, in the Nigerian case, the substantial problems associated with the great growth of primary education—an expansion which was contrary to the recommendations of the Ashby Report—would be taken as an instance of the over-emphasis on education, which has ultimately resulted from unrealistic manpower targets.

"Furthermore, some thinkers would argue that the education system in developing countries ought specifically to be biassed in a rural direction, and that the whole emphasis of the manpower planners' approach has been to over-emphasise formal education as against informal education, and to over-emphasise education for urban environments as against education which is truly nation-building. Now if we take this reasoning, which underlies the debate which has been specifically about African education in the last ten years or so, and apply it to Europe, we see much the same kind of argument taking place. A similar dichotomy about content and structure is implicit in much of the discussion now going on in (Britain) and in the rest of Europe."

What, in summary, are the main arguments that command widespread assent?

The major explanation of the increases in educational expenditure in recent years is undoubtedly related to the social pressures for more education and for the inclusion of the lower socio-economic groups into the formal education system. These "social pressures" embody not only a desire for education purely considered as education, but they embody ordinary economic calculations of the relationship between higher income and education. The dichotomy between "social" and "economic" demands for education is hard to draw and it is difficult to say whether the pressure for education which has been experienced in recent years may be categorised as more social than economic. Education affects social relationships. Education affects people's outlook on life. It gives to people both a general acculturation and special vocational skills. It is the combination of these social relationships, skills and outlooks, with the managerial structure, the government and above all physical capital, which together affects the rate of growth. In what follows an attempt is made to lay emphasis upon the complementaries.

One of the major causes of economic growth is the international migration of skills, abilities and technologies. Williams, in his contribution to the discussion of the "brain drain" and the alleged technological gap between Western Europe and North America, emphasises this: "R and D is important for growth but the idea that a country's growth depends on its own R and D overlooks the great importance of the international movement of ideas, of machines which embody the results of R and D, and of capital transfers to make possible the use in various countries of technological and managerial inventions made elsewhere."[1] Much of the work on the "brain-drain" has implicitly overlooked this

[1] Williams, B. R., *Technology, Investment and Growth*, London, 1967, p. 4.

valuable point; and it is to be hoped that research will pay far more attention to it in future.

A different approach

If this chain of reasoning is followed, a prospect develops of linking economic growth to education, technology and skill in a different way. Four relevant questions were posed by one of the authors in an earlier paper:[1]

1. What is the complementarity between the development of education, the progress of technology, and innovation embodied in new investment in plant and equipment?
2. In the light of this analysis, what kind of skills are required by advanced technologies? Specifically, do they precede technological innovation and capital investment, in optimal conditions, and if so, how many and what skills should be provided in advance?
3. How should such skills be measured and classified?
4. What is the role of the manufacturing sector in introducing advanced technologies in developing countries? Is it a reservoir of skills which may later be used to develop skills in other sectors? Or are its skills specific to its own technological circumstances.

In what follows a brief sketch of the approach implied by these questions is given.

A distinction can be made between the skilled people in an advanced economy and the highly educated. The majority of people with qualifications above the minimum are non-technically, non-scientifically-prepared. Therefore, the majority of teachers, executives and similar sorts of people appear in the non-technical sectors. Further, there are some qualified people (e.g. nurses) who are complementary to technically or scientifically qualified personnel. A number of graduates who are not scientists are employed in technically-oriented managerial roles because their jobs arise in technologically advanced economies.

While there are good reasons for distinguishing the highly-educated from the technically qualified, the distinction is a blurred one. It can be asserted, however, that a high proportion of educated people in most countries have had an education which was primarily non-technical in its orientation. Data from the under-developed countries suggests that their education systems are less technically oriented than those in advanced countries. "On-the-job" acquired skills are quantitatively more important than those springing from education in the skill mix of the industrial labour force.

Skill acquisition properly understood therefore *follows* investment rather than precedes it. In other words, education is not a necessary prior condition of a skilled labour force according to the evidence of the nature of the existing labour force.

This reasoning arises from a comparison of the disposition of the "educated" population in the labour force, and of the stock of "skilled people" in the labour

[1] Vaizey, J., in *Planning for Advanced Skill and Technologies*, UNIDO, New York, 1968.

force in different countries. A time-series of the evolution of the labour force suggests that, while there has been a notable development in the numbers of technically qualified members of the labour force with higher education qualifications, there has been an even bigger development in the labour force of those with higher education qualifications but who are not technically qualified.

If the hypothesis is to be developed, that in general skills tend to "follow" rather than to lead, then the next matter to be considered is the relationship between occupation structure, skill-mix, and capital intensity.

The potential rate of incorporation of new technology into plant and equipment depends ultimately upon the rate of gross investment. The rate of incorporation of new technology will depend upon the rate of investment in new capital and the rate of scrapping of old capital.

Productivity may gradually rise however even without the incorporation of a "new" technology. Small adaptations of equipment may have cumulative effects on technology which are significant.

An analogy may well be drawn with the stock of skills. The rate of withdrawal from the labour force and the rate of recruitment affect the total stock of new skills. Learning "on-the-job" and "learning-by-doing" are also important, as Arrow and others have pointed out.

Thus two situations may be defined which inhibit the introduction of new technologies:

1. new capital (or labour) may have an old design (or skill);
2. the existing situation may require the old design. But even so the old capital (or labour) can yield bigger productivity gains (the Horndahl effect) without any changes in technique.

Thus, a new skill introduced into our existing situation may be rendered nugatory while an existing skill may yield productivity gains.

What is the effect on this situation of a new scientific discovery? How does it get incorporated into the economy?

A great deal is known about "R and D". As one of the existing authors has said:[1]

"If we turn to research proper, certain clear distinctions have generally been made. There is research directly sponsored by a sector of the economy (e.g. atomic energy, space or oil); and there is research which just goes on under its own steam and may later have an application (e.g. the effects of biochemistry on drug therapy, and consequently on the development of the pharmaceutical firms). Clearly this research effort has, so to speak, a series of inner logics of its own. It is accidental, one supposes, whether the development of capital, of labour and of research happens to coincide; and it is impossible to say, except by a good many case histories, which comes first: gross investment, new skills or research breakthroughs. It is sufficient to say that there are several extreme positions:

1. Capital-intensive industries using little skill and little research (public utilities).

[1] Vaizey, J., in *Planning for Advanced Skills and Technologies, op. cit.*

2. Skill-intensive industries using little capital and little research (education).
3. Skill- and research-intensive industries (pharmaceuticals).
4. Skill- and capital- and research-intensive industries (aerospace).
5. Labour-intensive industries that require little skill, capital or research (small retailing)."

The research intensive industries have been the major pace-setters. Purely labour-intensive industries have declined, while skill-intensive industries have grown. But the most characteristic high yields of productivity have been in fairly capital- and skill-intensive industries, using little research (automobiles).

This taxonomy can be used as a basis for an elucidation of the place of education in technological advance. Research often leads to more skill-intensive techniques and usually to more capital-intensive techniques as well. The big advances will often be at a later stage, however, with a series of small correlative breakthroughs which are the result of "experience".

The nature and direction of physical investment seem in the past to have determined the nature of the demands for skills. (They are, of course, bound to determine the size of the demand). The projection of the nature, size and direction of these investments is therefore a prior condition of a projection of skill requirements.

It is no doubt true that the availability of skills has helped to determine the choice of capital equipment. But it is fairly easy to acquire many skills; it is difficult to design complexes of machinery. "Technology" has been traditionally conceived of as a matter of machines rather than of skills.

For these reasons (that "technology" has meant machines, and that skills have been relatively easily acquired) the study of choice of technologies has been predominantly concerned with capital.

In the discussion of factor proportions, homogeneity of factors has usually been assumed; and when heterogeneity has been assumed, it has been wholly (so far as we are aware) of capital, in particular the discussion of lumpiness. The labour force has been disaggregated for the study of wage-determination, but not for substitutability of labour and capital (which is where the work in the choice of technologies has been relevant). The supply of appropriate skills has (properly, in view of what has been said above) been a subsidiary one.

As one of the present authors has argued "it is clearly not inherent in their work that this should be the case. Just as 'capital' can be broken up into many discrete pieces of equipment (as developed in the work of Sen, Chenery and Mathur[1]) so that as Riskin[2] puts it, we can assume a '... multiplicity of specific inputs required for the production of any given commodity; the uneven rate at which these inputs become scarce as the scale of production expands; and the different proportions in which the inputs are required by different techniques', it must inevitably follow that the labour force can be so divided into many specific inputs".

[1] Mathur, G., _Planning for Steady Growth_, Oxford, 1965, esp. pp. 137-54 and 320-27. Also Sen, A. K., _Choice of Techniques_, Oxford, 1960; Leibenstein, H. and Galenson, W., Investment criteria, productivity and economic development, in _Quarterly Journal of Economics_, August 1955, pp. 343-70.
[2] _Planning for Advanced Skills and Technologies, op. cit._

But the inherent weighting problem is what weight is to be applied to different kinds of skill. Further, how "lumpy" are skills—what specificity of skills to specific techniques actually prevails? Crucial to the discussion, too, is what education and training is necessary to produce these skills. Though Tinbergen and his collaborators have used a physical capital model as the basis for their work on the labour force, they have not dealt with it in those specific terms.

On the second point, one authority has said "There is reason to believe that there is a high degree of complementarity between a certain type of production method and the kind of labour force needed for it. In other words, a certain level of technology and hence a certain level of productivity is represented by a specific kind of organisation and a specific kind of capital equipment that is made to work by a labour force whose occupational composition is well defined."[1]

If the preceding argument is followed, then the physical capital structure is what determines the pattern of skills.

But on the other points, the physical model has to be used with care. A model for the labour force which is derived directly from models of capital involves assumptions about skills and their relation to education which need to be investigated. Evidence suggests that many skills are not as discrete and specific as pieces of capital equipment are. As one of us has argued elsewhere[2] "Many people can do, more or less well, a wide variety of jobs: there is an element of improvisation, of 'make do and mend', about labour which is impressive. There are, of course two extreme instances where this is not the case: in highly developed skills, like surgery, or piloting aircraft, where specific skills are reinforced by legal constraints on who may exercise them; and in poor countries where roles in production are culturally assigned and nobody may perform another role. But in the bulk of economies, the majority of skilled and semi-skilled jobs fall somewhere between these two extremes; and, above all, this is the case in manufacturing industry. Thus the models tend to exaggerate the likelihood of skill bottlenecks, because they underestimate the substitutability of skills. But, further, they take for granted that the educational and training background which prevails in advanced countries is a *necessary* background for the exercise of those skills."

If this line of reasoning is followed, then it would follow that high levels of education at all levels are not necessary for economic growth, except in so far as the attitudes of the population need to be altered in order to make it possible for them to acquire skills.

To revert to the prior question: on what basis should the measurement and classification of skills be put? Classification by minute observation of the occupational distribution gives results of great complexity, but with a high degree of specificity. Training can be matched to these skills. This approach is widely used in industrial training. Measuring skill by educational background gives broader definitions but less specificity. According to Zymelman:[3]

[1] UNIDO Symposium: *Planning for Advanced Skills and Technologies*, New York, 1968.
[2] Vaizey, J., in *Planning for Advanced Skills and Technologies, op. cit.*
[3] UNIDO Symposium, *op. cit.*

F

"The linking of productivity to formal education ignores variables in the causality process between productivity and 'human resources'. A high educational level does not produce automatically a higher level of output, unless this higher level of education is a result of 'higher' occupational mix, such as more professionals and less labourers. It is, therefore, of little use to link directly productivity or income *per capita* to formal education for planning purposes. This research points to the necessity of (further) research in a vital area, that of inquiring into the different ways or paths of skill acquisition especially at the blue collar skilled worker level, and acquiring better data on the 'human functions' involved in production." The relationship between skill and educational background may not be determined by technical but by social factors and therefore cannot be properly classified by such criteria as "educational level". This is not to say that approximations may not be made, as Timar argues:[1]

"The average complexity (educational level) of labour can be approximately measured by a system of coefficients, which also takes into account, in addition to the length of time necessary to attain the different levels, the direct and indirect costs of education and training. This method makes perceptible the importance of the more highly qualified labour force. The complexity of labour measured with such a method (or with any other method) is higher in countries with more developed industries." That is, it is possible, in Timar's view to relate productivity to the skill-mix, and the skill-mix to educational background, and to weight the skill-mix by the costs of education.

The earlier sections of this Report have indicated, however, the extreme complexity of measuring costs (which include income foregone) and therefore, as one of us has commented: "This method of measurement of costs does not give the arithmetic ratios of skill intensity that would be necessary for the planning model to give unambiguous answers."

Since the measurement, classification and weighting of skill is not unambiguous, it follows that the relationship of the education system to the economy (which is an indirect one) cannot be easily traced.

To resume the argument. To postulate a rate of economic growth for any economy which requires a given distribution and size of the capital stock, and of the labour force, must entail a fixed technical coefficient between skills and capital, and between both and output. It is then possible to derive physical investment levels and educational output levels, after making allowance (in the case of physical capital) for the withdrawal of obsolete and worn-out capital, or (in the case of the labour force) the death or retirement of the workers, provided, in the case of labour, that there is a fixed relationship between skills and educational background.

In the short run in educational systems there are reasonably stable relationships between various levels of education. It can therefore be held that the analysis of the relationship between the growth of gross national product, labour and capital inputs, and productivity leads to an optimal model of the education system.

---

[1] UNIDO Symposium, *op. cit.*

But if what has been argued here is correct, then this analysis just presented is not only loosely argued (and yet to be proved) but it detracts strongly from the real problems of the relation of education to economic growth. In particular, it under-rates on-the-job training, specific vocational training, and "experience", and exaggerates the extent to which formal education is necessary for economic growth. It also (just as important) avoids a consideration of the problem of the content of education, and its distribution between groups and individuals.

On this basis, it seems more satisfactory to rely on the more general considerations discussed above.

12 Trends in resource use: England and Wales

THIS chapter traces the evolution of public educational spending in England and Wales, and also its composition at various dates in order to indicate certain trends in resource use. The importance of public spending in relation to total outlays has always been overwhelmingly large in recent times. It accounted for an estimated 90% of total current outlays until about 1950, and since then its share has risen, surpassing 95% about 1965.[1]

The long-term trend in real public expenditure on education in the United Kingdom has been steadily upwards, as Table 12.1 shows. This increase has been accompanied by an increase in monetary expenditure which was roughly proportional in the pre-Second World War period when prices were fairly steady (although there were rises and falls in various sub-periods, as the table implies). The post-war increase in prices has, however, been the occasion of an extremely sharp tendency towards rising monetary expenditure, which between 1948 and 1965 rose more than twice as fast as real expenditure.

As a proportion of national income, public education expenditure tended to grow during peace time, e.g. from 1.2% to 2.4% in the 1920-1935 period. It fell to 2.0% and 1.7% in the war years of 1940 and 1945 respectively, but rose to 2.5% in 1948, 2.8% in 1955 and 4.1% in 1965.

The increase in real expenditure shown above is arrived at after deflating the various sectors of education by special educational price indices. These have the effect of reducing the growth of expenditure to a greater extent than would a conventional index of the cost of living, or of final output. For instance, the implicit price index in the above table (1948=100) was 247 for 1965, while the consumer index was 171 and the final output index 175.[2]

The composition of this increasing expenditure shows certain trends which are of significance in terms of the hypothesis advanced in this book, which stated that increased educational demand would be largely for higher levels of education, which had high unit costs. It was shown that enrolments and expenditures were forecast in most countries to rise relatively slowly at the

---

[1] See estimates made in Vaizey, J. and Sheehan, J., *Resources for Education*, London, 1968, especially Chapters 6 and 8.

[2] This tendency is also found elsewhere. For instance, in the Federal Republic of Germany, taking 1954=100, the education price index was 157.0 in 1965, the cost of living index 118.2 and the GNP price index 128.1 (see Palm, Gunter—*Die Kaufkraft der Bildungsausgaben*, Freiburg, 1966, p. 66). It is accounted for by the rising real incomes of teachers, which together with inflation means a rapid rise in money costs of teachers who are the most important cost item in education.

TABLE 12.1 *Trends in current net public educational expenditure in the United Kingdom: 1920-1955*

Year	Expenditure at current prices (£m.)	Index (1948=100)	Expenditure at 1948 prices (£m.)	Index (1948=100)	Current expenditure as percentage of National Income
1920	65.1	30	100.2	67	1.2
1925	84.1	39	141.3	66	2.1
1930	92.8	43	152.9	71	2.3
1935	92,7	43	158.4	74	2.4
1940	107.5	50	154.9	72	2.0
1945	143.9	67	144.6	67	1.7
1948	215.3	100	215.3	100	2.5
1950	272.0	126	263.0	122	2.7
1955	410.6	191	300.0	141	2.8
1965	1,114.9	518	451.4	210	4.1

Source: Vaizey, J., Sheehan, J., *Resources for Education*, London, 1968, Tables VIII and X.

Notes: Although this chapter refers principally to England and Wales, the above table refers to the United Kingdom for purposes of comparison with National Income data. The trend for England and Wales would be rather similar, as it would refer to the greater part of the total population (86% in 1921, 88% in 1966) and of the population under 24 (86% in 1966). The National Income measurement used is Net National Product at Factor Cost. The educational expenditures relate to all publicly provided educational services (including further and Higher Education) by the Central Government and Local Education Authorities. In accordance with national accounting procedures, transfer items, such as aid to students, and superannuation, are excluded.

TABLE 12.2 *Composition of public education expenditure by sector: England and Wales, 1920-1967 (%)*

	1920	1930	1940	1950	1955	1965	1967
Primary . . .	57.4	56.4	54.8	37.3	38.9	28.1	27.5
Secondary . .	20.0	19.4	19.1	27.4	28.3	32.2	31.7
Teacher training .	0.9	0.8	0.6	2.0	1.7	3.4	3.9
Further and adult .	5.0	4.9	4.9	7.5	7.9	12.2	12.5
Universities . .	5.2	5.9	6.7	8.0	8.2	9.9	10.5
Special schools . .	2.3	2.5	2.7	1.5	1.9	2.0	2.0
Meals . . .	0.4	0.5	1.1	7.2	6.2	5.9	6.0
Health service . .	1.8	2.8	3.4	3.5	2.1	1.8	1.7
Administration and inspection . .	7.1	7.0	6.8	5.7	4.9	4.5	4.4
Total . . .	100.0	100.0	100.0	100.0	100.0	100.0	100.0

Sources: 1920-1965: Vaizey, J., Sheehan, J., *op. cit.*
1967: *Statistics of Education*, London, 1967, Vol. 5, HMSO, 1968.

Note: Percentages may not add to 100.0 due to rounding.

primary level. Table 12.1 shows that similar trends were operative in England and Wales.

Table 12.2 immediately suggests fundamental differences between the pre- and post-war years. These are probably partly a result of the major educational reform contained in the Education Act of 1944, but are partly the result of autonomous long-term trends. In the pre-war years of 1920 and 1930, and in 1940, primary and secondary education between them accounted for about 75% of expenditure. Further and adult education were minor items (about 5.0%), and the welfare items (health, meals, special schools) showed a marked tendency to increase their share as did university expenditure. Real expenditure, as a whole, increased by about 65% in this period (see Table 12.1), and welfare items, which increased from about 4.5% to over 7.0% of the total, more than doubled in absolute terms.

There is a large change in the pattern by 1950. First, it should be remembered that in the 1940-50 period, real expenditure rose by nearly 150%, so that diminished shares in no cases meant reductions in absolute expenditure. Most notably, the combined share of primary and secondary was about 65% in 1950, even though secondary accounted for almost 27.5%. The share of primary education had decreased dramatically from 54.8% in 1940 to 37.3% in 1950. The share of teacher training (still small at 2.0%) had increased, as had that of school meals and further education. Universities also increased their share to 8.0%. The increased share of secondary education was undoubtedly caused by the 1944 reform, partly because of the abolition of elementary schools and the transfer to secondary education at 11+, and partly because of the raising of the school leaving age to 15, which became effective in 1947. The 1955 pattern is rather similar (total real expenditure in 1950-1955 increased by about 50%), except that primary education increased its share against the long-term trend. This could be accounted for by the post-war rise in births, which in 1955 meant high primary enrolments.[1]

Another significant change in the distribution of expenditure (and a 170% increase in the absolute volume of expenditure) had occured by 1965-7. The share of primary education fell yet further to about 28%—half its pre-war level—and was overtaken by that of secondary education (now about 32%). Welfare items showed relative declines (but substantial real gains), and teacher training increased its share to 3.9% in 1967, compared with less than 1% in the pre-war years. The most notable gains were made by further education which accounted for 12.5% of the current expenditure by 1967, as against 7.4% in 1950. The absolute increase (in real terms) was almost 58% in this sector between 1950 and 1965. The increase in university expenditure, though considerable, was not as great in relative or in absolute terms.

The remainder of this chapter deals principally with trends in the two most important sectors reviewed, primary and secondary schools. The current price data are based partly on previous work and have been extended and converted to

---

[1] Enrolment in maintained primary schools was 3,955,472 in 1950, 4,800,862 in 1955 and 4,273,101 in 1965 (*Statistics of Education*, 1966, Vol. I, Table 3).

constant prices using official educational statistics, and *Resources for Education* by J. Vaizey and J. Sheehan.[1]

What was the effect of the increased emphasis on secondary education which occurred after the Second World War on educational inputs? This question is important as a step towards any useful discussion of the productivity of education or of the production function in education. For the moment we shall not be particularly concerned with the output side. Inputs per student enrolled, and unit costs, will be the principal variables examined, as well as the composition of these costs and inputs at various dates. In this way, what is reasonably measurable will serve as a basis for later discussion of the measurability of outputs related to inputs—a much more difficult matter.

The trend of costs within each sector cannot be measured meaningfully in monetary terms, in view of the price trends already noted, and deflation by means of some general price index or a cost-of-living index does not have much meaning either, except in the vague sense of indicating the amount of resources diverted from other uses to education. Such an exercise raises more problems than it answers, especially when price indices are being put to a use for which they were never intended. Consequently, it will not be attempted here. Instead, a breakdown of expenditure is made according to end-use, and expenditure on the various items is deflated by a series of special price indices. This is basically the type of analysis carried out later, but on this occasion in an inter-temporal instead of an inter-country dimension. It is a more disaggregated form of the education-price index used in Table 12.1. Table 12.3 below shows the trend of real expenditure on primary education for the 1955-67 period, at 1955 prices.

TABLE 12.3 *Current expenditure per pupil in maintained primary schools at constant (1955) prices: England and Wales, 1955-1967 (£)*

Year	Administration	Teachers' salaries	Non-teachers' salaries	Teaching materials and classroom supplies	Heating, cleaning, lighting and maintenance	Other	Total
	a	b	c	d	e	f	g
1955	1.29	21.25	0.39	0.99	6.12	0.39	30.44
1960	1.78	22.64	1.84	1.32	7.44	0.51	35.53
1965	2.22	23.24	2.95	1.34	6.38	0.61	36.74
1966	2.24	23.48	3.16	1.70	6.89	0.77	38.24
1967	2.25	23.62	3.20	1.81	7.16	0.82	38.86

Sources: Resources for Education, op. cit., Table XIII. *Statistics of Education,* London, 1966 and 1967, Vols. 1 and 5, HMSO, 1968 and 1969.

This table shows that real current expenditure (i.e. real inputs) per student increased significantly and steadily during the 1955-67 period. However, the increase when measured at 1955 prices—27.7%—was a lot less than the increase in current terms, from £30.44 per pupil in 1955 to £74.71 in 1967, i.e. 145.4%. Apart from the administration item which was difficult to estimate accurately,

---

[1] A more detailed description of the methods used will be found in Vaizey, J., *The Costs of Education,* London, 1958.

some items showed large increases in real terms, notably non-teaching personnel (+720.5%), and teaching materials and classroom supplies (+82,8%), whereas heating, cleaning and maintenance rose by 17.0% and teachers' salaries, which were deflated so as to reflect the inputs of teachers per pupil, rose by only 11.2%, which has important implications. The "other" item rose quite rapidly; not much significance should be attached to this, as it probably reflects the balance of forces between the progressively more important transport item, which is included in column *f*, and minor changes in classification of other items. A comparison of the composition of expenditure, both in money and in real terms, helps to emphasize these tendencies more clearly, and to introduce some further considerations. This is given in Table 12.4:

TABLE 12.4 *Percentage of expenditure per pupil on various items at current and constant prices: primary schools, England and Wales, 1920-1967 and 1955-1967*
(Current prices)

Year	Administration	Teachers' salaries	Non-teachers' salaries	Teaching, materials and classroom supplies	Heating cleaning, lighting and maintenance	Other	Total
	a	*b*	*c*	*d*	*e*	*f*	*g*
1920	5.66	76.24	0.85	3.97	13.01	0.28	100.00
1938	5.85	72.65	0.94	4.01	14.75	1.79	100.00
1950	5.14	67.93	1.40	5.47	19.21	0.54	100.00
1955	4.24	69.81	1.28	3.25	20.10	1.28	100.00
1960	4.92	66.37	5.09	3.36	18.96	1.30	100.00
1965	5.95	67.76	7.89	2.97	14.11	1.34	100.00
1966	5.51	68.04	7.76	3.39	13.76	1.53	100.00
1967	5.59	66.94	7.96	3.60	14.27	1.63	100.00
(Constant (1955) prices)							
1955	4.24	69.81	1.28	3.25	20.10	1.28	100.00
1960	5.01	63.72	5.18	3.72	20.94	1.44	100.00
1965	6.04	63.26	8.03	3.65	17.37	1.66	100.00
1966	5.86	61.40	8.26	4.45	18.02	2.01	100.00
1967	5.79	60.78	8.23	4.66	18.43	2.11	100.00

Sources: As in Table 12.3.
Note: Percentages shown may not add to 100.00 because of rounding.

The constant price series cannot be extended farther back than 1955 because of lack of data. The percentage shown reflect the trends in Table 12.3 i.e. in constant price terms. Columns *b* (teachers' salaries) and *e* (heating et cetera and maintenance) decrease their shares, while the shares of columns *c*, *d* and *f* (non-teachers' salaries, classroom materials, et cetera) increase. These constant-price trends reflect the composition of inputs into primary education when looked at from the educational system itself.

The first part of Table 12.4 reflects the shares of various inputs in current prices. These shares diverge from the constant-price shares because of differential input-price movements. Column *b*, and to a lesser extent columns *a* and *c* (i.e. the administration and salaries columns) show (implicitly) higher price rises than the others; this is chiefly because they are either entirely or very largely personnel items, and during the 1955-67 period at least, personnel items rose in price more than goods and services in general,[1] and also more than most educational materials and supplies.[2] The most significant difference is that, in current prices, the share of teachers' salaries was fairly stable in the 1955-67 period, and even more so in the 1950-67 period. Non-teachers' salaries increased (almost as much as in constant prices), and the heating, cleaning, maintenance item (column *e*) decreased its share—whereas at constant prices its share was stable. However, if we look at the composition of current expenditure in 1920 and 1938 (available only at current prices), we see that there is a long-term trend for the share of teachers' salaries (76.24% in 1920) to fall, or at least that there was a tendency for it to fall during the pre-war and especially the war years. These figures (at least for the post-war period) imply that a constant proportion of current resources spent on primary education went to teachers' salaries. In conjunction with the constant price data and the implied price movements, what was a constant proportion from the aspect of public finance, or of opportunity cost, was a diminishing proportion from the aspect of inputs to the educational process.

There are some implications in this for any discussion of capital and labour intensive techniques in education. If by "labour intensive" is meant "teacher intensive" then column *b* in Table 12.4 is a suitable measurement, i.e. the share of teachers' salaries in total costs or inputs. On this reckoning, "teacher-intensity" remained more or less constant in the post-war years when measured in current prices, or cost terms. But when measured in volume or constant price terms, "teacher-intensity" fell. Furthermore, if one were to use a different type of measurement, say the relationship between teacher inputs and number of pupils (output), "teacher-intensity" could be said to have risen, i.e. the pupil/teacher ratio fell in primary schools from 30.9 in 1955 to 27.8 in 1967.[3] This, however, begs the question of quality measurement—always especially difficult on the output side—and the whole issue of effectiveness. It also shows the difficulties in measuring inputs unambiguously, at least for the purposes of economic analysis.

One conclusion which can be drawn is that elasticity of substitution between teachers and other inputs (or factors) appears to be approximately unity. Despite a price increase of over 100% between 1955 and 1967 in labour inputs, compared with an increase of less than 50% in the price of non-labour inputs, the relative share of teachers in total costs was approximately constant.

Furthermore, the evidence given in *The Costs of Education* (*op. cit.*), based on 1948 prices introduces further complications. For instance, taking 1948 as 100, the price index for teachers in primary and elementary schools stood at 65 in 1920. For all primary and elementary costs it was 67 in 1920—implying a not very significant difference between teacher and other inputs when compared with the 1955-67 trends. Thus it was in this period of approximately stable

---

[1] i.e. real earnings of labour increased.

[2] For evidence of this see *The Costs of Education, op. cit.*, and *Resources for Education, op. cit.*, also Edding, F., and Berstecher, D., *International Developments of Educational Expenditure, 1950-1965*, Paris, UNESCO-IIEP, 1969, Chapter 6.

[3] *Statistics of Education*, 1967, *op. cit.*, Vol. I, Table 3.

relative input prices that teachers' salaries fell—from about 76% in 1920 to about 70% in 1948—as a proportion of current-price inputs. However, the significance attached to this unexpected trend is diminished, if not eliminated, when one considers the major and prolonged depression (when teachers' salaries were cut), the disruptive effects of nearly six years of war, and the major changes in organisation brought about by the Education Act of 1944.

For secondary education, a broadly similar trend of real unit expenditure and of the composition of unit costs is evident. This is despite the widely diverging trends in enrolments and total expenditure. Whereas primary school enrolments fell from 4.3 m. in 1920 to 3.7 m. in 1945, and rose to 4.6 m. in 1955, only to fall again to 4.3 m. in 1965, secondary school enrolments fell from about 1.5 m. to 1 m. between 1920 and 1945, but in the post-war period showed a much greater increase, to over 2.8 m. in the mid-1960s. The main reason for this is that changes in compulsory attendance laws and other social forces influencing the length of education have had their impact chiefly on the maintained secondary schools. Bearing these aggregate trends in mind, the following table (Table 12.5) may be compared with Table 12.3 above.

The overall increase in real expenditure per pupil in secondary schools was 29.2%—compared with 27.7% for primary school pupils. The major item—teachers' salaries—increased less than the overall average, i.e. by 11.7% compared with 11.1% for primary schools. Thus the rate of increase for the major aggregates was fairly similar between the sectors, on a per pupil basis. The slightly greater rate of increase for secondary schools could be explained by the growing proportion of high-cost sixth form pupils, who were 3.2% of (maintained) secon-

TABLE 12.5 *Current expenditure per pupil in maintained secondary schools at constant (1955) prices: England and Wales, 1955-1967 (£)*

Year	Administration	Teachers' salaries	Non-teachers' salaries	Teaching materials and classroom supplies	Heating cleaning, lighting and maintenance	Other	Total
	a	*b*	*c*	*d*	*e*	*f*	
1955	3.13	33.24	0.75	3.41	9.59	2.89	53.01
1960	3.39	32.59	3.13	4.01	9.25	2.22	54.59
1965	3.74	36.06	4.71	5.49	11.29	2.53	63.82
1966	3.96	36.70	5.22	5.78	12.46	2.57	66.69
1967	4.18	37.13	5.34	6.15	13.15	2.64	68.59

Sources: As in Table 12.3.

dary enrolments in 1955, and 6.4% in 1967. The growth of non-teaching personnel expenditure is very high in both cases: 612% for secondary and 720% for primary pupils. Also, teaching materials and classroom supplied showed similar trends: an increase of 78% for secondary and 83% for primary pupils. The heating, cleaning, lighting and maintenance item showed a more rapid growth in the secondary sector (37% compared with 17% for primary): this may have been due to the greater importance of new buildings in the secondary sector. Such buildings often tend to induce extra maintenance expenditure.

When a comparison in made in Table 12.6 below, of the composition of unit expenditure in the secondary sector, some of the conclusions reached above are reinforced.

For secondary education, as for primary, the percentage of expenditure going on teachers' salaries was almost constant during the post-war period, when measured at current prices. Also, it was at a lower level (63% to 64%) than during the pre-war period (73% to 76%). Other trends were similar to those noted already for primary schools, notably the strong increase in the proportion of expenditure going to non-teaching personnel, and the fall in the proportion of heating, cleaning, lighting and maintenance.

Furthermore, the constant price trends were similar to those in primary schools: a fall in the share of real input accounted for by teachers and a rise in that of other personnel, teaching materials and classroom supplies. The heating and maintenance item increased its importance in constant price terms,

TABLE 12.6 *Percentage of expenditure per pupil on various items at current and constant prices: maintained secondary schools, England and Wales, 1920-1967 and 1955-1967*

(Current prices)

Year	Administration	Teachers' salaries	Non-teachers' salaries	Teaching materials and classroom supplies	Heating, cleaning, lighting and maintenance	Other	Total
	a	*b*	*c*	*d*	*e*	*f*	*g*
1920	6.08	75.88	1.40	3.96	12.33	0.34	100.00
1938	5.23	73.14	1.35	4.04	14.44	1.80	100.00
1950	5.46	64.04	1.49	7.60	19.74	1.66	100.00
1955	5.90	62.62	1.41	6.52	18.07	5.44	100.00
1960	5.93	63.74	5.46	6.44	14.87	3.57	100.00
1965	5.52	63.98	6.96	6.69	13.77	3.09	100.00
1966	5.37	64.58	7.08	6.38	13.74	2.84	100.00
1967	5.62	63.54	7.20	6.62	14.17	2.84	100.00

(Constant (1955) prices)

Year	Administration	Teachers' salaries	Non-teachers' salaries	Teaching materials and classroom supplies	Heating, cleaning, lighting and maintenance	Other	Total
1955	5.90	62.62	1.41	6.52	18.07	5.44	100.00
1960	6.21	59.70	5.73	7.35	16.94	4.07	100.00
1965	5.86	56.50	7.38	8.60	17.69	3.96	100.00
1966	5.94	55.03	7.83	8.67	18.68	3.85	100.00
1967	6.09	54.13	7.79	8.97	19.17	3.85	100.00

Sources: As in Table 12.3.

Note: Percentages may not sum to 100.00 due to rounding.

in contrast to its decreasing share in current prices. In primary schools, this item decreased both its current and constant price shares; in this case the relatively favourable price trends were not enough to offset the decreasing share of current expenditure. The overall pattern is, however, one of similarity between the time trends in the composition of unit costs at primary and secondary levels, whether this be measured in current or in constant price terms. The remarks made in the preceding paragraphs about the nature of technical change in education and its relationship to the seemingly unitary elasticity of substitution between inputs in the education process apply equally to secondary as to primary education.

While the evidence from the time series data on the composition of educational expenditure is inconclusive on the question as to whether or not education is becoming more or less labour intensive, nevertheless the trend noted earlier for total secondary education to increase in importance relative to total primary school expenditure, does imply decreasing labour intensiveness in all schools taken as a whole. Thus secondary education rose from 27.4% of all current education expenditure in 1950 to 31.7% in 1967, or by 493% in money terms, whereas primary expenditure rose only by 297%, its share of the total falling from 37.3% to 27.5%. The point is that throughout this period, the percentage of secondary expenditure (at current prices) going on teachers' salaries, which varied between 62.5% and 64.5%, was lower than the corresponding percentage in primary education, which varied between 67% and 70%. Consequently, the increasing weight of secondary education spending in the total implied a tendency for the overall importance of teachers' salaries to decrease somewhat.

If one takes the sum of columns c and d (i.e. teachers' and non-teachers' salaries), as an indicator of labour intensiveness, then there was a clear rise in the 1950-67 period—from 69.33% to 74.90% in the case of primary, and from 65.53% to 70.74% in the case of secondary education. In this case the lower level of the indicator (on average) for the increasingly important secondary sector would have merely tended to offset the increasing "labour-intensiveness" of the separate levels.

Finally, unit costs in primary schools, measured as a proportion of unit costs in secondary schools, varied between 54% and 58% in the post-1950 period. Insofar as secondary education was substituted for primary (notably in the transfer of some former elementary school 11+ pupils to the secondary sector), this was a cost-raising factor, although this is not reflected fully in the tables shown here, as an adjustment was made for the pre-war years, allocating some elementary school pupils over the age of eleven to the secondary sector. The more generous staffing standards, whether measured by achievements or by requirements, which prevail in secondary schools are a reflection of this. This factor seems to be peculiar to the post-war years. Evidence given by J. Vaizey[1] implies that in the 1920-38 period, unit costs were approximately equal in each sector—at least as far as the current public expenditure was concerned. It is, however, difficult to be precise about this because of the changes in educational organisation and finance which occurred after 1944. But whatever judgement is made on this point, the main sources of the increase in current costs are the increasing salaries of teachers at all levels and the increasing enrolments at the secondary level. This, because of price trends, does not necessarily reflect the increase in inputs, at least from the educational point of view. There was a significant increase in non-labour and non-teacher input per pupil in the 1955-57 period, but because of differential price rises the increase in monetary expenditure was reflected predominantly in increasing expenditure on labour items.

[1] *The Costs of Education, op. cit.* See the expenditure and enrolment figures in Tables xiv, xvi, xxxviii, and xxxix.

The analysis that has just been conducted suggests that the causes of changing unit costs need to be examined. Are the changes due primarily to changes in GNP, enrolments or prices? An attempt to answer this is given in the following paragraphs and in Tables 12.7 and 12.8. These tables give rates of change of expenditure per pupil, enrolments, prices and national income for England and Wales from 1920 to 1967. While direct comparisons of expenditures are not possible for the pre- and post-1944 years due to educational reorganisation, it should be possible to compare rates of change, as each period (before and after 1944) provides a consistent series of statistics.

It should be apparent from the beginning that the increase in input prices is the major source of expenditure increase at current prices, at least as far as the post-war (i.e. the 1948-67) period is concerned. For instance, 60% of the increase in monetary expenditure in Table 12.1 on all education (1948-65) was accounted for by increases in prices of inputs.

But the rates of growth of unit expenditure in money terms and in real terms vary widely between various sub-periods. Tables 12.7 and 12.8 show seven such periods, and the variations differ between primary and secondary education, whether for teacher or non-teacher items separately or all expenditure taken together.

A preliminary attempt was made to examine the relationship between enrolment changes, national income changes, price changes and various types of expenditure. This did not involve any formal statistical analysis (at least initially), as inspection of the data provided sufficient basic preliminary information for the purpose, and as only a comparison of the rank order of three sets of seven items was involved.

1. Comparing enrolment changes with current expenditure changes, one would not expect any strong correlation because of the effect of price changes, which affect expenditure in a way which is purely random with respect to enrolment changes. In fact, both for primary and secondary education there does not appear to be any significant association.
2. Comparing rates of change in national income with rates of change in expenditure (both at current prices), one would expect some positive association. This appears to be the case for both secondary and primary education. (As national income rises so may expenditure on education. On the other hand, if national income falls, as in 1920-25, education expenditure may be sticky downwards). However, the correlation must be considered largely spurious, in view of the way broadly similar price changes tend to be built in to both sets of observations. They tend to inflate or deflate both items simultaneously; thus no significance should be attached to this result.
3. For change in expenditure at constant prices (i.e. eliminating the influence of price changes) per pupil and changes in enrolments, one would expect a negative correlation. The hypothesis is that when enrolments increase rapidly, real expenditure per pupil may fall, or at best rise slowly. However, some of the correlation in the teachers' item may be spurious, as the

measure of real teaching input used involved (among other things) the teacher/pupil ratio, and therefore enrolments. When changes in these measurements (i.e. teachers) are ranked against changes in enrolment, there is bound to be some inverse correlation: enrolments are part of the denominator of one series and are the numerator of the other. There does seem to be a significant negative association of changes in real inputs and enrolments. Furthermore, this association is more pronounced for the *teacher* input item in primary (but not in secondary) schools, which is in accordance with the reservation just given.

4. Between changes in real national income and changes in real expenditure, one might expect (at least in the long term) some positive correlation, especially as international comparisons of income and unit expenditure appear to show strong positive association. However, such an association was missing from the data entirely (perhaps the periods chosen for comparison were too short). Furthermore, in the case of primary education, there was a distinct negative association, probably because there was a tendency for enrolments to fall in the pre-war years, which were mostly years of low growth in income.

5. Changes in prices and changes in unit expenditure at current prices show

TABLE 12.7 *Changes in unit costs, enrolments and national income at current and at constant prices: primary schools, England and Wales, 1920-1967*
(all figures annual % growth rates)
(Current prices)

Period	Expenditure per pupil			Enrolment	National Income	Prices
	Teachers	Other	Total			
1920-25	+5.82	+3.91	+5.46	−1.01	−6.52	−6.67
1925-30	−0.16	+1.67	+0.10	+1.98	+0.94	−2.44
1930-35	−0.10	+0.42	+0.00	−2.53	−1.13	−1.75
1950-55	+7.90	+6.03	+7.31	+3.07	+7.65	+5.42
1955-60	+7.88	+11.35	+8.98	−1.83	+6.67	+3.57
1960-65	+6.48	+5.15	+6.04	+0.34	+6.59	+3.07
1965-67	+8.47	+10.52	+9.14	+2.57	+5.35	+3.61

(Constant (1948) prices)

Period	Expenditure per pupil			Enrolment	National Income	Prices
	Teachers	Other	Total			
1920-25	+6.82	+10.54	+7.49	−1.01	+0.16	—
1925-30	−0.22	+1.46	+0.11	+1.98	+3.38	—
1930-35	+1.02	+2.68	+1.37	−2.53	+0.86	—
1950-55	−0.47	+2.20	+0.33	+3.07	+2.65	—
1055-60	+1.88	+7.00	+3.14	−1.83	+2.17	—
1960-65	+0.52	+1.12	+0.67	+0.34	+3.30	—
1965-67	+0.82	+5.77	+2.85	+2.57	+1.79	—

Sources: Vaizey, J., *The Costs of Education, op. cit.*; Vaizey, J., Sheehan, J., *Resources for Education, op. cit.*; *Statistics of Education*, London, 1967, Vols. I and V, HMSO, 1968; *National Income and Expenditure*, London, 1966 and 1969, HMSO, 1966 and 1969.

Notes: National Income is Net National Product at Factor Cost. Price changes are measured by an index of final output prices.

a strong positive association. This is to be expected in view of the trend noted earlier for price increases in the 1948-67 period to account for about 60% of the total increase in monetary educational expenditure. There is not much reason for price changes to affect real expenditure, except insofar as monetary expenditure is "sticky". Partly because of the large salary element, expenditure is sticky in a downward direction, and thus falling prices may lead to large increases in real expenditure. This appears to have been the cause of the exceptionally large increase in real expenditure in the 1920-25 period (despite the increase in secondary enrolments and the low increase in real national income).

TABLE 12.8 *Changes in unit costs, enrolments and national income at current and at constant prices: secondary schools, England and Wales, 1920-1967*
(all figures annual percentage growth rates)
(Current prices)

Period	Expenditure per pupil			Enrolment	National Income	Prices
	Teachers	Other	Total			
1920-25	+4.98	+3.12	+4.63	+1.78	—6.52	—6.67
1925-30	—2.36	+0.70	—2.07	—5.19	+0.94	—2.44
1930-35	+1.11	+3.22	+1.53	+6.36	—1.13	—1.75
1950-55	+7.11	+8.43	+7.59	+2.46	+7.65	+5.42
1955-60	+7.30	+6.28	+6.93	+7.30	+6.67	+3.57
1960-65	+9.00	+8.77	+8.92	+0.70	+6.59	+3.07
1965-67	+9.83	+10.90	+10.22	+0.24	+5.35	+3.61
(Constant (1948) prices)						
1920-25	+9.58	+13.11	+10.27	+1.78	+0.16	—
1925-30	+3.07	+4.76	+3.44	—1.59	+3.38	—
1930-35	—1.26	+1.79	—0.55	+6.36	+0.86	—
1950-55	—0.01	+1.56	+0.49	+2.46	+2.65	—
1955-60	—1.00	+2.09	+0.56	+7.30	+2.17	—
1960-65	+2.04	+4.76	+3.17	+0.70	+3.30	—
1965-67	+1.48	+6.45	+3.67	+0.24	+1.79	—

Sources: As in Table 12.7.
Notes: As in Table 12.7.

The results of this exercise are negative and possibly disappointing. When the changes in unit expenditures are ranked against price movements for the various periods, the association (for current expenditure) is much stronger than any of those examined above. Therefore, we return to the original conclusion that price changes (especially post-war price rises) have been the main growth factor in current costs per pupil in England and Wales. Expenditure per pupil measured in real terms appears to be influenced somewhat by changes in enrolment, and other factors are difficult to isolate. The long-run increase in real income, (despite the lack of correlation for the 5-year periods) and changes in policies and outlook are almost certainly important but almost impossible to measure.

A falling price level may be accompanied by a relatively stable level of monetary expenditure. This occurred in the 1920-35 period, which therefore showed the greatest increase in real expenditure (especially as enrolments *decreased* at the primary level). However, this is a phenomenon which has been absent for over 30 years (on any significant scale), and is likely to remain so. The rise in prices (especially teachers' salaries) which accounted for most of the rise in current-price unit costs in England and Wales is by far the largest single influence on unit costs.

PART FOUR
Costs

How are costs measured and how should they be compared? Many attempts have been made to do both. In this Part a methodology is established which enables comparisons to be properly made.

13 The methodology of projections and forecasts of educational costs: I

PROJECTIONS imply the continuation of some already existing trend; their validity in the context of educational or economic planning is to be doubted as they assumed implicitly that existing trends are not subject to radical alteration, an assumption quite contrary to the very notion of planning. Forecasts depend on certain definite assumptions which may involve a radical break with existing trends. This section is not concerned with the differences between forecasts and projections as such, but merely with the cost calculations which are the result of forecasts or projections, and an essential part of the process of educational planning.

Whether as a result of social demand trends or of manpower forecasts, future enrolment is the basis for most educational expenditure forecasts. Teacher requirements are derived from enrolments, and these, together with the projected or forecast increase in GNP per head (itself probably part of the earlier manpower forecasting procedure), the increase in current expenditure on non-teacher items, and the need for capital expenditures, are used to estimate future total expenditure. Sometimes unit costs are estimated as a result of the forecasts or projections; sometimes they play a more instrumental role in making the forecasts or projections.

The work of the OECD in this field chiefly centres on manpower forecasting. The nature of manpower forecasting, its assumptions, and its shortcomings are noted elsewhere. The financial aspects of educational planning and manpower forecasting are dealt with in the OECD volume *Financing of Education for Economic Growth* (OECD, Paris, 1966), in the MRP and EIP projects and the various reports associated with them, and with the reports on educational planning in Latin America.

An article by the Netherlands Economic Institute uses two equations to estimate enrolment in developing regions by 1975. One derives enrolment *indirectly* from the "required" stocks of manpower of various levels (N^1, N^2, N^3, et cetera) of education needed to produce a certain level of GNP per head, making allowance for replacement needs.[1] The following equation is used, with empirical testing for 23 developing and developed countries:

$$N^i = \alpha_0 Y^{\alpha_1}\left(\frac{Y}{P}\right)^{\alpha_2}$$

[1] Financial aspects of the educational expansion in developing regions, in *Financing of Education for Economic Growth*, pp. 59-72.

where N^i = labour stock educated to the ith level

Y = National Income (1957 U.S. Dollars are used)

P = Population.

When income per head has a positive influence on N^i (α_2 positive) this signifies that a rich country can afford more students at level i. Where the opposite occurs (α_2 negative), the former trend is offset by the increased productivity of manpower stocks. In fact α_2 is negative.

The second equation is similar in form:

$$n^i = \beta_0 Y^{\beta_1} \left(\frac{Y}{P} \right)^{\beta_2}$$

where n^i = enrolment at ith level.

In this (second) case a direct estimate of enrolment was made on the basis of a regression equation with data from 27 countries.[1] The indirect (manpower stocks) and direct estimates vary in their results, the former being much larger for Africa and much smaller for India than the latter. For Latin America and the rest of Asia the divergences are not quite as striking.

Assuming a certain economic growth rate and deriving enrolment requirements by the direct method, the financial implications are examined. Existing current and capital expenditure per student in Africa, Latin America, India and the rest of Asia is used as a basis for standard unit (per pupil) costs for primary, secondary and higher education in 1975. The observed data refer to 1960, and the 1975 unit costs are (approximately) averages of 1960 costs. No allowance is made for the effect of economic growth on unit costs (even though it is noted that unit costs tend to vary with the level of income). This procedure could be partially justified on two grounds: (i) because teachers are comparatively high in the income hierarchy of low-income countries, their position may deteriorate as income rises—however there are also considerations against this view; (ii) if what one wants to measure are real inputs or real expenditure rather than real or financial costs, increasing income per head will not of itself affect the outcome— but the object of the article is to measure financial aspects. The paper proceeds directly from present enrolments and unit costs to future enrolments and unit costs (using practically the same measurement of unit costs for present and future dates). It does not examine teacher requirements, possible teacher shortages, teachers' salaries, et cetera, and their effect on costs.

The Mediterranean Regional Project (MRP) has been the occasion for a large amount of literature on various aspects of educational planning. The general financial aspect of MRP is dealt with in an article by the Secretariat of the OECD Directorate for Scientific Affairs.[2]

For primary education, population trends and the desired pupil/teacher ratio are the main determinants of future current expenditure. For other levels of education, the planned rate of economic growth and the resulting manpower and

[1] *Op. cit.*, pp. 66-71.

[2] *Educational Expenditures in the Countries of the Mediterranean Regional Project*, in "Financing of Education for Economic Growth", OECD, Paris, 1966.

educational requirements determine future expenditure. In general, calculations are made in 1961 prices and the target year is 1975. In each of the six countries (Portugal, Spain, Greece, Turkey, Italy and Yugoslavia) educational expenditures are expected to increase at a higher rate than GNP. In Greece, Portugal, Spain, Italy and Yugoslavia it is expected that education will account for an increasing share of government expenditure.[1] In Turkey, where total government expenditure is itself expected to increase rapidly relative to GNP, education will account for a more or less constant share.

The following general assumptions were made for the forecasts:

1. Teachers' incomes are expected to rise at the same rate as GNP per head.
2. The 1961 ratio of teaching costs to other current costs is expected to remain constant.
3. Capital expenditure is based on cost per pupil place at various levels. Replacement is expressed as a percentage of the 1961 stock of buildings with some extra allowances for unfit buildings, overcrowding and population movements.

There are some variations from these assumptions in different countries; these will be noted when the OECD country reports are analysed later. It may be remarked that during a period of rapid expansion, assumption (1) may not account fully for the increasing demand for teachers, or for improvements in the qualifications of teachers. Assumption (2) may need to be modified if the production function in education changes as GNP per head rises.[2]

The MRP projections, their financial implications and some of the assumptions involved are examined in an article by John Vaizey, which also includes a general discussion of the relation between education, skills, and economic growth.[3] Although the burden of educational expansion in real terms (buildings, teachers, withdrawals from the labour force, et cetera) may be high, the most important limitation may be a fiscal one—in view of the trends already noted in the Directorate for Scientific Affairs paper.

Financial projections will depend on educational and (where a manpower planning approach is adopted) on detailed manpower statistics. The educational statistics, apart altogether from the private sector and on-the-job training, about which very little is known, may contain errors and may be deficient for planning (as opposed to administrative) purposes. Statistics which classify manpower by skill and educational level often simply do not exist. Errors in these statistical areas will lead to errors in graduate, teacher and building requirements. There are three further important problems outlined in Vaizey's paper:[4]

[1] In the absence of any definite long-term plans for total government expenditure this statement should be regarded as provisional. A long term plan might well indicate a rapid rise in total government spending (as in Turkey, and in OECD countries generally) and change the assumed relationships.

[2] i.e. the relation between teacher and non-teacher inputs for a given output, during a period when teacher inputs tend to become dearer relative to non-teacher inputs in accordance with assumption (1) in this paragraph. The production function in education is analysed later.

[3] The financial implications of the Mediterranean Regional Project, in *Financing of Education for Economic Growth*, OECD, Paris, 1966.

[4] *Ibid.*, pp. 389-90.

1. The identification of budgetary outlays—especially in the aided sector.
2. The application of unit cost data to planning. Present unit costs may well be a reflection of an inadequate educational system and thus (apart from all problems concerning the reliability of the data) may be inadequate as a basis for planning.
3. The relative price of educational goods. The trend of teachers' salaries relative to other income, the productivity of the building industry, the price of other (current) educational expenditure, will all influence unit costs. The productivity of school building especially may be improved by intelligent planning.

Financial estimates of educational expenditure may understate the growth of the real burden, as incomes foregone will rise as the National Income in general rises. This item of cost is "a . . . notional psychological, subjective cost, but it has a very real effect in helping to determine people's attitudes to opportunities for education".[1]

An OECD publication on educational planning methods deals with further aspects of the analysis and projection of costs.[2] It is presupposed that for projections of the cost of real resources in monetary terms the following estimates have already been made for each level and type of education:[3]

1. the present and future numbers of pupils and students,
2. the present and future numbers of teachers and professors,
3. the present and future numbers of schools, classrooms, universities, etc.

Financial forecasts are made in the general framework which views educational planning as a process of estimating the number of pupils or students at each level (the basic raw-material inputs), the amount of real resource inputs necessary to transform these into "finished products" and finally the monetary cost of these real resource inputs. The two main (and complementary) phases of the planning process are the analysis of past expenditures and the projection of future expenditures.

The analysis of past expenditures

First, for public expenditures there are problems of definition arising out of "non-educational" (often cultural) expenditures by education ministries or authorities, and likewise educational expenditure by non-education authorities. Secondly there is the problem of what type of expenditure to include, and a budgetary rather than an economic approach is adopted which includes expenditures on goods and services, student aid and maintenance expenditures, and "indirect" expenditures such as administration.[4]

The breakdown of expenditure is primarily in terms of end-use, i.e. teachers' salaries, maintenance, materials, equipment, rent and taxes, administration

[1] *Ibid.*, p. 393.
[2] *Methods and Statistical Needs for Educational Planning*, OECD, Paris, 1967.
[3] *Ibid.*, p. 69.
[4] Thus, by implication, measurements of income foregone are excluded.

et cetera. Detailed teacher-salary information giving variations in earnings by sex, rank, qualification, length of service, level of education, et cetera, is needed. Price indices for the major items of expenditure (but especially for teachers) are needed. If possible, the amount and distribution of expenditures by end-use should be given separately for private, public, urban, rural, large, small, old and new schools at each level of education.

At a given level, educational expenditure may vary with the quantity of educational effort. This is difficult to measure; the number of pupils (or of teachers) is often used as an indicator. It may also vary with the price of the resources used, and projections, while usually made in terms of constant prices, will have to assume a rise in teachers' incomes (or prices) as income per head generally rises. From one point of view therefore, the constant price assumption is not consistent; from another the assumption is really one of the changing *relative* prices of capital and labour which would occur when there is economic growth, irrespective of any change in the general price level. Lastly, qualitative changes will have an effect on the level of expenditure. For teachers, changes in the qualifications of the teaching force or in its age/sex composition are mentioned. (However, one may remark that it is difficult to see in what way age/sex factors affect quality, except perhaps for an element of "learning-by-doing". The effect is primarily a *price* effect). For other items, changes in building and teaching methods and standards, improved maintenance of buildings and equipment, and wider curricula are the principal indicators.

To aid this analysis several technical coefficients, or measures of unit costs, are suggested in *Methods and Statistical Needs for Educational Planning*: salary per teacher (according to age, sex, specialization et cetera), cost per pupil place, non-teaching cost per pupil, cost per unit of various major items of equipment.[1]

Projections of future expenditures

Projections of current expenditure based simply on expected enrolments at various levels are not enough, as expenditure is related to real resource inputs rather than to enrolment. In addition it is necessary to take account of the number of teachers and the rate at which their salaries will rise, making allowance, where possible, for changes in their age or qualification structure. Non-teacher items often cover a large range of goods and services, so the degree of disaggregation used in projections may not be large. All this refers to global projections for a given level or type of education; further analysis will depend on the purpose of the projection: whether the effect of urbanisation or of a planned movement towards larger schools, or of an increased proportion of newer schools et cetera is being investigated. However, in nearly all cases the breakdown of current expenditure by end-use appears to be accepted by the OECD work as fundamental.

Projections of capital expenditure for a given level of education should have cost per pupil place as its basis. This has the advantage of being a measurement

---

[1] This equals total current expenditure, minus teachers' salary and superannuation expenditure.

which can be used under varying conditions. Furthermore, legal cost limits (and therefore some statistics) are often on a per pupil place basis. Regional statistics and projections are desirable as account must be taken, not only of the *net* increase in enrolment, replacement needs, and the elimination of overcrowding, but also of internal migration trends. The method of estimating capital expenditure from the cost of providing new classrooms, laboratories et cetera is deficient because:

1. Classrooms (et cetera) are not homogeneous and may vary considerably in size.
2. Cost per classroom may be a function of the size (or location) of the school in which it is placed.
3. The distribution of class-sizes, as well as the average class-size, must be known. Reliance on average class-sizes comes to the same thing as using the cost per pupil place method.

To which one may add a fourth reason:

4. The use of various new teaching methods may well diminish the importance of the traditional class and classroom.[1]

The financial aspects of educational expenditure projections, for which public and private expenditure must be distinguished, are also dealt with briefly in *Methods and Statistical Needs for Educational Planning*.[2] If the burden on public resources is seen to be greater than desired, various measures may be taken to reduce it:

1. Tapping additional sources of revenue (international aid, fees, loans, other private resources).
2. Manipulation of some input prices, e.g. teachers' salaries.
3. Changes in certain coefficients used for forecasting (student/teacher ratios, capital cost per pupil place, etc.) which change the amount of resources or inputs needed.
4. Changes in enrolment plans, which scale down all outputs and inputs.

In the OECD Mediterranean Regional Project, most of the literature (apart from the papers by the Directorate of Scientific Affairs and by J. Vaizey, mentioned previously) is concerned with aspects of manpower requirements rather than with costs. For instance R. Hollister's review[3] is largely a description and critique of the manpower requirements approach to educational planning, and even the appendix[4] on methods and data used in the MRP refers to projections and forecasts of output and productivity trends, to the resulting forecasts of occupational structures, and to their conversion to educational requirements.

---

[1] See *Children and their Primary Schools* (The Plowden Report), Part I, Chapter 28, HMSO, London, 1967.
[2] *Op. cit.*, pp. 81-2.
[3] Hollister, R., *A Technical Evaluation of the First Stage of the Mediterranean Regional Project*, OECD, Paris, 1967. A further critique of the manpower requirements approach is found above.
[4] Hollister, *op. cit.*, Appendix I, pp. 85-98.

While these matters (especially productivity trends and their effect on future teaching costs, if one assumes that the trend of teachers' salaries will be in some way influenced by the trend of incomes in general, for which estimates of sectoral and aggregate productivity trends are necessary) may be related in various ways to the cost projections there is no discussion of educational unit costs as such in Hollister's review.[1]

In the various country reports of the MRP, expenditure projections are made. The Spanish report for instance, analyses the educational system as it was in 1961-62, and projects its likely development (under existing policies) to 1975; then it derives educational needs for 1975 on the basis of economic growth and manpower-requirements forecasts; then it examines the scope for improving the efficiency of the system through reduced wastage, better use of physical and teaching resources, and various other forms of reorganisation.[2] Finally it makes an expenditure forecast for 1975.

In making this forecast it is noted that statistical deficiencies are especially severe in two vital areas: teachers' salaries and school building costs. Furthermore projections were made of public and private expenditures together, so the implications for public finance are not clear.

Teachers' salaries and the total number of teachers are used to estimate the salary expenditure at each level of education in 1967, 1971, and 1975. The base year is 1963, and salaries are expected to increase by a very large amount (over 50% in real terms) between 1963 and 1967. From 1967 to 1975 salaries are expected to increase at more or less the same rate as income per head. In general it is pointed out that the large increases in salaries in the 1962-67 period is necessary because of the relatively low pay of teachers. Primary teachers' salaries have been increased by 73% "in the last two years".[3] At the secondary and higher levels the very substantial increases expected for some grades of teachers in the 1963-67 period are not expected to be unduly cost increasing as the purpose of the increases is to enable more teachers to teach full-time. (In general, the number of hours worked by teachers is not known so unit cost estimates are very difficult to make).

Having estimated the total salary bill at each level, a series of coefficients was used to relate total teaching costs to total current costs. Thus for primary education, teaching costs are assumed to be 90% of current costs, for vocational training 75%, general secondary education 80%, teacher training 80%, technical secondary 75%, medical and scientific higher 70%, other higher education 80%. These coefficients are (apparently) the result of estimation rather than the extrapolation of any observed trend.

Current expenditure *per pupil* at constant (presumably 1962) prices is given in Table 13.1 below; the estimated *total* expenditure at each level was available for certain post-1967 years only.

---

[1] This will be seen in the following paragraphs where various cost projections are analysed. Especially interesting are the Irish EIP Report (*Investment in Education*, OECD, Dublin and Paris, 1966) and the Portuguese MRP Report.

[2] *The Mediterranean Regional Project: Country Reports, Spain*, OECD, Paris, 1965.

[3] *Mediterranean Regional Project, op. cit.*, p. 139. It is not stated whether this is in real terms or money terms or whether the period referred to is 1961-3, 1962-4 or 1963-5.

Table 13.1 shows large increases in unit costs between 1962 and 1975. These amount to over 300 per cent for primary education, over 100 per cent for general secondary education, and about 180 per cent for higher education. The result of this is to lessen the disparity in unit costs somewhat: whereas in 1962 the ratio between primary, secondary general and university (excluding medicine, science and technology) costs per enrolled pupil was 1: 6.5: 7, in 1975 the ratio is expected to be 1: 3.3: 4.8.

The increase in unit costs is principally a result of the reduction in the pupil/teacher ratio,[1] the increasing real income of teachers and the assumption of a fixed relationship between teaching and non-teaching costs which has the effect of bringing about "an important increase of current expenditure, which will cover both traditional expenses and those incurred by new teaching methods . . . especially . . . audio-visual methods which will be indispensable to make up for the scarcity of teachers".[2] No *precise* judgments could be made on the trend of the pupil/teacher ratio, but the main cost-increasing item at the primary level is the increasing real income of teachers (especially in the 1962-64 period). Unit costs do not increase as quickly in the more rapidly expanding 2nd and 3rd levels because the increases in teachers' incomes are to be accompanied by a transition to more full-time work. As primary teachers are nearly all full-time already, the increase in incomes, while necessary for recruitment purposes, cannot bring corresponding increases in teaching hours. Consequently the increase in unit costs for primary education is much greater than for any other sector.

TABLE 13.1 *Spain: Projected current expenditure per pupil 1962-1975*
(Thousands of Pesetas)

	1962	1964	1967	1971	1975
Primary education . . .	1.0	2.6	2.9	3.5	4.1
Vocational training . . .	5.5	7.0	7.6	9.1	10.8
General secondary education .	6.5	8.7	9.5	11.3	13.5
Technical secondary education .	4.0	10.4	11.4	13.4	16.0
Primary teacher training . .	5.2	7.4	8.1	9.7	11.5
Higher education:					
Science faculties and higher					
technical colleges . .	10.0	17.9	19.6	23.4	27.9
Medicine	10.0	17.9	19.6	23.4	27.9
Other faculties . . .	7.0	12.5	13.7	16.3	19.5

Source: The Mediterranean Regional Project: Country Reports, Spain, OECD, Paris, 1965, p. 141.

Note: Administrative expenditure, accelerated vocational training, and agricultural training are not included.

As data concerning the utilisation of school buildings and the cost per pupil place were almost non-existent, projections of capital expenditure in Spain were

---

[1] This ratio is not known properly for primary schools as the number of teachers teaching in each school is counted. Some teachers teach in more than one school, so there is a danger of double-counting.

[2] *Ibid.,* pp. 139-40.

to be regarded as rough guides only. Present capacity was estimated by the number of pupils enrolled and for secondary and higher levels of education, this was adjusted to "maximum capacity", i.e. allowance was made for present under-utilisation. Unit costs of new buildings were estimated; for primary and secondary general education it was assumed that existing cost data were used. The gap between "maximum capacity" and enrolment needs was used to indicate building requirements. In addition, 20% was added to the capital budget for each year of the 1964-75 period for renovation purposes. Unit costs were assumed to remain constant thoughout the 1964-75 period. As the main needs for primary and secondary general education had to be met before 1968 the bulk of the increase in capital expenditure would be in the early years of the planning period.

The result of these forecasts is given in the projections for total education expenditure which are reproduced in Table 13.2 below:

TABLE 13.2 *Spain: Projected total expenditure on education 1962-1975*
(Constant prices)
(Thousands of Millions of Pesetas)

Year	Current expenditure	Capital expenditure	Total expenditure	% of GNP	Annual rate of increase of total expenditure (%)
1962	12.5	1.5	14.0	1.8	
1967	30.2	4.9	35.1	3.3	20.2
1971	45.1	5.8	50.9	3.9	9.7
1975	61.1	4.8	65.9	4.0	6.7

Source: The Mediterranean Regional Project: Country Reports, Spain, OECD, Paris, 1965, p. 145.

Note: GNP is assumed to grow at the rate laid down in the first economic plan between 1962 and 1967. Thereafter a 6% rate of increase is assumed.

The annual average rates of increase in total expenditure are very high; 20.2 per cent in the 1962-67 period, 9.7 per cent in the 1967-71 period and 6.7 per cent in the 1971-75 period. The 400 per cent increase in the current expenditure component (from 12.5 to 61.1 thousand million Pesetas) is due largely to the increases in unit costs noted in Table 13.2. The trend of capital expenditure is much more uneven, with a projected fall in the 1971-75 period.

The higher rate of increase in the earlier years of the plan is due mainly to the rise in teachers' salaries (both absolutely and relative to other forms of income) foreseen in these years and because of the heavy needs for immediate capital expenditure. However the whole projection, it should be remembered, was made on a very inadequate statistical basis and should be regarded as a mere indication of the trends necessary to realise certain objectives.

By way of contrast with Spain, there is the MRP report for Yugoslavia, a country more accustomed to planning, and in which some statistics are quite good. Also, there is practically no private education.[1]

[1] *The Mediterranean Regional Project: Country Reports, Yugoslavia, OECD, Paris, 1965.*

Current expenditure in Yugoslavia is largely a function of the number of teachers, and these are expected to increase more rapidly than enrolments, at all levels, especially in the years 1965-75. Taking 1962 as the base year, the total expenditure on teachers' salaries is expected to rise by 12.7% per annum between 1962 and 1975 at constant prices. This assumes a 6% rise in teachers' real incomes each year, the balance being due to increased numbers. The 6% rise in real income is the same as that assumed for the whole labour force; in other words (unlike Spain) there was thought to be no need to provide for an improvement of teachers' relative status if educational targets were to be met.

Other current expenditure was expected to rise at 12.7% per annum (at constant prices) between 1962 and 1975 also, i.e. at the same rate as expenditure on teachers. This is in contrast with the 1958-62 period when non-teaching expenditure increased at a lower rate than teaching expenditure. In Table 99 of the report the projected increase in real current non-teaching expenditure per pupil is set out for various levels of education. The increase varies widely for the different levels and types of education; for instance it is nearly 250% for primary education, but only 70% or so for the Gymnasia. The reason for this variance is not explained, but it may lie in the projections of capital expenditure.

No estimates of cost per pupil place are given in the capital expenditure projections. Instead, the existing stock of school buildings is expressed in terms of square metres: 8.5 million m^2 (1963). Total construction in the 1963-75 period is put at 12.7 million m^2; depreciation (at 1.58% of the existing stock of buildings, per year) is 2.0 million m^2. The result is a stock of buildings amounting to 19.2 million m^2 in 1975. From this, estimates are made of (i) school space per pupil in 1962 and 1975 and (ii) total expenditure during the plan period. In moving from area to money measurements, no explicit mention is made of unit costs (though some assumptions must have been made to carry out the exercise). It is notable that in projecting capital needs the Yugoslav report mentions[1] the objective of eliminating the shift system in primary and secondary schools, whereas the Spanish report[2] tentatively proposes a much more *intensive* use of existing school buildings in secondary and higher education.

The result of the Yugoslav projections is that current teaching and non-teaching expenditures grow at the same rate, while capital expenditure grows faster. In 1962 total expenditure was 3.79% of Yugoslavia's GNP, of which teachers' salaries account for 2.14%, other current expenditure 0.64% and capital expenditure 1.01%. The 1975 figures are total expenditure 5.21%, teachers salaries 2.91%, other current expenditure 0.86% and capital expenditure 1.44% of GNP. It may be remarked that the latter estimate for capital expenditure is very high, being nine times the volume of capital expenditure in 1960.[3]

The less intensive use of some school buildings which will result from such a capital programme will no doubt account for part of the large rise in non-teaching costs in primary education. Although the structural and institutional framework

[1] OECD, *op. cit.*, p. 115.

[2] *Op. cit.*, p. 142.

[3] Also, at 1.44% it is a high percentage of GNP. The corresponding figure for Great Britain was about 0.9% in 1965, at a time when capital expenditure had been expanded rapidly.

of Yugoslavian education differs widely from that of Spain, the methods of forecasting are essentially similar, and so are the difficulties: lack of adequate statistics of teachers' salaries by age and qualification, and lack of information on building costs.

Projections have been made of Irish educational expenditure for the OECD EIP project.[1] Here only total educational expenditure and primary (National) school expenditure will be considered. Other sectors are often privately financed to a considerable extent and projections involve judgments about future policy which are not of much general interest.[2] In general it was assumed that policy would have little relative effect on overall primary enrolment (about 95% of which is in the National Schools, i.e. schools almost entirely financed by the State). The increase in enrolment between 1962 and 1971 was expected to be 2%, and the net increase in the number of teachers 8%.[3] Also taken into account was the increasing proportion of qualified teachers (a cost-increasing factor) which was however expected to be partly offset by the increase in the proportion of relatively low-paid young teachers. The introduction of certain new State grants for school maintenance was also allowed for. For projection purposes the various educational items were combined with economic growth and productivity trends given in the Irish *Second Programme for Economic Expansion*.[4] Two main conclusions were drawn:

1. Average salary per teacher was expected to rise by 3.5% per annum in real terms. This was the same as the then projected overall rate of productivity *per capita* growth in the economy for the 1961-70 period. Teachers' relative incomes were not expected to change, as any scarcity was due simply to lack of training facilities. Together with the rise in teacher numbers this gave a total increase in salary expenditure of 47% in the 1962-70 period. Superannuation expenditure was expected to increase by 30% in the same period.[5]

2. Current non-teaching expenditure (i.e. on goods and services) financed by households and school localities was not expected to increase in real terms. Public expenditure (on heating, cleaning, repairs, transport, books, et cetera) was expected to increase however, taking into account the effect of the then (1964) educational policies. The method of projection was as follows: first, the trend of current expenditures was ascertained in real resource terms (i.e. at base-year prices). Secondly a price rise of 1.2% per annum was added. This was in line with the Second Programme for Economic Expansion's projected increase of productivity in the service sector of

[1] *Investment in Education in Ireland*, OECD, Dublin and Paris, 1966, especially Part I, Chapter 5, and Part II, Appendix 5.

[2] In fact, subsequent changes in policy regarding the financing of secondary education have made the actual projections obsolete, though not the analyses and other considerations which lie behind them.

[3] In this section the National schools only are included in Irish primary education.

[4] Dublin, Stationery Office, 1964.

[5] As there is a non-contributory superannuation scheme, all superannuation expenditure is included. This is in line with the concepts laid down by, Edding, Friedrich, *Methods of Analysing Educational Outlay*, UNESCO, Paris, 1966 (see p. 17).

2.3% per annum and an increase in real incomes of 3.5% per annum.[1] Therefore a price increase of 1.2% per annum was necessarily implied.[2]

Thus the Irish expenditure projections were explicitly and directly connected with an overall economic plan (ignoring all manpower aspects for the moment). This led to an important methodological difference from the MRP projections. The difference lay in what was meant by "constant prices". The Irish report explained its use of the term as follows: "It may be objected that since . . . projections . . . assume rises in teachers' salaries and other items, then they cannot be in constant prices. The difficulty arises because of the ambiguity as to whether the term 'constant' applies to the price level in general or to each price taken separately. It is in the former sense that the term is intended here. It is assumed that the general price level remains constant, but that within this general constancy there are relative price changes. The specific assumption is that prices of educational items (teachers et cetera) are expected to show a relative rise leaving other items (such as manufactured products) to show a relative fall."[3] It may be remarked that this type of "constant price" projection was possible only in the context of an overall economic plan or programme which projected sectoral and total productivity trends, as well as making some specific assumption about income trends—in this case the assumption that real income was to rise everywhere in line with aggregate productivity and that relative price movements were to effect the necessary intersectoral redistribution of income. The MRP type of projection involves a forecast of overall economic growth, from which the growth of teachers' salaries (in real terms) is derived. But it does not involve any explicit assumption about physical productivity in the services sector.[4] There is merely the implicit assumption that the price of teachers diverges from the constant base year prices of other educational inputs at the same rate as the growth of income *per capita*, in other words that these educational goods and services do not change in price relative to *all* goods and services. Thus, the Irish report assumed:

1. that the price of teachers would rise at 3.5% per annum relative to the price of all goods and services.
2. that the price of non-teacher current educational expenditure items would rise at 1.2% relative to all goods and services.

whereas the MRP-type projections make assumptions similar to (*a*) but would make a zero price-rise assumption as far as (*b*) is concerned. Another difference

---

[1] The Second Programme for Economic Expansion was subsequently suspended, as some of the assumptions on which it was based (e.g. EEC membership for Ireland before 1970) were not realised. This does not affect the point at issue in this section; any future economic plan would have essentially similar implications.

[2] On the assumption that non-teacher current inputs into education come from the services sector. Do books, teaching aids et cetera fit into this category?

[3] *Investment in Education*, Part II, OECD, Dublin and Paris, 1966, pp. 250-51.

[4] Except the Portuguese MRP report where this question is considered. See Chapter V of *The Mediterranean Regional Project: Country Reports, Portugal*, OECD, Paris, 1966, pp. 173-76, where the relation of teachers' salaries to GNP per head is analysed in the light of sectoral and aggregate productivity forecasts given in Table 3, p. 43 of the same report.

is that the MRP forecasts cover a longer period—generally up to 1975 or 1976, whereas most of the forecasts in the Irish report were for 1970-71.

The main conclusions[1] of the Irish report were:

1. That public educational expenditure would rise from 75.9% to 79.9% of total educational expenditure, and from 3.8% to 4.6% of National Income between 1962 and 1971.
2. That total current costs per primary pupil would rise from £24.6 to £35.3 (at "constant" prices) due to the (relative) rise in input prices and the increasing quantity of non-teacher inputs per pupil.
3. That primary schools would account for a smaller proportion of total current educational expenditure in 1970-71 (41.8%) compared to 1961-62 (47.9%).

These trends were generally in line with the MRP forecasts despite the differences in methodology mentioned above and despite the fact that (unlike the MRP) they were simply projections, based on the continuance of (then) existing policy.

For capital unit costs (i.e. costs per pupil place) it was assumed that prices would remain constant, in the absence of any other information. In addition the report included a cost-effectiveness study of National Schools. Very small schools (with one or two teachers) have high unit costs—capital and current—and are no more effective than larger schools. A movement towards larger schools would lessen the need for extremely low pupil/teacher ratios in some schools and would consequently leave room for reducing the extremely large classes found in some of the larger urban schools, without increasing current unit costs.

The EIP report on education in the Netherlands bases most of its projections on social demand rather than on manpower factors.[2] In Chapter VIII of the report targets are given for enrolment, teaching staff and classroom construction. The target years are 1970 and 1975 and the base year is 1965. There is only a very brief discussion of the method used to project current expenditure.[3] It is assumed that average teachers' salaries will rise at 3.5% annually, in real terms, which is the same rise as forecast for real incomes generally. This is basically similar to the assumptions in most MRP countries and to the Irish report. In other words the unit cost projections are linked to the overall projected rate of economic growth. If teachers are to maintain their position in the income hierarchy, then real and money income per teacher (and therefore cost per teacher) must rise at approximately the same rate as overall income per head. For non-teacher current expenditure per pupil the rate of increase which took place during the 1950s was assumed to continue during the 1965-75 period. This increase was 5 per cent per annum in real terms.[4] This would entail a greater increase in non-teaching expenditure, i.e. an increase in the proportion of non-teaching expenditure in total current expenditure, were it not for the fact that the expected decrease in the

[1] *Op. cit.*, pp. 102-4.
[2] *Educational Policy and Planning in the Netherlands*, OECD, Paris, 1967.
[3] *Ibid.*, pp. 116-20.
[4] In this context "real terms" means constant base year (1965) prices—as in the MRP projections—and not the special "constant price" projections noted above for the Irish EIP projection.

pupil/teacher ratio (from 35:1 to 28:1 in primary schools, and from 29:1 to 23:1 in secondary modern schools, between 1960 and 1975) is expected to offset this trend, with the result that the proportion of non-teaching expenditure in total current expenditure is expected to fall.

The forecasts of costs and expenditure analysed above were all for developed countries. In all cases they were linked with forecasts of economic growth, not only because of manpower factors but because of the effect on costs of rising teachers incomes. As education is so labour intensive, and as teachers account for nearly all of the labour employed in education (accounting for as much as 85% of total current expenditure), teachers' salaries have a marked impact on the level of costs. It was assumed in nearly all of these forecasts (Spain being the exception) that teachers would maintain their position in the general hierarchy of incomes, implying that teacher shortages were (or at least were regarded by the planners as) largely a result of lack of training facilities or other elements on the supply side. This is also evident from the Robbins report and from other forecasts of teacher requirements and supplies in the United Kingdom. For the developing countries the problem can be more complex, as the next chapter shows.

14 The methodology of projections and forecasts of educational costs: II

MANY UNESCO and IIEP publications deal with educational costs and planning in the developing countries. Some of them have a more general application, for instance Friedrich Edding's UNESCO publication,[1] which first discusses the choice of unit and the various possible breakdowns of expenditure and then proceeds to deal with methods of forecasting current and capital expenditure, giving some examples of how this is done.[2]

First, it is observed that expenditure on teachers' salaries is the major component of current costs. Secondly, teachers' salaries are a fairly constant percentage of current expenditure in current *money* terms.[3] This leads to a projection of teachers' salary expenditure as a basis for forecasting. Thus, the number of teachers and the salaries they receive must be ascertained. For the number of teachers the following formula is used:

$$\frac{n_{st}.n_{hst}}{st/c.n_{ht}} = n_t$$

where n_{st} = number of students
$\quad n_{hst}$ = number of hours per week spent by students in class
$\quad st/c$ = number of students per class
$\quad n_{ht}$ = number of hours per week spent by teachers in class
and, $\quad n_t$ = number of teachers.

The formula is one of aggregate student-hours divided by aggregate teaching-hours. Next comes the problem of estimating average teachers' salaries in the projection year. Edding shows how teachers' incomes have in the past risen with output per head in general: in the Federal Republic of Germany, for instance, Gross Domestic Product per person employed rose by 8.9% per annum, while teachers' salaries rose by 8.7% per annum, in money terms. In real terms between 1950 and 1962 the growth rates given are 5.4% and 6.5% respectively.[4] Thus teachers' incomes may be presumed to rise in accordance with general productivity trends, according to Edding, if they are to maintain a competitive position in the labour market. Having obtained a projection of future expenditure on

[1] *Methods of Analysing Educational Outlay*, UNESCO, Paris, 1966.
[2] *Ibid.*, Chapter 5.
[3] Examples are given for the Federal Republic of Germany—Edding, *op. cit.*, pp. 36-7. The implications for real *expenditure* and real *costs* may be different.
[4] Edding, *op. cit.*, p. 37. This means that different deflators were used for teachers' and for aggregate incomes. This apparent discrepancy is not explained.

G

teachers, total current cost may be calculated: "Assuming that the proportions (between teachers' salaries and other current expenditure) found in the base year remain constant, 20% to 40% may have to be added to the total amount of teachers' salaries in respect of other current outlay in order to get a forecast of *total* current outlay. Dividing this amount by the level of enrolment forecast (or average daily attendance, or whatever the concept might be) we obtain the unit outlay for a projected year".[1]

This is a rather rudimentary method of projection, although it is a widely accepted one, being basically similar to much of the costing methodology in the OECD projects discussed in the previous chapter. Edding discusses how a more detailed analysis of past expenditures may give greater insight into the likely future course of events. Thus (using the consumer price index to change monetary into real expenditure) the increase in total expenditure can be attributed to (*a*) increased enrolment; (*b*) general price increases and (*c*) increases in teachers' real incomes and in other real expenditure. Further, expenditure can be broken down into teachers' salaries, operation of plant, maintenance of plant, books and other instructional materials, and other types of expenditure; next the price trends for each of these items can be calculated, and finally the increase in real inputs can be derived from this. Edding found that in the Federal Republic of Germany between 1950 and 1962 prices of teachers rose by 137%, of books et cetera by 66%, of operation of plant by 50%, of maintenance of plant by 83% et cetera, the aggregate price increase being 124%. This trend is similar to that found by J. Vaizey for education in the United Kingdom,[2] and in general a rise in the *relative* price of teachers (irrespective of any increases in the general price level) is to be expected as long as there is a sustained rise in income per head. This analysis of past expenditure in order to derive real input trends is also used elsewhere in this book.

On the methodology of analysing price trends of personnel inputs, Edding says that difficulties will arise primarily because of the effect of length of service on quality. Teachers' salaries usually vary with the level of qualifications and the length of service attained. While it is usually taken for granted that the level of qualifications is an indicator of quality, the same cannot be said for length of service. Learning by doing may be offset by obsolete training, and if this is the case any rise in teachers' salaries due to an increase in the age of the teaching force cannot be regarded as an increase in teacher inputs—any more than general price and salary-scale rises. In fact the age-structure of the teaching force does not usually change rapidly, so the practical problem is not very great.[3] In general then, the rise in average teachers' salaries between two dates is partly a reflection of general price rises, and partly a rise in average real incomes. Assuming no change in the *structure* of the incremental salary scale the divergence of salary rates from average earnings over the period will reflect the difference in experience (i.e. age-structure) of the teaching force. Thus the increase in real earnings

---

[1] Edding, *op. cit.*, p. 40.

[2] In *The Costs of Education*, London, 1958.

[3] Another problem, not mentioned by Edding, is the introduction of extra allowances (such as are found in British secondary schools) for certain responsibilities.

can be further broken down.[1] For pricing non-personnel inputs the general formula (for input i) is given by Edding as:

$$P_i = \frac{\Sigma p_n q_n}{\Sigma p_0 q_n}$$

where subscript 0 denotes the base year and n the terminal or given year. Thus terminal-year price weights are used. Naturally, as much information as possible (covering very many sub-indices) should be used in the calculation, but published price indices may sometimes be the only ones available.

For forecasting capital expenditure, Edding starts with a review of past expenditure, analysed on a per pupil place basis, and broken down by size and type of school and by type of expenditure (site works and building, equipment, design costs, et cetera). This is important as the composition as well as the size of a school building programme may affect costs. For forecasting, changes in the following should be considered:[2]

1. the general level of prices and incomes.
2. productivity in the building and equipment industries.
3. pedagogic theory and practice.
4. the general standard of comfort.

If by (1) is meant general changes in the price level, then it may be remarked that it would be more consistent with the methods used in projecting current expenditure if constant prices generally were assumed, making only specific corrections for productivity trends in the building industry, and for whatever policy decisions corresponding to (3) and (4) which are assumed.

Many of the UNESCO-IIEP African research monographs deal with the financial and cost aspects of educational planning. The most notable example is Tanzania, where educational and economic planning are more integrated and where more data is available than in many other African countries.[3] It is planned that secondary, technical, higher education, and teacher training will be developed in accordance with manpower needs. On the other hand, the development of primary education will be determined largely by financial limitations—in practice this means that the present (1964) enrolment ratio of about 50 % in lower primary education age-group will not be increased significantly.

J. B. Knight has analysed educational expenditure in Tanzania and has made projections of future expenditure.[4] The projections are largely derived from the Tanzanian 5 year development plan (1964-69). In making these projections some factors arise which are especially important when dealing with developing countries:

1. There is a significant foreign contribution to educational expenditure, especially to expatriate post-primary teachers' salaries.

---

[1] Or rather added to, if the teaching force is getting younger
[2] Edding, *op. cit.*, p. 50.
[3] See Skorov, George, *Integration of Educational and Economic Planning in Tanzania*, UNESCO-IIEP, Paris, 1966.
[4] *The Costing and Financing of Educational Development in Tanzania*, UNESCO-IIEP, Paris, 1966.

2. Teachers are relatively (to other occupations) very highly paid. This is partly connected with the use of expatriates from richer countries and partly with imitated or inherited foreign salary structures.
3. There are large salary differentials between different grades of teachers, especially at the primary and lower secondary levels.
4. There are large differences in unit costs between different levels and types of education (and between lower and upper primary education)—see Table 14.1 below.
5. Boarding costs are a significant part of total costs at all levels (except lower primary)—especially in Tanzania where the population density is low and where over 95 % of the population is in rural areas.

Factors (1) and (2) are connected; (2) is cost increasing in the sense that it means high input prices, but its impact is lessened by (1). Factors (2) and (4) are also connected, especially at the primary level where the use of grade A teachers affects costs;[1] as a result, the financial implications of policy decisions concerning staffing requirements or the relative size of different levels of education are more important than in developed countries: for instance while an extra lower secondary pupil in England and Wales would cost the same as 2 primary pupils, in Tanzania the cost would be nearly equivalent to 7 primary pupils (excluding all boarding costs). Factor (5) is cost increasing in the sense that the quantity of inputs per pupil is increased; while boarding costs may be looked on as merely transferring a private cost into an explicit public expenditure, the extremely low level of income in Tanzania when compared with boarding costs per pupil suggests that extra inputs are, in fact, used—for example children in boarding schools are better fed.[2]

In projecting educational expenditures for the plan period (1964-69), unit costs were estimated taking account of the following:

1. "Incremental creep", due to the ageing of the teaching force, which was estimated at about 2 % per annum for post-primary education.
2. The planned replacement of certain lower grades of teachers, and the trend in the pupil/teacher ratio.[3]
3. Real salaries were not to increase (even though the Plan forecasts an overall rise of 2.6 % per annum in Consumption per head).
4. Additional primary classes were to be in day schools, and additional secondary classes in boarding schools.
5. Only Primary Standards 1 and 2 were to be organised on a half-day attendance basis.

No comprehensive estimates of projected unit costs were given, but as the pupil/teacher ratio and certain other aspects of policy were cost reducing, and as real incomes of teachers were presumed not to rise, the following table (14.1) of unit costs in 1963 is not unrepresentative of unit costs during the plan period.

---

[1] Teachers with 12 years' Primary and Secondary Education plus 2 years' training.

[2] See Knight, *op. cit.*, p. 42.

[3] As there are no untrained teachers in the public primary schools of Tanzania the problem and cost of upgrading the teaching force is not as great as in some other African countries.

TABLE 14.1 *Tanzania: Current cost per pupil of different educational levels, 1963*

	Primary standards				Secondary forms	
	I-II	III-IV	V-VI	VII-VIII	1-4	5-6
Length of course (years) .	2	2	2	2	4	2
Total enrolment .	. 262,400	224,700	69,500	35,100	16,420	760
COST PER PUPIL (£)						
Salary:	2.8	6.3	7.3	14.8	50.3	130.3
of which overseas .	—	—	—	—	6.8	16.7
of which local . .	2.8	6.3	7.3	14.8	43.5	113.6
Equipment . . .	0.5	0.5	1.3	2.0	5.0	15.0
Other	0.4	0.4	0.7	1.4	6.6	8.0
Total excluding boarding	3.7	7.2	9.3	18.2	61.9	153.3
Boarding . . .	—	—	15.4	15.4	24.0	24.0
TOTAL . . .	3.7	7.2	24.7	33.6	85.9	177.3
TOTAL LOCAL COSTS	3.7	7.2	24.7	33.6	79.1	160.6

Source: Knight, J. B., *The Costing and Financing of Educational Development in Tanzania*, UNESCO-IIEP, Paris, 1966, p. 71.

Note: Costs for Primary standards I and II are for half-day attendance only. In 1963 the Tanzanian £ was equal to the £ Sterling.

The above Table (14.1) shows that between different levels of primary and secondary there are very wide variations in unit costs. While total current costs per pupil (excluding boarding costs) ranged from £3.7 to £18.2 in primary schools (costs varying directly with age and standard), the range in secondary schools was from £61.9 to £153.3 per enrolled pupil. Depending on the basis of comparison the ratio of current unit costs between secondary and primary forms can be as high as 40:1. This is much higher than the corresponding ratio in the more developed countries; for instance the ratio in Spain (see Table 13.1 in the previous chapter) was about 7:1 in 1962 and was expected to decline rapidly in the following decade. The above table shows that local costs were 100% of total costs in primary education; for lower and upper secondary education, local costs amounted to 92.1% and 90.6% of the total respectively, the balance coming from external aid.

If new primary classes are to be for day pupils and new secondary classes for boarding pupils, then the unit cost differences between primary and secondary education will be all the greater. The overseas cost component is higher for technical education than for both levels of secondary education shown in the above table; in the technical schools teaching cost per pupil is £100.2, of which £41 is financed from overseas; in the Technical College £64.8 of a total unit teaching cost of £119.5 is financed from overseas. As the University College at Dar-es-Salaam was opened only in 1961, it was not possible to be very definite about unit costs; for instance with the build-up of numbers actual current cost per student fell from £1,262 in 1964-65 to £623 in 1966-67.

The Tanzanian forecasts assume a lowering of unit costs in some sectors of education because of the substitution of day for boarding schools—at least as far as marginal pupils are concerned. This will apply mainly to upper primary education where enrolment increases are expected. Also increases in the pupil/ teacher ratio, especially in higher education, are expected to lower unit costs. In addition, the assumption that teachers' salaries remain constant in real terms (except for movements on the incremental scale) implies a lack of upward pressure on unit costs which is assumed in projections for other countries. Whether this is a realistic or feasible assumption in the light of a general *per capita* increase in consumption during the same period is, however, questionable.

Forecasting current educational expenditure in Uganda[1] also involves the use of present (i.e. 1964) unit costs at different levels of education, together with future enrolment plans.[2] As the resulting expenditure forecast (in 1964 prices) is about 16% greater than the allocation planned for education in the overall econo- mic development plan, the Ugandan educational planners are seeking ways to cut unit costs (rather than enrolments). Obvious areas for cost-cutting are uni- versity education and grade III teacher-training, where present unit costs are high due to small enrolments.

In the African studies, a lesser rise in unit costs is assumed than in those studies and forecasts which concern the developed countries. While this implies a diminution in teachers' relative income it should be remembered that teachers are relatively very highly paid in Africa and that the development of African education should reduce the great scarcity of teachers somewhat, and lead to a replacement of expatriate teachers, who have to be highly paid. On the other hand, there is the necessity of upgrading the primary teaching force in many countries and the fact that there are very few replaceable expatriates in the primary education sector at present. Also, in the Tanzanian case, a separate allowance was made for "foreign" costs, and the assumption was made that purely African salary levels would not increase in real terms, which might be more realistic if a surplus of university graduates were expected.

P. H. Coombs summarizes the rising trend of educational enrolments and expenditures in many countries and comments on the high levels of expenditure necessary (especially in developing countries) to achieve declared targets.[3] By 1970 it is estimated that many African countries will be spending nearly 7% of GNP on education, while the Latin American and Asian groups will spend 5.4% and 4.3% respectively. Even then, enrolment at the primary level will be only 71% of the total relevant age-groups in Africa and 74% in Asia. In Latin America it should be 100%. Furthermore, these projections assumed a 5% economic growth rate for Latin America and 4.39% growth rate for Africa. In fact, the rate of growth seems to be falling short of this target, so the problem has become greater.

As projections of educational expenditure are usually part of an educational or

[1] Chesswas, J. D., *Educational Planning and Development in Uganda*, Chapter 7, UNESCO- IIEP, Paris, 1966.

[2] Unit costs are in many respects similar to Tanzania, with a very large gap between primary, secondary, and higher education. However, the estimates are not as detailed or as reliable as those quoted for Tanzania.

[3] *The World Educational Crisis—A Systems Analysis*, UNESCO-IIEP, Paris, 1967. Especially Part II.

economic plan of the government, most of the expenditure projections are the work of governmental or intergovernmental agencies. In the United Kingdom, however, the National Institute for Economic and Social Research has published a forecast of the size and structure of the British Economy in 1975.[1] While subsequent economic events have made the forecast an almost impossible one, still the target date could be set at, say, 1980, and the forecast would once again be fairly realistic. At any rate the growth of educational expenditure tends to develop its own momentum, and the estimates of expenditure in this book by J. Vaizey and R. Knight are of interest despite subsequent policy changes, some of which affect expenditure more in the intervening years—for example the postponement of raising the minimum school leaving age from 1970-71 to 1972-73.

In general the Vaizey and Knight forecasts involve much greater expenditure than official British estimates, mainly because they assume not only the continuance of present and declared policies, but also because they assume that all major existing deficiencies in the educational system are to be eliminated by 1975. The expenditure forecasts involve firstly, estimates of enrolment, of teacher requirements and of school buildings, at each level of education.

Increases in enrolment at each level and type of education (including nursery schools) are deduced from population trends, voluntary changes in enrolment (nursery schools and staying-on after the school leaving age), statutory enrolment changes (raising the minimum school leaving age and introducing part-time education instead of full-time for 5-year-olds). For further and higher education —including teacher training—the effects of the Industrial Training Act and of the increased demand for teachers are allowed for.

The increase in teacher numbers between 1960 and 1975 also takes account of the above factors, with additional provision for lowering the size of all classes to a maximum of 30 pupils. This latter factor accounts for over 1/3 of the total increase in teacher numbers. The total increase in the teaching force will be 73% in nursery, primary and secondary schools; for the 3–4-year-old age group it will be 97%, for the 5-year-olds 23%, for the 6–10$^2/_3$-year-olds 90%, for the 10$^2/_3$–14-year-olds 35% and for the over 15s 240%. The number of teachers in all further education will increase by over 100%, and in higher education by over 200%.

The forecasts of the costs involved in implementing this expansion are based on measures of unit costs. The unit in this case is cost per teacher, and not cost per pupil, as in many other forecasts. The method of forecasting was as follows. The basic assumptions were constant prices of goods and services, and a growth rate of 3.1% per annum in teachers' incomes. This growth rate was derived from the growth projections made for the British economy in the earlier part of the book.[2] Of total costs per teacher in primary and secondary schools, about 2/3 is accounted for by personnel, and 1/3 is spent on goods and services. As it was assumed that the former component (per teacher) would rise by 3.1% per annum, and as the latter component (again on a per teacher basis) would remain constant in volume (and therefore in value), the aggregate increase in costs per teacher would be the weighted average of the personnel and non-personnel items, i.e. about 2%

[1] Beckerman, W. and associates, *The British Economy in 1975*, Cambridge, 1965.
[2] Beckerman and associates, *op. cit.*, Chapter 3.

per annum. A similar type of forecast was made of costs in higher and further education. As personnel (which is the cost-increasing item) has a lower weighting in the inputs to these sectors, the increase in costs per teacher is lower, i.e. 1.5% per annum. The results of these forecasts are summarized in Table 14.2.

The increase in total current expenditure on education is almost 100% in 15 years, i.e. from £799m. in 1960 to £1,593m. in 1975. In some sectors—higher and further education, and teacher training—the rate of increase is even higher, and there is also a high increase (over 200%) in the volume of maintenance grants, which tend to be associated with these sectors. Teacher training is the fastest-growing sector, with an increase of over 300% in real expenditure.

TABLE 14.2 *Current public expenditure on education in the United Kingdom 1960-1975* (£ m.)
(at 1960 prices)

						1960	1975
Schools	.	.	.	.	.	509	920
Further education		.	.	.	.	68	166
Universities*	.	.	.	.	.	63	177
Teacher training.		.	.	.	.	8	34
Miscellaneous	.	.	.	.	.	56	90
Imputed rents	.	.	.	.	.	66	114
Maintenance grants	.	.	.	.	.	29	92
TOTAL	.	.	.	.	.	799	1,593

* Including the Colleges of Advanced Technology which are now Universities.

Source: Beckerman, *op. cit.,* p. 484.

Notes: Miscellaneous expenditure includes administration, health, recreation, inspection etc. Private expenditure is excluded; it was less than 10% of the total in 1960 and is expected to decrease as a proportion.

The projections of enrolment and of teacher numbers, on which the expenditure figures are based, seem to be on the high side, especially as the raising of the school leaving age did not occur in 1966 as assumed, and therefore the trend towards increased "staying-on" will hardly be as marked. Furthermore, it is hardly likely that class-sizes will be reduced as much as indicated. In any event economic difficulties look like interfering with education expansion in the medium term. However, the expenditure forecasts may not be correspondingly optimistic. The rate of increase of 2% in expenditure per teacher at each level of school education assumes that all of the increase in real expenditure will be absorbed by the 3.1% increase in teachers' salaries, leaving non-teacher current expenditure per teacher constant. Due to the fall in the pupil/teacher ratio, non-teacher expenditure *per pupil* would rise in real terms, but not by as much, certainly not by as much as in the past.[1] The combination of optimistic enrolment and teacher forecasts with a conservative expenditure-forecasting procedure may well produce a result which will be close to the actual course of events. Of course

[1] See Vaizey, J. and Sheehan, J., *Resources for Education,* London, 1968, for an account of the rapid rise in real non-teacher expenditure in the United Kingdom before 1965.

all the above forecasts were in constant 1960 prices and any checking would have to apply a method of deflation corresponding to the constant cost concepts used in the forecasts themselves.

Because teachers account for such a high proportion of educational expenditure, obviously forecasts of the number of teachers (as well as forecasts of pupil numbers) are an important part of any cost projection. The rapid rise which is forecast in the enrolments of many countries implies a rapid rise in teachers' numbers, especially if it is desired to improve on present staffing practices at the same time. This increase in the size of the teaching force has repercussions on other sectors of education; it makes increased demands on the teacher-training colleges and the universities, and the output of the secondary school system must in turn be large enough to provide the increased intake demanded by the higher level institutions. Perhaps the most comprehensive analysis of this problem is found in the ninth report of the National Advisory Council on the Training and Supply of Teachers.[1] This report first considers the demand for teachers for a 20 year period (to 1985-86) taking into account population changes, changes in the minimum school leaving age, likely increases in enrolment beyond the school leaving age, and staffing standards. Staffing requirements are not set simply by the pupil/teacher ratio *per se*, but rather by the pupil/teacher ratio implied by the requirement to eliminate classes over a certain size. This required a detailed analysis of the deployment of teachers and pupils in the schools, the result being that pupil/teacher ratios of 26.3:1 and 19.7:1 were required to eliminate junior classes of over 40 and 30 pupils respectively.[2] To eliminate senior classes of over 30 pupils, a ratio of 15.7:1 was necessary. On these assumptions the demand for teachers increases rapidly, from 358,000 in 1968 to between 508,000 and 581,000 in 1986.[3]

In order to increase the supply of teachers, the report modified the Robbins report proposals for an increase in the intake of the colleges of education from 25,000 per year in 1966 to 40,000 in 1974. Firstly the rate of expansion of the colleges should be increased so that the 40,000 intake target would be achieved by 1971.[4] Secondly the proportion of male students in the colleges should be increased from about 30% to 40%; this would yield a considerable increase in the number of teachers because of the lower wastage rate for men. In addition it was assumed that there would be a continuation in the trend for more married women to return to teaching after an absence of some years and that this would be helped by greater opportunities for part-time teaching. The supply of university graduate teachers (going mainly to secondary schools) was expected to increase from about 6,000 to 8,000 per annum between 1963 and 1968, and to remain at that level until 1975. After 1975 there should be a large increase, to 13,700 by 1986. The supply of graduate teachers is more difficult to forecast than the supply from the training colleges, and the report acknowledges this. Graduate teacher supply is assumed to be a function of total graduate output, and

---

[1] HMSO, London, 1965.

[2] See report *op. cit.*, Appendix C.

[3] Depending on whether it is required to have a maximum class size of 40 or 30 in primary schools.

[4] *Higher Education* (Cmnd. 2154) HMSO, London, 1963.

especially in later years it is related also to the number of training courses available for graduates. The result of these proposals is to increase the teaching force by over 100% between 1963 and 1968. The report is best summarized by the following table:

TABLE 14.3 *Estimated supply and demand for teachers 1963-1986 England and Wales* (Thousands)

	1963 (Actual)	1968	1972	1976	1978	1981	1986
DEMAND							
1. S.30 + J.40	334	358	420	461	477	491	508
2. S.30 + J.30	—	—	—	530	545	562	581
3. SUPPLY	280	324	380	440	479	540	636
Surplus (+) or Deficiency (−)							
4. S.30 + J.40	−54	−34	−40	−21	+2	+49	+128
5. S.30 + J.30	—	—	—	−90	−66	−22	+55

Source: Ninth Report of National Advisory Council on Training and Supply of Teachers, HMSO, London, 1965.

Notes: J.40=Maximum of 40 in primary classes
J.30=Maximum of 30 in primary classes
S.30=Maximum of 30 in secondary classes together with satisfactory staffing standards for 6th forms.

The table shows clearly that even with the large increase in teacher numbers there is a deficiency until at least 1978, or until nearly 1986 if it is desired to eliminate all junior classes of over 30 pupils (see line 5). By 1986 there would be a sufficient number of teachers to improve staffing standards still further, or to expand nursery education. The forecasts were checked for consistency with secondary education enrolments; it was found that there would be enough secondary pupils to supply the universities and the colleges of education while maintaining the present levels of qualifications of entrants. The Vaizey and Knight projections imply a higher number of teachers for 1975; this is because they assume that all classes of over 30 pupils will be eliminated by that date. Thus, the lower number of teachers forecast by the ninth report of the National Advisory Council on the Training and Supply of Teachers implies a lower level of expenditure (other things being equal) than is forecast by Vaizey and Knight. Whatever the policy with regard to teacher recruitment, it is clear that the expansion in teacher numbers will be large over the next 20 years, that changes in admissions policy to, or in the size of, the colleges of education will have a sizeable effect on teacher numbers only after some time has elapsed,[1] and that the number of teachers which policy

[1] For instance "the ninth report", *op. cit.,* presumes that the expansion of the colleges of education will be complete by 1971. but nevertheless it is clear (see Table 38, p. 69) that the deficiency of primary school teachers (who come almost entirely from the colleges of education) will be overcome only by about 1986—a lag of 16 years. Policy decisions were taken in 1965 that would tend to bring teacher supply nearer the Vaizey and Knight figures for 1975.

may dictate will have a decisive effect on future expenditure. These considerations apply to every country; they have been illustrated for England and Wales because it is for these countries that the most far-reaching and detailed forecasting has been done.

15 The problem of international comparisons of unit costs

INTERNATIONAL comparisons of educational expenditures are rendered difficult by the variety of price and income structures in different countries. Previous studies either make no allowances for this, or avoid *direct* unit-cost comparisons, or make partial adjustments (using exchange rates based on purchasing power parities). One study[1] deals more thoroughly with this problem, and although its main concern is not education, it provides a methodological basis for international comparisons.

In the OECD publication *Financing of Education for Economic Growth*, (OECD, Paris, 1966) there are six papers which deal with international aspects of expenditure and costs. Some of these are concerned mainly with projections of expenditure in various countries; they are reviewed here only in so far as they make *international* financial, price or monetary comparisons.

The first of these papers, by the Netherlands Economic Institute[2] is an attempt to work out the financial implications of certain enrolment targets for Africa, Latin America, Asia[3] and India.

For Africa, arithmetical averages of recurrent expenditure per pupil and of capital expenditure per pupil place were obtained from public budget and similar sources, for Primary and Secondary education in each of 25 territories or countries. The year to which these calculations refer is not stated, but as 1960, is the base year for the enrolment calculations, it is presumably the year to which the financial data refer also. Similar cost data were obtained for 19 Latin American countries. However the capital costs (and all Higher Education costs) were taken from estimates made at the Santiago de Chile Conference held under the auspices of UNESCO in 1962. Estimates (very rough) were also made of Indian and other Asian costs.

The way in which this data was used to make forecasts of expenditure is not the concern of this part of the analysis. What is interesting is that all the unit costs were expressed in U.S. Dollars, using official exchange rates (one presumes that official rates were used, in the absence of any contrary indication). No allowance was made for different factor or product prices, and the following table which compares the African and Latin American data shows that the

---

[1] Gilbert, M. and associates, *Comparative Products and Price Levels*, OEEC, Paris, 1958.
[2] *Financial Aspects of Educational Expansion in the Developing Regions: Some Quantitative Estimates*, in OECD, *op. cit.*, pp. 59-72.
[3] "Asia" here excludes India, Japan, Mainland China and (presumably) non-European USSR.

generally higher levels of *per capita* income in Latin America are not reflected in higher unit costs.

TABLE 15.1 *Current and capital expenditure per pupil in Africa and Latin America* (U.S. Dollars)

Region	Recurrent expenditure per student			Non-recurrent expenditure per student place		
	First level	Second level	Third level	First level	Second level	Third level
Africa . . .	28	251	1,000	59	529	4,000
Latin America .	23	257	600	65	300	1,200

Source: Netherlands Economic Institute paper, in "Financing of Education for Economic Growth", OECD, Paris, 1966, Tables 4.2.1, 2 and 3.

It may be concluded that:

1. Use of purchasing power parities would have altered the comparisons both within the "regions" and between them.
2. The method used for comparison does not bring out the effect of the relative levels of teachers' salaries. They may well be *relatively* lower in Latin America than in Africa and this would account for the low current unit costs in Latin America.
3. For third level education African unit costs are high because higher education (which is only in its infancy in Africa) imports foreign personnel and standards.[1]

A paper by D. Blot and M. Debeauvais[2] is of interest, not because it compares *unit* costs, but because in analysing the link between public expenditure on education and Gross Domestic Product for 104 countries using 1961 data, an attempt is made to correct for international differences in purchasing power. Blot and Debeauvais use regression analysis and find high correlation between educational expenditures and income. They have two reservations in the course of their analysis:

1. When analysing countries in groups according to income levels "it is possible to 'prove' divergent theories through judicious manipulations of the figures".
2. As there is reason to believe that the phenomena under study may not be stable over time, cross section analysis is doubtful as far as operational results are concerned. Elasticities based on time-series data are quite different in magnitude.

The most relevant part of the Blot-Debeauvais paper from the point of view of the present study is Table 6 which lists population, GDP and public education expenditure for 104 countries. All the expenditure figures are in U.S. Dollars; the rates of exchange used are not official IMF rates but a form of purchasing

---

[1] Foreign teachers are also one of the reasons for the relatively high salaries and unit costs of first and second level African education.

[2] Educational expenditure in developing areas: some statistical aspects, in *Financing of Education for Economic Growth*, OECD, Paris, 1966, pp. 73-83.

power parity derived from United Nations sources.[1] These exchange rates are also given in the table. They are an improvement on IMF rates, which do not necessarily reflect the relative purchasing power of various currencies for various reasons (not the least of which is because the rates are managed or controlled by the various national or international monetary authorities for policy reasons which often bear no relation to international price movements). Therefore, in using exchange rates which do attempt to reflect price movements, the Blot-Debeauvais measurements are an improvement on other more conventional ones. The international comparisons in the following chapter of this report use similar special exchange rates, which are discussed at length.

A paper[2] by Seymour Harris compares proportions of National Income in various countries (mainly OECD countries and the USSR) spent on education. His cross-section analysis confirms that educational expenditures are income-elastic. Apart from demographic factors, higher *per-capita* incomes are associated with higher enrolments. There are two factors however which he omits from his analysis, and which *might* explain some of the discrepancies that arise:

1. The position of teachers in the hierarchy of incomes generally, will influence the proportion of expenditure on education.
2. Variations in the *quality* and *qualifications* of (say) primary teachers should also be taken into account.

These two problems, the relative income of teachers, and the definition of teachers, are dealt with later; a further reservation is that Harris deals only with 22 fairly high-income countries. The income-elasticity of educational expenditures would appear to be different if a wide cross-section, including the very low-income countries, is taken. This is also related to the question of *relative* incomes of teachers (and to international flows of teachers and financial aid, to some extent).

Paul Senf, in a paper which forecasts educational and public expenditure in five European countries (Germany, France, Italy, Belgium and the Netherlands), expresses present and forecast public expenditure in U.S. Dollars, using official exchange rates.[3] However, when he deals with educational expenditure projections, the analysis is in terms of the share of public or of total expenditure in each country. No analysis of projected unit costs, or of the effect of teachers' salaries et cetera, is made. While no allowance is made for general purchasing power differences, the fact that five European countries (four of which have fairly similar levels of income per head) are compared, probably lessens any distortions which may occur in the use of official exchange rates.[4]

[1] *Yearbook of National Accounts Statistics*, United Nations, 1963, Table 3B.
[2] Public expenditure on education, in *Financing of Education for Economic Growth*, OECD, Paris, 1966, pp. 103-49.
[3] Financial implications of the expansion, by 1970, of public and educational expenditures in five countries of the European Economic Community, in *Financing of Education for Economic Growth*, OECD, Paris, 1966, pp. 337-67.
[4] M. Gilbert says that the differences in price level and structure between many European countries are too small to justify a precise ordering (*Comparative National Products and Price Levels*, OEEC, Paris, 1958). Furthermore these differences appear to have lessened between 1950 and 1955, and with the advent of free trade in Europe could be expected to lessen further.

F. Edding's article "Expenditure on education: statistics and comments" makes some careful international comparisons of expenditure.[1] Firstly, the general rising post-war trend of the share of education in National Incomes is demonstrated (for developed countries mainly, as these happen to have the best statistics). This does not give rise to any general exchange rate problems, as the comparison is entirely in terms of percentages. Secondly the National Income *per capita* and the education expenditure *per capita* are given for 24 countries in terms of United States Dollars, using official exchange rates. There is a very high correlation between these two sets of expenditures (as we should expect, given the extreme differences in Income *per capita* levels).

The final section of Edding's article deals with the proportion of educational expenditure (1) in different uses and (2) at different levels of education. Also the proportion of expenditure financed by different levels of government is analysed. The latter point is not of much interest here; each country will have a pattern of financing dictated by administrative, geographical, social and constitutional factors, and international comparisons are difficult. The former comparison, is however, important and interesting:

1. *Educational expenditure by end-use*: First, detailed historical statistics are given for Germany 1925-60.[2] The proportion of capital to total expenditure shows a marked long-term rise, from 4.9% in 1925 to 5.4% in 1935 to 22.7% in 1955 and to 26.9% in 1960. Expenditure on teachers' salaries is a falling proportion of current expenditure, which transfers (pension payments) show a slight rise. The residual "other current expenditure" moved from 14.9% in 1925, to 0% in 1935[3] to 13.8% in 1955 and to 21.4% in 1960. Secondly a number of African, American, Asian, Oceanic and European countries are compared for 1959. It would seem that the coverage of the data is not uniform and that comparisons between individual countries would not be in order. However, some general trends may be observed. Latin American countries had a comparatively high proportion of current non-teaching costs. For Asia and Europe the proportion fluctuated widely—from about 3% to nearly 40%. There is no clear trend of teaching costs as a proportion of total or of current costs. In fact the variations are so wide (and apparently so random and unexpected) that the coverage of the data must be far from uniform.[4] With economic growth, the growth in teachers' incomes (if they are not to fall very rapidly in the income hierarchy) is a major cost-increasing item. There is no reason why the cost of non-personnel items should increase at a similar rate. Therefore much of the increase in real expenditures on

---

[1] Reprinted in Robinson, E. A. G. and Vaizey, J. (eds.), *The Economics of Education*, London, 1966.

[2] See Edding, *op. cit.*, p. 44. From 1950-60 the statistics refer to the Federal Republic of Germany, including West Berlin. Transfer payments are included throughout.

[3] A time, when, according to Edding the depression led to drastic pruning of educational expenditure which, unlike teachers' salaries, could be cut. At this time the proportion of the German National Income spent on education was falling. Cf. Edding, *op. cit.*, p. 26 and p. 28, Table 1H.

[4] This could easily arise due to the inclusion of welfare or transport items, or possibly to the way in which grants to the "aided" sector are treated.

education should be on non-personnel items. The measurement of these trends is discussed further in the following chapter. Edding also observes that the "secular increase of the share of non-salary expenditure is important, because in this section it can be expected that real costs per unit may decrease. This is the field where the advantages of mass production can be made useful for education. The personnel expenditure per teacher and for other staff members on the contrary is bound to increase. It has more or less to follow the rise in average real income. If teachers are in short supply, their salaries are likely to rise faster than average income. If there is a surplus of teachers, a lowering of the pupil/teacher ratio may cause an increase of total personnel expenditure, even though salaries may not follow the movement of average of real income".[1]

2. *Proportion of educational expenditure at different levels.* As the institutional structure of education differs widely, so too will the coverage and structure of educational statistics differ, thus making direct international comparisons difficult. There are however some time trends in the distribution of educational expenditure in different countries which are sufficiently marked and widespread to be of interest.[2] The period covered is from the first decade of the twentieth century to 1955-60, and expenditures are classified under primary, secondary, higher and other. For some countries secondary is divided into general and professional/technical education, and for one country (Belgium), teacher training is an additional subdivision of secondary education. The proportion of primary expenditure shows a strong tendency to fall in nearly all cases, and secondary expenditure has an equally strong tendency to show a proportional rise. Higher education accounts for a rising share of expenditure in only two countries: the United States and India. As might be expected, India shows significantly different trends to the other countries; higher education gains, professional and technical education loses, and the other sectors of education maintain more or less constant shares in total educational expenditure.

To these findings of Edding may be added J. Vaizey's analysis[3] of educational expenditures in the United Kingdom which also shows a falling trend in the share of primary education and an expansion in the share of higher levels. It also shows a rising share of capital expenditure in the total—especially for the post-war period when *real* capital expenditure was enlarged by favourable price movements.

An article[4] by M. C. Kaser is important for international comparisons because it touches on certain points which will be seen later to be of considerable importance. The coverage of Kaser's comparisons is confined to "Industrialized

---

[1] Edding, *op. cit.*, p. 47.

[2] See Edding, *op. cit.*, Tables 6, A-G. The countries analysed are Germany, the United States, the Netherlands, Belgium, Italy, India and Sweden.

[3] *The Costs of Education*, London, 1958. Esp. pp. 74, 86 and 185-98 (Tables XIV-XXXI); also Vaizey, J. and Sheehan, J., *Resources for Education*, London, 1968, pp. 136-7.

[4] Education and economic progress: experience in industrialised market economies, in Robinson and Vaizey, *op. cit.*, pp. 89-173.

Market Economies"—i.e. Northern and Western Europe, North America and Japan.

Estimates are made for total and *per capita* GNP in local currencies and in U.S. Dollars at current and at constant prices. The estimates were made from official and private sources covering 1900-01 to 1958-59, but in some cases (France, Canada, USA and England and Wales) go back to 1870—or earlier. Index number problems arise (*a*) in the price indices for time-series of GNP where resort is made to inevitably imperfect compromise solutions, and (*b*) in the price-weights used to compute purchasing-power parities where the 1955 rates computed by Gilbert and Kravis[1] were used.

The relationship between GNP *per capita* and second level and third level enrolment are examined and found to be of positive significance. However, when it comes to comparing various money outlays with GNP there is little or no association. Expenditure per pupil and salaries of teachers are expressed in terms of "aliquots"—i.e. as fractions of GNP *per capita*. The lack of correlation between educational expenditure (in aliquots) and GNP *per capita* may be due to deficiencies in the data, according to Kaser. In particular, public expenditure on, or subsidies to, aided schools may not be given uniform treatment. The main conclusion drawn from this comparison is interesting and important: "there is lack of evident improvement in this (qualitative) parameter,[2] whereas a rise in *per capita* GNP is linked with the quantitative (increment in secondary and university numbers in relation to primary enrolments, and fall in student teacher numbers).[3] If all these parameters are comparable, the implication is of diminishing costs per unit of educational output (or rising educational quality per unit of costs)". However "the figures obtained for teacher salaries, on the other hand, defy interpretation".

What is most important is that both of these measurements—educational unit costs and the level of teachers' salaries—should be considered jointly. In making international comparisons this report will deal with the influence of the teachers' position in the incomes hierarchy on unit costs. One way of ranking and comparing the position of teachers is the "aliquot" measurement used by Kaser. It has the advantage of being based on fairly widely available statistics; however, these statistics—especially for labour force and National Income—are unreliable for many less developed countries.

Thus two considerations must be borne in mind: (1) general differences in purchasing power, which are corrected by the exchange rates used by Kaser and other authors, and (2) specific differences in the prices of inputs—notably teachers—which may be allowed for by comparing and adjusting (or standardising) "aliquot" measurements—or some similar indicator of relative prices— according to the base level of some particular country.

The adjustments to be made will vary with the purpose of the comparisons. If

[1] See Blot and Debeauvais, *op. cit.*, for similar 1961 parity rates (derived from *UN Yearbook of National Accounts Statistics 1965*) which in turn rely on Gilbert and Kravis' work.

[2] i.e. the expenditure per pupil (at all levels) in relation to GNP *per capita*.

[3] This presumably is the pupil/teacher ratio. Earler (*op. cit.*, p. 123) Kaser lists this as a *qualitative* parameter, thus giving rise to some confusion. Also total enrolment in relation to the population or to certain age groups is not considered.

we want to compare the burden or cost of *money* expenditures (whether total, per pupil, class, et cetera) then the first adjustment—for *general* purchasing power differences—is the relevant one. However, if we want to analyse expenditure further and compare *real expenditures* (in terms of teachers, school buildings et cetera) rather than costs, or if we want to compare the trend of real inputs,[1] then the second adjustment—for variations in the prices of *educational goods*— is also relevant. Here we are concerned with the international rather than the inter-temporal aspects of comparisons, and thus United Nations and OECD work is of great interest.

A study by Milton Gilbert and Irving B. Kravis of 1950 exchange rates has been re-written as a study of 1955 parity rates, products and prices, between the United States and Western Europe.[2] The European countries included are Denmark, United Kingdom, Norway, Belgium, France, Netherlands, Germany and Italy. Comparisons are also made between the 1950 results (obtained in the earlier study) and 1955.

The Gilbert and Kravis study is centred round a detailed break-down of Gross National Product of the countries concerned. There are 33 main categories listed and further subdivisions were made in order to arrive at price and quantity estimates for these, using census, budget and other statistical data supplied mainly by the statistical services of the countries concerned. The various categories of expenditure were put into three main groups:

1. Consumption, which includes all personal consumption as well as current education and health expenditures, public and private.
2. Investment (gross capital formation), which includes changes in stocks, and net exports.
3. Government, which is composed mainly of general administration and defence.

As a rule, market prices were compared, the exceptions being items subject to heavy selective taxation, such as tobacco and alcoholic beverages et cetera, where factor-cost ratios are also shown.

Because of the index number problem several types of international comparison are made. For the comparisons of National Products and of the Consumption, Investment and Government groups, total and *per capita* expenditure is calculated using United States price weights, the price weights of the European country concerned, a geometric average of the two, and in one case, official exchange rates.

The basis for this analysis is a more detailed series of comparisons in which product levels and purchasing power rates are given for each of 33 components

---

[1] Just as comparing the time-trend of inputs involves special indices of teachers' salaries and other goods (cf. Vaizey, J., *The Costs of Education*, London, 1958), so international comparisons involve a type of index measuring the *relative* prices of inputs in various countries. We are concerned with teachers only, because of the statistical problems involved, because there is reason to believe (from preliminary evidence) that teachers' incomes vary widely in different countries (relative to other incomes), and because teachers are quantitatively the most important single input in education.

[2] Gilbert, Milton and associates, *Comparative National Products and Price Levels*, OEEC, Paris, 1958.

of GNP, using USA and European price and quantity weights for each country. The unit of account is US Dollars. Thus there are two series of binary comparisons with the USA as a base.[1]

In general these comparisons show that official exchange rates do not correspond to purchasing power equivalents, either for large aggregates such as GNP or for much smaller items. The official exchange rate of European currencies (per US Dollar) was in general higher than the purchasing power equivalent (i.e. prices in Europe tended to be lower when reckoned at official exchange rates). This was true in general[2] whether European or USA quantity weights were used, even though one might expect USA quantity weights to show a higher European price level.[3]

Similarly, the comparisons of National Product show that official exchange rates exaggerated the discrepancy between USA and European income *per capita* levels. In some cases for 1950, GNP for European countries measured at USA price weights was nearly twice the level measured at official exchange rates. Again USA price weights narrowed the difference in income levels much more than European price weights (because a large weight was given in the latter to, say, food which is relatively dear in the USA and a small weight was given to, say, automobiles which are relatively cheap in the USA). A trend common to all these comparisons was that the discrepancies for Italy—by far the poorest country compared—in price and income structures were larger than for other countries, generally. Also, discrepancies were in general greater in 1950 than in 1955, which is to be expected in view of the greater rate of growth of real income *per capita* in Europe in the 1950-55 period, in view of the more pronounced inflation[4] which Europe also experienced (when compared with the USA), and finally in view of the relative absence of the disruptive influences of the second world war and of the Korean War.

There are large differences in the purchasing power of domestic currencies for the various components of GNP and these differences follow definite trends. First, investment enjoys a price advantage in European countries which is slightly less than that of GNP as a whole. However, if investment is broken down we find that:

1. *Producers' durables* are relatively much dearer in Europe, and (at USA quantity weights) appear to be *absolutely* more expensive also.
2. *Residential Construction* is relatively cheaper in Europe than in the USA (relative to both all investment goods and to GNP).
3. *Non-Residential Construction* is relatively similar in price in Europe and USA.

Secondly, government expenditures are relatively much cheaper in Europe. If

[1] There is also a set of comparisons using average European price and quantity weights. These comparisons are not as detailed as the binary comparisons and do not deal specifically with education, so we do not deal with them here.

[2] Except for the purchasing power of the French franc in 1955, measured at USA quantity weights.

[3] Because, contrary to normal market expectations, a high weighting would be given to goods *relatively* dear in Europe and a low weighting to goods *relatively* cheap in Europe.

[4] Especially in France, which, as a result, provides the only example (in 1955) of where the internal purchasing power of a European currency was less than that of the US Dollar.

such expenditures are split into "Personnel" and "Other", we see that the Personnel item, for both civil and military items is especially cheap in Europe, where purchasing power is between three and six times the USA level, "Other" expenditure (i.e. on goods and services) is relatively cheaper in Europe too, but the difference is not nearly as great as for Personnel.

Thirdly, while consumption as a whole is *relatively* similar in price in Europe and the USA, there are large divergences in several of its components. Consumers' durables are notably expensive in Europe, and health, education and housing are relatively inexpensive. Other items follow less pronounced trends. Low current housing costs are probably partly a result of the low construction costs noted above.

In general it is found that the labour intensive items are relatively cheap in Europe (some food items, clothing, health, education, government personnel, residential construction), and the capital intensive items are relatively dear (consumers' and producers' durables, et cetera). This is what we would expect, as incomes in general by any indicator are much higher in the USA than in Europe. Clearly this has important implications for education (which is highly labour intensive); the "normal" expectation would be for education to be relatively dear (relative to other goods and services, i.e.) in richer countries, but this could be offset in so far as teachers' incomes do not rise with other incomes, and thus the position of teachers in the income hierarchy is seen to be a matter of great importance.

Here, it is helpful to set out in detail the method used[1] to compare "real" educational expenditure, and the price levels relevant to education, for Denmark, Norway, Belgium and the Netherlands.[2]

Public and private expenditure on education are included in all cases, but administrative expenditures are excluded. Expenditure is divided into two categories:

1. *Personnel.* The quantity weights were made on the basis of teacher numbers. The price weights were based on average salaries. In each case teachers were divided into three levels, according to the ages of the pupils whom they taught: (1) Primary (under 12 years), (2) Secondary (12 to 18 years), and (3) Higher (over 18 years).
2. *Expenditure on goods and services.* Price weights were derived from prices of other categories of goods. No quantity indicators could be obtained directly, so (presumably) an average was calculated from the total expenditure and price data.

As a result, three tables are derived. These make comparisons of purchasing power (on teachers and other educational goods) for the countries concerned. Quantity comparisons are also made, on a *per capita* (of *total* population, not enrolment) basis, i.e. price indices are used to estimate the number of teachers and the amount of real resources *per capita* allocated to education. These are given in Tables 15.2, 15.3 and 15.4 below.

[1] Gilbert and associates, *op. cit.*, pp. 141-3.
[2] The comparisons for France, Germany, Italy and the U.K. are given in the earlier work of Gilbert and Kravis, *op. cit.* (pp. 200-7 of French translation.)

TABLE 15.2 *Per capita quantity comparisons of teachers*
(Number of teachers per head of population. Index: USA=100)

	1950					1955			
	United Kingdom	France	Germany	Italy	Denmark	Norway	Belgium	Netherlands
All education	71	79	49	72	68	74	118	81
Primary education . . .	108	117	73	95	90	96	144	129
Secondary education . .	55	75	41	76	47	53	110	39
Higher education	32	7	18	9	57	63	57	49

Sources: 1950 Data: Gilbert, M. and Kravis, I., *An International Comparison of National Products and the Purchasing Power of Currencies*, OEEC, Paris, 1954.
1955 Data: Gilbert, M. and associates, *Comparative National Products and Price Levels*, OEEC, Paris, 1958.

TABLE 15.3 *Purchasing power equivalents of various currencies on teaching personnel* (Units of National Currency per Dollar (USA quantity weights))

| | 1950 | | | | | | 1955 | | |
	United Kingdom (£)	France (Old Fr.)	Germany (DM)	Italy (Lire)	Denmark (Kroner)	Norway (Kroner)	Belgium (B. Fr.)	Netherlands (Guilder)
Primary education . . .	0.171	112	1.87	191	3.35	2.98	19.9	1.48
Secondary education . . .	0.161	119	1.98	164	3.95	3.52	32.4	1.71
Higher education . . .	0.145	132	1.71	136	2.72	2.43	27.6	1.05
Aggregate purchasing power parity . . .	0.288	313	3.63	577	5.94	6.58	44.9	2.93
Official (IMF) parity . . .	0.357	350	4.20	625	6.91	7.14	50.2	3.81

Sources: As in Table 15.2 on p. 203

Table 15.2 (p. 203) is simply a quantity comparison; there is no weighting for price structures. It obviously reflects the demographic patterns of the countries listed, especially as far as the primary level is concerned, as enrolment at this level was quite comprehensive. For higher (and in some cases for secondary) education the *per capita* quantity of teachers is notably low in Europe; for instance France in 1950 had only 7% as many teachers in higher education per head of population as did the USA. Such a discrepancy is obviously greater than any demographic differences, as are the corresponding indices of higher education teachers per head of population in Italy (9%) and Germany (18%). This table as such does not give any information on unit costs; for this guides to purchasing power are necessary, and these are given in Table 15.3 below.

Table 15.3 shows the relative purchasing power of various currencies when applied (*a*) to teaching personnel at different levels of education and (*b*) to all goods and services. It also shows, by way of contrast, the IMF official rate of exchange. The table uses USA quantity weights throughout; this means that the prices of teachers, and of goods and services were weighted according to the relative quantities of these teachers, goods and services used in the USA. If European weights were used, the aggregate purchasing power parities would diverge even further from the IMF parities.

Table 15.3 leaves some questions unanswered. It does not give any definite indication of the relative position of teachers in the income hierarchy of any country. More important, as the basis for the table is a calculation of average salaries of all teachers at various levels of education, the question of the definition of a "teacher" and teachers' status in various countries is avoided. There is an implicit assumption that on the basis of a purely nominal definition "primary teachers" (or other categories) are compatible internationally. While it is almost impossible to remove every discrepancy in international statistics, two adjustments at least are desirable in this case. First, qualified and unqualified teachers should be distinguished and weighted averages used. Secondly, an adjustment should be made for age-structure differences in the teaching force.[1]

However, the value of Table 15.3 lies in the contrast between the various parities used for any one country. Even aggregate purchasing-power parities are inadequate for international comparisons of real *expenditure* on education (using "real expenditure" in an equivalent sense to "real inputs"); while official IMF exchange rates are completely misleading.

Tables 15.2 and 15.3 deal with personnel expenditure only; Table 15.4 attempts comparisons of expenditure on goods and services also. While data are available only on the comparisons of Denmark, Norway, Belgium and the Netherlands with the USA, there are useful conclusions to be drawn:

First, education seems to be a relatively more teacher (or labour) intensive process in the lower income area (Europe) compared to the United States.

Secondly, the index number problem, while by no means resolved, is not a great *practical* problem: USA and European price and quantity weights for

---

[1] This is important because planning and forecasting requires "standardised" costs. The sex-composition of the teaching force will affect costs also, but this is usually as a result of the different age-patterns of male and female teachers.

TABLE 15.4 *Quantity comparisons and purchasing power equivalents (all levels of education) 1955*

	Quantity comparison (*per capita* USA = 100)		Purchasing power equivalents (Units of domestic currency per U.S. Dollar)	
	U.S. Price Weights	National European Price Weights	U.S. Quantity Weights	National European Quantity Weights
Denmark				
Personnel . . .	66	65	3.47	3.39
Goods and services .	46	46	7.03	7.03
Norway				
Personnel . . .	71	70	3.09	3.04
Goods and services .	55	55	5.73	5.73
Belgium				
Personnel . . .	111	107	26.80	26.90
Goods and services .	29	29	57.20	57.20
Netherlands .				
Personnel . . .	74	79	1.48	1.57
Goods and services .	23	23	3.34	3.34

Source: Gilbert, M. and associates, *op. cit.*

Note: The term *National European* price or quantity weights means that the price or quantity weights applicable to each country were used. There is no question in this example of using average European price or quantity weights, although these are used by Gilbert and associates for some types of comparisons.

education give rather similar results. Whether this result would hold if the weighting allowed for different qualification structures in the teaching force is another matter. A lot would depend on the countries chosen.

Thirdly, the purchasing power equivalents, when compared with Table 15.3 show that for expenditure on goods and services, aggregate purchasing power parities are a reasonably good basis for comparison (unlike for comparisons of personnel expenditure).

Thus, the work on international comparisons of expenditure and costs points to the need for certain considerations to be taken into account:

1. The index-number problem, which will necessitate at least two sets of comparisons and which is (in principle) very difficult to solve.
2. The fact that comparisons of real expenditures or inputs will necessitate special purchasing power equivalents (especially for personnel expenditure, but ideally for each item of expenditure).
3. The position of teachers in the general hierarchy of incomes will therefore be a very important factor (which directly affects the purchasing power equivalent) and therefore the determinants of teachers' salaries need further study if reasonable forecasts and plans are to be made.
4. More attention will have to be paid to the definition of a teacher and to the qualification structure of the teaching force in different countries; simple, unweighted averages are not enough.

16 Inter-country comparisons—theoretical aspects

BROADLY, the problem is one of separating out the notion of a common unit of costs, implicitly fixed in *absolute* terms, from costs presented as relative shares, or proportions, of output or income. Opportunity cost refers, of course, to the latter; most accounting data deals with the former.

In many countries, although the schools are partly financed by the local authorities, the bulk of the finance comes from the central government. The central government often pays teachers' salaries (the major item of current expenditure), the local authorities pay for school maintenance, cleansing, heating, (about 10% of current expenditure). Capital expenditure contains a greater element of local finance, however. This varies according to certain circumstances. It follows, therefore, that standards of building, the number (and qualifications) of teachers, their salaries, and other conditions of education are (to a degree at least) standardized over various regions of the country. As a consequence of this, differences in unit costs (and in other variables) between various regions reflect the pupil/teacher ratio and class size (generally smaller in rural areas), and also the relative cheapness of building and maintenance in rural areas. But leaving this on one side, it is necessarily the case that the proportion of regional national income devoted to education is greater in the low-income (i.e. rural, usually) areas than elsewhere. This is the consequence of national uniformity of educational standards, which entails a high degree of uniformity of expenditure.

This may be illustrated by taking two regions, A with a relatively high real income and B with a relatively low income per head. It is assumed that trade effectively equalizes prices in A and B. Teachers in A and B receive equal money (and real) incomes. Thus they are relatively higher in the income-hierarchy of B than they are in A. Also, as they account for the bulk of educational expenditure, the proportion of resources devoted to education will be higher in B than in A. If it is assumed that the *efficiency* with which educational resources are used does not vary between A and B, then unit costs will be equal in both regions. These assumptions entail both unequal and equal opportunity costs, which are measured by the amount of alternative output—as measured by educational expenditure—foregone. It is this paradox that has led to confusion.

Now, the assumption may be dropped that teachers' money (and real) incomes are equal, but let them fall in B so that teachers in B now have a similar position in the income hierarchy as teachers in A. Still assuming similarity of educational systems, it can be said that the proportion of income spent on education will tend to be *equal* in A and B. Unit costs are now *lower* in B (the low-income area) than in A. If income per head in B is 50% of income per head in A, then the opportunity cost of a teacher in B will be only 50% of what it is in A, as prices are still equal, but teachers' incomes vary with regional *per capita* incomes.

Next, the equal teachers' money income assumption is restored but the *price* equalization assumption discarded. Other things remaining equal, prices will move so that the £x paid to teachers in A and B will purchase (say) 20 units of goods in A and only 10 units of goods in B.[1] Using the expenditure on teachers as the guide to unit costs, region A will have higher costs than region B. While teachers' money incomes (and money costs) have remained the same their real incomes (and real or opportunity costs) have changed. This change in teachers' real income has worsened their position in the region B income-hierarchy, *relative to the position of teachers in the region A income-hierarchy*. As the teachers in region B started out in a favourable position when compared with those in region A, the result is that the movement of teachers in the income-hierarchies of the two regions is convergent.

It is now supposed that neither teachers' incomes nor prices in general are equalized in A and B, then nothing *a priori* can be said about either the level of unit costs or the proportion of regional (or national) income allocated to education in A and B, even if the organization and efficiency of the educational systems of A and B are similar (an unlikely possibility in such separated regions). What it is necessary to know is the level of teachers' *real* income in A and B, or more generally (to take non-teaching costs into account) a measure of *real* expenditure on education in both regions. If A and B have different currencies then a purchasing-power parity rate of exchange is needed to compare real expenditure and real costs. This may differ from official exchange rates. In so far as teachers' incomes are *relatively* high in the low income regions, then these regions will have a tendency to devote larger shares of resources to education than the high income regions. It is this case which corresponds to the real world—for international comparisons at least—but the more abstract series of assumption in the previous paragraphs serve to clarify some of the issues involved.

One can extend these arguments further.

For instance, if there are two communities A and B, in *every* respect similar (including income *per capita*), save that in A teachers had higher salaries than in B, then unit costs would be higher in A than in B, because teachers in A commanded greater resources for the same output or effectiveness. However, if output (assuming it could be measured) were correspondingly greater in A, then unit costs would no longer be greater in A. However, the composition of national output would now be different; it would include more education in A than in B.

If the outputs are now varied further, and A and B are assumed to differ in many respects, it can be said that the national outputs are equal, only if, were the composition (i.e. quantity weights of components) of output to become identical, they would add up to the same total of output. (This is what the classical economists sought to do by measuring all output in corn, or some similar commodity). But what may be counted as *identical output* on this basis might also be rated as less or more in A or B if the tastes of consumers in A and B differ. This is almost

---

[1] i.e. equal money incomes will imply unequal real incomes.

certain to be the case when the distribution of national income differs in two countries. If the national income of A is distributed in favour of a class which prefers personal services, and if the national income of B is distributed in favour of a class which prefers mass-produced manufactures, then a national output heavily weighted towards mass-produced manufactured goods will satisfy B more than A.

Thus, while teachers in A may be relatively better paid than teachers in B (and thus unit costs in A higher than in B), it is not possible to say that by lowering the position of teachers in A the national income will be greater unless the gainers in A can compensate the losers (i.e. teachers) and unless the original is agreed by all (including teachers) to be sub-optimal. Unit costs in A are higher, and more is spent on education in A merely in the sense that some inputs (teachers) are dearer, but not in the sense that a change in teachers' salaries would of itself change either educational output or total output. While this analysis has been dealing explicitly with the proportion of total resources or inputs allocated to education, the initial assumption of similarity in price levels and price structures (apart from the educational sector which we considered) implies that costs and expenditures are directly related to the allocation of resources.

This is a local application of a general principle, that where uniform standards are applied, the proportion of resources going to education is *higher* in the poorer areas than in the more prosperous ones, and, in so far as local resources are involved, the expansion of education is greatly limited by this factor alone. Alternatively, in so far as education is nationally or internationally financed, expansion is limited by the availability of public funds to be distributed from the more prosperous to the poorer areas. This is exemplified in the case of the developing nations by the movement of teachers from richer to poorer countries, where these teachers are paid expatriate salaries and consequently absorb a high proportion of resources. It follows, too, that teachers with a uniform rural/urban salary scale, are of a relatively higher status in poorer areas than in the more prosperous areas. Teachers are near the bottom end of the salary structures of the professional classes.

For instance, in Ireland (1965) the maximum salary for a married male teacher was £1,490. For a civil service Executive Officer it was £1,600, and for a Higher Executive Officer (which is arguably a more relevant grade for comparison) £2,060. Other middle grade executives in semi-state companies earned from £1,600 to £2,000 maximum. Professional groups such as doctors, lawyers and graduate executives undoubtedly earned more (although it is difficult to give the earnings of groups such as doctors and lawyers who are mostly self-employed). The notable thing is that the educational qualifications necessary for teachers are higher than for most occupations for which rates of pay are quoted above.

The application of uniform salary scales over different regions and areas may make it difficult to match the supply and demand of teachers. Obviously there are more disutilities (for most people) involved in working in some areas than in others. Hence a single teacher-supply target, derived from a projection of enrolments and from pupil/teacher ratios, class-size targets et cetera may be meaningless in certain conditions. Thus, in the United Kingdom, where the overall supply and demand situation with respect to primary teachers is one of shortage, certain areas, such as Sussex, have a surplus of available teachers and are limited in their recruitment by a Department of Education quota. Other areas (around Birmingham, for example) suffer from an acute shortage of teachers. Hence the recommendation of the Plowden Report[1] for an extra allowance for teachers in educational Priority Areas—areas which are poorly provided with teachers and schools. In Ireland also, it may even be the case that rural areas in the West are attractive to teachers. This could be due not only to pleasant working conditions and surroundings (when compared with an urban school having large classes) but also to the enhanced relative income (and other) ranking which the teacher enjoys in such an area.

An important, if negative, conclusion is now arrived at because if country A has a professional class that is relatively more highly remunerated than that of country B, and therefore the unit costs of all (or most) of its professional services are higher than those of B, then it can be shown that (1) A spends more than B on services as conventionally measured and (2) it only spends the same (or possibly even less—under certain assumptions) in terms of real resources or inputs, when the difference in relative prices which we assumed, is allowed for.

In making international comparisons for expenditure on goods which do not enter into international trade, the traditional solution in international trade theory may be vindicated. This is that the prevailing official rate of exchange is not a reliable guide to real expenditure, unless there are perfect markets and (within each country) perfect mobility of factors, full employment and perfect competition, and that if these conditions are not fulfilled, a purchasing-power parity rate of exchange should be employed. In fact, perfect mobility and perfect competition et cetera are not the rule in most countries and therefore there is needed a purchasing-power parity exchange rate—like that developed by Milton Gilbert and used in much OECD work for international comparisons.[2] Purchasing-power parities between two countries can be calculated on two bases: the first which weights prices in each country according to the structure of final output in country A, and the second which uses the structure of output in B for weights. Thus it is possible to compare educational expenditure (and from this to derive a comparison of unit costs, however these may be defined) in a number of different ways (supposing there are two countries, A and B):

1. In real terms of physical units (in this case teachers, equipment, et cetera).
2. In monetary terms using the market rate of exchange for currencies.
3. At purchasing-power parity rates of exchange. There will be at least two such rates, depending on whether quantity weights of A or B are used as a basis for comparison.

[1] *Children and their Primary Schools*, HMSO, London, 1967.
[2] *Comparative National Products and Price Levels*, OEEC, Paris, 1958.

PART FIVE

Productivity

"Education is the last pre-industrial revolution industry." This kind of remark is often heard, particularly as the pressure on resources grows. What would it mean to say that educational efficiency had improved, or that productivity had risen? This Part examines the notion of productivity in education, a sector of the economy which resembles other important sectors.

17 The "production function" in education

RESOURCES go into education. The "education process" takes place. Education has effects. None of these is easy to assess or measure. Nevertheless, there is something that can be said about each. The analogy with the production function is easy to draw, but the notion of the production function is not as simple as it seems. In a production function there are not only analytical problems but serious problems of measurement of labour and capital. It is not the present intention to review the analytical problems but rather to try to indicate that even if the formulation were analytically satisfactory, there are overwhelming statistical problems, and that these two difficulties—analytical and statistical—combine to obscure rather than to clarify the questions that are at issue.

What are inputs to education? Principally labour—teachers' labour. In two succeeding chapters, a thorough analysis is made of the supply and demand for teachers and of their salaries. Capital in education takes the form principally of buildings. Later there is a case-study of the development of educational building. But education does not only involve teachers, non-teaching labour, equipment and buildings. Pupils and students are not raw material—like iron ore in a crucible—but a living part of the educational process. How can their "input" be assessed? Attempts have been made to evaluate their potential labour time (the so-called income forgone hypothesis), but they have been analytically and statistically unsatisfactory. The problem is a genuine one—for students make a contribution, and assume the contribution must be capable of being meaningfully presented—but it is difficult to see a solution. Perhaps the wrong question has been put? It is suggested, towards the end of this analysis, that this is what has happened, and it follows therefore that an alternative solution to the dilemma may be found.

What is the problem that is being tackled by the use of the analogy of the production function? It is part of a series of analogies with other economic concepts—capital, returns and productivity among them—which have come to the fore in recent years, and the analogies have been trying to explain, first, what determines the costs of education and secondly (and for the greater part), what is the place of education in a modern economy. Since there are divergent views on what causes a modern economy to move, and since these views are also related to other views on the distribution of the benefits of the working of the modern economy, there are inevitably divergences in the explanation of what part education plays in all of this. So much is obvious, and it is explained (in a different context) earlier. The divergences of view about the notion of the production function have filled the pages of the learned journals for years. What can usefully be said about it in relation to education?

To begin at the beginning. Inputs to education change over time. The consequences of education change over time. It is difficult to evaluate the changes, and to assign to them unambiguous numerical indicators. The processes of teaching and learning change—and it is difficult to describe the process of change independently of the changes in the nature of the inputs and outcomes. A deeper involvement of the students in the process of education by the development of self-instruction techniques, for instance, changes the evaluation of pupils' time (or "input") and also allegedly affects their personalities (an "output")—input, process and output are all intertwined in a way that makes separation not merely difficult but positively misleading.

The analogy of education with industry is not an exact one. For one thing, industry for the most part has separable inputs, processes and outputs. There are technological relationships inside firms, and in industries, which are describable in engineering terms.[1] Its inputs and outputs are not only in this sense tangible, but they are bought and sold on the market. Its processes change partly as a result of changes in relative prices of inputs and outputs. Therefore, though the matter is in dispute, the combination of inputs (labour time, and the flow of service from capital) in a production function for a firm, or for an industry, expresses a technological relationship. What is the case with schools and universities? There are obviously different ways of teaching and learning. They can be described in pedagogic, psychological and sociological terms. They change, and the changes can be so described as well. What is terribly difficult is to value the inputs and outputs, and to ascribe shifts in the processes of learning and teaching to shifts in relative prices.

To recapitulate, inputs into education are difficult to evaluate. They are, perhaps, simpler than in some other sectors of the economy, but they include teachers' salaries—which are an administered price, not reflecting in any direct sense supply and demand considerations, and thus not reflecting scarcity—and students' time and efforts, which include income forgone and the net balance of pain and pleasure for being a student. "Input" is therefore a complex and ambiguous notion.

Some parts of educational output are unambiguous—the number of people who complete a school-life, the number of examination successes, et cetera. But the more the objectives of education are examined, the less easy they are to define, and to measure. A simple example must suffice. The incorporation of less socially-advantaged children into the secondary education system is desirable, yet because their attainments are inevitably lower than those of the socially-advantaged the average level of examination scores will tend to decline. Output is measured by examination results which point in opposite directions to those indicators that measure the rate of incorporation of disadvantaged children into the secondary education system. It has proved impossible to achieve a satisfactory indicator of total output—for the simple reason that education is a way of life and not just that the educational system happens to be a sector of

[1] Salter, W. E. G., *Productivity and Technical Change*, 2nd edn., Cambridge, 1966.

the economy. In practice this means that cost-benefit analysis, for example, can be applied only within sectors of education, and not between education and other parts of the economy, and that even in this instance non-additive iterative procedures rather than a summation must be used.

To test educational efficiency therefore, like has very carefully to be compared with like—as all cautious educational research, with its carefully-hedged conclusions, indicates. The notion of the general efficiency or productivity of the educational system, which could be said to have risen or fallen between, say, 1950 and 1960, is an evident absurdity. So, too, is the notion of "total factor productivity". As Harcourt[1] has said, commenting on Jorgenson and Griliches' review of overall factor productivity ". . . their measure of the rate of growth of total factor productivity (which, on their hypothesis, should be approximately zero) is a quantum index of growth in outputs, each weighted by its value share in total output, *less* a similar index of the rates of growth of input services, similarly weighted". In other words, a shift of total factor productivity is due to errors in measuring inputs. This is not a helpful procedure to assess what it is desired to assess—whether one way of teaching is more effective than another, and how much more or less does it cost?

Thus, questions are left which are susceptible to reasonable answers, although the obtaining of data to respond to them may not be an easy task. They fall under four headings:

1. How do teaching methods and learning procedures change?
2. What administrative procedures help or hinder the process of change?
3. In what sense is a change "effective"?
4. Does the change involve a greater or lesser use of resources than the use of existing processes of teaching and learning?

It will at once be apparent that these questions raise issues which are not only complex, but which involve assessments well beyond the scope of economics. Here an additional note of caution is necessary. It is surprising how the cautious results of investigators in other disciplines are used as firm assumptions in some work on the economics of education. For example, the nature/nurture controversy in intelligence and attainment is far from settled, and the combatants are still dealing each other what to the outsider seems like pretty powerful blows. Yet works appear in economics which, for instance, "standardise" earnings for ability and attainment as though the psycho-socio results were settled beyond further dispute. The crucial point, however, is that the first three questions are analogous to the technical—what might be called "engineering" —questions that arise in the production of a manufactured good. To answer them requires technical knowledge.

Even the fourth question, which appears to be more narrowly economic, has broader implications. The evaluation of inputs is only economically meaningful when compared with the resultant outcomes, and as has been seen, these outcomes are especially difficult to enumerate.

Inputs include:

[1] Harcourt, G. C., Some Cambridge controversies in the theory of capital, *Journal of Economic Literature*, Vol. 7, No. 2, June 1969, p. 379.

H

1. Capital services. These may be on a replacement cost, original cost, or present-value basis.
2. Salaries and wages, especially teachers' salaries. Teachers' salaries are administered prices, bearing little relation to market determined wage and salary levels (if, indeed, there are any significant number of such market determined levels). In addition, some payments (e.g. to some women) represent payment for an addition to the labour force of people with no alternative gainful occupation. The opportunity cost of such employment in market terms is zero, or low.
3. Students' time. This has for long been a matter of dispute. Prevailing wage rates for young people cannot be used, because (a) to do so assumes full employment and (b) it assumes a labour market that is totally unresponsive to major shifts in labour supply. It also assumes a net welfare effect (often misleadingly labelled "consumption") which is zero. This is an implausible assumption about the rising demand for education as it is at present composed.[1] The demand has been described as a "thirst" for education. It has been compared with a flood. It has not yet been compared with a casino.[2]
4. Other inputs. These vary, but include more straightforward elements, such as cleaners' wages, and equipment, where prices are more likely to be determined on the open market than teachers' salaries.

The notion of output is discussed at length elsewhere.

The changes that occur in education have consequences that can be evaluated pedagogically, socially, et cetera. The present concern is economic. In this part of the report an attempt has been made to highlight some significant recent changes in pedagogic procedures. What is suggested here is that the process of cost comparison can lead to a general strategy of educational innovation.

In studying the major new inputs into the new methods of education, the authorities are concerned chiefly with individual items of expenditure—such as a T.V. transmitter or something of that kind. Yet evaluation of a new system only makes sense, as a system, in relation to a closely defined output. Basically, the reason for undertaking a cost study of the new media of education is to compare the outputs of different systems, since ultimately the object is to say whether this system is "better" than that system—that is, that for a *given* output, fewer (or less scarce) resources are used.

To achieve this object it is not necessary to know in detail the relative effectiveness of the systems that are being compared, though it is helpful to have this information. Nevertheless, it is sufficient to make assumptions about the effective-

---

[1] For many students, education is a way of life. As Keynes said: "Most probably, of our decisions to do something positive, the full consequences of which will be drawn out over many days to come, can only be taken as a result of animal spirits—of a spontaneous urge to action rather than inaction, and not as the outcome of a weighted average of quantitative benefits multiplied by quantitative probabilities" (*The General Theory of Employment, Interest and Money*, London, 1936, p. 161). To argue that students think in terms of income forgone and the careful assessment of the discounted returns that it will yield to them is to argue that everything that they say and do, and everything that reporters and writers say they do, is a surface rationalisation of deeper currents which accord with market-oriented ideologies. It may indeed be so, for anything is possible in this world, but the principle of Occam's razor suggests not.

[2] *Op. cit.*, p. 159.

ness, which can be verified at a later stage. This course is further suggested by the reflection that the actual effectiveness of existing ("conventional") education is not at all precisely known. Economics may not be an exact science, but it is far in advance of some other social studies in the precision of its results.

In other words, the problem is to construct an analytical framework of assumptions into which various data can be filled, as and when seems appropriate.

There is sufficient evidence on the performance of the new methods to suggest that their effectiveness in certain circumstances is better, and in most circumstances is no worse, than that of the conventional systems. Therefore, the ruling assumption of this part of the report is that things are not worse when the new methods are used; or, to put it more positively, their effectiveness is assumed in ordinary circumstances to be equal to that of the existing methods. Thus, assuming that cost considerations are dominant, if the new methods are half the cost of the existing methods, there is an obvious *prima facie* argument for their use.

It is, however, possible to present stronger arguments than this, for it is well known that with the existing methods there are a number of crisis areas where the level of effectiveness is very low. Among these areas are the following:

1. The disenfranchised groups, such as the black Americans, the Puerto Ricans and the other minority groups, which the existing educational system notoriously neglects.
2. Allied to this are the ineducable groups. Their problems may be of genetic, social or psychiatric origin. It is closely allied to the ethnic-poverty problem (see 1. above)—and it is an area of education where needs are great, and the means of meeting them are few. In general, there is evidence that for this group there are new methods that are effective, and it is a matter for policy decision as to whether resources should or should not be devoted to alleviating the conditions of these depressed classes. (An analogy is with a cure for cancer. Doubtless if it costs $1 *per capita* for universal preventative vaccination, then a universal programme would be adopted. But suppose each treatment costs $100? Or $1,000? At what point would the trade-off occur?).
3. This pair of instances of the failure of existing methods is paralleled by the experience of early learning. It is fairly clear, now, that the evidence shows that the new methods can help very young children and there is some evidence (though not much) that early learning can overcome some, at least, of the social or genetic handicaps that affect certain minority groups in modern societies.

There are several areas of the curriculum, too, where it is known that the existing system of education performs indifferently. It does so chiefly because there are too few teachers or, where there are enough teachers, their performance is poor, or the subject is inherently one that demands presentation in a way that a teacher cannot, without aid, present it.

To take some examples from the existing curriculum:

(a) *Mathematics*. It is widely agreed that for most pupils the existing mode
   of mathematics teaching is a failure. There are indications that new methods
   can do better.

(b) *Languages*. The language laboratory and, to some extent, the T.V. system,
   represent a significant advance in the teaching of languages.

In both these cases, there are reasonable grounds for supposing that the
existing system in some degree fails, and that the new methods in some degree
succeed, either because they are absolutely more effective or because they are
able to perform where there is an absolute shortage of teachers.

The best example of this is the introduction of new subjects into the curriculum.

There are two revolutionary concepts where an absolute shortage of teachers
will prove a handicap to a realisation of the idea. These are:

1. education continuously throughout life; and
2. self-enthused study.

It is now banal to say that society and knowledge change so rapidly that
education will have to be life-long. It is platitudinous to say that this life-long
education will build upon a direct motivation to study which is itself the consequence of relatively prolonged and successful exposure to education. It is also
clear that the magnitude of the demand for further study (which, in principle,
will equal a significant part of the total life of the greater part of the adult
population), will pose enormous demands for teachers—and not just teachers,
but teachers of the right calibre. It is in this context that quantitatively the new
methods may well have their biggest contribution to make. This is already
observable in the areas of staff-training (e.g. in the armed services and in industry),
and of what is euphemistically called "enrichment".

There are two crucial areas where a contribution of a strategic kind may be
made by new educational techniques. The first is that as the education system
as a whole expands, the quality of certain parts tends to fall (though, in general,
standards rise with expansion). In some parts of the world—e.g. India and
Latin America—the expansion has been so rapid that the quality of almost all
parts of the system has fallen. The second is that of teacher education and
training.

It is generally agreed that there is a crisis of "quality" in education throughout
the non-communist world; it follows, therefore, that in some areas the effectiveness of education by conventional methods is falling rather than remaining
constant. It also follows *ex hypothesi* that as the needs for education change,
and the curriculum changes in consequence, the teachers will grow less and less
able to cope, and that in consequence, as a logical corollary, their effectiveness
will decline.

It is further generally agreed that the key to raising the effectiveness of the
existing methods, and to the successful implementation of the new methods, is
teacher education and training. When people talk about a crisis of "quality" in
education, what they mean is either that the teachers are inadequate, or that
they are ill-prepared. It follows, therefore, that in order to raise the quality of

teaching, two steps have been advocated: (1) to raise the salaries of teachers which, with a given budget, entails a reduction in the number employed, (though it is not obvious that this would have the desired effect), or (2) a radical attack on the problem of teacher education. Clearly, the new educational techniques are relevant to both these questions, in the sense (*a*) that it is possible that by releasing financial resources, they may enable salaries to be raised (the logic of this is that they will release the less able teaching staff, and that smaller numbers of more highly qualified people can cope with the same enrolments of students), and (*b*) that it enables groups of teachers, or teachers in training, to be reached from a central point where instruction and demonstration of a high quality can be offered.

In the light of this general analysis it is possible to reach certain tentative conclusions:

—that the new techniques are competitive in price for a number of situations;
—that certain methods are *not* competitive in price for many situations;
—that the new techniques can perform in some circumstances where existing media are performing inadequately.

Further, it is possible tentatively to identify certain techniques that can be used, singly or in combination, to attack particular problems. This is explained in detail in the reports of the Nuffield Resources for Learning project, some of which are summarised in Chapter 19.

On this basis a diagram is tentatively proposed

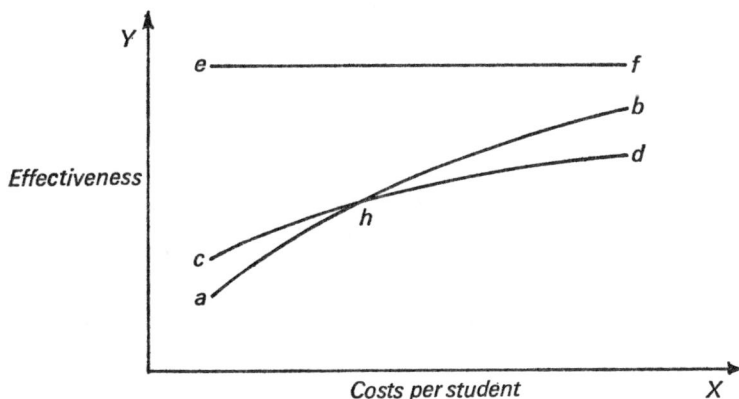

FIG. 17.1

The *Y* axis measures educational effectiveness in a given area by certain criteria that can be specified, if necessary. (It is not necessary to define the criteria as being always the same: a large number of diagrams can be drawn to represent effectiveness of different criteria—e.g. test scores, reports by teachers, reports by consultants, reports by parents, reports by students, et cetera *ad inf.*). Costs, on the *X* axis, are defined simply as the costs of a particular system at different levels of operation. ("System" is a defined combination of inputs).

In the illustration given here, the line *ab* reflects the effectiveness of the existing systems. It is a hypothetical case, but reflects what intuitively seems to be the case—that as costs rise (e.g. as the pupil/teacher ratio declines) effectiveness rises, but at a diminishing rate, till improvement ceases. The lines *cd* and *ef* reflect two different new media systems, which have a high initial cost, but which in one case rise immediately in effectiveness, in that case to intersect the curve *ab* at *h*. In this instance, by reading the diagram it is possible to delimit the area where the use of the media could usefully be considered. A boundary curve can be inserted to indicate where the economic costs are so high that the effectiveness or otherwise of any system is no longer of interest or concern.

This chapter has been about inputs and outputs. The notion of technological relationship between inputs has been shown to have some relevance to educational decision-making. Studies have shown how difficult it is to get the true costs of different ways of teaching accurately compared. The real problem of educational innovation is probably an administrative rather than an economic one.

18 The productivity of education

In a market economy, it will therefore often occur that the cost of a given product will rise (that is, physical productivity will fall); but since more will be charged for it, the total money product will also rise. Physical productivity may fall, but the money value of output will rise. In the non-market sector, where output is measured by inputs, only the physical productivity will fall.

Yet it has been said that productivity in English secondary education and in British universities has fallen. The first point may well be, "So what?", as has been said above. If a hospital is made more comfortable, then its productivity will have fallen by definition. If the British Museum is more beautifully and expensively arranged, its productivity will have fallen. In other words, if education falls into that part of the nation's life where productivity is not a relevant criterion, then it serves little purpose to measure it.[1] As education "improves" its productivity will fall; it has been falling since the nineteenth century when public education began, in the sense that the pupil/teacher ratio has steadily fallen. If education were sold, its price would rise, and so the value of its output per worker would appear to rise, and in one sense its productivity would rise. But its physical productivity, together with that of almost all the luxury or service sector, has been falling; though its "efficiency" has been rising.

Leaving this on one side, however, the case as presented has flaws. One study of British secondary education attempts to measure productivity trends in education.[2] It examines inputs and outputs in the 1950-63 period, and concludes that total factor productivity declined by approximately 2.5% per annum.[3] Ambiguity in the measurement of inputs and outputs suggests that this may be an over-precise conclusion.

One of the principal questions posed by Blaug and Woodhall was: "annual expenditures on secondary education have risen since 1950 from about £50 per pupil to £150 per pupil. Was this increase largely due to the costs of better quality education?".[4] The answer, of course, is "yes". The greater part of the increase in unit costs at every level of education in the post-Second World War period was due to price inflation, which is not directly related to productivity.[5, 6]

[1] In this work the word "efficiency" has been used, but in the restricted sense of comparing two or more closely related situations.
[2] Blaug, M., and Woodhall, M., Productivity trends in British secondary education, 1950-63, in *Costs and Productivity in Education*, Paris, UNESCO-IIEP, 1967.
[3] The rate of decrease varied between 1.1% and 3.1% per annum, the variation being due principally to different output measures. This, as will be seen, is of some significance.
[4] Blaug, M, and Woodhall, M., *op. cit.*
[5] See Vaizey, J. and Sheehan, J., *Resources for Education*, London, 1968, and Edding, F. and Berstecher, D., *International Developments of Educational Expenditure, 1950-1965*, Paris, UNESCO-IIEP, 1969, for other examples.

The authors substitute the word "objectives" for the word "outputs".[1] This is potentially a serious matter, as it presupposes that the "objectives" chosen for measurement correspond to what people—pupils, parents, teachers and policy-makers—really want to achieve. "Objectives" can easily be imposed as a proxy for outputs, and such measured objectives may be quite arbitrary, or at best partial, in which case it would be nonsense to maximise their achievement in isolation. Furthermore, the various objectives may be non-additive, or even, over a range, conflicting.[2] This means that an arbitrary index number must be used, arbitrary in the sense that it has no necessary general consensus behind it. "Objectives" is not therefore a synonym for physical output.

Another example of ambiguity is in finding that "it takes more *resources* today to produce a secondary school leaver of given quality than it did in 1950".[3] This is ambiguous (apart from the danger of confusion with the statement on rising unit costs already quoted) in the sense that the word *resources* as used here is taken to mean opportunity cost, or real cost to society. Such costs are usually measured by the money costs of various input items deflated by suitable price indices. But the *raison d'être* of the Blaug Woodhall study is *presumably* the measurement of productivity as the ratio of outputs to inputs, i.e. as an *internal* measurement. Internal and external measurements of productivity must be carefully distinguished. Internal measurements are concerned with ratios, and external measurements with real resources and costs measured by units determined for the economy in general.[4] The input measurements used by Blaug and Woodhall are deflated by individual special input price indices, and tell nothing about the opportunity cost of such inputs, and therefore nothing about resources, except in the sense that they give a time series of resource inputs measured at the prices ruling in a certain base year. They have relevance to costs in the base year only; for other years they are simply index numbers.

However, the principal statistical criticisms of the recent estimates of productivity change are concerned with the criteria used to measure inputs and outputs.

Inputs are measured partly on the conventional basis of adding together teachers' salaries, other current expenditure, and an imputed annual value of capital costs, each item being deflated by an appropriate price index. In addition, pupils' time is valued according to earnings foregone. The procedure is described as follows: " ... the Crowther Committee estimated that in 1957 the average earnings of 15–16-year-olds were about £200 a year. The Robbins Committee made a similar estimate of the earnings forgone by students in teacher training

---

[6] Unless perhaps a price rise were due to factor scarcities. This does not seem to be the case with education, despite the oft-proclaimed shortage of teachers. Educational input prices did not rise exceptionally—they rose as part of a general wage and price inflation. Furthermore, the price of the principal input—teachers—being administered, its response to scarcities may not necessarily be what simple micro-economic theory would suggest.

[1] See Blaug, M. and Woodhall, M., *op. cit.*, p. vi-2.

[2] For instance, increasing the participation of certain social groups may conceivably conflict with the achievement of some purely academic goals in secondary education.

[3] Blaug, M. and Woodhall, M., *op. cit.*, pp. vi-1 and vi-2 (italics added).

[4] To avoid such confusion, it might be better always to speak of *internal efficiency* and *external productivity*.

and further education colleges in 1962-63; their estimate was £540 a year. By interpolating from these figures for 15 and 18-year-olds, and by taking account of the average earnings of *all* young people over the decade of the 1950s, we can estimate the earnings forgone by schoolchildren in each age group since 1950 . . . The imputed money value of pupil's time must be deflated by an index of juvenile wage rates to provide an estimate of the real value of pupils' time".[1]

If the principle of including income forgone as a cost or input item is acceptable, then a procedure like that described in the preceding paragraph is not necessarily invalid, though there may be doubts about the process of interpolation for such crucial data: for reasons already given, however, the principle is not fully acceptable, and the input measurement given is therefore questionable. But if the income forgone hypothesis is accepted for the sake of argument, then the additional task of reconciling the input measurements thus constructed with the various output measurements remains. Even if input measurements are taken as valid in themselves, they are not necessarily directly comparable with other independently constructed output measurements.

A similar issue arises when the "length of schooling" index of output is considered. In this case the number of school leavers is weighted according to their ages when leaving. As the average age has tended to increase by a significant amount, the resulting index shows a higher rise than the unadjusted number of leavers. The reason for using such an index is, according to Blaug and Woodhall, that economic criteria (such as those which have just been considered), might be rejected by "teachers who value learning for its own sake, rather than for its vocational implications. According to this point of view, school-leavers might be weighted by the length of their schooling, rather than by their future earnings. This method of weighting assumes that one of the aims of schools is to foster a desire for education, and so measures their success in terms of the number of pupils persuaded to stay at school beyond the statutory age".[2]

Neglecting the insufficiency of such a critierion, which has already been mentioned, the implication of this is that time spent in school is to be regarded as useful and good in itself. But the use of income forgone measurements on the input side implies the opposite, namely that time spent in school has a disutility which is to be measured in terms of the earnings which would otherwise accrue. If time spent in school is valued for its own sake, then earnings forgone or earnings actually earned are irrelevant on input and output sides alike and should be excluded from both. (One could, perhaps, get out of this dilemma by arguing that the *result* of time spent in school rather than time itself was desired for its own sake. But this, besides being conceptually tortuous, introduces an arbitrary dichotomy between utilities and disutilities, associating the latter uniquely with schooling. The two are in fact inseparable).

While these indices may each be valid indicators in terms of themselves they are not necessarily comparable with other independently measured indices. Further, in the absence of a *numéraire*, the measurement of "output" is never "objective" in the sense that it would be universally or widely acceptable.

[1] Blaug, M. and Woodhall, M., *op. cit.*, pp. vi-22 and 23.
[2] Blaug, M. and Woodhall, M., *op. cit.*, pp. vi-14.

Therefore there are some important qualifications to be made to attempts to measure productivity in education. First, because of the difficulty in giving operational meaning to the concept of "total factor productivity" which has already been noted, the policy implications of falling productivity, as defined by Blaug and Woodhall are not clear. One could argue either (*a*) that the effort, effectiveness, ability of teachers—or possibly pupils—was falling, or (*b*) that the utilisation of capacity had fallen—say due to absenteeism, smaller age-cohorts, over-building or over-staffing. The important point is not so much the actual presence of either of these causes during the 1950-63 period as the need to make a correct diagnosis of the cause of apparently decreased productivity if appropriate remedies are to be applied. Thus if (*b*) were in fact the cause of apparently falling productivity, then to propose more capital intensive and presumably more cost-effective teaching methods (which is quite commonly done) could lead to even lower productivity. The intensive must be distinguished from the extensive margin.

Also, as "costs" or inputs are defined to include pupils' income forgone, it follows that more pupils are absorbed, the more will productivity fall, unless other inputs are reduced. It would be possible, for example, to hold productivity constant by reducing the number of teachers as the number of pupils rises. A point needs to be noted here. Not only is the reasoning such as to restate in paradoxical form what is self-evident and acceptable, but the implication as to the measurement of output is worthy of reflection.[1] For, if society (through its representatives, parents and the students themselves) decides to keep more students at school then this must be thought by them to be a positive contribution to welfare. Yet the result of this decision appears, in these calculations, purely as a negative. Of course, in conditions of full employment (which are far from being prevalent in the United States where this type of reasoning has its origin), young people who stay at school lose earnings at that time. This can be represented as a negative. On the other hand, the community, their families and the young people themselves *choose* to stay at school, and presumably in some sense enjoy it. If calculations are to move away from money costs, they must move to an assessment of all utilities and disutilities, not merely of those disutilities associated with income forgone. Thus a positive utility figure should be added to the national output.

Since 1950 the pupil/teacher ratio in England and Wales (and in many other developed countries) has fallen; classes are smaller. This gives benefits to teachers and taught, which would appear in the total utility of educational output. (The disutility of work would decline, thus reducing "costs"; the enjoyment of school would rise, thus increasing the sum of utilities that equals "output").

As there are more teachers per student, output measured simply by the number of graduated students per teacher is arithmetically certain to fall. To get output up, that is to say to keep productivity per teacher constant or

---

[1] Part of this paradox is no doubt due to a confusion between stocks and flows. For instance, Blaug, and Woodhall, *op. cit.*, for most of their work measure "output" in flow terms (adjusted graduates) and "inputs" in stock terms (i.e. unit costs). Only at the end of their paper do they allow for this error. This leads to some confusion.

rising, the output has to be weighted. One way to weight it is to add a factor for the positive utility of being in, and teaching in, smaller classes.

It can also be weighted by the subject mix of secondary schools, examination results, et cetera. It cannot, of course, allow for the fact that as education extends over those previously considered ineducable, the average examination results are bound to decline below the level they would have been at, and the subject mix is bound to change. It is fair to say that the pedagogic benefits associated with smaller classes may be smaller than they were thought, or even non-existent, as some research suggests, but these indices cannot show this fact, if it is a fact, which needs to be discovered directly.

The criterion that cannot be used without great difficulty is the expected future earnings of pupils receiving secondary education, for all this calculation shows is that as education spreads to the lower paid sections of the community, the average earnings at constant prices of its products will fall, unless there is a flattening of the income distribution curve.[1] If, as seems probable, earnings patterns represent a complex of socio-economic factors, then a direct socio-political decision—for example, equal pay for women—can have a major and fortuitous effect on the "yield" of education measured by this criterion. In other words, it is extremely dangerous to use an existing income distribution to project a lifetime earnings profile forty years ahead.[2] It also implies that education given to the poor is useless unless it leads to immediate social mobility of the educated. But to imply that the educated will "rise" is to say that the social structure remains unchanged—which is also to say that the mass of the poor will always be uneducated.

It is insufficient to say that, since earnings represent marginal physical productivity, therefore relative earnings (if they could be projected) would measure the relative social yield of different labour inputs. A fallacy appears to have crept into the reasoning, even on its own terms. Neo-classical wage theory has always held that for the firm wage rates are given (settled by supply and demand or by the law), and that the amount of work is varied by the entrepreneur, till the marginal revenue product equals the marginal cost; and under perfect competition, the marginal revenue product will equal the value of the marginal physical product. Therefore, according to this view, if the law raises women's wages the number of women employed will fall, since the wage-rates are given, but not the amount of work. This reasoning would allow for such considerations as that a rise in women's status could indirectly raise their productivity, and it could also reduce imperfections (irrationalities) in the labour market. But suppose, as unemployment rises, the government raises demand and restores the previous level of employment. The reasoning is faulty. It does not allow for macro-economic action to maintain full employment; marginal productivity doctrine is (what its name implies) a partial equilibrium, and it assumes that a macro-economic situation is unaffected by what goes on in the sector considered.

---

[1] As economic growth occurs, real earnings will rise for everybody. If a proportion of this is attributed to education, as the reasoning suggests, then the rising real earnings must be allowed for in the calculations.

[2] Only actuaries ever do this seriously, which is why pension funds are often out of balance.

There is considerable evidence that education has but little effect on social mobility, and it follows therefore that many of the assumptions on which calculations of the economic "yield" of education has been based must have been fallacious. But it is not upon this point alone that the main objections to this mode of reasoning are directed. It is rather upon an examination of the notion of "input" and of the notion of "output", both of which have been shown to raise major difficulties, and the results of the examination appear to cast legitimate doubt on the basis of such calculations as those of the productivity of English secondary education during its period of rapid development.

Nothing that has been said should discourage attempts to assess the effectiveness (using that term to include the health, happiness and comfort of pupils and teachers) of different modes of education, and of resource use in the schools.

In conclusion, certain broad generalisations may be made on the basis of a commonsense notion of relative effectiveness. Take the problems of education in the developing countries. Manifestly, the inputs are much lower than in rich countries. For example, in Portugal in 1965, $(US)29 was spent on each primary school child; $192 in England and Wales, $103 in Ireland and $292 in Quebec. Using British price weights, the figure for Portugal becomes $95, for England and Wales $192, for Ireland $110, and for Quebec $244. Despite the levelling effects of a revised price index, the inputs are very different.

It is almost certain that the outcomes are much lower. Evidence of drop-out rates, for example, and casual inspection, will suggest that the education is in many ways far less effective in less developed than in developed countries. (This may be due to lack of family support, the inappropriateness of the education system to the socio-economic conditions, or sheer educational inefficiency. Whichever it is, the cause of the ineffectiveness does not affect the point at issue). Thus inputs and outcomes are relatively low in the developing countries. This is generally true of many sectors of their economies—agriculture, especially— and it reflects both their poor factor endowment and the low productivity that results from this low level of skills and modern capital. Whether or not the productivity of education (in the sense of the ratio of inputs to outcomes) is higher or lower in the developing or the developed countries it is not possible to say, since unambiguous index numbers of inputs and outcomes do not exist.

It seems intuitively probable that as inputs rise, however, outcomes do not rise *pari passu*—there are many reports of falling rather than rising standards. It looks as though developing countries may go through a phase, perhaps a lengthy phase, in which inputs rise but outcomes do not, followed by a period of consolidation in which "productivity" begins to pick up.

Behind this idea is a notion that there is a "critical mass" for education where, after a few years, it begins to "work": families accept its disciplines, the schools settle into a rhythm which accomplishes, more or less effectively, the goals, high or low, that they set themselves. In such circumstances, easily recognisable to experienced teachers and administrators, though hard to be exact about, it is not straining language to describe "productivity" as rising. If the analogy is thought useful, it could be said that fuller utilisation of plant and the gradual improvement of staff and students will lead to market improvement in outcomes, with relatively constant inputs over the years. Thus, one answer can be given to those who ask the question: how does productivity change in the developing countries? It is that it falls during rapid expansion and rises during periods of consolidation. The answer in terms of policy decisions is thus essentially a conservative one—consolidation is desirable on productivity grounds. But there is a more radical question: can modern techniques be used to accelerate productivity rises?

To that the answer is more complex and—probably—disappointing. In the first place there is widespread evidence that most pedagogically desirable improvements—better trained teachers, better buildings, more books, and more favourable pupil/teacher ratios—are cost-raising. Modern technology, from the television to the computer, is at best no cheaper than "conventional" techniques and often more expensive. Yet productivity does not depend on inputs alone, but on the ratio of inputs to outcomes. Both pedagogically-desired reforms, and modern technology certainly improve some outcomes. Whether they increase output *pari passu* with the increase in inputs is debateable.

The problem is complex. To adopt modern pedagogic methods is to adopt an expensive education system. In a developing country such a system will be even costlier than it seems, because its productivity will be low, owing to the inappropriate backgrounds of the students and of the teachers. Failure rates, for example, will be high.

It is to these sort of questions that the analysts of productivity should properly apply themselves.

19 New techniques in education

Introduction

EDUCATION uses a great deal of labour—teachers, students and others. Technological change has largely passed it by. In comparison with the manufacturing sector of the economy and, to a lesser extent, with certain parts of the service sector, education looks like the part of the economy where time has stood still. As technological change consists largely in making labour go further, and as the relative costs of labour tends to rise compared with other elements of production, it follows that the unit costs of teaching will inexorably rise: improvements (reductions) in the pupil/teacher ratio, of course, add to the increase in unit costs.

Admittedly in some countries the use of resources in education has changed. In Britain, for example, in 1920 76% of the costs of education were labour costs: in 1965 they were 58%. Within the total of expenditures, there was a rise in the proportion spent on ancillary staff (from 7% to 12% between 1920 and 1965).

In Britain, at least, it seems that development and use of new techniques has speeded up in recent years, with an increasing realisation that to be really effective, teaching aids have to be accompanied by changes in the organisation of teaching. In this chapter we report on the results of a study[1] of three of the innovations that have taken place in Britain. The study was basically one of costs: the explicit assumption made was that the net additional educational benefit of the innovations was nil. There is strong evidence that the benefits are, in fact, positive, but in the absence of any definitive results the conservative assumption had to be made. The three types of project reported on are the use of educational television in schools, the use of teaching machines, and the development of teaching "packages" for use in schools. At present these three projects are in an infant stage of development and thus in addition to establishing the present costs of these projects estimates were made of the future level of costs, when the various methods are used on a larger scale. Throughout the study particular attention was paid to the possibility of substituting teachers by either non-teaching staff or by other resources. In other words, the question was asked, are the effects of educational innovation to reduce the rate of increase of educational costs?

[1] Vaizey, J., Hewton, E. and Norris, K., *The Costs of New Educational Technologies*, Lisbon, 1971.

The use of teaching machines

The use of teaching machines is not new: they are used extensively in the United States and are used industrially to give instruction to individuals or to very small groups. In British schools, however, their use to teach whole classes is something of an innovation. In the secondary school studied, the first and second year classes[1] were taught mathematics almost entirely by teaching machines. The actual procedure of teaching varied from group to group, but the machine was basic in all cases and work on the machine took up most of the students' time. The machine conveyed a branching programme and each student, for most of his five classes a week, worked with the machine at his own pace. From time to time students were called together for class discussion, and occasionally the student would devote his time to a practical exercise (e.g. construction of a model) away from the machine. The teachers devoted most of their time in class to speaking to students individually. The organisation of teaching had thus completely changed.

The machines and the programmes were rented. Work schedules and exercises were, however, prepared by the mathematics staff at the school. This preparation was largely carried out in leisure time. From the point of view of the costing study this created two problems—the enumeration and the valuation of the hours spent in this preparation. In retrospect the time taken to prepare schedules and exercises for two years was estimated as 1,200 man hours, the normal working year of a teacher. This time could be valued at nil (all leisure) or the cost of teacher (to replace those preparing the material). As in the long run part-time effort is unlikely to be sustainable on this scale, the latter valuation was used for development costs. The development costs were amortised over seven years.[2]

On these assumptions, the use of this method of teaching added about £20 to the annual cost of teaching mathematics to each of the five hundred children involved. This represents an increase of about 85%. The costs of using teaching machines on an experimental, small-scale, basis such as this are clearly misleading. The development costs are spread over a small number of units, there is little scope for saving in teacher time, and the machines are rented on too small a scale to effect any reduction in the rental.[3] Further, no account is taken of the indirect benefits of experimentation such as the development of expertise and the encouragement and assistance given to others. The present costs were thus used as a basis for estimating the costs of teaching mathematics by machine to all classes in a large number of schools. The situation taken was one where 10,000 machines were rented: this would imply that schools with a total of 60,000 pupils would be involved. In this situation the additional unit costs of teaching mathematics by this method fall to rather less than £5: this is an increase—over traditional methods—of about 20%. The reduction in unit costs from their small-scale level comes from the three sources suggested above. The

[1] With the exception of two remedial groups.
[2] An interest rate of 8% was used in amortisation calculations throughout the study.
[3] 110 machines were rented by the school, although the local authority rented 260 machines.

development costs per pupil become negligible and the annual rental per machine and associated programmes falls by nearly two-thirds. Finally, some saving in teacher costs is assumed. It is considered not unrealistic that five mathematics teachers could be replaced by two teachers and one ancillary, thus reducing labour costs by nearly 50%. If this reorganisation does not occur—and it must be seen as a possible change, rather than a probable one—then the additional unit costs become about £9 a year.

Even where machines are used on the large scale envisaged in the last paragraph, and even on the most optimistic assumptions about teacher savings, teaching machines add about 20% to the costs of teaching mathematics. To be economically worthwhile, the educational "output" would have to increase by at least 20%. This must be considered unlikely, although it is clearly not possible to substantiate this surmise.

However, in many schools, severe difficulties are being experienced in obtaining teachers of certain subjects, notably science and mathematics.[1] The fact that traditional methods are significantly cheaper is of limited importance if the teachers are not available. A further, and cheaper, alternative is to dispense with the machines and use the programmes in book form. This possibility is considered next.

The development of teaching packages[2]

As part of the Nuffield Resources for Learning Project, there exists a group of teachers, known as the Hive, employed full time in the preparation of material to be used in secondary schools. The Hive's basic task is to prepare material and build it into a programme which pupils can follow individually, using where necessary audio and visual aids also equipped with material forming part of the course. Each programme is prepared for a year's study in one subject at a given level. Programmes have been prepared for Mathematics, English, Science, French and Social Studies. There is in each programme generally a core of material which most pupils work through, but provision is also made for the more and less able pupils by the inclusion of alternative or extra material which the faster or slower worker may choose, usually with the guidance of the teacher. The programme[3] thus embodies the ideas of the programme writers in written material (booklets and worksheets), master tapes, pictures, photographs, prints, slides and references to textbooks, films, and other tapes which the schools using the programme may obtain for themselves. The term used to describe the materials and any necessary equipment such as tape-recorders is the package. This is what the pupils work from and work on, and the study is on the costs of the package. As in the previous section, the costs of preparing packages at present were considered first.

---

[1] *The Shortage of Science and Mathematics Teachers*, London, Royal Society, 1969.

[2] This part of the study was largely undertaken by Mr. Eric Hewton.

[3] The distinction should be drawn between programmed learning and the kind of programmes prepared at the Hive. Although a Hive programme may observe some of the principles of programmed learning at times, there is no general intention to produce either a linear or a branched programmed learning course.

The cost of a package can be divided into the costs of developing the programme, and the costs of materials and equipment used in the package. Each member of the Hive produced on average one programme a year. On this basis, the total costs of producing a programme, including the writer's salary, clerical and administrative costs and overheads, was estimated at £4,500. Amortised over five years this gives an annual development cost per programme of £1,125. The development costs do not vary significantly between subjects: material and equipment costs, however, vary significantly, reflecting the attitudes and methods of those responsible for preparing the packages. In a situation where 1,300 pupils, in twenty schools, use the packages, the material costs vary—when savings on books normally used have been deducted—from about £500 to about £1,800. The result is that the total additional costs per pupil in this situation vary from £1.26 to £2.23.

On the basis of these calculations of the situation where only 1,300 pupils use the packages, it was possible to extrapolate to situations which may obtain when the system is extended beyond its present experimental stage. The situation chosen was one where 10,000 children are involved. Assuming that, as at present, only third year children used the packages, this would involve 300-350 classes, and between 50 and 100 secondary schools. Many education authorities have this number of third year pupils within their area. In this situation the unit costs fall significantly as the development costs are spread over more users and unit costs of printing decline. The additional unit costs are estimated to vary (between the same subjects) from £0.4 to £0.8. This would represent an increase in the costs of teaching these subjects of between 1 % and 6.5 %, with an average increase of just over 3 %.

Viewed strictly from a cost point of view, further reductions in the unit costs of packages could be secured by enlarging the number of schools served by one Hive. In the limit this would imply one central Hive for all schools centering their teaching around this method. However, it is thought that the size of unit described above is the maximum that could operate without losing many of the advantages of this method, and that in fact it may be rather more realistic to think in terms of smaller, rather than larger, units. The advantages that would be lost with more schools using the material of any one Hive are those that arise out of the co-operation of the participating teachers with the members of the Hive. With smaller Hives, visits to schools and co-operation with teachers are facilitated and there is a greater chance of feedback and, perhaps most important, a sense of involvement. Creating packages for smaller, or regional, groups of schools gives greater scope for flexibility, less standardisation and in some cases, e.g. in social studies, the ability to cater for local needs. Too much duplication of effort could be prevented by links (formal and informal) between the various Hives.

The effect within the schools using the material prepared by the Hive is largely to alter the structure of teaching groups, or units. Pupils work individually and at different paces which can lead to more re-thinking of the concept of a class. More of the teachers' time will be devoted to individual tutoring and discussion, diagnostic testing and evaluation, and considerably less to "class teaching" and to the preparation of lessons and material. It is possible that children in different age groups may be working on the same material, thus it may be necessary to think in terms of larger groupings and perhaps team teaching. A crucial point is the effect this will have on teacher requirements.[1] In the costs derived earlier, it was assumed that no change in teacher requirements occurred. However, in a similar situation in Sweden it is assumed that the subsequent re-grouping of class units will lead to a reduction in teaching costs.[2] There it is estimated that the most likely grouping will be units of 80 to 90 pupils: these pupils, previously taught by three teachers, could now be taught by two teachers and one assistant. This saving is more than enough to offset the costs of the packages. In Britain any saving arising from this source would be smaller, as an ancillary is paid about half the salary of a teacher compared with a fifth in Sweden. Those participating in the scheme in Britain do not feel that any significant substitution against teachers is likely to occur and thus it was not taken into account in the costing exercise.[3] When highly qualified staff are in short supply, however, the use of packages means that such staff can be utilised to their fullest advantage.

It is estimated, then, that when material is produced on a moderately large scale the unit costs of teaching each of the subjects using the packages will rise by an average of about 3%. There is some possibility that small savings in teaching costs could occur as a result of re-grouping classes within the school.[4]

Educational television services

A major innovation in education in Britain in recent years has been television. It has also been widely used throughout the world, especially in developing countries.[5] In Britain, educational programmes are produced and transmitted by the national television companies and also by some local education authorities: it is the latter with which this section is concerned. Three educational television services (ETV), each serving a city, were studied.

The three services differed considerably in several ways. Although all the services were established within the last five years, two were set up deliberately to provide an ETV service, one had a dual purpose—to provide an ETV service and to train technicians and engineers. The type and variety of programmes, however, differed widely as did the extent to which filmed material—as distinct from material produced by the service—was used. Despite this the unit costs of the services were, in 1968/9, reasonably similar. Several types of unit cost can be calculated for ETV services, two of which will be considered here. The most obvious calculation is that of annual cost per school pupil. Two of the ETV

---

[1] See Chapter 22.

[2] *Report on I.M.U. Mathematics:* O.E.C.D. Centre for Educational Research and Innovation, 1969 (mimeographed).

[3] Cf. the previous section.

[4] This depends, of course, on large rooms being available. Changes in the method of teaching imply changes in the design of schools.

[5] See *New Educational Media in Action: Case Studies for Planners*, Vols. I, II and III, UNESCO-IIEP, and *The New Media: Memo to Educational Planners*, Paris, UNESCO-IIEP, 1967.

services produced and transmitted programmes for universities and colleges as well as for schools: on various assumptions the cost of the programmes for schools can be estimated. This is then divided by the total population of the linked schools. The weakness of unit cost per school pupil in assessing the costs of using television as a teaching aid is that it does not distinguish between those schools and pupils who watch the programmes and those who do not. All the services had some audience figures and from these an estimate was derived of the cost per student hour. In this calculation the total cost is again the cost of the programmes produced for schools, and this is divided by an estimate of total audience hours. The unit cost series were estimated for 1968/9 and for the early 1970s when each of the services will have reached a definite stage in their development. The range of the results is presented in Table 19.1: all figures are in 1969 prices.

TABLE 19.1 *Range of unit costs of three educational television services* (£)

	1968/69	1972 (estimated)
Annual cost per school pupil . . .	1.4-2.2	1.5-2.0
Cost per student hour	0.2-1.9	0.1-1.9

These figures should be compared with a unit cost figure for all schools of £140.[1] Thus the costs of the ETV services are equal to an addition to unit costs of from 1.0-1.5% in 1969, and in 1972 of between 1.1 and 1.4%. The range of costs gives a slightly misleading impression, as in two of the services the trend of costs is strongly downward, but in the other unit costs are expected to increase due to a decision to add to the variety of programmes. The reductions are largely due to the expansion of the potential audience as more schools are linked. By 1972 however, all services will have linked all schools in their respective areas. Any further expansion would have to come from an extension into other areas; two of the services have large nearby centres of population that may be linked.

Conclusions

The studies summarised above have been of a partial nature. The question that has been asked is, if one change takes place in the method of teaching, what is the effect on costs? The answer in each case is that costs are increased as little compensatory change takes place. Admittedly the increase in costs from the use of learning packages is small, but nonetheless the method adds to costs. The effect is based on the presumption, however, that educational benefits arise from these new methods. These have not as yet been systematically enumerated, let alone evaluated, so any form of cost effectiveness analysis is not possible for these studies.[2] Certainly the percentage increases in costs—with the

[1] This excludes, as do the ETV estimates, an imputed capital cost.
[2] See Chapter 18.

exception of the use of teaching machines—would appear to be within the possible range of educational improvement, and with the general demand for better education may be implemented on a larger scale.

A more interesting question is to ask the effect on costs if these, and other changes, occur simultaneously. A situation is envisaged later where schools become resource centres, with teachers, audio-visual aids, learning packages, closed circuit television, and perhaps computers. It would seem that this would simply increase costs even more unless savings are made in teaching costs and building costs. Teaching costs account for about a half of all school costs, and unless an increase in the pupil/teacher ratio occurs as a result of the use of new methods, then these must necessarily add to total costs. From the partial studies it seems unlikely that any teacher substitution will occur—certainly none has yet taken place. Thus for new methods to be used on a wider scale, the decision will have to be taken that the educational benefits are worth the resulting increases in costs.

20 Capital and educational building

MORE capital is used in education than the customary figures of educational expenditure would suggest. The main form of capital is, of course, buildings, though more and more equipment is being used and stocks of materials are growing.

In analysing the capital structure of education, therefore, it has seemed worthwhile to take a particular instance—that of England and Wales—where important and much-heralded improvements have occurred in architecture, in order to analyse factors affecting trends in outlays.

In estimating the costs of educational building, a look has first to be taken at certain educational trends which are occurring, and which will affect the nature of the buildings put up.

The first trend is the rapid increase in numbers of pupils and teachers, requiring a considerable investment in physical capital. During the period 1945 to the present, something like £3,000 m. has gone into the construction of new schools and colleges of all kinds.[1] Not only have big sums been involved, but in this field significant advances have taken place in building practice and in educational usage: education saw the first innovations in new procedures of control which have had the effect of getting a far higher productivity out of the building industry. The prices of school buildings have remained more stable than most other prices. This favourable treatment of educational building is one aspect of the rapid expansion of education in Britain in the last twenty years. It has become a major enterprise. In the 1960s about 3 to 4 per cent of investment went into education—and total educational outlays were running in the later 1960s at between 5 and 6 per cent of the GNP. The number of teachers had risen from 231,000 to 279,000 between 1956 and 1964. The number of pupils had risen from 5.4 m. to 7.7 m. over the period 1950 to 1965,[2] in England and Wales, in primary and secondary schools.

[1] The capital outlays on new buildings and works in education have been divided as follows (i.e. Gross Domestic Fixed Capital Formation in Education):

£m. (current prices) (UK)

	Universities	"Other education"
1955	7	87
1960	23	123
1965	87	192
1970	101	302

Source: National Income and Expenditure, 1966, Table 61 and 1971, Table 57.

The expansion continues. By 1980 or so, there will be 10 m. or so pupils and students; the number of teachers will have increased from 280,000 in 1965 to nearly double in 1980.[1] In the National Plan and the work associated with it, a requirement for about 500,000 new school places annually—half for replacement—or roughly double the present total during the next decade—was envisaged.[2] In other words, no falling-off in the demand for educational building was likely because, although the rate of growth of the education system as a whole, though still high, is likely to be less in the 1970s than in the 1960s, the replacement demand is still substantial.[3]

[2] The growth in the number of teachers was as follows:

Teachers in maintained primary and secondary schools:
England and Wales

	(000)
1954	231
1959	261
1964	279
1970	329

Source: Vaizey, J.; Sheehan, J., *Resources for Education*, 1968. Also *Statistics for Education*, 1967, Vol. 5, and 1966, Vol. 6 for 1967 data.

[1] The change in the number of pupils and students in aided schools in England and Wales has been as follows: (000)

	Primary	Secondary	Universities
1920	4,305	1,685	46
1930	4,532	1.407	46
1950	3,955	1,696	85
1965	4,273	2,819	169
1969	4,789	2,964	211

Source: Vaizey, J., Sheehan, J., *Resources for Education*, 1968. Also *Statistics of Education*, 1969, Vols. 5 and 6.

[2] The projections for students and teachers were as follows (they have subsequently been revised upwards):

	Pupils (m.)	(England and Wales)	
	1963	1972	1986
Juniors . .	4.1	5.2	5.7
Seniors . .	2.8	3.5	4.5
Total . .	6.9	8.7	10.2

Source: Ninth Report of the National Advisory Council on the Training and Supply of Teachers, 1965, Table 5.

[3] It was estimated in Beckerman, W. and associates, *The British Economy in 1975*, 1965, Chapter 14, by Knight and Vaizey, Table 14.20, p. 491, that in 1962, the percentage of places in schools built at different times was as follows:

Post war	46
1920-44	14
1900-19	9
Pre 1899	31
	100

On the assumption that all schools built before 1900 need replacement, which is not unreasonable, and allowing for building since 1960, a ten-year programme would require about 250,000 places a year.

In forecasting the rate of growth of education and of educational expenditure, the first step is to forecast the general level of economic growth, because what happens to the whole determines to some degree what happens to the part. There seems little doubt that whatever happens in the short and medium run over the next three or four years, within twenty years from now the total level of the national income, in real terms, will be at least double what it is today.[1] Even during extremely unfavourable periods in economic history, the rate of the Gross National Product in real terms has rarely been less than one per cent a year,[2] and only occasionally has it been negative, as in the great slump of 1931-33. There are grounds for believing that if the economy were properly conducted, the rate of growth could be four or five per cent a year, steadily, with few breaks. Thus, in general, it is safe to say that there will be a substantial and rising amount of building going on. Of this growth in the Gross National Product, it is not unreasonable to predict an increase in building. In the National Plan, investment would have risen from 18 % to 20 % of the GNP; and building would take a high proportion of this.[3] How much of this will be for education? As was pointed out in the figures just given, education has been one of those sectors which has taken a large part of total building activity since the end of World War II. There are reasons for thinking that other competing demands will be more prominent in the future than they have been over the last twenty years or so. These other competing demands include building for roads, hospitals and other medical care, housing and other social facilities, some of which have been relatively neglected until recently. It is fair to say that, housing apart,

[1] According to Beckerman, W., and associates, *The British Economy in 1975, op. cit.,* Table 1.1.

Alternative indicators of growth rates, 1950-62:
percentage annual average compound trend rates (constant prices)

	GNP	GNP per head of population	GNP per head of employed labour force
Austria	6.0	5.8	4.9
Belgium	2.8	2.2	2.5
Canada	3.6	0.9	1.9
Denmark.	3.8	2.9	3.2
France	4.4	3.5	4.2
Germany.	7.2	6.2	5.1
Ireland	1.3	1.7	2.6
Italy	6.3	5.7	4.7
Netherlands	4.9	3.6	3.5
Norway	3.6	2.7	3.4
Portugal (1955-1965). . .	5.9	5.1	5.1
Sweden	3.7	3.1	3.2
United Kingdom . . .	2.6	2.1	2.0
USA	3.0	1.3	2.0

Source: Policies for Economic Growth, Paris, OECD, 1962; General Statistics and Manpower Statistics, 1950-1962; and appendix Table 1.1. Data for Portugal supplied by Portuguese research team.

[2] The lowest rate of growth in Britain since 1947 was in 1966; and the national income per head actually fell from 1920 to 1923; 1929 to 1932; 1940 to 1941; 1945 to 1947.
See Deane, P. and Cole, W. A., *British Economic Growth, 1688-1959.*

[3] The National Plan proposed a rise in investment from £5.8 b. in 1964 to £8.0 b. in 1970, and in building from £2.9 b. to £4.0 b., over the period 1964-1970.

the bulk of social service building since 1945 has fallen in the educational field. It is a matter of doubt as to whether this great rate of growth, which education has experienced, will continue in the future. If one looks at the 1965 National Plan, for example, it will be seen that the hospital building requirements are tremendous. It would seem likely that education would probably be stabilised at this present high level: some even predict a fall.[1]

Thus, within this total of building for the social services, which is likely to be at a substantial and growing rate, it may be prudent to assume that one will see a more moderate rate of growth in educational building than has been customary in the late 1940s, the 1950s and the 1960s. But this rate of outlay is still likely to grow.

The next problem is concerned with the likely trends in the development of the structure of education. How will the building be divided up between primary, secondary and higher education? It is known that the number of pupils will grow, both because the age cohorts now coming in to the primary schools are on average bigger than those at the higher end of the secondary school, and above all because of the sustained increase in the rate of enrolment in secondary education and higher education, beyond the compulsory leaving age. This increase is, of course, due to a complex interaction of various social and economic factors, and it may be accelerated or slowed down by the comprehensive reorganisation of secondary schools, and by the eventual raising of the school leaving age; but in general the evidence, both from this country and from elsewhere, is sufficient to suggest that there is likely to be a fairly steady increase of the order of $1\frac{1}{2}\%$ of each age cohort per year, for the forseeable future, enrolling in post-compulsory education.[2]

This inevitably means that by the late 1980s the English and Welsh education service will, in terms of numbers, resemble that of California at the present time. That is to say that there will be provision for nursery education for three- and four-year-olds; that most young people will go to school at the age of 5 or 6; they will stay at school until 17 or 18, and a high proportion, perhaps as many

[1] At constant prices, it was suggested in Beckerman, W. and associates, *op. cit.*, that current outlays on education by public authorities would rise from £799 m. in 1960 to £1,593 m. in 1975, and investment from £147 m. to £289 m. Thereafter, it was implied, investment would probably fall off.

[2] The Beckerman figures (*op. cit.*) by Knight and Vaizey are as follows:

(000)

	Students and pupils (United Kingdom)		
	1960	1975	1986*
Under 5	235	616 ⎱	
Age 5	756	1,060 ⎬	5,717
All other primary	4,241	5,375 ⎰	
Secondary, under 15 . . ⎱		3,407 ⎱	
15 and over . . . . ⎰	3,575	1,587 ⎰	4,497
Further education	325	650	
Higher education	176	515	

* *Ninth Report of the National Advisory Council on the Training and Supply of Teachers*, 1965, Table 5.

as two-fifths, or even more, will stay on into some form of further and higher education; of these a third or more will probably go on to graduate work. This means that the bulk of the new building for extra pupils will probably be for the higher age groups, or for nursery schools; apart from that which is for replacement of out-of-date buildings, or for families that have moved to new housing developments.[1]

Thus the likely weight of work for new buildings will be for pupils and students in the age groups 16 and above and, especially, in the most rapidly expanding part of the education system, further education (including the polytechnics).

Now, as to the *nature* of educational building, a common factor in all the discussion that is taking place about secondary and higher education enables one obvious conclusion to be drawn. It would be widely agreed that the emphasis in the reform of the educational structure is on the desirability for flexibility within the system, so that pupils can move easily from one kind of course to another kind of course. Further, the relationship of individual schools and colleges implies a system in the sociological sense, a system within which the relative standing and place of individual institutions may well change fairly frequently. The sort of thing in mind is a speeding up of the process by which a secondary school may become a technical college, and then a university, and then a specialised institute—all in the space of two generations.

There has been a pronounced attack upon the autonomy of the individual school, college or university in the last twenty years, and it may be thought that there will be a movement away from the notion that an institution, once established, will remain the same for ever, or—at least—for a very long time.[2] Of course, it is much easier to talk about flexibility than to work out in detail the arrangements which are necessary to ensure that there *is* flexibility; and if one may put it negatively rather than positively, it is extremely improbable that any institution in secondary education or in higher education, which is currently in operation, will remain substantially unaltered in its scope and function over the next twenty years. What does "purpose-built" mean in this context? That seems to be a major question.

But there are other and even more important changes taking place in education—changes which again, like the structural changes, have managerial and architectural consequences. The content of education, the subjects that are taught, the curriculum generally, is in a state of ferment.[3] Increasingly, there

---

[1] The relative growth over the period 1960-1975 is:

a quarter for the child population of primary age;
more than double for nursery places;
a stable secondary population under 15;
a tripling of the post-15 places;
a doubling of further education;
a tripling of higher education.

This is in terms of student numbers. The standards may rise or fall. The 1975 targets will not be achieved, but by 1980 they probably will be. (Beckerman, W. and associates, *op. cit.*).

[2] See Vaizey, J., *Education for Tomorrow*, 5th edn. 1969.

[3] The leading body in this field in England and Wales is, of course, the Schools Council whose successive Reports are cumulatively affecting opinion.

are arrangements for looking at the curriculum as a whole and for proposing changes in the curriculum at all levels. Changes are being introduced at an increasingly rapid rate. One thinks, for example, of the proposals for the reform of the sixth form curriculum; one is aware of large proposals for the reform of the whole secondary curriculum inside the comprehensive school. Increasingly, the impact of the new universities on the older universities has led to the adoption of new kinds of joint honours courses. There is a radical re-structuring of technical education going on, under the auspices of CNAA and the training boards which have been set up under the Industrial Training Act. Less talked about, but even more remarkable are the changes that are going on in the teacher-training field.

These changes, even more than the structural changes, mean that the whole development of specialist teaching accommodation in all fields of education is in grave danger of being made redundant before it leaves the drawing board. It may well be, for example, that a subject which hitherto has loomed very large in the curriculum, at a particular level of education, may virtually die out, and be replaced by another. This is probably going to be the case with Latin, and perhaps traditional chemistry, in the academic secondary school. On the other hand, other subjects, either not very much taught at present, or not taught at all—one thinks of Sociology and Russian—may come in quickly. In the primary school, clearly, there will be an increase in mathematics and modern language teaching. The architectural implications of these changes in the curriculum seem again to point in the direction of flexibility and the need to face up to frequent change.

The administrative consequences of curriculum reform are equally impressive, because what one needs is a continual mechanism for keeping the curriculum under review, and for ensuring that the right kinds of teaching are available at the right stages in a pupils' development. Hitherto, the curriculum has been designed because certain teachers were available, who taught certain stated subjects, largely for certain pre-determined examination objectives. In future people will first tend to define the pedagogic objectives, then find the teachers, and then set the examinations. A radical re-structuring of the curriculum in this fashion carries with it radical implications for the overhaul of the administration of education.

This change is closely, symbiotically, related to a further development. It concerns the whole method of teaching.[1] In the primary schools, certainly in the infant schools, the revolution has broadly taken place.

Now the revolution in teaching will undoubtedly be much longer in coming than it was in medicine because, after all, the problems of curing illness are more susceptible to scientific investigation and to technical—that is to say pharmacological—intervention than education is; for one thing, so many of the aims of education are inchoate and extremely hard to specify. But, in so far as there are aims in education which can be formulated concisely and specifically attained—for example, that a child should be able to read a foreign language by a given age, or that a child should be able to read its own language at a given age—increasingly research and technological development is going to throw up

[1] See Vaizey, J., *The Economics of Education*, 2nd edn. 1963.

new ways of aiding the teacher in his or her work. Some of these ways we already know; television is perhaps the most obvious but possibly the least useful of them. There is the teaching machine, which makes use of programmed learning, which in turn is based upon a particular kind of psychology; there is computer-assisted learning, which reinforces in the way that the programme does, the learning process; there is the language laboratory; there are a whole series of these new developments, many of which are only faintly on the horizon at the moment.[1]

The school becomes a place where an individual child works at its own pace individually, helped by teachers. The child comes together with other children only when it is important for groups of children to be together because they have to learn to live and work as a group, or because it happens to be the easiest way to impart a particular kind of information, or to give them a common stimulus, or things of that kind. In other words, the emphasis within the school must be upon flexibility of lay-out; there will be a need for quiet places for teachers to work with individuals or small groups of children, there will be needs for large places where big groups can congregate; the school needs to be organised in such a way that children can move quickly, easily and quietly from one bit of it to another; the sign-posting must be good.

This conception of the flexibility of education is quite new. It means getting away from the system of classes, and groups, and moving more to the concept of the pupil whose needs are continually diagnosed, so that a whole battery of educational resources may be directed at him (to use an unfortunate metaphor). What is meant is a closely-monitored environment that will respond almost immediately to signs of growth, so that he can develop in freedom and security, without having to conform to somebody's notion of what a "typical" child of his age needs to do.

This idea of education, spelled out for the individual in quite specific terms, is utterly different from the formal educational structure of the past, where every child goes to school after his fifth birthday and must stay at school until the term after that in which he reaches his fifteenth birthday; a structure in which he "goes up" from class to class, automatically, year in year out, and proceeds from the primary to the secondary school at 11 (or under Plowden at the age of 12), and begins French at 8, and drops geography at 14, and so on. It is a movement towards a much more flexible system, in which children go to school when they need to go to school, and don't go to school when they don't need to go to school—very much the sort of approach the old-style "progressive" educationists adopted.

It is a concept of school that represents a way—perhaps the most hopeful way—of meeting the urgent social need to help children coming from deprived families and deprived social areas. Attempts to overcome deprivation seem to point towards such measures as earlier attendance at school for the more deprived children, and special treatment when they are there. This implies an intense individualisation of the educational process for the more deprived

---

[1] See Vaizey, J., *Education in the Modern World*, 2nd edn., 1969.

children. The message of the Newsom and Plowden Reports is precisely this, and it is also what has been found in the United States in the War on Poverty; to overcome deprivation, you have to devise individual treatment.[1]

Reflecting on all this, and thinking about education both in this country and elsewhere as it develops over the next twenty years, increasingly one sees the school as a resource centre. It is a place where teachers and other specialists are gathered together, where a library, not only a collection of books but a collection of tapes, films, video-tapes, is available; where there is a closed-circuit television. One thinks of the school as a workshop, where teachers develop specialised curricula, experiment with new teaching techniques, where they diagnose the needs of individual children—in other words a school increasingly becomes like a very good medical centre or hospital where a whole range of specialists is brought to bear upon the extraordinary diverse needs of individuals. And increasingly the division between different groups of children, whether by age, by ability, or by any other criterion, will become less relevant to their education precisely because education is becoming much more individualised. This will probably become one of the paradoxical consequences of the introduction of new technologies into the educational system.

If development along these lines does take place, and the local schools become far more an educational centre, what is the boundary between the school, on the one hand, and other community facilities on the other hand? To take an actual example, if a secondary school has a good library, it is often (not always but often) staffed by members of the local authority library service, and the books are interchanged on a loan scheme with the public library. Is there some advantage to be gained in siting a branch of the public library in the school, and allowing local people to make use of the school library? If the school has sports facilities (for example a swimming pool), is it not economical and sensible to make it available to the parents as well as to the pupils, to the apprentices at work as well as to the sixth-form pupils going on to do "A" level and on to the University? If the school has specialists in modern languages, as it does, and many of them teach in the evening at evening classes, is there anything to be said for making the language laboratories available at all hours of the day for whatever local people happen, at that time, to be taking modern languages? Where does the school end, and where does it begin?

Calculation of capital costs

In this section trends of cost per pupil-place and other aspects of capital unit-costs in various countries will be examined. The United Kingdom is used as a basis for the comparisons for two reasons: first because the amount of information available for other countries is nearly always far more limited; second, bacause certain cost-reducing techniques and planning procedures apply in the United Kingdom[2] which may be of more general interest.

---

[1] See the *Plowden Report, op. cit.,* and *Half our Future,* 1963.

[2] The actual figures quoted below will, however, apply to England and Wales unless otherwise stated.

Capital costs are related to building costs and to the rate of interest. Building costs are a function of policy decisions on standards, input prices and productivity in the construction industry. It is difficult to get a precise quantitative estimate of the influence of these variables on educational capital costs. In what follows a brief description of trends in the United Kingdom will be given.

First the interest rate, which will be taken for the purposes of this discussion as the yield on long-term government securities, has generally shown an upward trend during the past 25 years. This has been most notably the case in the 1948-52 period when there was a change of government and of monetary policy, and in the 1964-69 period. In the United Kingdom the rate has risen from approximately 2.5% to 9% in the post-war period (with many fluctuations around the trend). In many other countries the rate has not risen as much, notably in Portugal, where it was approximately 6% in 1969. However the upward trend is evident in almost all countries, and it has a significant effect on capital costs.

Secondly, building standards are important, when one takes into account the fact that decisions on surface area per pupil, number of pupil-places per class, provision of laboratories and all kinds of specialised rooms come under this heading. Decisions are also taken about construction methods in conjunction with standards. Thus the third influence, that of productivity in the building industry, is linked with the second. This is especially the case in the United Kingdom, where construction cost per place fell in the 1948-55 period despite a rise in material and labour costs. It is significant that this occurred when detailed planning of educational and constructional standards was introduced; a rapid rise in productivity was the result. Productivity also rose in other countries, but usually not enough to offset rising input prices.

The fourth influence, input prices, is mainly cost increasing. This is especially so with respect to labour inputs, and price indices for most other materials show a significant rise. For instance, cement prices in the United Kingdom rose by 58% between 1924 and 1950, and by 23.8% between 1954 and 1963.[1] In the earlier period the price rise was significantly less and in the latter period greater than for a selection of 28 manufacturing industry price changes. Also, prices of bricks rose even more; by 101% between 1924 and 1950 and 21.9% between 1954 and 1963.[2] In other countries it is likely that material prices also rose; it is certain, from statistics of wages and earnings, that the price of labour (which is an important item in the construction industry) rose. There has been a big rise in labour costs.

It seems likely that interest rates, labour and materials prices, and building standards were cost increasing in nearly all countries. Productivity increases offset this to some extent, but not usually enough to lower total construction costs—the significant exception is England and Wales for a period, as will be seen. Still less have *capital* costs been offset, as the rate of interest has in general

[1] Salter, W. E. G., *Productivity and Technical Change*, 2nd edn., Cambridge, 1966, pp. 107 and 197.
[2] Salter, W. E. G., *loc. cit.* The sample of 28 manufacturing industries, while not randomly chosen, was found to be reliable. (*Op. cit.*, Appendix B).

risen sharply. In all of what follows, building or construction costs must be distinguished from capital costs—the latter is an annual figure which represents amortisation payments or costs over a certain period at a certain rate of interest, and is thus comparable with current costs. The former is a lump-sum figure—or is paid over two or three years—and is not directly comparable with recurrent costs.

In calculating capital costs the following procedure is used. Estimates of building cost per pupil place are first obtained for the year for which unit costs (both current and capital) are being estimated. This is then expressed as an annual sum by using a procedure similar to that adopted by United Kingdom local education authorities. The life of buildings is assumed to be 60 years, and the appropriate discount rate $(x\%)$ is taken as approximating to the current or recent yield on long-term government securities. Capital cost is thus the annual sum of interest and principal necessary for a loan equal to the total building cost, over a period of 60 years at $x\%$.[1]

Such a calculation of capital costs—on what is in effect a replacement-cost basis—gives a capital cost total which is greater than that given by other methods. Historic cost measurements are generally much lower, because of the secular increase in costs, and because of the writing-off of some old buildings (in the present case those greater than 60 years), which have zero capital costs. Also the use of education authority or government loan charges (i.e. interest payments) for capital cost calculations are lower, for similar reasons. Historic costs are equivalent, in a sense, to average capital costs for the educational system: they represent weighted average capital charges on a capital stock of various vintages. What then is the justification of using a replacement cost figure which is higher than the usual average measurements—especially as the current unit cost figures are averages?

Principally, this procedure is justified because past capital costs are sunk costs, irrelevant to current decision-making. In this sense they are analogous to rents. What is relevant is the present cost of educating pupils and providing places, i.e. corresponding to the marginal cost. In the case of current costs, increased enrolments or participation will mean expenditure on teachers, materials and other items which correspond closely to present overall *average* expenditures (subject perhaps to short-term restrictions on teacher supply and hence decreased marginal cost if the increase in enrolment is unforeseen). All in all, current educational costs are fairly similar, whether average or marginal. Not so with capital costs, which provide a link between the past and present, as Keynes has pointed out, and which being past are beyond the influence of the present. Similarly, when looking ahead it is only necessary to consider the long term rate of interest *at the time when buildings are being built and financed.* Any subsequent variations in the interest or discount rate (i.e. during the 60 years assumed lifetime of the building), are also irrelevant, as costs are sunk and beyond any influence. Thus for statistics of capital costs to have operational

---

[1] This procedure is similar to that used in a detailed cost study of English secondary schools, *A Report on Unit Costs in Secondary Schools*, by Keith Norris and John Vaizey (London, Acton Society Trust, 1969).

significance, replacement cost calculations are appropriate as they approximate more closely to marginal costs than other measurements.

For the years studied here, 1955, 1960, 1965 and 1967, the rates of discount used will be 5%, 5.5%, 6.5% and 6.5% respectively for the United Kingdom, figures which approximate to the long-term rate of interest in those years. It is not possible to go beyond such approximations, as the cost limits applying to school buildings listed for these years may apply to buildings actually financed within a year or so of the date given. Where possible unusual fluctuations in the rate of interest were allowed for. It is not intended here to enter into the controversy concerning the social discount rate, which should properly be applied in this case.[1] The yield of long-term government bonds, while not an ideal measure in theory, is the best practical one and commands a fairly wide understanding and consensus.[2]

In the tables below, a 3.5% discount rate will be used for Portugal in 1955, 1960, 1965 and 1967. For Ireland the rates are 4%, 4.5%, 6% and 6.5% respectively. The calculations are in terms of current prices throughout. This is because constant price figures would properly deflate both interest rates and building costs to base year prices—or rates. They would not be fully compatible with a similarly deflated current expenditure series. On the other hand, if deflation to a constant price series did not take account of interest rate changes, the term "constant prices" would be misleading and the series would have little relevance or meaning. Consequently comparisons are best made in current prices throughout, with emphasis on the *proportion* of total annual costs per student accounted for by capital and various current items.

Table 20.1 shows that the share of capital costs in total costs declined in Portuguese primary education, and in British primary and secondary education. However, it rose slightly for Irish primary education. Table 20.2 suggests an explanation for these trends, when the price indices of current and capital expenditure are compared. Generally, the current expenditure index rose relatively to the capital index (taking 1955 as 100 the current index for Portugal was 145 and the capital index 85; for British primary education the indices were 171 and 159 respectively, and for British secondary education 178 and 162). The exception, Ireland, had fairly similar price rises for current and capital items (1955 = 100; 1965 = 177 for current and 172 for capital items). Thus it appears that declining relative prices were responsible for the declining share of capital in total unit costs in Portugal and Britain. Where relative prices were almost constant, the capital share showed a slight rise. Of course when *building* costs are compared with current costs, very large divergences in relative prices are

[1] This subject has been dealt with by W. J. Baumol, who clarifies much of the confusion which has arisen. See On the social rate of discount, *American Economic Review*, Vol. LVIII, September 1968.

[2] As Prest and Turvey (Cost benefit analysis: a survey, *Economic Journal*, Vol. LXXV, December, 1965) remark, the issue is one both of pure theory (mainly interest-rate theory) and of practice (what are the imperfections of the capital market?). The questions of risk, externalities and the effects of taxation also complicate matters. They conclude that "whatever one does, one is trying to unscramble an omelette, and no one has invented a uniquely superior way of doing this". In practice, there has been a tendency to take the long-term interest rate on government debt (i.e. the cost of borrowing to the government) and leave it at that.

TABLE 20.1 *Capital costs in relation to total unit costs: Portugal, Ireland, England and Wales* (U.S. dollars at current prices)

		Teachers	Other current	Capital	Total	Capital as % of total
			Costs per pupil			
1955	Portugal (Primary) . . .	11.42	2.05	5.91	19.38	30.52
	Ireland (Primary) * . .	56.03	7.07	15.22	78.32	19.43
	England and Wales (Primary) .	69.44	30.04	29.07	128.95	22.55
	England and Wales (Secondary)	108.63	64.84	50.53	224.00	22.56
1960	Portugal (Primary) . . .	21.77	3.07	4.48	29.32	15.27
	Ireland (Primary)* . .	68.44	8.76	18.48	95.68	19.31
	England and Wales (Primary) .	101.80	51.58	32.23	186.61	17.81
	England and Wales (Secondary)	155.05	88.20	59.48	302.73	19.65
1965	Portugal (Primary) . . .	25.06	3.51	5.27	33.84	15.59
	Ireland (Primary)* . .	92.00	11.16	26.02	129.18	20.14
	England and Wales (Primary) .	129.97	61.84	43.14	234.95	18.36
	England and Wales (Secondary)	222.48	125.26	76.75	424.49	18.08
1967	Portugal (Primary) . . .	...	...	...	...	...
	Ireland (Primary)* . .	...	...	...	...	...
	England and Wales (Primary) .	152.94	75.54	44.62	273.10	16.34
	England and Wales (Secondary)	268.41	154.04	81.22	503.67	16.13

* Capital costs for Ireland were estimated as follows: exisiting cost data was for the 1957-1962 period. This was taken to represent 1960 costs. In the other years an estimate was made, allowing for a unit cost increase of 2% per annum. No direct estimates of unit building or capital costs could be found at the time.

Sources: Investment in Education (*op. cit.*), Part II, pp. 256-58. Also, *Statistics of Education*, 1967, Vols. 1 and 5. Additional information for Portugal supplied by the Portuguese team and from *Contas do Ano Económico de 1966*, Lisbon, Junta do Crédito Público, 1968, and *Anuário Estatistico*, Lisbon, 1967, I.N.E., 1968.

Note: Capital costs throughout are calculated on an assumed life of buildings of 60 years.

TABLE 20.2 *Price indices of building and capital and current unit costs: Portugal, Ireland, England and Wales*

	Portugal			Ireland			England and Wales					
							Primary			Secondary		
	Build-ing	Capi-tal	Cur-rent	Build-ing	Capi-tal	Cur-rent	Build-ing	Capi-tal	Cur-rent	Build-ing	Capi-tal	Cur-rent
1955	100.00	100.00	100.00	100.00	100.00	100.00	100.00	100.00	100.00	100.00	100.00	100.00
1960	71.63	71.63	149.53	110.63	121.38	120.00	105.40	113.93	131.66	108.54	117.32	135.90
1965	85.12	85.12	145.12	122.13	170.96	177.27	125.95	158.55	170.71	128.94	162.30	178.17
1967	...	...	...	...	...	...	130.29	164.01	192.25	136.45	171.76	201.40

Sources: As in Table 20.1.

Note: These indices are explained more fully in the text. The building-cost index (and the capital cost index which is derived from it) does not allow for quality change, as it is based simply on cost per pupil-place. An index based on cost per square metre might come closer to the ideal—but quality change is properly measured in more dimensions than area. The current cost indices do allow somewhat for quality change. They are not simply indices of current (money) costs per student. They are the implicit price indices used to convert current money expenditures to current real expenditures, i.e. weighted indices of the prices of various current inputs.

found in all cases. The tendency is for building costs to show large relative declines. This is partially offset by interest rate increases, so that capital costs show, in general, a much smaller relative decline. The exception is Portugal where interest rates were maintained at a low level by Government financial policy, thus maintaining capital costs in education at a low level, and accounting for a substantial decrease in the share of capital as a proportion of total unit costs (from 30.52 % in 1955 to 15.59 % in 1965). Almost all of this decline occurred in the 1955-60 period when the price index for current costs rose from 100 to 150, and the capital cost index fell from 100 to 72. In the 1960-65 period, capital costs rose and the price index of current costs fell slightly, so that the share of capital in total unit costs was almost constant.

In general it seems that capital costs are between 15 % and 20 % of total unit costs, and that the rate of interest has an important influence on fluctuations in this proportion. One would expect general inflationary pressures, whether cost or demand-determined, to have some common influence on current and capital costs, and thus not to vary the proportion markedly. The rate of interest may fluctuate independently of these pressures to an extent, although it is also true to say that high interest rates and inflation have been associated in the past twenty years. Another source of fluctuation is the trend of productivity in construction, as it appears that these are certain times (e.g. Portugal in the 1955-60 period) when productivity can rise rapidly.[1] Such increases are usually over a limited period and appear to be due to innovation and reorganisation in the construction industry. Similar trends are not evident in current costs because of the nature of the educational process which makes "productivity" an elusive concept, usually subject to gradual long-term changes arising out of educational method, and to a limited degree the increasing use of educational aids. In building the scope for mechanisation and the incorporation of new techniques is more evident.

The share of capital cost is, of course, ultimately dictated by standards of building and standards of education, which determine current costs. Therefore it is difficult to state any precise general conclusion on the magnitude of this share. But because of the interest rate changes and productivity trends discussed, there is obviously scope for considerable fluctuations in capital costs (more so than current costs, almost certainly) and therefore in the proportion of total costs accounted for by capital.

---

[1] Another example is in England and Wales during the 1948-55 period when there was a rapid increase due to reorganisation of the educational building industry, leading to an absolute decline in building costs, despite inflation of input prices. This is analysed further in *The Costs of Education, op. cit.*

I

PART SIX

Teachers

The remaining Part is about the supply and demand for teachers. Teachers' salaries are the biggest item in educational costs and therefore this study has importance from that point of view. But the whole question of how teachers' salaries are settled is relevant to a broad issue which has been much discussed. This is the issue referred to above, as to how salaries are settled in that part of the economy, largely publicly owned, in which most well-educated people are employed.

21 Teachers and their salaries

In this chapter the remuneration of teachers in six Western European countries is described. They are Austria, Denmark, England and Wales, Ireland, Portugal, and Sweden. To avoid giving a mass of figures, data for each country are given for the more important salary grades but even so it is often difficult to give a clear picture of teachers' salaries. The multiplicity of grades and variations according to age, sex, seniority, region and type of school make it impossible to write in terms of the average teacher. Particular attention is given to differential payments to teachers. At the end of this chapter an attempt is made to place teachers' salaries in the context of incomes in general in each country: also, where possible, descriptive comparisons are made in the section dealing with each country: these only refer to male teachers. Because the situation *within* each country is considered and the aim is not to make financial comparisons *between* countries—although some obvious conclusions do emerge— the financial data have simply been converted to a common currency, sterling, at official exchange rates ruling at the time to which the data refer, August, 1967. The more sophisticated methods of conversion, described earlier, have not been used.

The salary structure in six countries

In *Austria*, teachers are civil servants and their salaries are fixed with respect to those in the rest of the civil service: they are paid 5-6% more than the lowest paid civil servant with the same educational background, the extra 5-6% being paid to offset the lack of promotion opportunities. There are five salary scales: in each there are 17 incremental points spread over 34 years' service.

TABLE 21.1 *Teachers' salaries: Austria, 1967*

	£
Female handicraft	467-940
General primary	568-1,293
Upper primary and special school .	593-1,510
Compulsory vocational . .	624-1,540
Secondary general and vocational .	739-1,978

There are no subject differentials and the only additional payment to the above scales is through overtime. By law, teachers can be required to teach up to 7 hours a week more than the normal teaching load: they are paid 6% of their weekly salary for every hour, whereas the monetary value in terms of basic salary of an extra hour is between 4 and $5\frac{1}{2}\%$ of salary payments to general compulsory teachers, and 8% in the case of general secondary teachers are for overtime: thus it can be seen that in these grades about 1-$1\frac{1}{2}$ hours a week overtime is the average.

Promotion prospects are poor:[1] a teacher cannot move out of a salary scale into a higher one without taking examinations to obtain the necessary qualifications. Hence upward mobility is restricted. The only real career prospect is to become a headmaster:[2] 11.7% of all posts are headmasterships, although about a third of these are in one or two teacher schools, often in remote regions; if these are excluded, then the proportion of headmaster posts is reduced to about 7%.

As in other countries, it is difficult to give hard and fast comparisons with other salaries. Generally, the situation seems to be that at the top of the scale salaries are not uncompetitive with industry, but that younger teachers are paid badly. For example, a graduate on entering a firm would be paid about £1,286 which is at least £535 more than he would receive in teaching. This non-competitiveness obtains despite the recent narrowing of the difference between the top and bottom of the teacher salary scales.

In *Denmark* it is necessary to distinguish between folkeskole and gymnasium teachers: the latter are graduates, the former have only teacher training.

Folkskole teachers are civil servants: their salary scales differ regionally; there are three scales: (1) urban type schools outside Copenhagen municipality; (2) rural type schools outside Copenhagen municipality; (3) schools in Copenhagen municipality.

Teachers in the first two groups of schools are paid roughly equally—although promotion prospects are better in group (1)—but pay in Copenhagen schools is about 10% greater. The figures below, for four important grades of folkeskole teacher, are for group (2).

TABLE 21.2 *Teachers' salaries: Danish folkeskole, 1967*

Grade	Salary	Length of scale: years
School principal	£2,088-2,466	9
Senior teacher	1,762-1,960	6†
Assistant teachers*	1,191-1,573	12
Infant class teachers	1,081-1,332	14

* The position of senior teacher assumes 15 years previous service.
† Excluding infant class teachers.

Gymnasium teachers can either elect to be civil servants or can hold contract appointments. The latter are more highly paid but have less security: increasing numbers are opting for contract appointments and thus most civil servants are of some seniority.

In both types of schools, overtime working occurs. In folkeskole the standard

---

[1] *Study on the Demand for and Supply of Teachers: Austria*, OECD, Paris, 1969.
[2] i.e. Director.

TABLE 21.3 *Teachers' salaries: Danish gymnasia, 1967*

Grade	Salary	Length of scale: years
Adjunkts. . . .	£1,367-1,949	12
Lektors	2,142-2,530	9
Super lektors . . .	2,804-2,963	—
Rektors	3,112-3,253	—
Contract teachers . .	1,582-3,150	25

Note; The position of lektor assumes 15 years' previous service.

teaching load is 32 hours per week. Any teaching in excess of this counts as overtime and is paid as such. In folkeskole, overtime is paid 20% more per hour than normal teaching. The incidence of overtime working is given in Table 21.4.

TABLE 21.4 *Percentage distribution of weekly hours worked in excess of standard load: Danish folkeskole, 1967*

	Men	Women
0	7.1	15.7
1–4	28.3	36.0
5–8	33.3	13.9
9–12	18.9	3.0
13–20	8.3	4.7

Source: Study on the Demand for and Supply of Teachers: Denmark, op. cit., p. 82.

Notes: a) Totals do not sum to 100, as some teachers worked less than standard load.

b) Figures refer to schools outside Copenhagen: in Copenhagen slightly more overtime is worked.

One point of interest is that men work more overtime than women. The average male qualified teacher works 7 hours a week overtime: the result is that his annual salary is 26% higher than indicated in Table 21.2.

In gymnasia, salaries bear even less relationship to the salary scales, due largely to overtime working and partly to the granting of "extra time" to some subjects and classes. To understand clearly the system of payment, it is necessary to explain how the total number of wage hours per week is calculated for each teacher. For each class the teacher takes, his weekly wage hours are calculated as follows: there are three components. First, the number of hours he taught the class. To this is added "extra time": this is allowed for certain subjects, for example physics, and for certain grades. Thus, for example, 8 hours spent teaching 3rd gymnasium classes counts as 9 wage hours. Finally, time is granted for homework correction: this is normally 9 minutes per pupil per week. Thus total wage hours for each class equals hours taught plus extra time plus homework correction time. This calculation is carried out for each class taught and hence the teacher's total weekly wage hours are derived. The standard week is 24 hours:[1] any wage hours in excess of this are paid at overtime rates. Overtime

[1] With reductions for seniority.

working occurs on a large scale: male teachers work on average 11.5 hours a week overtime, and female teachers 5.5 hours a week. The salary implications are best illustrated by considering a first year male contract teacher working the average 11.5 hours overtime. The effect is to increase his annual salary from the £1,582 given in Table 8.3 to £2,861: overtime thus accounts for nearly 45% of his salary.

Earnings are thus closely related to work done. It is not surprising that the provision of promotion posts is not considered to be important. Posts of principal in folkeskole, for example, comprise only 3.2% of all teacher posts in such schools and the number of more lucrative posts in municipal schools will decline as the average size of school increases.

The opportunities for overtime earnings make it difficult to compare teacher earnings with other earnings. Thus a graduate entering a gymnasium earns (according to the salary scale) 13% less than a graduate entering the civil service. But clearly if he works an average amount of overtime, bringing his hours worked per week to $35\frac{1}{2}$, then the teacher is considerably better off. Earnings in gymnasia must be considered competitive, at least with those ruling in the civil service.

In *England and Wales* alone of the countries considered, the same salary scale applies in all maintained schools. Salaries are fixed by negotiation between the management—representatives of local authorities—and teachers' unions. The single unified salary scale was, in 1967, from £800 to £1,500, with fourteen annual incremental points. Payment above the basic scale is made (1) for above minimum qualifications. Graduates with less than a second class honours degree receive an extra £100 a year, and those with second or first class degrees receive £220 over the basic scale. For certain types of training, notably graduates who have teacher training, £50 a year is paid; (2) to holders of posts of responsibility or heads of department. These payments vary from £125 to £700 a year: the distribution of these posts is heavily biased towards the bottom of this range.

Head teachers were paid up to £4,110, their salaries being based on size of school.[1] There is no subject differential and as the teaching load is not defined, there is no overtime working. Teachers in London receive £70 cost of living allowance.

Promotion possibilities must be considered quite good, although they vary considerably according to sex, qualifications and type of school. England and Wales provides data which also serves to illustrate a point that will be discussed subsequently: that even where there are few explicit differentials (say between men and women) in salary scales, the system operates to provide them. Table 21.5 gives the percentage of male and female, and graduates and non-graduates holding certain status in primary and secondary schools. Non-qualified teachers[2] are excluded throughout.

---

[1] In a small sample of secondary schools, average salaries of headmasters were found to be £2,868. Norris, K. and Vaizey, J., *A Report on Unit Costs in Secondary Schools*, Acton Society Trust, 1969 (mimeographed). As primary schools are smaller, salaries there are considerably lower.

[2] Non-qualified teachers comprised 2.2% of the teaching force.

TABLE 21.5 *Percentage distribution of teachers of various grades: England and Wales, 1967*

	Primary schools		Secondary schools		All schools	
	Graduates	Non-graduates	Graduates	Non-graduates	Graduates	Non-graduates
Men						
Head teachers	36.3	32.9	8.8	2.7	10.8	14.5
Responsibility posts	21.9	32.0	72.2	65.1	68.5	52.1
Assistant teachers	41.8	35.1	19.0	32.2	20.7	33.4
Total	100.0 (2,836)	100.0 (34,054)	100.0 (35,068)	100.0 (53,314)	100.0 (37,904)	100.0 (87,368)
Women						
Head teachers	9.1	10.7	4.0	1.5	4.8	7.9
Responsibility posts	11.0	17.2	60.6	47.1	52.8	26.3
Assistant teachers	79.9	72.1	35.4	51.4	42.4	65.8
Total	100.0 (3,500)	100.0 (98,633)	100.0 (18,717)	100.0 (42,620)	100.0 (22,217)	100.0 (141,253)

Source: Statistics of Education, 1967, Vol. 4, *op. cit.*, p. 46.

Note: Responsibility posts include deputy head teachers, heads of departments, and holders of graded posts.

The average salaries that arise as a result are shown in Table 21.6:

TABLE 21.6 *Average salaries of teachers: England and Wales, 1967*

		Primary schools	Secondary schools
Men	Graduates. . .	£1,647	£1,778
	Non-graduates . .	1,501	1,399
Women	Graduates. . .	1,375	1,615
	Non-graduates . .	1,249	1,239
	Graduates. . .	1,497	1,721
Men and women	Non-graduates . .	1,314	1,328
	All teachers . .	1,322	1,469

Source: Statistics of Education, 1967, Vol. 4, op. cit., pp. 56-7.

From Table 21.5 it can be seen that, for men, the chances of promotion, that is of holding a post of responsibility or of becoming a head teacher, are good. Only 20.7% of male graduates, and 33.4% of male non-graduates, received no payment above the basic scale. Women have a much worse chance of promotion. The major reason for this is that administrative responsibilities tend to be assumed by those working between the ages of twenty-five and thirty-five: yet this is when a high proportion of married women leave (temporarily) to have children. The result is that although men and women have identical salary scales, women earn less than men. This is shown by Table 21.6, where in every case male earnings are greater.

Most graduates (93.9% of male graduates and 84.2% of female) teach in secondary schools. In secondary schools their chances of promotion are much greater than that of non-graduates (see Table 21.5) but this is not the case in primary schools. To demonstrate the effect on their earnings in secondary schools, it is necessary to separate the differences between graduate and non-graduate earnings into two parts: that which is due to payments for qualifications and that due to them having better promotion prospects. Using data showing the distribution of good honours graduates who receive £220 a year for their degree, and other graduates who receive £100, and using data of the proportion of graduates who receive payment for teacher training, this separation is presented in Table 21.7.

TABLE 21.7 *Graduate differentials in England and Wales:*
secondary schools, 1967

	Men	Women
Total differential	£379	£376
Qualification differential . .	204	206
Promotion differential . . .	175	170

Source: Statistics of Education, 1967, Vol. 4, op. cit.

Thus nearly a half of the excess of graduate over non-graduate earnings are due to their better chances of attaining a headmastership or a post of responsibility.[1] In this case, then, although there is an explicit gradaute differential, the ruling differentials are considerably in excess of this.

A male graduate entering teaching receives a salary roughly equal to those ruling in the civil service and the private sector, but his very low annual increments mean that his salary becomes increasingly uncompetitive. For non-graduates comparisons are more difficult to make, but the maximum of the scale appears rather low.

Salary scales in *Ireland* in 1967 were exceptional in two respects. There was a separate scale for married men (cf. the scale for unmarried men and for women), and secondly not all salaries were paid out of public funds. In secondary schools the state laid down an incremental salary scale, but schools were obliged to make payments in excess of this out of their own funds of between £300 and £400. This is an important element in the total salary of lay secondary teachers.[2] The average salary of a secondary teacher was £1,280, 24% of which came out of school funds.

There were six incremental salary scales:

1. National (primary) teachers:

married men . . . . . . £822-1,542 (17 increments)
women and single men . . . . £659-1,229 (17 ")

Additional payments of between £24 and £124 were made for degree qualifications.

2. Secondary teachers:
married men . . . . . . £692-1,403 (16 increments)
women and single men . . . . £522-1,070 (15 ")

Secondary teachers were also paid a "basic" salary of £300-£400 depending on years of service and a payment of £110 was made to those possessing an honours degree.

3. Vocational teachers:

married men . . . . . . £942-1,610 (16 increments)
women and single men . . . . £754-1,285 (15 ")

Additional payments to vocational teachers took the form of "Special Class Allowances" of either £280 or £475.

The resulting average salaries were as follows:

National teachers £1,140
Secondary teachers £1,280
Vocational teachers £1,160

Although there is no explicit subject differential in secondary schools, the

[1] This could be explained through age, but the age distribution of graduate teachers is not markedly different from that of non-graduates; graduates tend, in fact, to be slightly younger.

[2] Religious teachers are omitted from this analysis as they are, in effect, outside the labour market. Most salary payments accrue not to the individual but to the religious community of which he is a member.

extra payments out of school funds enable schools to offer more to (say) scarce science teachers than to others. Thus the allocation of these payments to some extent reflects market forces.

The graduate differential in the scales is small. Promotion prospects are poor: many head teacher posts are in very small rural schools and in secondary schools the more senior posts often go to religious, rather than lay, teachers. Salaries are generally considered to be non-competitive: teachers were paid less than those with equivalent qualifications who were employed in the rest of the public sector.

In *Portugal* the private sector is much larger than in the other five countries. This is particularly true in academic and general secondary education, where about 50% of enrolments are in private schools. The percentage of unqualified teachers is also significantly higher than in the others, in Portugal, although this proportion has declined in recent years. However, in this description and in the subsequent comparisons, only qualified teachers in the public sector are considered. Salary scales are shown in Table 21.8.

TABLE 21.8 *Teachers' salaries in Portugal: 1967*

		Salary range	Increments
Primary	Probationary teachers . . .	£233	none
	Regular teachers	322-442	3
Secondary:	Teachers under contract . .	525-652	2
Lyceum*	Auxiliary and probationary teachers	724	none
	Regular teachers	815-1,177	2
Secondary:	Teachers under contract and *adjuntos*	525-652	2
Technical	Auxiliary teachers . . .	525-725	none
schools	Regular teachers	814-1,177	2

* Academic and general schools.

Increments are received at 10 year intervals. The primary teacher begins his career as a probationary teacher, in which position he remains for at least one year. During this period his holidays are unpaid and so, at the most, he is earning for $9\frac{1}{2}$ months per year.[1] The time he remains in this position does not count towards any increment. It is only taken into consideration when probationary candidates are to be chosen for promotion to the higher category. In the selection of the people who pass to the regular teacher scale, priority conditions, e.g. marital status, are established. Because of the shortage of teachers, earnings are often greater than indicated by the salary scales. Thus the average earnings of primary teachers in 1967 were £366.

In secondary schools regular staff have a degree, two years of post-graduate work and a teachers' training certificate. Teachers under contract and *adjuntos* only teach certain subjects such as singing, domestic science, and various other practical subjects. Auxiliary teachers are those waiting for a vacancy on the

[1] This has been allowed for in Table 21.8.

establishment of regular teachers. Heads and deputy heads of schools receive additional annual payments of between £12 and £30.

The earnings of teachers are compared with the earnings of civil servants in Table 21.9.

TABLE 21.9 *Average annual earnings of teachers and civil servants in Portugal: 1967*

Primary teachers	£366
Secondary teachers	779
Civil servants: 1) with qualifications similar to those of primary teachers	557
2) with primary education only	257
3) with degrees	1,629

Teachers' earnings are significantly lower than those of civil servants with similar qualifications. The discrepancy is most marked in the case of those with a degree. Their average earnings in the civil service are over twice those in teaching. The discrepancy is, in fact, greater than this, as to be a secondary teacher it is necessary to have not only a degree but further academic qualifications. These differentials are not significantly different from those existing in 1950.

The salary situation in *Sweden* is complex: there are 31 salary grades, the more important of which are given below. The salaries are determined by negotiation between the government, represented by a special board, and teachers' unions.

Increments are usually received after 3, 6 and 9 years' teaching.[1] There are a number of posts receiving payment in excess of the above scales. About 14% of teachers are heads of departments and receive an extra payment of £166 or £207, and a further 10% of teachers receive other additions to their salary.[2] About 2½% of all teaching posts are headmasterships. There is some paid over-

TABLE 21.10 *Salaries in the more important teacher grades: Sweden, 1967*

PRIMARY	
Lower departmental	£1,586-1,866
Middle departmental.	1,866-2,194
Special teachers in middle department . . .	2,315-2,721
VOCATIONAL TEACHERS	2,078-2,445
SECONDARY: ACADEMICALLY TRAINED SPECIAL SUBJECT TEACHERS	
Senior master	3,199-3,759
Assistant master	2,721-3,376
HEADMASTERS: DIRECTORS OF STUDIES	3,606-4,881*

* There is more than one scale; the range is shown here.

Notes: Sweden is divided into three areas, between which salaries differ slightly. The middle class is given here.

[1] The assistant masters' scale is over 15 years.

[2] Many of these responsibility posts and head of department posts were created in 1964: hitherto promotion prospects were very poor.

time working: the standard teaching load varies according to type of school, being, for example, 30 hours a week in primary schools and rather less in secondary. Overtime is paid at the same rates as normal teaching.

Teachers' salaries seem to be comparable with those in the civil service: a senior master has the same salary as graduates in the third (usually final) promotion level, and headmasters of large schools earn the equivalent of divisional heads in the civil service. Earnings of other teachers are also comparable to those of civil servants with equivalent educational backgrounds. Salaries in the industrial sector are comparable for younger teachers, but at senior levels those in industry earn more than civil servants and teachers.

Teachers' incomes relative to all incomes

In this section an attempt is made to place teachers' salaries in the context of all other incomes, in each of the countries that have been considered. There are some conceptual and many practical problems involved in this exercise. The first of these is to decide on the average teacher.

Two comparisons were made, one for primary teachers and one for secondary. Where figures were available for the average salary of primary or secondary teachers, these were used. The weakness of this method is that it reflects not only the salary scale but the age distribution of the teaching force: against this it can be argued that the age distribution is not likely to change quickly over time—the tendency being, as education is an expanding industry, for the average age of teachers to decline slowly over time. The advantage of using average salaries is that it reflects the distribution and remuneration of posts of responsibility, head teachers, et cetera. In countries for which average teacher salaries were not available, estimates have been made: where information on the age structure of the teaching force was missing, mid-points on salary scales have been used. A further problem is whether to include overtime earnings: these arise in Austria, Denmark, and Sweden. An objection to its inclusion is that it is the result of teacher shortages, and its incidence will therefore disappear as the teacher supply position improves. However, to exclude overtime earnings in Danish gymnasia would be completely to misrepresent salaries, and in general overtime is voluntary. Thus, overtime earnings have been included. The figures are for male and female earnings: the basic scales are the same but allowance has to be made for men working more overtime, and tending to hold a larger proportion of incremental posts. The comparison is for men and women, but subsequently a separate comparison is made for each for England and Wales: the data prevent this comparison being made for the other countries. The basis of the figures given in Table 21.11 are explained beneath the table. The figures refer only to qualified teachers.

To indicate the level of teachers' salaries relative to those of others, some standard of comparison has to be selected. Ideally this would be the earnings in the rest of the public sector, and in the private sector, of those with equivalent qualifications to various grades of teacher, but this data is not generally available. The second best would be to compare teachers' salaries with all salaries, but

TABLE 21.11 *Average salaries of qualified teachers: 1967* (£)

	Primary	Secondary
Austria	£1,026	£1,477
Denmark . . .	1,734	3,512
England	1,322	1,469
Ireland	1,140	1,280
Portugal	366	779
Sweden	1,887	3,419

Notes:

Austria: primary: weighted average of mid-point of each primary scale (see Table 21.1) plus allowance for overtime, which accounts for 48% of salary.

secondary: mid-point of scale plus allowance for overtime (8%).

Denmark: primary: weighted average of mid-point of each of the four primary salary scales (see Table 21.2) plus allowance for overtime (and underload) working: overtime accounts for 9.4% of the salary.

secondary: weighted average of the five secondary scales (Table 21.3) plus allowance for the average hours overtime worked by male and female teachers. Overtime accounts for 31.2% of total earnings.

England: figures for average salaries from *Statistics of Education*, 1967, Vol. 4, *op. cit.*, pp. 56-7.

Ireland: figures for average salaries supplied by the Department of Education.

Portugal: figures for average salaries supplied by the Portuguese team.

Sweden: primary: weighted average of mid-points of lower and middle department scales. Overtime working is on a very small scale and is ignored.

secondary: weighted average of the three scales plus allowance for heads of department allowances and overtime. Overtime accounts for 6.3% of total salary.

again this data is not known for all countries, so the choice becomes between all earned incomes, all incomes, or income *per capita*. The first has been chosen: it is preferred to all incomes, as teachers in general come from those socio-economic groups without significant property holdings, but it should be remembered that their place in the total income scale will be lower than that in the earnings scale. The weakness of income *per capita* for purposes of comparison is that there are significant differences between countries in the proportion of the population that is working. In larger cross-section studies, income *per capita* is usually used, because of lack of other data, but in these six countries data on earnings is available. The comparison made is a crude one between the average teacher, as defined above, and average earned incomes in non-agricultural sectors: for Austria the earnings data exclude commerce, for Portugal it is manufacturing only, and for Sweden the data refer to manufacturing and mining and quarrying. The results are presented in Table 21.12.

These figures have to be interpreted with a great deal of caution, but some general points can be made. Because the income distribution curve in all countries is skewed, if teachers were placed on the curve, their position in relation to

TABLE 21.12 *Ratio of teachers' salaries to average earnings in non-agricultural sectors: 1967*

	Primary teachers	Secondary teachers
Austria . . .	1.4	2.1
Denmark. . .	1.3	2.7
England . . .	1.5	1.7
Ireland . . .	1.7	2.0
Portugal . . .	2.2	4.5
Sweden . . .	1.5	2.7

Sources: Teachers' salaries; see notes to Table 21.11.
Other earnings: *Year Book of Labour Statistics,* Geneva, 1967, International Labour Office, 1968.

median earnings would be higher than the ratios suggest. The skewness of the income distribution has also to be taken into account before it can be said, on the basis of these figures, that, for example, secondary teachers should be easier to recruit because of higher relative remuneration in (say) Denmark than in Austria. In Portugal, casual observation suggests a highly skewed income distribution, and this may partially explain the apparent paradox that although the ratios are higher for Portugal for both primary and secondary teachers than for any of the other countries, the teacher shortage is most acute there. That is, although teachers appear highly paid in relation to the average worker, in relation to qualified manpower teachers' relative salaries may not be as high as in the other countries. Added to this, of course, is the fact that the total pool of qualified manpower is very small, and the recent rapid expansion of the educational sector[1] has simply led to an absolute shortage of qualified manpower. Thus Portugal is omitted from the subsequent comparison.

The obvious point about the primary comparison is the uniformity between the five countries: the arithmetic average of the ratios is 1.5 with maximum deviations of only 0.2. From this the cautious suggestion is made that primary teachers occupy more or less the same place in the earned incomes scale in the five countries, and it would be expected that the magnitude of the recruiting problem might not be too dissimilar. This is supported by the fact that in all countries, the shortage of primary teachers is expected to be eliminated in the near future. Given that a high proportion of primary teachers are women, the ratios in Table 21.11 also understate the place of primary teachers in the income scale. For although women teachers earn less than men (although the basic scales are the same), the female earnings in the whole economy are less than those of men by a greater amount. Complete data are only available for England and Wales: the comparison is between female earnings in primary schools and average female earnings in non-agricultural sectors.[2] The resulting ratio is 2.0, as compared with 1.5 in Table 21.11.

The results for secondary teachers are less clear cut. The differences between

[1] Due partly to the current extension of compulsory schooling.
[2] To isolate the effect from differences in hours worked, the figure for female earnings was calculated on the assumption that females work the same number of hours as men.

countries are greater, varying from 2.7 to 1.7 (Portugal is again excluded from the comparison). Denmark, where teachers would appear to be comparatively well paid,[1] has the most acute shortage of secondary teachers: this, and the fact that the casual comparisons made in the text of the first section of this chapter suggested that teachers' salaries were competitive with those elsewhere for qualified manpower, also suggests that remuneration may be less important in teacher supply than would have been expected.

Differentials in teachers' salaries

In this section, other aspects of the remuneration of teachers in these countries are considered. Attention is largely paid to the existence or non-existence of differentials, both explicit and implicit. An explicit salary differential is one embodied in the salary scales, an implicit differential is one produced through allocation of incremental posts and of promotion. The difference is clearly brought out if the pay of men and women teachers is considered.

Equal pay for women obtains in the six countries surveyed, with the partial exception of Ireland, and in fact throughout Western Europe. Thus there is no explicit sex differential. However, women teachers do, in fact, earn less than men: see Table 21.6 for figures for England and Wales. There are several ways in which this implicit sex differential can come about. Women form a much larger part of the primary teaching force than of the secondary. Primary salary scales are lower than secondary salary scales, except in England, and thus the average earnings of women are lower. However, even within each type of school, women's salaries are lower. This is partly explained through differences in the amount of overtime worked: in each country where overtime is paid, women work fewer hours than men, thus reducing average earnings.[2] It can be objected that these differences in earnings are not, in the strictest sense, differentials and that the principal cause of the implicit differential is that many women leave teaching temporarily between the ages of 25 and 35, and therefore tend not to assume posts of responsibility. Hence men dominate these posts and have higher salaries. Figures for England are given in Table 21.5, where it is shown that the proportion of women remaining on the basic scale is about twice that for men. Experience in Denmark is the same: although 50% of all teachers are women, only 2.8% of school principals, 16.4% of deputy principals, and 1.5% of head teachers are women.[3] Implicit pay differentials against women are, of course, not confined to teaching: in occupations in England where equal rates of pay prevail, women's earnings are about three quarters that of men.

In only two of the countries were there subject differentials. In Ireland the extra payments made to teachers out of school funds are used, to some extent, to attract certain scarce categories of teacher. Figures are not available as to the size of the resulting differential, but it is not likely to be large. In Denmark,

---

[1] The salary includes a large proportion (31.2%) of overtime earnings, but because of the method by which the "standard" teaching load is calculated, actual hours worked are not significantly higher than in the other countries.

[2] See, for example, Table 21.4.

[3] *Study on the Demand for and Supply of Teachers: Denmark, op. cit.*

as part of the complex method of calculating the teachers' work load, it was seen that some subjects were granted "extra time" so that teaching in those subjects was more remunerative. However, here again the resulting differential in average earnings is not likely to be large. Implicit subject differentials occur in countries with no explicit differential, and accentuate explicit differentials where these are present. There are several reasons for this. Firstly, in subjects where teachers are (relatively) scarce, the opportunities for overtime will be greater. In Danish gymnasia teachers of chemistry, physics, and mathematics worked 44.5%, 40.4% and 35.3% respectively of their hours as overtime. This was more than teachers of any other subject, the average for all subjects being 27.1%. In Swedish secondary schools, mathematics and science teachers also worked more overtime than any other subject teachers (except Greek). Secondly, in subjects where there is a shortage of teachers, then promotion prospects are better and early on in their careers teachers have a very high chance of receiving payments above the basic scale. Finally, as schools strive to fill posts in such subjects, they are forced to accept teachers of low quality. Thus, even ignoring the previous factors mentioned, a teacher of any given quality will earn more in some subjects than in another. In fact, in subjects where teachers are relatively easy to recruit, teachers of a higher quality will be paid less.

Regional differences in salary scales are present in only one country (if the cost of living allowances paid to teachers in London and Copenhagen are excluded). In Sweden in an attempt to eliminate regional differences in teacher supply, "shortage posts" have been established: in these teachers are exempt from certain conditions, e.g. a teacher can be appointed to a permanent post even though he lacks the normally necessary two years' experience. The effect is thus to raise salaries in these regions.

Finally, there are primary/secondary and graduate/non-graduate differentials. In each of the countries surveyed, there is a graduate differential. In England and Wales, the graduate is given a payment for his degree, irrespective of the type of school he teaches in, whereas in the other countries it appears as a primary/secondary differential (which does not exist in England and Wales). Noting this exception, we discuss these two differentials together. The size of the differential can be seen by expressing average salaries of secondary teachers as a multiple of the average primary salary.

TABLE 21.13 *Secondary/primary salary ratios: 1967*

Austria	.	.	1.4
Denmark	.	.	2.0
England and Wales	.		1.1
Ireland	.	.	1.1
Portugal	.	.	2.1
Sweden	.	.	1.8

Notes: See notes to Table 21.9.

The ratio partly reflects differences in the training period necessary for primary and secondary teaching, and partly differences in overtime working: this latter influence is particularly strong in Denmark and to a lesser extent operates in Austria and Sweden. Over time, as educational requirements for primary teachers are upgraded, the tendency is for secondary/primary differentials to narrow.

A final factor of some importance in teachers' salary scales is the implied career structure of the profession. This is compounded of the rate of progression of the basic scale and the probability of receiving some payment over the scale and the size of such payments. It further depends on the earnings of those with equivalent qualifications outside the profession. More detailed statistics would be necessary to make substantive statements about this.

22 Estimation of the supply of and demand for teachers

WE have discussed various methods of projecting and forecasting the future growth of the educational system, in terms of enrolments. It was seen that in most countries estimates of future enrolments were normally derived from projections of the social demand for education, although in some cases manpower needs were taken into account. Assuming that the enrolment estimates are accepted as a basis for policy, those responsible for the future development of the educational system require the enrolment estimates to be translated into demands for educational inputs. They are thus in a position to identify, and correct, any shortage (excess) of supply of the inputs. Here only one type of input, teachers, will be considered. Further, as the training requirements of teachers in higher education are rarely specified rigorously, only school teachers are considered.

The methodology of teacher supply and demand forecasts will be described and two such forecasts, for Norway and England and Wales, will be examined in some detail.

Criteria for estimating the demand for teachers

To estimate the future demand for teachers the future school population must be converted into teacher requirements. Basically pupil/teacher ratios are applied to the forecasts of the school population by age group. The problem facing the forecaster is to calculate the pupil/teacher ratios which depend on a number of variables that are particularly subject to government action, e.g. maximum class size. As will be seen, the forecaster often has a choice for a given variable between the optimum value, the value embodied in (say) statutory requirements, the present value, or some combination of these. Often the impression is gained that forecasters look over their shoulders at the supply position before choosing the value of the demand variable to be used: thus a sort of constrained set of values emerges. The demand for teachers is not calculated independently of the supply.

The aim, then, is to derive pupil/teacher ratios (for each age group, or level of schooling) to apply to estimates of the future school population.[1] The following are some of the more important factors to be considered in the estimation of the ratios:

[1] To be useful, these have to be for ten or fifteen years hence and hence so do the pupil/teacher ratios.

1. *Class size.* In most countries there is some notion of the optimum size of class. This may be embodied in some quasi-legal requirement as, for example, in England and Wales where from 1944[1] until 1969 maximum class sizes in primary schools should not have exceeded 40, and in secondary schools 30, "except where circumstances do not permit . . .". The fact that this was never achieved, and latest indicators are that it will not be until the late 1970s, guards one against putting too much emphasis on legal requirements. Elsewhere, commissions on education have recommended maximum class sizes,[2] and everywhere social and pedagogic pressures are towards a reduction in class size. Despite some evidence, which seems to be questionable, that small classes are not more effective than large classes, the bulk of opinion among primary school teachers is that a class of forty is too big for the effective use of the pedagogic methods now considered desirable. The feeling in secondary schools is less clear-cut, due to their diversity, but in most countries a concensus emerges as to maximum desirable class size. In any event, in most forecasts class size plays a key role in assessing the demand for teachers. Recently there has, however, been some dissatisfaction with this method: ". . . we do not think that this represents the most satisfactory method of formulating the objective of staffing policy. The concept of classes of roughly equal size as the basic pattern of school organisation will increasingly have to be modified, as new methods and techniques of teaching come to require a more flexible organisation with scope for considerable variations in the size of teaching groups".[3] Notable among the relevant new methods is team teaching: the effect of the new techniques on class size has been discussed. Additionally, concern with the number of classes (which may be a small percentage of all classes) that are oversize[4] may obscure the average size of class. Also, concern with size of classes as registered may detract attention from the more important size of classes as taught.[5] However, clearly, size of class must remain of crucial importance in deriving pupil/teacher ratios, although flexibility in the interpretation of the term is desirable. It may be preferable, for example, to have teachers of high quality with large classes rather than small classes taught by poor teachers.

2. *Size of school.* Small schools are generally inefficient (in the purely technical sense) in their use of teachers. This can be demonstrated by reference to the following data for Ireland (Table 23.1):

Teaching cost per pupil in the small schools is, in most cases, significantly higher than the average for all schools. This cannot be explained by the slightly above average salaries that were earned in three out of the four classes of small school. The latter is simply a function of age and qualifications, whereas the higher teaching cost per pupil is a direct result of lower pupil/teacher ratios.

---

[1] 1944 Education Act (Regulations).

[2] In, for example, Norway.

[3] *The Demand for and Supply of Teachers, 1963-86* (Ninth Report of the National Advisory Council on The Training and Supply of Teachers), London, HMSO, 1965, p. 9. This will subsequently be referred to as the *Ninth Report*.

[4] However defined.

[5] These and other influences are considered more fully later, in the section on the forecasts for England and Wales.

K

TABLE 23.1 *Teaching cost per pupil in a sample of 595 national schools, by teacher size and centrality of school: Ireland, 1961-1962*

Centrality	School size (Number of teachers)						Average salary* per teacher
	1	2	3	4-6	7 and over	All schools	£
	Teaching cost per pupil (£)						£
Cities . . .	21	31	22	19	12	13	669
Large towns (1,500 and over)	51	27	20	16	14	15	659
Small towns . .	49	26	21	16	—	20	720
Villages . .	39	21	22	21	—	22	709
Rural . . .	34	27	23	20	—	26	688
Total . . .	37	26	22	18	12	17	679
Average salary per teacher (£) .	631	708	733	719	632	679	

* In capitation schools the total grant divided by the number of teachers, excluding super-numeraries.

Source: Investment in Education, Dublin, Stationery Office, 1966, p. 235.

The larger the average size of school or, to be more correct, the smaller the number of small schools, the fewer the teachers required for any given school population. A rapid reduction in the number of such schools has helped alleviate teacher shortages in Denmark: there the maximum size of class is 28 and where this is exceeded the practice is to split the class in two and create a new teaching post. The reduction from 4,443 in 1951 to 2,002 in 1967 of the number of muni-cipal rural schools has meant that the class size requirement has less effect on the demand for teachers.[1] As small schools are more common in rural areas it follows that migration to towns eases teacher requirements. In countries where the agricultural sector is still large, internal migration becomes a factor not without importance to educational forecasters.

3. *The amount of time spent in "full class".* This is closely connected with the relationship between class sizes and pupil/teacher ratios referred to above. The tendency in many Western European countries in recent years has been to intro-duce more flexibility especially into secondary education. Pupils have more choice of minority time subjects (e.g. vocational subjects to prepare them for the labour market), while at the same time maintaining a core of major subjects taken by most pupils which provides a general education and facilitates transfers between schools and between classes in schools. The corollary of wider choice is smaller classes as taught. In Copenhagen schools 4% of teacher demand arises from this choice. In most studies[2] this tendency, although recognised, seems not to be an integral part of the forecasts. Admittedly this may be an

[1] *Study on the Demand for and Supply of Teachers: Denmark*, OECD, Paris, 1969.
[2] Cf. those for Denmark and Norway, *op. cit.*

area where it is relatively easy[1] to save on teachers if supply becomes tight, or to deploy teachers if the supply situation is easy. Hence it provides a safety margin. This comment applies, however, to some degree or other, to all of these influences on the ratio. It raises the issue, of whether the pupil/teacher ratio is based on what is educationally desirable or on what is thought to be feasible; this is discussed further in the assessment at the end of this chapter.

This issue raises also the problem of how teaching is actually conducted. The study on Resources for Learning at the Nuffield Foundation seems to point in certain directions. An increasing amount of technological equipment is being brought into schools so that between the traditional concept of a teacher, a piece of chalk, a blackboard and forty children, there is a considerable volume of equipment of all kinds. This ranges from programmed learning texts, to learning machines, and up to television and computers. The impact of this could be to speed up the individualisation of learning. Increasingly, the progressive educational thesis is being accepted that each pupil should have his own curriculum, his own methods of work, his own pace of work, and that the teachers' function is to help him to proceed along a path specially designed for him, so far as this is feasible. Modern methods and technology may make this ideal more feasible for the average child. The impact of this doctrine on pupil/teacher ratios is two-fold. It has the effect of breaking up the traditional teaching group and re-arranging it from time to time into larger groups and from time to time into smaller groups: one suspects that the effect here is to increase teacher requirements. On the other hand, the use of such equipment opens up the possibility of teacher substitution: in many countries at the moment, where such methods are in the experimental stage, this is not so and hence there is a net addition to teacher needs and hence to costs, but it seems highly likely that as educational expenditure continues to rise some teacher substitution will occur. The net effect of the two influences is difficult to assess: the answer probably depends on the time scale. In the near future it will increase teacher requirements but in the long run demands for checking educational expenditure will lead to increasing teacher substitution. Either way, in several countries this is becoming a factor that will have to be taken into account of in long-term forecasts, although as yet there is little evidence of this.

4. *Teaching loads.* Here again a teacher is badly defined, for the number of hours in attendance at school and the number of hours spent teaching can vary within wide limits. The difference between the two is comprised of the number of hours set aside for marking, preparation, and relaxation and, perhaps more important, the amount of aid the teacher is given in secretarial, clerical and policing work. These can be very important factors, although forecasting likely changes is not easy. One influence is the strength of teachers' unions. In Norway, the demands of teachers for a reduction in the length of the working week is being integrated into the forecasts. Another is the pressure for cost reductions: ancillaries are cheaper than teachers and this may lead to a more effective use of teachers.[2]

---

[1] Although presumably at some "educational" expense.
[2] Especially as teachers account for such a high proportion of total costs.

Some examples of demand forecasts

Two teacher demand forecasts, for England and Wales and for Norway, are now described. Some explanation of the choice of these countries is required. England and Wales have been chosen because the Ninth Report[1] discusses in some detail the relationship between class size and pupil/teacher ratios. The Norwegian[2] projection is interesting, as it provides a range of results based on different assumptions concerning variables that are within the scope of government policy.

In England and Wales, official forecasts are made at, or revised at, regular intervals but discussion will be centred around the Ninth Report. Later forecasts are contained in the U.K. contribution to the OECD study, and in the annual statistical report of the Department of Education and Science:[3] these are largely based on the assumptions made in the Ninth Report. The Ninth Report's estimation of future school populations has already been described in Chapter 7, and here we are solely concerned with the resulting demand for teachers. In the Council's Seventh Report, uniform pupil/teacher ratios were applied to the whole secondary sector, and further, the previous ratios had been derived from classes as registered rather than as taught. The Ninth Report recognised the weaknesses of this method and to provide data, a survey was carried out in secondary schools: classes were divided into three groups—those in which pupils were (mainly) under 15, over 15 but not in Sixth Form, and Sixth Form. For these groups the average size of class as taught was found to be 27, 20 and 10.6 respectively. The Council thought that the position in Sixth Forms was satisfactory and in fact that some increase in efficiency (increase in pupil/teacher ratio) might be expected as Sixth Forms continued to increase in size, and the remaining analysis is concerned only with the first two groups. The relationship between the average size of class (l) and the pupil/teacher ratio (R) is expressed as:

$$(R) = \frac{lk}{mj}$$

where k = proportion of all teachers class teaching
m = average number of teachers engaged in teaching a class[4]
j = the proportion of all pupils receiving class teaching,

which can be re-written as $(R) = Fl$, where $F = \dfrac{k}{mj}$.

It was assumed that the values of F calculated for 1964 (January) would remain constant, i.e. constant until 1986. This is a curious assumption because

[1] *Op. cit.*

[2] *Study of the Demand for and Supply of Teachers. A Case Study in the Application of Teacher Demand and Supply Models in Norway*, OECD, Paris, 1969.

[3] *Statistics of Education*, London, 1967, Vol. 4, HMSO, 1968, pp. 77-91.

[4] The meaning of this term may not be immediately clear: it is perhaps best explained by saying that the value of m will usually be close to one, i.e. most classes are taught by one teacher at a time.

it abstracts from every influence on pupil/teacher ratios except class size. It seems highly improbable that the size of schools, numbers of ancillaries provided, technology et cetera would remain constant for over 20 years. If there is any truth in the saying that education is the last major industry not to have experienced its "industrial revolution" and that it is entering it now, some decrease in teacher needs per school population would be expected on these grounds.[1] However, the values of F^2 were then applied to average class sizes adjusted to eliminate classes over 30 in size. The resulting pupil/teacher ratios were 16.7:1 and 14.5:1 for the two age groups respectively. When the school leaving age is raised to 16 in 1972/3 the distinction between these two groups will cease to be meaningful, and thus for subsequent years a weighted average of the two is used, 16.3:1. In primary schools the pupil/teacher ratio to eliminate classes of over 40 was calculated as 26.3:1. Thus those pupil/teacher ratios, for primary, secondary except Sixth Form, and Sixth Form class, are arrived at and applied to the estimated school populations to derive the demand for teachers.

The Council indicated that it was not altogether satisfied with this method and the Department of Education and Science is examining new approaches. Its discussion centred around the problem of oversize classes and whether too much emphasis was being placed on it. "If it is right to focus attention on the unduly large classes, it is wrong to ignore what happens to the rest of the system." And later . . . "It may be unduly theoretical to envisage an ascertainable optimum size of class for schools of different types, but, short of this, there can be little disagreement that the aim of securing a more effective deployment of teachers would be well served if all class sizes were brought nearer the average."[3] In subsequent forecasts the above ratios are used to derive teacher demand, although no attempt is now made to identify any given limit on the size of class with a particular pupil/teacher ratio.

The Norwegian forecast where the effect of some of the other variables affecting pupil/teacher ratios is demonstrated, is now described. The model used by planners in Norway is of some complexity and the presentation in the text of the report deals with five factors, which are thought to be responsible for virtually all changes in teacher demand:

1. Number of pupils
2. Hours taught in full class
3. Extra hours
4. Class size
5. Teaching obligations.

An outline of the report is given here to illustrate the extent to which alterations in assumptions can affect the end result. As the authors emphasise the assumptions are in effect assumptions concerning decisions to be made by

[1] J. Vaizey and R. Knight suggest that a 10% improvement in the efficiency with which staff are utilized, might not be unreasonable, in their contribution to: Beckerman, W. and associates, *The British Economy in 1975*, Cambridge, National Insitute of Economic and Social Research, 1965, pp. 458-96.

[2] .7798 for classes for pupils under 15, and .8119 for those over 15 but not in Sixth Form.

[3] *Ninth Report, op. cit.*

political bodies. To avoid complicating the exercise with estimates of voluntary enrolment ratios we present the forecasts for compulsory education, presently being extended from 7 to 9 years' duration. For each variable, except (1), three values are given, the most optimistic[1] that could reasonably be expected in the light of present policy is labelled b_1, c_1 et cetera, the most pessimistic labelled b_2, c_2 et cetera, and the present situation b_0, c_0 et cetera. We consider each of them in turn: the statistics are presented separately in Table 23.2 which also distinguishes between school grades 1-6 and 7-9.

1. *Number of pupils.* From the point of view of this exercise the demographic data on which these are based are taken as datum. This alone, with no change in staffing standards, yields an increase in the demand for teachers of 35,000 by 1985.
2. *Hours taught in full class.* This simply means the total number of hours each pupil is actually taught each week. The optimistic forecast embodies the recommendations of a recent Royal Commission.
3. *Extra hours.* This largely refers to the additional teaching hours caused by the division of classes into two or more groups: a minor element is time spent by teachers on administration. In Norway, division of classes has been a major cause of the rising demand for teachers. At present extra hours are 6.3 hours per week in the lower grades, and 18.9 hours per class in the upper grades. These totals are subject to two pulls: some official opinion is that it should be possible to operate with fewer divided classes, but against this there is the tendency, especially at higher levels, to offer more choice, which increases the division of classes. The moderate alternative (c_1) assumes that these influences offset each other and that the present situation endures. The pessimistic alternative is based on the assumption that further division of classes will occur, that these will be an increase in administration and supervision time,[2] and that there will be paid leave for training.[3]
4. *Class size.* The alternatives presented are, again, well within the limits provided by likely policy changes.
5. *Teaching obligations,* i.e. hours worked per week. The moderate alternative (e_1) is that which would arise if the demands of the Teachers Association were met, and e_2 is rather more generous in its reduction of teaching obligations.

A combination of the alternatives yields interesting results. The extrapolation of the existing situation, i.e. the result of solely demographic factors, gives an additional demand for teachers in 1985 of 35,000. Now compare this result with a combination of all the optimistic alternatives, and with all the pessimistic alternatives: the figures are in the final column. The first point to notice is that the final columns are not an addition of the alternatives: thus the summation of the teacher demands given by $b_1 + c_1 + d_1 + e_1$ yields a change of $-2,950$

[1] Optimistic in the sense of decreasing teacher demand.

[2] To 10% of teaching hours from the situation in 1965 of 7.5% in grades 1-6, and 5.5% in grades 7-9.

[3] As recommended by successive educational commissions.

TABLE 23.2 *Effects of various staffing standards on teacher requirements: compulsory education, Norway, 1985*

Hours taught per week in full class				"Extra" hours per week				Class size				Teaching obligations (Hours per week)				Extra teachers required 1985 over 1965
a	b	c	d	a	b	c	d	a	b	c	d	a	b	c	d	
b_0	22.7	36.0	—	c_0	6.3	18.9	—	d_0	19.5	24.9	—	e_0	33.0	25.0	—	35,000
b_1	23.0	30.0	−2,500	c_1	6.3	18.9	—	d_1	21.9	25.7	−2,400	e_1	30.0	25.0	+1,950	31,500
b_2	25.0	33.5	+800	c_2	15.0	28.0	+7,250	d_2	19.5	22.1	+2,050	e_2	28.0	24.0	+4,150	53,000

Column headings: (a) The alternative assumptions
(b) Values for school grades 1-6
(c) Values for school grades 7-9
(d) Difference in teacher requirements from that yielded by number of pupils and present staffing standards.

Source: Study of Demand for and Supply of Teachers: Norway, op. cit.

over the "0" alternative and hence the extra teachers required in 1985 would appear to be 32,050 (35,000−2,950) rather than the 31,500 shown. Thus the consequences of simultaneous variation of the alternatives are not a simple addition of the partial consequences. For example, the decrease in the hours taught per week in full class gives greater effect to the increase in class size: similarly in the last row of the table the effect on demand for teachers of the increase in extra hours is accentuated by a reduction in teaching obligations. It is seen that the extreme alternatives yield a demand for teachers 68 % greater than the optimistic, and 51 % greater than that based on demographic factors alone. The report comments that the demographic estimates themselves can be taken as accurate within 7 %, which emphasises the importance of the political variables. This is the point: the forecasting process becomes an exercise in forecasting political behaviour because the wide range of variation in the resulting estimates is "fully due to variations in assumptions concerning decisions by responsible political bodies in the course of the next twenty years. This provides an illustration of the dilemma facing those who want to forecast future developments in the labour market for teachers".

Analysing the supply of teachers

Having estimated the demand for teachers, the other side of the forecasting process is to compare this with estimated supply and ultimately to take steps, where possible, to correct any imbalance.

In most countries the training of teachers is directly or indirectly undertaken by the state, which to some extent facilitates forecasting. In forecasting future supply it is useful, and usual, to distinguish between two groups. First, primary school teachers and teachers in secondary education whose training is of less than degree standard. The supply of such teachers is largely determined by institutional factors: they receive a training very specific to teaching and experience is that a high (and relatively constant) proportion enter teaching when their training is completed. The second group comprises teachers whose training is at university, their qualification normally being a degree, and those whose qualifications are highly competitive with a degree and not specific to teaching. The supply of these teachers is to some extent dependent on conditions in the labour market for graduates. For both groups, in-service wastage is an important factor in the supply situation.

We consider first the supply of the first group, basically non-graduates.[1] The institutional arrangements for training teachers vary from country to country, and clearly the names applied to such institutions similarly vary. We will use the English term "college of education" to apply to institutions whose object is the production of teachers: the other important characteristic will be that the award will be of less than degree equivalent. Thus in virtually all countries teacher training is looked at educationally and administratively as a

---

[1] In England and Wales some students now read for the (four year) Bachelor of Education degree. In so far as most holders of this degree (which is, as the title suggests, quite specific to education) will presumably enter teaching, it does not invalidate the distinction, for the purposes for which we have made it.

problem of the schools rather than as a full, integral part of higher education.

The output of non-graduate teachers is seen, in forecasts, as a direct function of the number of places available in colleges of education. The justification for this is that historically the colleges have always tended to have more suitable qualified applicants than places available. The proportion of those completing courses who enter teaching is high—85% would be a realistic figure for many Western European countries—and hence the annual recruitment of non-graduate teachers is easily calculated.

In the case of graduate teachers, the crux of the forecasting problem[1] is to estimate the proportion of graduates who will enter teaching after a short course in teacher training. The proportion fluctuates annually as is shown by the following figures:

TABLE 23.3 *Graduates entering maintained schools direct, as a percentage of the relevant output of home graduates of Great Britain*

		1958/9	1959/60	1960/1	1961/2	1962/3
Men	Mathematics and Science	17.0	18.7	14.7	14.3	14.9
	Arts	24.8	25.9	26.7	22.6	22.5
Women	Mathematics and Science	22.9	26.7	26.6	25.7	23.6
	Arts	35.0	35.6	34.6	32.4	30.6

Source: Ninth Report, op. cit., p. 56.

The evidence is that a similar situation obtains in (at least) the OECD countries. The proportions vary annually with no clearly discernible trend. Teaching has to compete with industry, the civil service, and of increasing importance, with higher education, for the annual output of graduates. Conditions in these other sectors clearly influence the numbers choosing teaching (initially) as a career, but not much is known about the way such influences operate. All the forecaster can do is to take a view: past figures will provide some sort of guide but it is clear that forecasts of graduate teacher recruitment must be subject to fairly wide margins of error.

Thus the forecaster arrives at an estimate of total teacher recruitment: he now has to take into account in-service wastage in order to derive the annual net addition to the teacher supply. It is true to say that the problems of keeping teachers in the profession are as great, if not greater, than in attracting and recruiting them initially. The scale of in-service wastage can be illustrated with a further reference to England and Wales: there it has been estimated that to increase the teaching force (in the very short run) by 12,500 requires the recruitment of an additional 40,000 teachers. A complexity of wastage rates are required: for each age group (fairly narrowly defined) of teacher wastage rates are required for graduates and non-graduates, and for men and women. For obvious reasons wastage rates for women are significantly higher than for men, but so also are re-entry rates, a further variable that is of importance.[2] Wastage

---

[1] As the future output of graduates—given the excess demand for University education—is also largely a function of buildings.

[2] Men who leave the profession rarely return.

rates by age group do not seem to follow any clearly defined pattern and past trends in wastage generally do not provide much help to the forecaster.

Not much is known of the quantitative importance of the many influences on wastage (except perhaps for women), and even *a priori* reasoning about the direction (let alone the extent) of future changes, can give contradictory results. For example, consider wastage rates among men. As education becomes more professionalised, one can argue that the rate of withdrawal from the teaching profession into other occupations will tend to decline. One of the major problems of labour mobility in contemporary society is the degree to which demarcation lines have been drawn between the various occupations which are necessary to the efficient functioning of that society, but which tend to become rigid and barriers to change. If one accepts the importance of relative salaries then some estimate of their likely movements also becomes an integral part of the supply forecast. Thus, faced with various influences the forecaster, as far as one can tell from published estimates, usually projects past trends where these are at all discernible making allowance for any future changes that are highly probable, e.g. if marriage rates are expected to increase this should clearly be allowed for in forecasts of female wastage rates.

The supply of teachers next year is equal to the present stock plus recruitment minus wastage from the stock, and thus the supply in future can be derived. Thus far discussion has been of qualified teachers, but varying proportions of the teacher stock are unqualified.[1] In England and Wales in 1967, 2.2% of all teachers were unqualified: 10.5% of Irish primary teachers were unqualified in 1963, and 26.4% of primary teachers in Portugal (1961). If the aim is to eliminate unqualified staff by (say) the terminal forecast date, then the present numbers of such staff have to be deducted from the existing teacher stock. Where the proportion of unqualified staff is large, complete elimination may not be feasible and some less ambitious objective is included in the forecast. This is another example of forecasters being forced to choose between optimum and feasible situations.

Given the estimates for teacher demand, it is thus possible to identify future surpluses or shortages of teachers. This is done not only on a global scale but also for different types of school and ideally also for teachers of different subjects—but breakdowns of this degree are rarely attempted.

Demand, supply and "shortages"

Estimates of the teacher supply position have in most cases predicted teacher shortages in the future. The notion of a teacher "shortage" must be examined more closely. This has been said to exist when there is an adequate number of teachers to attain desired staffing standards. Another possibility is that although staffing standards, as reflected by pupil/teacher ratios, are maintained the

---

[1] The precise meaning of this term varies. A qualified teacher normally possesses some minimum academic qualifications plus teacher training. But, for example, handicraft teachers who are fully competent may, on the above criterion, count as unqualified. The term thus has to be treated with caution.

quality of teachers is reduced. That is, in order to fill colleges of education, entry requirements may be relaxed, and standards within colleges are reduced so that the average quality of teachers falls.[1] So a shortage of teachers is now defined as a lack of teachers of desired quality: the host of problems in the interpretation of "desired quality" is abstracted from. A third possibility is a combination of both of the above. So far we have not mentioned price. If it is assumed, for the moment, that prices move in the market for teachers in such a way as to eliminate any excess demands, the following definition of a teacher shortage emerges: a shortage of teachers of desired quality to maintain desired staffing standards at any given price.

From this definition, and for other reasons to be discussed below, it will be appreciated that forecasts of teacher shortages have to be interpreted with some caution. The bare figures can be misleading and constant reference should be made to the assumptions on which the forecasts are based: the assumptions not only include the pupil/teacher ratios used and wastage rates, but also of course all the assumptions underlying the enrolment projections. In this brief survey of the results of several recent forecasts it is not possible to list all of the relevant assumptions, but some points of interest emerge. In England and Wales two forecasts of the supply and demand balance are published because of uncertainty over the future pattern of wastage rates: a shortage of teachers is estimated to continue until 1978 on one forecast, and 1980 on the other.[2] These figures also serve to illustrate one key assumption in the English forecasts, and in those for most developed countries; that finance will not be a limiting factor in the employment of teachers. This may not always be the case. There may be occasions when on the assumptions inherent in a forecast there is a shortage of teachers; yet because finance is at that moment a limiting factor, the current output of qualified teachers may not be fully absorbed into schools, i.e. teachers will be unemployed.

In Sweden shortages are likely to be eliminated by the early 1970s[3]; this is again based on a complex of assumptions, but two points are of interest. Rapid pedagogical change and educational development is occurring in Sweden, which means that more trained teachers are required outside schools, with the implication that within schools higher pupil/teacher ratios are feasible, and are used in the forecast.

In many countries the expectation is that shortages of primary teachers will be eliminated before those of secondary school teachers. In Denmark for example, supply and demand for *folkeskole* teachers is expected to balance in about 1975, although because of the prevalence of overtime working and its acceptance by teachers, the shortage up to 1975 will be more apparent than real. In the *gymnasia*, however, the shortage of staff will continue into the subsequent decade.[4]

---

[1] Although in several Western European countries the supply of college places acts as a constraint.

[2] *Statistics of Education*, 1967, Vol. 4, *op. cit.*, p. 84.

[3] *Study on the Demand for and Supply of Teachers: Sweden*, *op. cit.*

[4] *Study on the Demand for and Supply of Teachers: Denmark*, *op. cit.*

Estimates made for the six Mediterranean Regional Project countries forecast a shortage of primary teachers until the mid 1970s and of secondary teachers for some years after them. The supply figures are, however, based on highly optimistic assumptions and the forecast dates for balance in the supply-demand position are correspondingly optimistic.

Thus these recent global forecasts expect a deficiency in the supply of teachers at least in the near future. Within the overall figures there are structural shortages, for example of science teachers, which are likely to continue for much longer. These structural shortages and possible remedies for their elimination have been dealt with earlier.

It can be argued that given the methods of estimation the forecasting of a shortage is nearly inevitable. First, if there has been an increase in the proportion of the population enrolled at school, or such an increase is expected, then the rate of growth of the school population will be greater than the rate of growth of the population of colleges of education and universities. In other words, "the projections tell us more about the age structure of the population than anything very relevant to the questions of teacher supply".[1] Secondly, Hansen argues the projections embody some hoped for improvement in the quality of teachers, so that there appears to be a shortage of qualified teachers larger than if the existing quality had persisted. In Western European countries, as has been seen, the norm is to project the existing quality situation, and this does not apply. Thirdly, some improvement in staffing standards is often embodied into the projections and this gives a similar result. It has been shown above that most aspects of staffing standards can be reduced to a single figure, the pupil/teacher ratio: smaller classes, fewer "oversize" classes, shorter teaching hours, et cetera, all imply lower pupil/teacher ratios. In fact, most concern has been with class size but however derived, staffing standards can be expressed in terms of pupil/teacher ratios. Now if forecasts of future school populations are taken and the problem of differing pupil/teacher ratios in different school grades is abstracted from, the demand for teachers can be shown on the following diagram as a rectangular hyperbola:

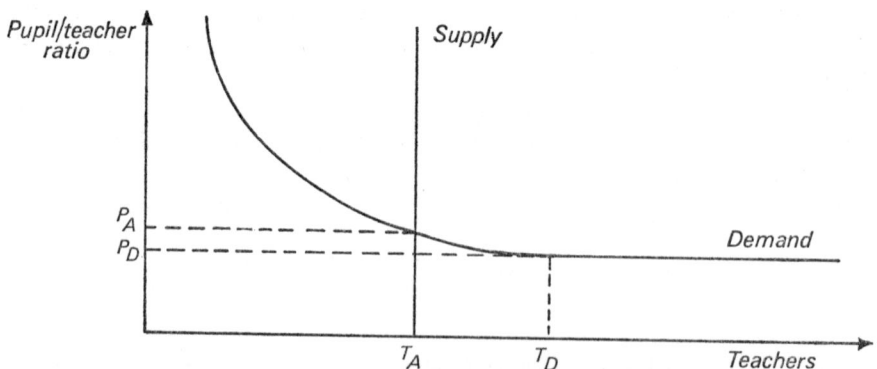

Fig. 23.1 Graph showing the demand for teachers.

[1] Hansen, L., Educational plans and teacher supply, *Comparative Education Review*, October 1962, p. 137.

It has this shape as the area under the curve at any point is $\frac{P}{T} \times T = P = $ constant as given by enrolment projections.

Forecasts either project existing staff standards (pupil/teacher ratios) into the future or, more usually, as these are considered inadequate, use some "desired" ratio. Assume the latter is the case, and call this ratio P_D, then the demand for teachers is T_D. Now say supply in the terminal year of the forecast is less than T_D, say T_A hence the actual pupil/teacher ratio is P_A. Although there is a shortage of teachers in the terminal year in the sense that at desired standards supply was less than demand, unless P_A is some very high figure, the shortage does not prevent the educational process from continuing, i.e. every class has a teacher. Of course, if the pupil/teacher ratio in the base year of the forecast was greater than P_A, then although the forecast yields a shortage of teachers, by base year standards there is a surplus. The variability of pupil/teacher ratios thus provides a safety margin for educational planners, and indicates that it is perhaps supply that is the dominant partner in the relationship. That is, as shown on the diagram, the enrolment projections fix the position of the demand curve and the supply of teachers then determines the pupil/teacher ratio. The task of the educationalist then becomes one of devising a means of making the pupil/teacher ratio workable. Since projections of enrolments are themselves subject to a great deal of uncertainty, forecasts of teacher demands are unlikely to be accurate. This may not in itself be serious for, as has been argued, the educational system has in this respect a great deal of flexibility: class sizes can be varied as can teaching loads and the amount of overtime worked. This is not to argue that the forecasts are not worth making—clearly the system is only flexible up to a point—and given the time lags in the training of teachers some estimate of future requirements is essential. If organisational changes continue to occur in schools, and if pedagogical and technological change takes place, however, the pupil/teacher ratio will become an increasingly imperfect tool. Organisationally more non-teachers may be brought into the school and clearly account must be taken of the increasing number of teachers who contribute to teaching from outside the school, such as those producing programmes for educational television, and those producing programmed instruction material. As such instructional material is used on an increasing scale, reference to those in schools only will have increasingly less meaning: at the moment it seems that only in Sweden is recognition taken of these developments in forecasts of teacher demand and supply.

Models of the educational system

This final section briefly describes the place of teacher flows in models of the educational system. Earlier in this book the derivation of future enrolments using educational models was outlined, and most models contain teachers as another part of the educational system and hence the future balance of teacher requirements and supply can be seen. It was argued earlier that the main advantage of educational models was that since they integrated all the various sectors of the system, the implications of changes in one sector for another were clearly brought out. This merit is clearly of importance in the case of teacher flows, as the educational system provides not only the demand for teachers but itself produces teachers. It was also argued that a principal weakness of the models was that they offered no solution to the estimation of some key parameters, and indeed being mechanistic the values imputed to such parameters took on even more importance. In the case of estimating the future social demand for education, the key parameter was the vector of transition probabilities—the probability that someone in a process would be in the subsequent process next year—or enrolment ratios. Yet the estimation of these was the most difficult part of the forecasting exercise. The situation is precisely the same in estimating teacher requirements. The crucial estimate is of pupil/teacher ratios, as these ratios to a large extent sum up the future values of class size, teaching load, and number of choices offered to pupils as well as ideally—but rarely in practice—reflecting pedagogical and (educational) technological change. In educational models pupil/teacher ratios are of critical importance, but the way out of the difficulty is often to assume that they will remain constant, which of course abstracts from all educational change.

To illustrate these points an outline of the economic input sector of one educational model is given. The model chosen is that of Stone,[1] since it is amenable to summary and seems to clearly bring out the strengths and weaknesses of such models. Earlier the derivation of future enrolments, based on a social demand approach, by this model was described. It was seen how, starting from demographic (birth and survival) flows and on assumptions about the time path of transition probabilities, the future output of graduates,[2] a vector g, and the future number of pupils in each process, a vector s, could be derived. The main purpose of calculating future enrolments is to make sure that the economic inputs are available at the right times and in the right quantities.[3]

There are two influences upon these inputs, activity levels and educational technology. To demonstrate: if X is a matrix whose row elements represent the inputs—paper, buildings, teachers et cetera—and whose column elements represent educational processes, then if X is divided through by activity levels, s, then a co-efficient matrix, U, is derived:

$$U = X_s^{-1}.$$

If the row sums of X are denoted by x then

$$x = U_s.$$

Thus given that future values of s have been calculated, then required values of x are known. One can also calculate the actual and expected future values of x and compare the two flows. This can be done either on the assumption that the elements of U remain constant—one column of U represents pupil/teacher

[1] Stone, R., A model of the educational system, *Minerva*, Vol. III, No. 2, Winter 1965, pp. 172-86.
[2] Those who leave the system from any process.
[3] The assumption of the social demand approach is that the system will adapt to pupil demands.

ratios—or assumptions about future possibilities can be introduced into the model.

Stone divides the economic inputs into material supplies, buildings and labour. The latter, which is largely composed of teachers, is likely to constitute the main bottleneck. The equations for the future supply and demand for teachers are presented.

The demand for teachers, e_d is given as:

$$E\, e_d = A\, E_s,$$

where A is a partition of U representing teacher/pupil ratios, s is the vector representing the number enrolled in each process, and E is an operator which advances by one time period the variable to which it is applied. The supply of teachers, e_s, is given as

$$E\, e_s = (I - \hat{c})\, e_s + B_g,$$

where $\hat{c}$ is a vector whose elements represent wastage rates for each type of teacher, and B is a matrix showing the proportion of each type of graduate, g, who take up the various types of teaching. Thus the equation states that next year's supply of teachers (of each type) equals those remaining from this year's stock plus new entrants to the profession. Thus future flows of supply and demand are derived; but the derivation depends crucially on the values given to teacher/ pupil/ ratios (A), wastage rates (c), and the proportions of leavers entering teaching (B). The model cannot in itself project these and so obviously all the difficulties described earlier in the estimation of the future value of these variables remain unsolved. This weakness is, perhaps inevitably, present in all models.

Since the models can incorporate the same estimates of the future value of these parameters as those that are used in separate teacher forecasts, there is a net gain in using them, as their advantages remain. As the models become more sophisticated, the benefits increase.

Selected bibliography

This work is drawn from *The Economics of Educational Costing*, Vols. 1-3, published by the Gulbenkian Foundation, Lisbon, 1969-71.

General economics

Abramovitz, M., The sources of economic growth in the United States and the alternatives before us, (Review of Denison's article), *American Economic Review*, Vol. LII, no. 4, 1962.

Arrow, K. J., The economic implications of learning by doing, *Review of Economic Studies*, Vol. III, no. 80, 1962.

Barback, R. H., *The Pricing of Manufactures*, London, 1964.

Baumol, W. J., *Economic Theory and Operations Analysis*, New Jersey, Englewood Cliffs, 1965.

Baumol, W. J., On the social rate of discount, *American Economic Review*, Vol. LVIII, no. 4, 1968.

Carter, C. F. and Williams, B. R., *Industry and Technical Progress*, Oxford, London, 1957.

Denison, E. F., assisted by Jean Pierre Poullier, *Why Growth Rates Differ*, Washington D. C., The Brookings Institution, 1967.

Friedman, M., Savage, L. J., The utility analysis of choices involving risk, *Journal of Political Economy*, Vol. LVI, August 1948.

Galenson, W. and Leibenstein, H., Investment criteria, productivity and economic development, *Quarterly Journal of Economics*, Vol. LXIX, no. 3, 1955.

Graaff, J. de V., *Theoretical Welfare Economics*, Cambridge, 1957.

Hahn, F. H. and Matthews, R. C. O., The theory of economic growth: a survey, *Economic Journal*, Vol. LXXIV, no. 296, 1964.

Harcourt, G. C., Some Cambridge controversies in the theory of capital, *Journal of Economic Literature*, Vol. 7, no. 2, 1969.

Hicks, J., *Capital and Growth*, Oxford, 1965.

Johnston, J., *Econometric Methods*, New York, 1963.

Jorgenson, D. W. and Griliches, Z., The explanation of productivity change, *Review of Economic Studies*, Vol. XXXIV, no. 3, 1967.

Kaldor, N. and Mirrlees, J. A., A new model of economic growth, *Review of Economic Studies*, Vol. XXIX(3), no. 80, 1962.

Keynes, J. M., *The General Theory of Employment, Interest and Money*, London, 1936.

Knight, J. B., The determination of wages and salaries in Uganda, *Bulletin of the Oxford University Institute of Economics and Statistics*, Vol. 29, no. 3, 1967.

Kuznets, S., *Modern Economic Growth: Rate, Structure and Spread*, New Haven and London, 1967.

Long-term Economic Growth 1869-1965. A Statistical Compendium, Washington D.C., U.S. Department of Commerce, Bureau of the Census, 1966.

Lydall, H. F., *The Structure of Earnings*, Oxford, 1968.

Marris, Robin, *The Economic Theory of "Managerial" Capitalism*, London, 1964.

Marshall, Alfred, *Principles of Economics*, London, ed. C. W. Guillebaud, 1961.

Mathur, G., *Planning for Steady Growth*, Oxford, 1965.

Myrdal, Gunnar, *Economic Theory and Under-developed Regions*, London, 1957.

O.E.C.D., *Policies for Economic Growth*, Paris, 1962.

Petty, Sir William, *Essay Concerning the Multiplication of Mankind*, 2nd edn., 1986.

Pigou, A. C., *The Economics of Welfare*, 4th edn., London, 1962.

Prest, A. R., and Turvey, R., Cost benefit analysis: a survey, *Economic Journal*, Vol. LXXV, no. 300, 1965.

Ranis, G., Factor proportions in Japanese economic development, *American Economic Review*, Vol. XLVII, no. 5, 1957.

Reder, M. W., The theory of occupational wage differentials, *American Economic Review*, Vol. XLV, no. 5, 1955.

Robinson, Joan, *The Accumulation of Capital*, London, 1956.

Robinson, Joan, The production function and the theory of capital, *Review of Economic Studies*, Vol. XXI, no. 2, 1953-4.

Salter, W. E. G., *Productivity and Technical Change*, 2nd edn., Cambridge, 1966.

Sen, A. K., *Choice of Techniques*, Oxford, 1960.

Smith, A., *The Wealth of Nations*, Vols. I and II, London, 1964.

Solow, R. M., Technical change and the aggregate production function, *Review of Economics and Statistics*, Vol. XXXIX, no. 3, 1957.

Solow, R. M., Investment and economic growth: some comments, *Productivity Measurement Review*, November 1959.

Solow, R. M., Investment and technical progress, in *Mathematical Methods in the Social Sciences, 1959*, K. J. Arrow, S. Karlin and P. Suppes, (eds.), Stanford, 1960.

Solow, R. M., Technical progress, capital formulation and economic growth, *American Economic Review*, Papers and Proceedings, Vol. LII, no. 2, 1962.

Thomas, Brinley (ed.), *The Economics of International Migration*, London, 1958.

Vaizey, J. (ed), *The Residual Factor and Economic Growth*, Paris, OECD, 1965.

Williams, B. R., *Technology, Investment and Growth*, London, 1967.

Expenditure on education

Blot, Daniel and Debeauvais, Michel, Educational expenditure in developing areas: some statistical aspects, in *Financing of Education for Economic Growth*, Paris, OECD, 1966.

Edding, Friedrich, *Methods of Analysing Educational Outlay*, Paris, UNESCO, 1966.

Edding, F. and Berstecher, D., *International Developments of Educational Expenditure 1950-1965*, Paris, UNESCO-IIEP, 1969.

Final Report, UNESCO/ECA Conference of African States on the Development of Education in Africa, Addis Ababa, 1961.

Harris, Seymour, Public expenditures on education, in *Financing of Education for Economic Growth*, Paris OECD, 1966.

Hewton, E., Norris, K. and Vaizey, J., *The Costs of New Educational Techniques*, Lisbon, 1971.

Investment in education

Knight, J. B., *The Costing and Financing of Educational Development in Tanzania*, Paris, UNESCO–IIEP, 1966.

Martins, C. M. Alves, Alguns aspectos do ensino em Portugal, *Análise Social*, nos. 20-21, Vol. VI 1968.

Netherlands Economics Institute, Financial aspects of the educational expansion in developing regions: some quantitative estimates, in *Financing of Education for Economic Growth*, Paris, OECD, 1966.

Norris, K. and Vaizey, J., *A Report on Unit Costs in Secondary Schools*, London, Acton Society Trust, 1969 (mimeographed).

O.E.C.D., *Economic Aspects of Higher Education*, Paris, 1964.

O.E.C.D., Education investment and planning programme, in *Educational Policy and Planning in Sweden*, Paris, 1964.

O.E.C.D., *Financing of Education for Economic Growth*, Paris, 1966.

O.E.C.D., *The Mediterranean Regional Project: Yugoslavia, Italy, Greece, Spain, Portugal, Turkey*, Paris, 1965.

O.E.C.D., *Methods and Statistical Needs for Educational Planning*, Paris, 1967.

Palm, Gunter, *Die Kaufdraft der Bildungsausgaben*, Freiburg, 1966.

Poignant, R., *L'Enseignement dans les pays du Marché Commun*, I.P.N., Paris, 1965.

Secretariat of the OECD Directorate for Scientific Affairs, Educational expenditures in the countries of the Mediterranean Regional Project, in *Financing of Education for Economic Growth*, Paris, OECD, 1966.

Senf, Paul, Financial implications of the expansion, by 1970, of public and educational expenditures in five countries of the European Economic Community, in *Financing of Education for Economic Growth*, Paris, OECD, 1966.

Stigler, G. J., *Employment and Compensation in Education*, New York, NBER, Occasional Paper no. 33, 1950.

Vaizey, J., *The Costs of Education*, London, 1958.

Vaizey, J., Financial implications of the Mediterranean Regional Project, in *Financing of Education for Economic Growth*, Paris, OECD, 1966.

Vaizey, J., and Sheehan, J., *Resources for Education*, London, 1968.

Education and capital theory

Aukrust, O., Investment and economic growth, *Productivity Measurement Review*, February, 1959.

Becker, G. S., Investment in human capital: a theoretical analysis, *Journal of Political Economy*, Vol. LXX, no. 5, Part II, 1962.

Becker, G. S., *Human Capital*, New York, NBER, 1964.

Blandy, Richard, Marshall on human capital: a note, *Journal of Political Economy*, Vol. LXXV, no. 6, 1967.

Blaug, M., The rate of return on investment in education in Great Britain, *Manchester School of Economic and Social Studies*, Vol. 33, no. 3, 1965.

Blaug, M., An economic interpretation of the private demand for education, *Economica*, Vol. XXXIII, no. 130, 1966.

Blaug, M. and Woodhall, M., Productivity trends in British secondary education, 1950-1963, in *Costs and Productivity in Education*, Paris, UNESCO-IIEP, 1967.

Bowman, Mary Jean, Human capital: concepts and measures, in *Economics of Higher Education*, Selma J. Mushkin (ed.), Washington, U.S. Department of Health Education and Welfare, Office of Education, 1962.

Byatt, I. C. R. and Cohen, A. V., An attempt to quantify the economic benefits of scientific research, *Science Policy Studies*, no. 4, London, HMSO, 1969.

Correa, H., The economics of human resources, *Contributions to Economic Analysis Series*, Amsterdam, 1963.

Grubel, H. B. and Scott, A. D., The international flow of human capital, *American Economic Review*, Vol. LVI, no. 2, Papers and Proceedings, 1966.

Hansen, W. L., Total and private rates of return to investment in schooling, *Journal of Political Economy*, Vol. LXXI, no. 2, 1963,

Henderson-Stewart, D., Estimate of the rate of return to education in Great Britain, *The Manchester School of Economic and Social Studies*, Vol. 33, no. 3, 1965, appendix to Blaug's article, The rate of return on investment in education in Great Britain.

Knight, J. B., The determination of wages and salaries in Uganda, *Bulletin of the Oxford University Institute of Economics and Statistics*, Vol. 29, no. 3, 1967.

Merret, S., The rate of return to education, a critique, *Oxford Economic Papers*, 1966.

Morris, V. and Ziderman, A., The economic return on investment in Higher Education in England and Wales, *Economic Trends*, 1971.

Mincer, J., On-the-job training: costs, returns, and some implications, *Journal of Political Economy*, Vol. LXX, no. 5, Part 2, 1962.

Renshaw, E. F., Estimating the returns to education, *Review of Economics and Statistics*, Vol. XLII, no. 3, Part I, 1960.

Schultz, T. W., Capital formulation by education, *Journal of Political Economy*, Vol. LIII, no. 6, 1960.

Schultz, T. W., Investment in human capital, *American Economic Review*, Vol. LI, no. 1, 1961.

Schultz, T. W., Investment in human capital: reply, *American Economic Review*, Vol. LI, no. 5, 1961.

Shaffer, H. G., Investment in human capital: a comment, *American Economic Review*, Vol. LI, no. 5, 1961.

Sjaastad, L. A., The costs and returns of human migration, *Journal of Political Economy*, Vol. LXX, no. 5, Part 2, 1962.

Smyth, J. A. and Bennett, N. L., Rates of return on investment in education: A tool for short-term educational planning, illustrated with Ugandan data, *The World Year Book of Education, 1967*, London, 1967.

Thomas, Brinley, The international circulation of human capital, *Minerva*.

Vaizey, J., Towards a new political economy? Or some problems of some aspects of economics in the light of "human resource" concepts, in *The Residual Factor and Economic Growth*, Paris, OECD, 1965.

Walsh, J. R., Capital concept applied to man, *Quarterly Journal of Economics*, Vol. XLIX, February 1935.

Weisbrod, B. A., Education and investment in human capital, *Journal of Political Economy*, Vol. LXX, no. 5, Part 2, 1962.

Wolfle, D. and Smith, J. G., The occupational value of education for superior high school graduates, *Journal of Higher Education*, April 1956.

Economic statistics

Beckerman, W. and associates, *The British Economy in 1975*, Cambridge 1965.

Deane, P. and Cole, W. A., *British Economic Growth 1688-1959. Trends and Structure*, Cambridge 1962.

Denison, E. F., *The Sources of Economic Growth in the United States and the Alternatives Before Us*, Supplementary Paper no. 13, New York, Committee for Economic Development, January 1962.

Denison, E. F., Measuring the contribution of education (and the "residual") to economic growth, in *The Residual Factor and Economic Growth*, Paris, OECD, 1965.

Gilbert, M. and associates, *Comparative National Products and Price Levels*, Paris, OEEC, 1958.

Gilbert, M. and Kravis, I. B., *An International Comparison of National Products and the Purchasing Power of Currencies*, Paris, OEEC, 1954.

The Growth of World Industry 1938-1961. International Analyses and Tables, New York, UN, 1965.

Instituto Nacional de Estatistica, *Anuários Estatísticos*, Lisbon.

Irish Second Programme for Economic Expansion, Dublin, 1964.

Junta do Credito Publico, *Contas do Ano Económico de . . .*, Lisbon.

Kendrick, J. W., *Productivity Trends in the United States*, Princeton, N.J., NBER, 1961.

National Income and Expenditure, Dublin.

National Income and Expenditure, London, HMSO.

O.E.C.D., *Manpower Statistics*, Paris.

O.E.C.D., *Wages and Labour Mobility*, Paris, 1965.

Routh, G., *Occupation and Pay in Great Britain, 1906-1960*, Cambridge, 1965.

Royal Commision on Equal Pay, London, HMSO, 1947.

Stone, J. R. N., Input-output and demographic accounting: a tool for educational planning, *Minerva*, Vol. IV, no. 3, Spring 1966.

Stone, J. R. N., Stone, G. and Gunton, J., An example of Demographic Accounting; the School Ages, *Minerva*, Vol. VI, no. 2, Winter 1968.
Yearbook of Labour Statistics, Geneva, International Labour Office.
Yearbook of National Accounts Statistics, New York, United Nations.

Educational economics

Arrow, K. J. and Capron, W. M., Dynamic shortages and price rises: the engineer scientist case, *Quarterly Journal of Economics*, Vol. LXXIII, no. 2, 1959.

Becker, G. and Chiswick, B., Education and the distribution of earnings, *The American Economic Review*, Vol. LVI, no. 2, Papers and Proceedings, 1966.

Blank, David M. and Stigler, George J., *The Demand and Supply of Scientific Personnel*, New York, NBER, 1957.

Blaug, M., Peston, M. and Ziderman, A., *The Utilization of Educated Manpower in Industry*, London, 1967.

Bowman, Mary Jean, The costing of human resource development, in *The Economics of Education*, J. Vaizey and E. A. G. Robinson (eds.), London 1966.

Campbell, R. and Siegel, B. N., The demand for higher education in the United States, 1919-64. *The American Economic Review*, Vol. LVII, no. 3, 1967.

Chiswick, B., Minimum schooling legislation and the cross-sectional distribution of income. *Economic Journal*, Vol. LXXIX, no. 315, 1969.

Correa, H. and Tinbergen, J., Quantitative adaptation of education to accelerated growth. *Kyklos*, XV, 4, 1962.

Eckaus, R. S., Economic criteria for education and training. *Review of Economics and Statistics*, Vol. XLVI, no. 2, 1964.

Eckaus, R. S., Education and economic growth, in *The Economics of Higher Education*, Selma J. Mushkin (ed.), Washington D.C., U.S. Department of Health, Education and Welfare, 1962.

Edding, F., Expenditure on education: statistics and comments, in *The Economics of Education*, J. Vaizey and E. A. G. Robinson (eds.), London, 1966.

Hansen, W. L., The "shortage" of engineers, *Review of Economics and Statistics*, Vol. XLIII, no. 3, 1961.

Hollister, R., *A Technical Evaluation of the First Stage of the Mediterranean Regional Project*, Paris, OECD, 1967.

Jewkes, J., How much science? *The Economic Journal*, Vol. no. 277, March.

Kaser, M. C., Education and economic progress: experience in industrialized market economies, in *The Economics of Education*, J. Vaizey and E. A. G. Robinson (eds.), London, 1966.

Morgan, J. N. and David, M. H., Education and income, *Quarterly Journal of Economics*, Vol. LXXVII, no. 3, 1963.

O.E.C.D., *Educational Policy and Planning in the Netherlands*, Paris, 1967.

Schultz, T. W., *The Economic Value of Education*, New York and London, 1963.

Schultz, T. W., Education and economic growth, in *Social Forces Influencing American Education*, Chicago, 1961.

Skorov, George, *Integration of Education and Economic Planning in Tanzania*, Paris, UNESCO-IIEP, 1966.

Unido, *Planning for Advanced Skills and Technologies* (Symposium) New York, 1968.

Vaizey, J., *The Economics of Education*, London, 1962.

Vaizey, J. and Robinson, E. A. G. (eds.), *The Economics of Education*, London, 1966.

Education

Anderson, C. A., A skeptical note on the relation of vertical mobility to education, *American Journal of Sociology*, Vol. 66(1), May 1961.

Bowles, Samuel S., Towards equality of educational opportunity, *Harvard Educational Review*, Vol. 38, no. 1, 1968.

Burt, Sir Cyril, *Age, Ability and Aptitude*, London, 1954.

Chesswas, J. D., *Educational Planning and Development in Uganda*, Paris, UNESCO-IIEP, 1966.

Children and their Primary Schools, The Plowden Report, London, HMSO, 1967.

Coleman, James, The concept of equality of educational opportunity, *Harvard Educational Review*, Vol. 38, no. 1, 1968.

Coleman, James, *et al.*, *Equality of Educational Opportunity*, Washington D.C., U.S. Department of Health, Education, and Welfare, 1966.

Committee on Higher Education, *Higher Education*, Report of the Committee appointed by the Prime Minister under the chairmanship of Lord Robbins 1961-63, London, HMSO, 1965.

Coombs, P. H., *The World Educational Crisis—A Systems Analysis*, Paris, UNESCO-IIEP, 1967.

The Demand for and Supply of Teachers, 1963–1986, Ninth Report of the National Advisory Council on the Training and Supply of Teachers, London, HMSO, 1965.

Douglas, J. W. B., *The Home and the School*, London, 1964 and 1969.

Dyer, Henry S., School factors and equal educational opportunity, *Harvard Educational Review*, Vol. 38, no. 1, 1968.

Education Act of 1944, London, HMSO, 1944.

First Report of the Public Schools Commission, London, HMSO, 1968.

Floud, J. E., Halsey, A. H. and Martin, F. M., *Social Class and Educational Opportunity*, London, 1956.

Half our Future, The Newsom Report, London, HMSO, 1963.

Hansen, W. L., Educational plans and teacher supply, *Comparative Education Review*, October 1962.

Husen, T., *Talent, Opportunity and Career*, Stockholm, 1969.

Instituto Nacional de Estatistica, *Estatística da Educação*, Lisbon.

Jencks, C. and Riesman, D., *The Academic Revolution*, New York, 1969.

Jensen, Arthur R., How much can we boost IQ and scholastic Achievement?, *Harvard Educational Review*, Vol. 39, no. 1, 1969.

Kerr, Clark ..., paper to the Australian Conference on Planning in Higher Education, Armidale, N.S.W., August 1969 (unpublished).

Layard, R., King, J. and Moser, C., *The Impact of Robbins*, London, 1969.

Lesser, G. S. and Clark, D. H., Abilities of children from different social class and cultural groups, *Monographs of the Society for Research in Child Development*, Vol. xxx, no. 4, 1965.

Ministry and Department of Education and Science Annual Reports, London, HMSO.

Ministry of Education, *15 to 18*, Report of the Central Advisory Council for Education, under the chairmanship of G. Crowther, London, HMSO, 1959.

Moynihan, Daniel P., Sources of resistance to the Coleman Report, *Harvard Educational Review*, Vol. 38, no. 1, 1968.

New Educational Media in Action: Case Studies for Planning, Vols. i, ii and iii, Paris, UNESCO–IIEP, 1967.

The New Media: Memo to Educational Planners, Paris, UNESCO-IIEP, 1967.

Reports of the Burnham Committee, London, HMSO.

Report of the Royal Commission of Inquiry on Education in the Province of Quebec, Montreal, 1966.

Report on I.M.U. Mathematics, OECD, Centre for Educational Research and Innovation, 1969 (mimeographed).

Schools Council Report, London, HMSO.

Shaycroft, Marion F., *The High School Years: Growth in Competitive Skills*, Pittsburg, 1967.

Statistics of Education, London, HMSO.

UNESCO, *Report of UNESCO Director General to the UNESCO General Conference*, Paris.

UNESCO, *Statistical Yearbooks*, Paris.

United States Digest of Educational Statistics, Washington D.C., U.S. Government Printing Office.

Vaizey, J., *The Control of Education*, London, 1963.

Vaizey, J., *Education for Tomorrow*, 5th edn., London 1969.

Vaizey, J., *Education in the Modern World*, 2nd edn., London 1969.

Educational planning

Análise Quantitativa da Estrutura Escolar Portuguesa, 1950-59, (A Quantitative Analysis of the Portuguese Educational System), Lisbon, Centro de Estudos de Estatística Económica, 1963.

Armitage, P. and Smith, C., A computable model of the educational system, illustrated with British data, in *The World Year Book of Education, 1967*, London, 1967.

Correa, H., A survey of mathematical models in educational planning, in *Mathematical Models in Educational Planning*, Paris, OECD, 1967.

Debeauvais, Michel, Manpower planning in developing countries, *International Labour Review*, Vol. 89, no. 4, 1964.

Dressel, Paul L., Comments on the use of mathematical models in educational planning, in *Mathematical Models in Educational Planning*, Paris, OECD, 1967.

Moser, C. A. and Layard, P. R. G., Planning the scale of Higher Education in Britain: some statistical problems, *Journal of the Royal Statistical Society*, Series A, Vol. 127, Part 4, 1964.

O.E.C.D., *Educational Planning in the Netherlands*, Paris, 1966.

O.E.C.D., *Problems of Human Resources Planning in Latin America and in the Mediterranean Regional Project Countries*, Paris, 1967.

Stone, J. R. N., A model of the educational system, *Minerva*, Vol. III, no. 2, 1965.

Stone, J. R. N., A view of the conference, in *Mathematical Models in Educational Planning*, Paris, OECD, 1967.

Tinbergen, J., Educational assessments, in *Economic and Social Aspects of Educational Planning*, Paris, UNESCO, 1964.

Tinbergen, J. and Bos, H. C., A planning model of educational requirements of Economic development, in *The Residual Factor and Economic Growth*, Paris, OECD, 1965.

Manpower

Advisory Council on Scientific Policy, Committee on Scientific Manpower, *The Long-Term Demand for Scientific Manpower*, London, HMSO, 1961.

Advisory Council on Scientific Policy, Committee on Scientific Manpower, *Scientific and Engineering Manpower in Great Britain*, London, HMSO, 1956.

Advisory Council on Scientific Policy, Committee on Scientific Manpower, *Scientific and Engineering Manpower in Great Britain, 1959*, London, HMSO, 1959.

Advisory Council on Scientific Policy, Committee on Scientific Manpower, *Scientific and Technological Manpower in Great Britain, 1962*, London, HMSO, 1962.

Bombach, G., Long-term requirements for qualified manpower in relation to economic growth, in *Economic Aspects of Higher Education*, Paris, OECD, 1964.

The Brain Drain, Report of the Working Group on Migration, London, HMSO, 1968.

The Flow into Employment of Scientists, Engineers and Technologists, Cmnd 3760, London, HMSO, 1968.

Harbison, F. and Myers, C. A., *Education, Manpower, and Economic Growth*, New York, 1964.

Hunter, G., *High Level Manpower in East Africa, Preliminary Assessment*, London, 1962.

Hunter, G., *High Level Manpower, Requirements and Resources in Tanganyika* Dar-es-Salaam, 1963.

Hunter, L. C. and Robertson, D. J., *Economics of Wages and Labour*, London, 1969.

Johnson, H. G., The economics of the "brain-drain": the Canadian case, *Minerva*, Vol. III, no. 3, 1965.

O.E.C.D., *Education, Human Resources and Development in Argentina*, Paris, 1967.

Parnes, H. S., *Forecasting Educational Needs for Economic and Social Development*, Paris, OECD, 1962.

Payne, G. L., *Britain's Scientific and Technological Manpower*, London, 1960.

Peck, J. Merton, Science and technology, in *Britain's Economic Prospects*, Washington D.C., The Brookings Institution, 1968.

Report on the 1965 Triennial Manpower Survey of Engineers, Technologists, Scientists and Technical Supporting Staff, London, HMSO, 1966.

A Report on Manpower Education and Training in Zambia, Lusaka, 1966.

The Shortage of Science and Mathematics Teachers, London, Royal Society, 1969.

Study of the Demand for and Supply of Teachers: England and Wales, Paris. OECD, 1969.

Study on the Demand for and Supply of Teachers: Austria, Paris, OECD, 1969.

Study on the Demand for and Supply of Teachers: Denmark, Paris, OECD, 1969.

Study on the Demand for and Supply of Teachers: Norway, Paris, OECD, 1969.

Study on the Demand for and Supply of Teachers, Sweden, Paris, OECD, 1969.

Survey of High-Level Manpower Requirements and Resources for the Five-Year Development Plan, 1964-65 to 1968-69 (prepared under the direction of Robert L. Thomas), Dar-es-Salaam, 1965.

Thonstad, Tore, *Education and Manpower: Theoretical Models and Empirical Applications*, London, 1969.

Vaizey, J., The labour market and the manpower forecaster—some problems, *International Labour Review*, Vol. 89, April 1964.

Vermot-Gauchy, M., Supply and demand for engineers, in *Forecasting Manpower Needs for the Age of Science*, Paris, OECD, 1964.

Other

Geyl, Peiter, *Napoleon: For and Against*, London, 1965.

Medawar, P. B., *Encounter*, November 1969.

Index